Education, Environment and Sustainable Development

Education, Environment and Sustainable Development

Edited by

M.K. Satapathy

SHIPRA

ISBN: 978-81-7541-363-4

2010 Reprint Edition
(First Published in India in 2007)

Education, Environment and Sustainable Development

Published by:
SHIPRA PUBLICATIONS
115-A, Vikas Marg, Shakarpur, Delhi – 110092 (India)
Ph.: 91-11-65277210, 22500954 Fax: 22458662;

Head Office: LG-18-19, Pankaj Central Market, Patparganj, Delhi 110002
Ph. 91-11-65277210

Branch Office: 115, Munish Plaza, 20, Ansari Road,
Daryaganj, Delhi 110002; Ph. 91-11-65946453, 9810522367

Email: info@shiprapublications.com
Website: www.shiprapublications.com

Foreword

An unplanned human activity coupled with unabated consumption of natural resources has led to environmental degradation. In the present-day context, the issues related to global warming, sea level rise, climatic changes have become increasingly important concerns for the environmentalists. To overcome such a situation, which affects our environment, scientific management of natural resources and environmental protection needs to be emphasized.

The edited volume of "Education, Environment and Sustainable Development" by Prof. M.K.Satapathy has highlighted some of the major issues concerning our environment and sustainable development which, I am sure, would create an awareness and educate the people in general. At the same time, it would provide sufficient information to the researchers and students on the subject.

Pramod Tandon
Vice Chancellor
North-Eastern Hill University

Shillong

Preface

Ever since man appeared on earth, he has been harnessing the natural resources to meet his basic requirements. The phenomenal increase in human population followed by fast growing industrialization and urbanization in the last century has put tremendous pressure on the shrinking natural resources which are degraded much faster than before, raising threats to the survival of human beings. The environmental problems that we face are numerous and multifaceted: deforestation, soil erosion, biodiversity loss, degradation of marine resources, pesticide build up, environmental pollution, climate change, ozone depletion and more, some of which are of global environmental concern.

The developed countries have disturbed the environment because of excessive use of the natural resources, whereas in most developing countries the causes of environmental degradation are having roots in poverty, inequality and under-utilization of resources. Therefore, development must be accelerated with rational use of natural resources.

Development and environment are not contradictory. The environmental protection, resource conservation and economic growth are like two sides of the same coin—one can not prosper without the other. Sustainable development stresses the need to view environmental protection and economic growth as mutually compatible and not necessarily conflicting objectives. This implies that growth objectives should be compatible with natural resource base limitations and bio-spherical waste assimilation carrying capacities. The ultimate objective is to improve the quality of life of people on the planet.

From the historic UN sponsored conference on Human Development held at Stockholm in 1972, much emphasis has been given to human dimension of environmental protection and the need for environmental education. Education is seen from the process of adjustment to environment. In general the primary aim of environmental education is to enable citizens to understand and appreciate the complex nature of the environment as well as the role played by a properly managed environment in economic development. Only an informed, motivated and committed citizenary could provide the mass base necessary for the continued protection of the environment. So education, both formal and non-formal has an indispensable contribution to make. The task of education as a dynamic force is not only to develop a rational basis for study of the environment, but to equip people to make up their minds and activity in an informed way.

The UN conference on environment and development popularly known as Earth Summit (1992) in its agenda 21 gave importance to education, awareness and training. It stressed reorienting education towards sustainable development. Education is critical for promoting sustainable development and improving the capacity of people to address environmental and development issues.

In September 2000, 189 nations with 147 heads of states, while adopting the Millennium declaration having a framework of 8 goals and 18 targets, have unanimously stressed on eradication of poverty and promotion of environmental sustainability (Goal-7).

Further to promote awareness and diverse activities, UNO has declared 2005-14 as the decade of education for sustainable development and calls for people to do whatever possible to save the planet earth. This means that the journey towards sustainable development involves every one at every stage of life from early childhood to adult life. Realising the importance of environmental education in Indian context, the Hon'ble Supreme Court of India in their historic judgement directed that from the academic year 2004-05, environment should be taught as a compulsory subject at all levels (School/College/University) of education in our country in order to protect the life support system and promote peaceful and healthy existence.

In spite of the importance of the subject, very few books are available in the area of education and sustainable development. Keeping this in view the present book *Education, Environment and Sustainable Development* has been prepared with twenty selected chapters contributed by researchers working in the area of Environmental Education and Sustainable Development. Besides core areas such as environmental education at school and college level, sustainable development—Issues and concerns; various dimensions such as value education, teacher education programme, population education, women education, community participation, biodiversity conservation, role of mass media, etc. has been discussed in the context of sustainable development in the book. Informations in certain chapters has been supplemented with tabular and graphical presentations to promote easy understanding. I sincerely hope the book shall be found interesting and useful to students, teachers, academicians and researchers from the field of science as well as social science having interest in the field of environmental education as well as sustainable development issues. However, the responsibility of the facts stated, opinions expressed or conclusions reached in the chapters, is entirely that of the respective authors and not necessary of NCERT, NERRI or the Editor.

I express my deep sense of gratitude to Dr. T. Chancellor (U.K.); Prof. G. Ravindra and Prof. M.A Khader, NCERT, New Delhi; and Prof. D.S. Bhattacharjee, NERIE, Shillong, for their encouragement and inspiration. I am extremely grateful to all the contributors especially Prof. N.C. Datta, Prof. S.C. Santra, Dr. R.N Bisoyi, Dr. V. Jha, Dr. R. Ray for their interest and timely submission of the articles. I am thankful to my colleagues Drs. Aswani Garg and Rashmi Sharma, NERIE, Shillong, for their support and goodwill. Lastly I am thankful to my wife Dhanalaxmi for sharing some of her time for discussion during editing this book.

M.K. Satapathy

Contents

Foreword v

Preface vii

1. Man and Environment Human Dimension of Environmental Concerns and Sustainable Development 1
   M.K. Satapathy

2. Environmental Education Philosophy, Structure and Nature 8
   D. Dash and and M.K. Satapathy

3. Environmental and Ecological Programmes in Higher Education 28
   J.G. Ray

4. Perspectives of Environmental Education in College and University 41
   S.C. Santra

5. Environment and Sustainable Development Concept, Model and Principles 50
   Dipak De

6. Education for Sustainable Development: Issues and Concerns 60
   M.K. Satapathy and D. Dash

7. Education for Sustainable Development in the Context of Teacher Education Programme 77
   M.K. Satapathy and D. Dash

8. Equity, Environmental Conservation and Sustainable Development 92
   B.P. Sahu and P. Ghildayal

9. Need and Importance of Value Education for Environmental Conservation and Sustainable Development 111
   M.K. Satapathy and D. Dash

10. Biodiversity and its Conservation Strategies for Sustainable Development 122
    A.S. Dixit and M.K. Satapathy

11. Women's Education, Environmental Sustainability and National Development 140
K.K. Tiwari

12. Environment, Biodiversity, Conservation and Sustainable Development in the Perspective of Education 161
N.C. Datta

13. Understanding Microbes for Biosphere Sustainability 179
R.N. Bisoyi

14. Role of Mass Media in Promoting Environmental Conservation and Sustainable Development 192
B.N. Neelima

15. Ecological Concerns and Environment-friendly Agriculture 203
Shivadhar Singh

16. Indigenous Technology, Eco-friendly Environment and Sustainable Agriculture 228
P.S. Sivakumar, M. Nedunchezhiyan and R.C. Ray

17. Community Participation in Management of Forest Resources and Sustainable Development 253
N. Subba Rao

18. Women and Environment: The Gender Difference 272
Dipak De

19. Community Awareness for Sustainable Development: A Case Study from Bhubaneswar 281
A.K. Patra and Paramita Pramanick

References and Bibliography 291

Index 316

List of Contributors 323

1

Man and Environment

Human Dimension of Environmental Concerns and Sustainable Development

M.K. SATAPATHY

Environment is the sum total of all physical (non-living) and biotic (living) factors that surround and potentially influence an organism. In nature organisms survive, grow and reproduce in appropriate environments, interact with each other and are influenced by the whole complex of environmental factors. Man is an integral component of the environment and he influences and is influenced by the environment. From psychological view point, environment is the individual's life space, the totality of stimuli affecting an individual form the point of conception to the point of death. In normal conditions environment remains balanced and natural disturbances are seen as driving force in the evolution of ecological systems. However human population pressure and its divergent activities acting as external force(s) disturb the evolution process.

Till today nature, bounties are used and overused indiscriminately. In economic development, environmental assets are either not factored in economic costs or priced very inadequately. Besides, needs of outraging human population, developments in science and technology that made economic miracles has led to environmental disasters. Sustainable development seeks to correct the imbalance of the last few centuries. It tries to promote economic development without compromising the environmental issues. It conveys two main do's and don'ts: do not overexploit the natural resources and do recognise the rights of the future generations on resources available today.

The earth formed about 4.5 billion years ago and life first evolved within the first billion years. The age of mammals, the Cenozoic era, began 65 million years ago. The early humans (*Homo erectus*) appeared in about 1.65 million years ago in east Africa and the modern man (*Homo sapiens*) evolved only 90-100,000 years ago. It depended on nature for food gathering through hunting. It is only about 10,000 years ago that human being started growing food rather than merely gathering it from the wild state. If the existence of human beings as an independent species is equaled to a 24 hour day, we have been farmers for only about just seven minutes (Swaminathan, 1984). At the beginning of this farming practice, human population was very limited (about 5 million) and natural resources in terms of land, soil, forest, animal, etc. were plenty. With settlement and agriculture, the population started growing and by the 14th century the figure reached 500 million. Population reached 5 billion in 1987 increasing to six billion in 1999. With 2 per cent average annual growth, the population is projected to reach about 9.3 billion by the middle of this century. The accelerated population growth has intensified human use of planet's resources. As such most of the land surface on the earth and the oceans has come under the direct control of human kind. Even the outer space is not free from the human impact. This new attitude towards nature came with the idea of progress that advocated the superior role of humans as masters of nature.

Human beings and the natural world are on a coliusion course. Human activity has inflicted harsh and often irreversible damage on the environment and on critical resources. In the mad race to consume more, mankind is using up the earth's finite resources such as the top soil, water, forests, etc. far faster than the natural processes can regenerate them.

The millennium ecosystem assessment report released in 2005 has noted that since 1950, humans have changed ecosystems more rapidly and extensively than anytime in human history. Consequently, it has degraded 60 per cent of the world's grasslands, forests, farmlands, rivers and lakes. For example, the net loss of global forest cover during 1990s was about 94 million hectares. At present tropical forests are being cleared at the rate of 1 ha/second. About 6 million ha of agricultural land are lost due to soil degradation and desertification every year affecting 250 million people around the world. About 1.5 billion people representing one fourth of the world population have no access to safe drinking water and 45 million people in the world are affected by poor quality water. Because of urbanisation, and industrialisation, and wrong science & technology policy, at least one billion people around the world breathe unhealthy air and three million die annually from the effects of air pollution.

Further many, free ecosystem services such as maintaining the gaseous balance of the atmosphere and stable climate, regulating the hydrological cycle and moderating floods and droughts, building and maintaining the fertility of soils essential to agriculture, eliminating and detoxifying wastes, pollinating crops, controlling the vast majority of crop pests and disease vectors and supplying forest products, food from sea, etc. are being affected by human activity. About 50 per cent of the mangrove forests and wetlands that perform vital ecological functions of local ecosystem services such as flood and cyclone control have been destroyed. Recent natural disaster like tsunami in Asian countries bears testimony to it (Anonymous, 2005). It is often said: "If we do not keep account of what we take from the earth, one day the earth will seek on its due and will reply with a disaster—earthquake, tsunami or worse." (Chidambaram, 2005)

With destruction of habitats, there is collision between man and wild life. As such, worldwide 24 per cent of mammals, 12 per cent of birds, 25 per cent of reptiles and 30 per cent of fish species are endangered or threatened with extinction. This loss of diversity affects our food security, our ability to stay healthy and to adapt to a changing environment. (Ramamurthy, 2004; Bala Ravi, 2006).

The global environment is being stretched on one side by abject poverty and on the other side by affluence and development (Singh, 1982). To the millions of people in the developing world, the basic needs (food, fodder, fuel wood, shelter, etc.), the problems of daily existence are more important than environment degradation. On the other hand people of the prosperous developed world are more conscious about their luxury and comfort. Reckless consumption and materialism that fuel economic growth in the developed countries has played havoc with the global environment. Concentration of carbon dioxide gas in the atmosphere has started building exponentially because of industrialisation from 1800 onwards and the trend continues unbated (Rao, 1999) due to burning of fossil fuels like coal, and oil. Oceans and lakes of the world have been laden with toxic chemicals from factories and no longer sustain life. The rising mean temperature of the planet is altering the global weather (Schnedier, 1989). Ice layers of the polar regions are melting. The life protecting ozone layer in the upper atmosphere has been damaged. Struggle for resources threatens social stability across countries and communities. New health hazards are emerging and killer diseases are rearing their heads again as lifestyle and patterns of living getting changed. War, terrorism and preparation for these are demanding more material resources than those required for improving the life of the human being. As such, many environmental problems arise from the deliberate or inadvertent abuse, misuse and overuse of natural resources by mankind.

The full cost of the massive assault on the planet's systems has now become evident. Of the 24 ecosystems vital for life on earth, 15 have been seriously degraded or used unsustainably, raising questions (Ehrlich and Ehrlich, 2005) about the chances of environmental collapse. As such humanity is on a self-destructive course and the planet's ability to sustain future generations is questionable. Once, Gandhijee, the champion of non-violence said,

> "*The earth provides enough to satisfy everyman's need but not for everyman's greed*". People's mad rush for materialism is not only irreligious but also a criminal act (Khoshoo, 1998) against nature and humanity and all creations at large.

Realising the environmental concerns, large number of scientists, environmentalists, politicians, social workers and thinking citizens have come to a single conclusion:

> "*We are consuming natural resources at a rate much fister than that at which nature can regenerate them. We are polluting the environmental at a rate greater than its ability to absorb the pollution. This is an unsustainable way of living and it can only lead to an environmental and social catastrophe*". (Rajagopalan, 2005)

Towards 1960s the voice for environmental issues started surfacing. Books like Rachel Carson's *Silent Spring* (Carson, 1962) set the tone for an environmental movement. Before her death in 1964, she remarked:

> "Man's attitude towards nature today is critically important simply because we have now acquired a fateful power to alter and destroy nature, but man is a part of nature and his war against nature is inevitably a war against himself".

Many gatherings and conferences were organised from 1960 to voice against economic growth and environmental crises. As such in the last two decades there has been a tremendous increase (Dash and Satapathy, 2004) in the efforts in both public as well as private sectors to create environmental consciousness, sensitivity and values among the people. It has been increasingly realised all over the world that living a harmonious and healthy life on this planet earth is the man's greatest need and environmental assets need to be preserved, as on them the quality and indeed the very existence of life on earth depends.

The first International initiative to discuss environmental crises was the United Nations conference on Human Environment held at Stockholm (Sweden) in 1972. It assessed on a global scale the damage done to the environment and contemplated on ways and means of preventing and solving environmental problems. It also stressed the need for environmental education as one of the most powerful instrument in an all out attack on environment crises.

In 1981 addressing the first International conference on environmental education held at New Delhi, the then Indian Prime Minister, Late Mrs. Indira Gandhi, highlighted the need of environmental protection in the following words:

> "*Environmental Education is to arouse social consciousness and make community aware of the fact the good of the individual and that of the community are both harmed by ecological disruption*"

Later in 1983, World Commission on Environment and Development (WCED) was set up in 1983 with Gro Harlem Brundtland of Norway as its chairperson. The commission in its report '*Our Common Future*' (WCED, 1987) highlighted the concept of sustainable development and defined it as development that meets the needs of the present without compromising the ability of future generations to meet their own needs. The commission's main focus is that development and environmental conservation can go together. Further it stresses that it is the development that responds to the current needs of today's citizen and of the society at large without compromising and hindering the resources required to fulfill the development of tomorrow's citizens.

The quality of life for humans is linked to the quality of the environment that they share. It tries to secure health, happiness, prosperity and perfect harmony with natur, not only for the present but also for the foreseeable future. The Commission also suggested that human survival and well being could depend on the success in elevating sustainable development to global ethics (WCED, 1987. p. 308).

Twenty years after the Stockholm conference, the popularly known Earth Summit was held at Rio-de-Janeiro during 3-4 June, 1992 attended by a large number of heads of governments, NGOs, representatives of international bodies, industry, trade unions, local government and others. The Rio-Declaration (adopted by fully 128 states) came out with 'Agenda 21' a detailed action plan for sustainable development in the 21st century. It proclaims that: human beings are at the centre of concerns for sustainable development and that they are entitled to a healthy and productive life in harmony with nature (Principle 1); that the right to development must be fulfilled so as equitably to meet developmental and environmental needs of the present and future generations (Principle-3), that states should reduce and eliminate unsustainable patterns of production and consumption and promote appropriate demographic policies to achieve sustainable development and a higher quality of life for all people.

The Millennium Development Goals set by heads of state of 189 countries in 2000 has called for environmental sustainability, universalisation of primary education and reduction of poverty and hunger by half by 2015 (Sweetman, 2005; Samir, 2006). The Johannesburg (South Africa) gathering popularly known at Rio + 10 has called to the nations for more concrete action to promote sustainable development, and education has been given top priority.

An individual is the starting point of environmental degradation. If an individual believes in need and not in greed, and in comfort and not in luxury and ponders about what is enough for a comfortable life style, most of the problems can be solved. For example through use of biodegradable locally available materials (instead of plastics), use of taps instead of showers, damp curtains instead of coolers to bring down room temperature, planting trees, garbage segregation, water harvesting, land fillings, reusing and recycling of wastes, growing organic food, using public transport instead of personal vehicles, avoiding use of cracker and chemicals paints in festivals etc., an individual can share in the responsibility. A sustainable community can spring form responsible well informed individuals. Thus, sustainable life style of the individuals can lead to sustainable communities to sustainable nations and then to a sustainable world. We should not consider the earth as a property we have inherited from our forefathers. We have borrowed it from our children.

The human behaviour towards environmental systems sustains all of us on the planet earth. As such the future really is in our hand. The mankind can reverse the degradation of ecosystem and natural resources in coming decades but the changes in policy and practice required are substantial.

In a developing country, sustainable development must generate economic and social growth that is equitable with no or little effect on environment. The welfare of villages with development based on ecological economic principles and gender equality together with access to education, health care, livelihoods, credit and decision making are critical to the success of such eco-development (Kyoto, 1998). It needs people empowerment, participation and active involvement in decision making process through decentralised governance. In Indian context, because of the vastness of the area and prevailing eco-cultural diversity of the country, it is realised that there is an urgent need to develop programmes to address location/region specific concerns (Dhar *et al.*, 2002).

The most critical input for bringing about sustainability in a gamut of social, economic and cultural situations, is education which gives an individual knowledge, information, and understanding and above all stresses on ethics and morality leading to change in human thought and action (Westing, 1996).

Sustainable development needs that many other things be in place in society (Anonymous, 2002)—peace, human rights, equal rights for women, protection of children, employment opportunity, safe shelter and sanitation, education for all, food and nutrition and crucially a stable population. As such, a nation's ability to develop sustainably depends on the capacity of the people to understand the complexity of human environment interaction and their eco-friendliness. Women as the important and first environmental educators for young children can stimulate change in the behaviour that can lead to savings in food, water, energy consumption and ultimately in the protection of natural resources and bio-diversity (Dash, 2005). They can build a rational and far sighted attitude and values which can be deeply rooted in the minds of future generation.

Effective and meaningful environmental education is a challenge we must take seriously if our future generations are to enjoy the benefits of our national heritage. The way we plan today for public education on the environment will have dramatic effects on the future quality of life (Hudson, 2001). Without people's involvement no amount of effort can help sustain the environment. What has gone wrong today is that this essential element, the people's dimension, is largely neglected. However, things are changing. Environmental awareness has increased, in particular among students and the youth (Ghosh, 2004). Community based and voluntary organisations have been active in drawing public, regulatory, and sometimes judicial attention to environmental violations and issues. In a series of landmark judgments, the Hon'ble Supreme Court has filled in gaps in the legislative framework and enforcement machinery through jurisprudence.

2

Environmental Education
Philosophy, Structure and Nature

D. DASH AND and M.K. SATAPATHY

Today, the environmental degradation is a matter of great concern before mankind. Over the last few decades the delicate ecosystem of our planet is facing the danger of destruction due to the intervention of human beings. In the developmental race man has been ruthlessly consuming natural resources and polluting environment. The increasing level of water and air pollution, formation of ozone hole, acid rain, global warming, etc. are some of the issues of common concern. The earth is fast losing its treasure (Baliga, 1996). Several plant and animal species have already vanished from this earth and many more are on the verge of extinction. Forests are diminishing at an alarming rate, land masses are getting eroded and a climate change in different parts of the world is clearly due to global warming. The recent Tsunami bears testimony to it (Chidambaram, 2005; Swaminathan, 2005).

The reality is that the human being has considered the environment as a reservoir of resources but not as a vital component of our life. We have forgotten the conservation and preservation of mother nature. But the time has changed. Fortunately some people have realised this issue and are considering seriously to take some measures to save our endangered environment (Rao, 1999). These considerations have led to the creation of a number of organisations, especially among environment friendly nations, communities and individuals. Advancement of this ecological thought has awakened the whole mankind for the protection of nature and its sustainable existence. Environmental consciousness has become a serious theme for discussion and deliberation at global as well as national levels. To this process, much stress is being given on the environmental education to improve the environmental awareness and attitude of the people so that they can take care of the earth, our life support base. Effective and meaningful environmental education is a challenge to be taken seriously if we and our future generations (our children) are to enjoy the benefit of our natural heritage about the environment

Concept of Environmental Education

Environmental education is the education about the environment, education for the environment and education in the environment. While education about the environment includes concepts and skills (Fig. 2.1) that are necessary to understand it, education for the environment covers those aspects of education that covers conservation, preservation, and upgradation of the environment (Costanza, 1996). Education in the environment looks into education outside the classroom in the social and biophysical contexts in which it exists (Ayre, 1999). It supposes to teach a person to interact fully with the surrounding world and at the same time to improve his own inner world (Agarwal, 1997). It helps in the maintenance of life and health, in self-preservation and in the preservation of human race as a whole. It provides each and every person with

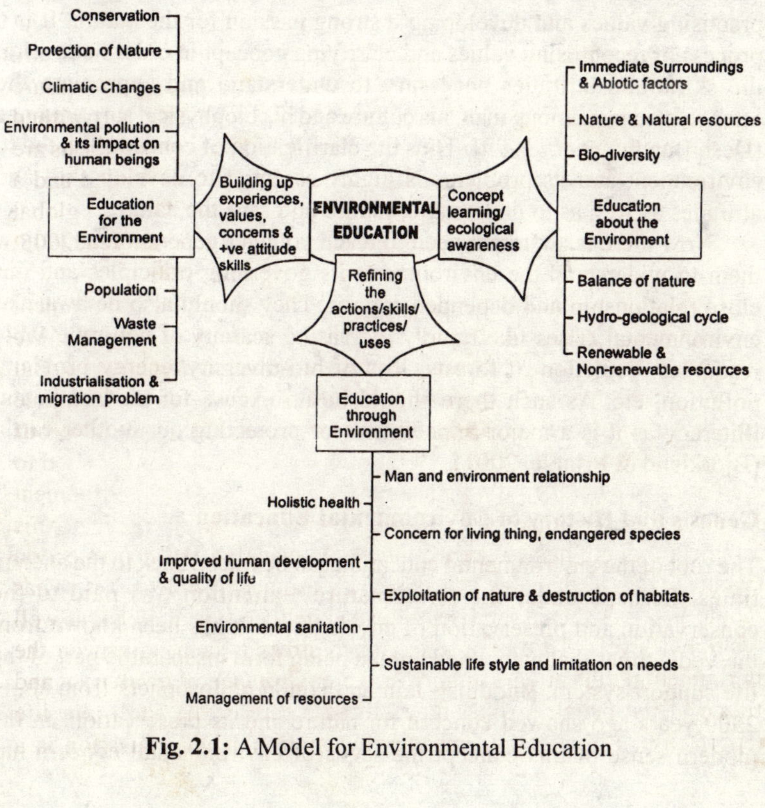

Fig. 2.1: A Model for Environmental Education

opportunities to acquire knowledge, attitudes, values, interest, commitment and skills to protect and improve our environment.

The definition of Environmental Education encompasses a variety of concepts and approaches. The most common definition given by the U.S. office of Education states:

> "Environmental Education is the process that fosters greater understanding of society's environmental problems and also the process of environmental problem solving and decision making. It involves development of skills and insights needed to understand the structure, requirements and impact of interaction within and among various environmental entities, subsystems and systems". (Kirk, 1992)

Being a vital component of efforts to solve environmental problems, it must stay relevant to the needs and interests of the community and yet constantly adapt to the rapidly changing social and technological landscape (Hudson, 2001). Environmental Education is a life long process that occurs in both planned and unstructured ways for recognising and practising values and developing a strong passion for the nature. It is a process of recognising values and clarifying concept in order to develop the skills and attitudes necessary to understand and appreciate the inter-relatedness among man, his culture and his biophysical surroundings (Desh Bandhu *et al.*, 1999). Thus the clarification of concepts related to environment and its problems is highly essential to develop skill and attitudes as well as to understand, realise and love the nature.

Now there is an urgent need to teach younger generation and allow them to understand the environment, its governing principles and our close relationship and dependence on it. They should also be aware of environmental crises like rapidly increasing scarcity of non-renewable resources, depletion of forests, loss of bio-diversity, energy problem, pollution, etc. As such there should be no excuse for environmental illiteracy as it is a major impediment for protecting our mother earth. (Bjorkland & Pringle, 2001).

Genesis and History of Environmental Education

The root of the environmental education can be traced back to the ancient times. Perhaps under the term "nature", attention was paid to the conservation and preservation of environment. It has been known from the Vedic times that nature and human being form inseparable part of the life support system. Buddhist, Jain and Hindu philosophers from about 2500 years ago showed concern for nature and its preservation. In the modern sense of this concept the seeds of environmental concern has been noted by Gorge Perkin Marsh in his book '*Man and Nature*'. He expressed deep concern that natural resources are limited and their over exploitation will put the man in danger. Publication of books like *Silent Spring* by Rachel Carson in 1962 and the *Limits to Growth* by Meadows *et al.,* in 1972 were significant landmarks in environmental education, as these publications started a hot debate on the environmental issues.

With increase in the knowledge of science and technology and initiation of industry, in the last part of ninetieth century as well as in the beginning of the twentieth century, there had been a rapid deterioration in quality of environment, which compelled the educationist, intellectuals, politicians and the common people to think about it resulting in the establishment of IUPN (International Union for the Protection of Nature), later changed to IUCN (International Union for the Conservation of Nature and Natural Resources). Disinger (1983) observed that the first use of the term environmental education was at an IUCN meeting in Paris in 1948. From the late 1960s the term began to be used increasingly and this was refined in the UK by the establishment of the Council for Environmental Education.

During the late 60s and early 70s the publication of books likes '*Silent Spring, Population Bomb, Pesticide Conspiracy*' etc. increased the public interest on environmental issues. The United Nation also took on its agenda to spread environmental consciousness among the common people. "Man and Biosphere Programme", World Conservation Strategy (WCS), publication of Red Data Book, etc. are some of the important achievements.

In June, 1972, the first UN sponsored conference on "Human Environment" held at Stockholm, assessed the damage done to environment on a global level and contemplated on ways and mean of preventing those. In its Principle 19, it gave emphasis to the human dimension of environmental protection and conservation (Saxena 1993), and stressed on the need for environmental awareness and education (Granta & Bhaskar Rao, 1998). This was the first international conference to identify education as an important means of addressing environmental issues (Recommendation 96). In pursuance of the recommendations of this conference. United Nations Environment Programme (UNEP) was created as an independent body. Subsequently, UNESCO in co-operation with UNEP launched the UNESCO-UN international Environmental Education Programme (IEEP) in 1975 at UNESCO Secretariat in Paris. IEEP aimed at assisting government, national, International and regional institutions to incorporate environmental education into formal and non-formal education systems and programmes. Though the Stockholm conference (1972) approved an action plan for the environmental protection, giving emphasis on various strategies including environmental education, the major recognition was given by Belgrade Charter, in Yugoslavia in 1975. The Belgrade Charter recognised the urgent need of environmental education and provided working frame of reference for designing and practicing environmental education programme.

The Tbilisi Inter-governmental conference on Environmental Education, was the follow up workshop, held at Tbilisi, Georgia in 1977. It outlined a substantive structure of environmental education, which was to become prototype of Environmental Education programme worldwide. It also clearly defined the goals, objectives and guiding principles of Environmental Education.

In 1977, the International Congress on Environmental Education, Tbilisi + 10 was held in Moscow and was followed by Jomiten Conference, Thailand. All these conferences had given emphasis to Environmental Education (EE) at local, national, regional and international levels and for all the age groups, inside and outside the formal school system. By the 1980s the term Environmental Education encompassed environmental studies, field studies, environmental science, environmental interpretation, urban studies, heritage education, conservation education, global environmental issues education and different interests promoted different aspects, often through separate organisations and groups. The Agenda 21 of famous Earth Summit (1992) held at Rio-de Janeiro also shows the implication for environmental education throughout the document (Anonymous, 1992). It also recommended that environmental and development education should be incorporated as an essential part of learning within both formal and non-formal education streams (UNESCO, 1998). In India first International Conference on Environmental Education was held at New Delhi in the year 1981. Addressing this conference, Late Mrs. Indira Gandhi, the then prime minister of India outlined the objectives of EE as:

> "*Environmental Education is to arouse social consciousness and make community aware of the fact that the goal of the individual and that of the community are both harmed by ecological disruption.*"

The concern for environment, a social issue got special recognition in the Brundtland Report of 1987. In this report '*Our Common Future*' environmental agenda acquired a new term called as sustainable development. It stresses that development should be aimed at improving the quality of life of all sections of the population, combating poverty, protecting environment and most importantly building the innermost capacity for mutual respect, tolerance, cooperation and peaceful co-existence (WCED, 1987). The focus has changed from the problems of the environment to those of the people (Sterling, 2005). Thus, after 1990 environmental education has changed to Environmental Education for sustainable development having two intimately linked goals.

- Education towards protection and enhancement of the environment, and
- Education as an instrument of development for improving the quality of life of human community.

Further, Millennium Development Goals (MDG) adopted by 189 nations in 2000 as a part of comprehensive development agenda stressed on environmental sustainability (Anonymous, 2004). The World Summit on Sustainable Development (WSSD) held at Johannesburg in 2002 noted that much of current education falls far short of what is required and calls for a new vision and deeper and more ambitious way of thinking about education (UNESCO, 2002).

Environmental Education: Indian Context

The imparting of Environmental Education is an age-old tradition and is a part of Indian culture and ancient civilization. In fact the father of the nation, Mahatma Gandhi, in 1937, launched the movement of basic education for the first time, which was perhaps the first serious attempt at relating education in school to local environmental needs. In the constitution of India the Directive Principles of State Policy on Environment has been articulated in Article 48A of the constitution introduced by the 42nd Amendment in 1977. It says that state shall endeavor to protect and improve the environment and to safe-guard the forests and wildlife of country. Likewise Article 51(A) laid emphasis on protection of environment as one of the fundamental duties of every citizen. Further the national concern for Environmental Education is reflected in the National Policy on Education (NPE, 1986) document. The document observes: "There is a paramount need to create a consciousness in the environment. It must permeate all ages and all sections of the society beginning with the child. Environmental consciousness should be there in the form of teaching in schools and colleges. This aspect will be, integrated in the entire educational processes."

The best that basic education had to offer was incorporated in the report of the education commission (1964-66) that laid emphasis on the internal transformation of education so as to relate it to the life, needs and aspirations of the nation. However, till 1970 special emphasis was not laid on organising learning experiences included in the curriculum to create awareness on environmental problems and their solution to inculcate habits of conserving nature and judicious use of natural resources (Panigrahi, 2004). Following publication of the Curriculum for the Ten year school—A Framework in 1975, National Council of Educational Research and Training (NCERT, 1974-77) developed syllabi, text books and other instructional materials through active involvement of national experts, experienced teachers, and representatives of state institutes of education. These were the influences, which created the appropriate climate of imparting the environmental education in India.

In 1986, when NCERT took up the responsibility of conducting massive teacher training programme, it recognised that environmental education was not merely a transfer of facts and information but required students to engage themselves in activities, in observation, in going out to nature, and that these needed to be integrated with the classroom environment. *The National Curriculum for Elementary and Secondary Education: A Framework* developed by the NCERT in 1988 has incorporated the major thrusts and recommendation of NPE relating to EE. The NCERT also developed the National Curriculum Framework for School Education (NCERT, 2000). It emphasised on preservation of natural environment including forests, lakes, river, and wildlife and compassion for the living creatures. It also includes issues of energy, environment, population explosion, water management, etc. under different contexts like frontline curriculum, indigenous curriculum, etc. The recent curriculum framework (NCERT, 2005) also puts equal or much emphasis on EE especially on hands on experience and project work and tries to put the concerns under habitat and learning.

The scheme "Environmental Orientation to School Education" is being implemented in the country since 1988 under the aegis of Department of Education, Ministry of Human Resource Development, to allow educational programmes in the schools to be fully harmonised with the local environmental contexts and concerns. NCERT (2001) has also published the document "Environmental Orientation to School Education: a Training Module" for eastern region". The document has brought local specificity and social relevance to environmental education for the benefit of teachers and teacher educators.

The Hon'ble Supreme Court of India in its historic judgment (18 December, 2003) directed that from the academic year 2004-05, environment as a compulsory subject should be taught at all levels of education (School, College and University) in our country. Following this NCERT (2004) has published the document "Environmental Education in Schools" carrying guidelines and syllabus for Environmental Education for different stages. The Centre for Environmental Education Ahmedabad (CEE, 1994) is also involved in spreading environmental awareness among children as well as general community. Besides these, many non-government environmental groups are working in India for promotion of environmental education. More than 700 environmental NGOs are active today throughout the country (Singh, 1998) in creating awareness about environment at all levels of the society besides developing study and resource materials for the purpose. The Centre for Science and Environment, New Delhi is regularly monitoring the environmental scenario of the country and bringing out its findings through its publication of the state of India's Environment. The Ministry of Environment and Forestry (MoEF) is the nodal agency of the central government for planning, promotion and co-ordination of environmental and forestry programmes. The MoEF accords priority for the promotion of non-formal environmental education and awareness among all sections of the society through diverse activities such as National Environmental Awareness Campaign, establishment of National and Regional museums of Natural history, setting of eco-clubs in schools, production and dissemination of films, audio-visuals, popular publications on the environmental issues, institutional awards etc.

The Environmental Education: Need and Objectives

Education in the recent past has been lopsidedly anthropocentric ignoring its eco-centric integration, for after all humans and their environment are inseparable and are utterly inter-dependent for mutual survival. Omitting the linkage for ecology with almost all other disciplines, has been the serious lapse in our education today. However in the context of national and international environmental crises, the need for environmental education is highly essential. It acts as a tool to influence knowledge, attitude and values for the improvement of environment and life support system. Therefore most of the educationists and environmentalists (Knimiller, 1983) give stress on the "Environmental Literacy" for all.

The goal of environmental education is to mould a child into an adult citizen who has strong emotional ties with nature (Mishra and Airen, 1994), and transforms child to a responsible person who can help in the maintenance of life and health in self-preservation and also in the preservation of mankind. It helps to identity the environmental crises that exist both in physical and social environment.

The ultimate objective of Environmental Education is to formulate a responsible attitude in the young mind towards sustainable development (Dash and Satapathy, 2004). The development of sharing and caring habits help them to grow as responsible persons for solving environmental problems in future. The principles of sustainable development, "live together" and "allow others to live" will create a broad minded, kind hearted human being who can easily take care of his own environment, without having a callous nature. Thus a child will come out from the cocoon of long years of getting environmental education with appreciation of planet earth, its beauty and an assumption of environment ethics (Ramesh, 1998).

The reason behind incorporating textbooks with large amount of information regarding environment, is to make it more functional than any other discipline we have studied so far. The disciplinary approach in science and social science is meaningless for majority of the students who drop out before or after completing the schooling or discontinue their education in the middle or high school level. The complicated definitions of science and mathematics, long structural and molecular formula of complicated compounds, details of the historical development have no use in their day to day life. Majority of them do not use this knowledge in future. On the other hand it is often seen that more than 50 per cent of the students often fail to identify the local trees, do not know the name of medicinal plants, values of trees for timber and fuel, etc. This explains the need for environmental education that acts as a powerful device to prepare children for future.

Thus environmental education sharpens the thinking and reasoning ability of the children for the betterment of environment as well as their own sake. It is highly essential for self-fulfilment and social development. The main objectives (UNESCO, 1985) behind it are:

- To create and infuse awareness about the numerous elements that make up the environment, of the total environment and its allied problems.
- To help them to acquire basic understanding of the total environment, its interrelationships with man including indigenous tradition and cultural practices related to the environment with a view to promote conservation and wise use of natural resources.
- To help learn a little more about the subject/topic in the lesson with specific reference to some environmental aspect.
- To help students to view environment as an integral part of what they are learning and doing.
- To develop sensitivity to and appreciation of the tremendous diversity in the natural and human world as adding richness to every aspect of life and learning.
- To help them to acquire social values including strong feelings of concern for the environment and the motivation for actively participating in its protection and improvement.
- To help them to acquire the skills for solving environmental problems.

The concept of man-nature interdependence highlights the dynamic nature of the relationship between human beings and environment. This should be the cornerstone of bringing about an understanding of environment leading action for sustainable development. Thus EE aims to "aid citizens in becoming environmentally knowledgeable, and above all, skilled and dedicated, willing to work individually and collectively, toward achieving and/or maintaining a dynamic equilibrium between quality of life and quality of environment" (UNESCO, 1990).

Environmental Education: As a Challenge for School System

Environmental Education, as we consider it to be a bunch of efforts to solve environmental problem, must look after the need and interests of the people, society and the nation. Thus it is a challenge for the environmental educators to handle the new generation tactfully coping with new knowledge and techniques to meet the demands of the changing social and geographical landscape. A solid base for environmental education already exists. Time to time it needs to be renewed looking into different age groups and different problems/concerns at different contexts. The way we plan today on environment and its protection for the children will have a great impact on their future quality of life as well as the quality of the nature. So it is often considered as a challenge before us. The NCERT (2004) document '*Environmental Education in Schools*' speaks that the implementation of EE in schools needs to be undertaken in a mission mode to prepare young minds to appreciate the importance of environment in a holistic manner not only for human survival but for all life forms on earth.

The right way of exposing students to environmental concerns is by giving equal emphasis to each and every aspect of environmental problems. The child should be well aware of major environmental concerns like deforestation, global warming, ozone depletion, industrial pollution, etc, as we call those as "loud emergencies" (UNICEF, 1989). Similarly she should also be exposed to the ongoing silent emergencies of environmental degradation like under nutrition, unsanitary surroundings, unsafe drinking water, premature death, poverty, sickness, and other crippling diseases. The protection of children from the negative consequences of these silent environmental threats is no less important than efforts to deal with the louder environmental emergencies especially in the developing countries like us. The neglect of these concerns can only accelerate the environmental perils, which threaten the human beings especially the younger generation.

Learning more about what we have done to the environment is not so much essential as what we can do for the care of it. The children should acknowledge the danger, and side by side learn how to overcome it so as to save the earth and mankind. Certain exciting opportunities should be given to the children for enhancing learning besides sharpening observation through actual experiences. Thus the environmental planners and educators must come up with new knowledge and techniques to fulfil the demands by preparing a well-defined and structured modern, curriculum that becomes relevant to the needs and interests of the community.

Environment is our source for developmental processes. But we often damage this environment through over-consumption that leads to waste, and pollutes the nature. Affluence is a major cause of environmental degradation. The affluent people consume more and are the major producers of household garbage, toxic industrial waste, automobile exhaust fumes, and commercial deforestation and so on. For children, affluence of this type is a threat to their future. From the very formative stages they should learn not to waste resources, consume essentials and help conserve the resources for future use. Environmental education should emphasise the principle of sustainable economy. Optimum resource consumption being economically viable is highly essential instead of over or minimum consumption. The children should be taught how to adopt a new approach to "do more with less" while safeguarding and improving the natural resource base for future.

Today's child is more intelligent and probably has wide access to information relating the environment than before. These media-inspired children may become highly effective managers for environmental protection if we ignite the spark on them by giving proper environmental education. Even if they are well informed regarding environment, they do not have actual experience with the natural world. On the other hand, in case of most of the rural based children, exposure to information is not sufficient but their association with nature is quite strong enough to create an instant desire to save the natural heritage and nature as a whole. Thus the environmental education should fulfil these objectives having similar goals but through different strategies.

The Structure of Environmental Education

The importance of environmental education in understanding, preventing and solving problems related to environment has been widely recognised all over the world. Evidences to this are a number of national and international conferences, seminars, workshops on the theme and efforts made by different countries in introducing the perspective and scope of environmental education at all levels of educational system. In spite of this, till now an effective curriculum (UNESCO, 1986) is yet to be prepared on Environmental Education that provides an 'experiential learning' to the children and helps to develop right kind of attitude and values. As such, there is an urgent need for a value based action oriented course of EE that would lead from knowledge to feeling and finally to appropriate action (NCERT, 2004).

Curriculum and Content

In the Indian situation environmental education has generally been visualised as a multi-disciplinary (Fig. 2.2) area of study. However the introduction of environmental education at school level has become mandatory. Accordingly, NCERT has played a pioneering role (NCERT, 1981) in the country in disseminating ideas about environment, environment crises and ways and means to overcome those in a number of ways. The National Curriculum Committee had recommended in the 1975 policy document "The National Curriculum for the Ten year School: A Framework" that a single subject environmental studies be taught at primary stage. It had proposed that in the first two years (Class I and II), environmental studies will look at both the natural and social environment while in Class III and IV, there should be separate portions for social studies and general science themes as EVS part I and part II respectively. Following the National Policy on Education (NPE, 1986), NCERT (1988) developed the "National Curriculum for Elementary and Secondary education: A framework—1998" which reflects the same approach for the teaching of environmental studies at primary stage. It viewed that "the school curriculum should highlight the measures for environmental protection and the prevention of pollution and conservation of energy".

According to the recommendation of the National Curriculum Framework for School Education (NCERT, 2000), environmental studies be taught as an integrated course for the entire primary stage, instead of two distinct parts devoted to science and social studies in Class III-IV. The subject the Art of Healthy and Productive Living, along with language and mathematics has been introduced at the level of Class-I and II. In Class-III and IV, environmental studies have become a separate subject. At the upper primary and secondary level, (in Classes VI-X) environmental education has been integrated in different subjects like social sciences, science and technology and languages. At the higher secondary level, besides the vocational education stream most of the topic related to environment are found in integrated form. The National Curriculum Framework (NCERT, 2005) has called for continuation of this integrated approach for environmental studies during the primary years. Some of the specific objectives of teaching environmental studies at primary stage as observed by the document are:

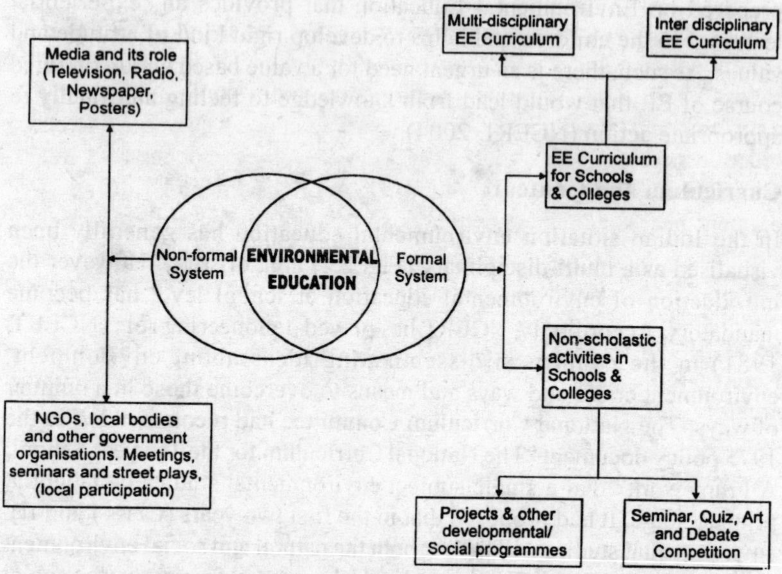

Fig. 2.2: Dimensions of Environmental Education

- To develop an understanding based on observation and illustration drawn from life experiences and physical, biological, social and cultural aspects of life and
- To nurture curiosity and creativity of the child by engaging the child in exploring and hands on activities to acquire basic cognitive and psychomotor skills through observation, classification, inferences, etc.

The infusion model of environmental education curriculum followed presently not only emphasises content, spreading in different disciplines (NCERT, 2005) but also on the development of awareness, attitudes and skills, on environment leading to action. The greening of text books (CEE, 1994) involves bringing in environmental prospective, concepts, information, data, questions, exercises, activities, visuals, etc. into the text books. True greening involves both in terms of the content what is written and the ways it lends itself to be taught. But its success is a question. The content related to environmental education is given in the textbooks of biology, chemistry, physics, geography, and languages, even in mathematics. However often it is marked that while transacting the curriculum in the class room the teacher tends to neglect the environmental education dimension of the subject curriculum. For example while dealing with pesticides in chemistry curriculum, the teacher may include pesticides, their chemical structure, synthesis, etc, but the most vital part is its application which is sometimes over-looked. "The correct use of pesticides", "ignorance of the people/farmers regarding its health impact," "the substitutes of pesticides": these are certain concepts that need to be included in subject curriculum. Sometimes the subject teacher does not give sufficient importance to the particular Environmental Education component because of their own education being based on traditional disciplines.

While infused in different subject curricula, it is often marked that environmental education content is not blended properly. It is found even in the NCERT textbooks that the infused materials do create incoherence and confusion in the curriculum. Environmental problems are not adequately defined in terms of their socio-economic and political determinants. This makes it unlikely that children will understand what they must do and how they should do it (Jackson, 2001).

The multidisciplinary model (Fig. 2.3) of environmental education may be suitable at primary stage, but its appropriateness decreases with increasing level of school system particularly at the higher classes. Tbilisi conference on environmental education recommended the guiding principles of environmental education that put stress on the disciplinary approach (UNESCO, 1998). It states that "environmental education should be interdisciplinary in its approach drawing on the specific content of

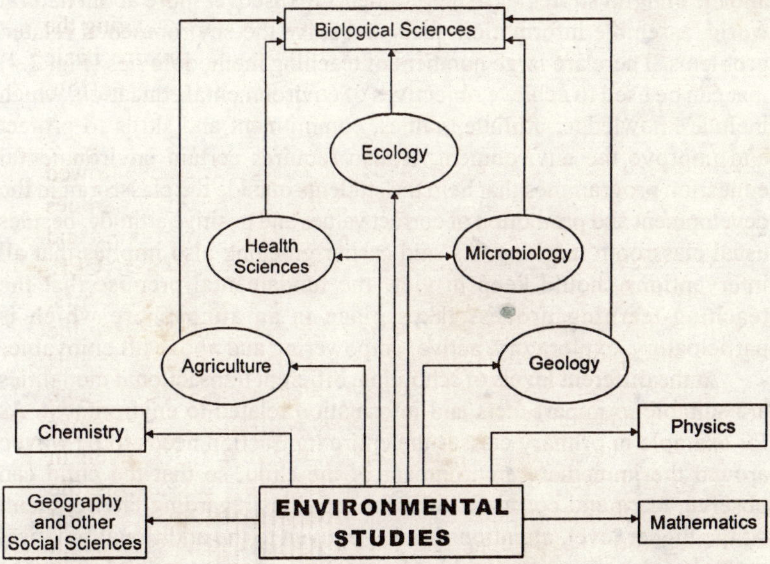

Fig. 2.3: Multi-disciplinary Model, to Teach Environmental Sciences

each discipline in making, possible holistic and balanced perspective". Interdisciplinary approach often suggested (NCERT, 2004) will help in more in-depth coverage on major environmental issues from local, national and international points of view, so that students receive proper insights into different environmental problems and concerns. However it is not easy to implement, as it would lead to curriculum load in the form of an extra subject. Further, it is necessary to reformulate the curriculum in other subject areas in order to avoid repetition, excess information load of incomprehension, etc.

Sometimes it is said (Prolix, 2004) that infusion of environmental education with biology curriculum is the best approach for teaching environmental education. Because of the similarities in the concepts, the environmental sciences can be properly blended with biological science. Further the integration may not impose an extra burden on the curriculum load of the student and side-by-side it will provide practical solutions of human suffering due to environmental destruction. Thus biologists must understand their responsibilities and should try honestly to infuse the environmental concerns on the student's mind along with their traditional biology teaching.

Pedagogical Issues

Effective environmental education requires the recognition of appropriate and meaningful strategies to help students to discover more about natural world, assemble information, facts and solve the environmental related problems. There are large numbers of teaching methodologies (Fig. 2.4) that can be used to achieve objectives of environmental education, which include knowledge, attitude, values, commitment and skills to protect and improve the environment. It also requires certain environmental education programmes that help the students outside the classroom in the development and promotion of correct values and positive attitude, besides usual classroom teaching. As said earlier greening also implies that all interventions should keep in view the fundamental premise that the teaching-learning process takes place in an atmosphere which is participatory, exploratory, active, empowering and above all enjoyable.

At the different levels of schooling, different transactional modalities are suitable to impart facts and information related to environment. As for example in primary classes the entire transaction needs to be woven around the immediate environment of the child, so that the child can observe, learn and correlate different activities regarding environment. At the higher level, attention should be given to the additional practical inputs besides classroom teaching by creating separate time slot and space within the total curriculum framework (NCERT, 2005). The practical

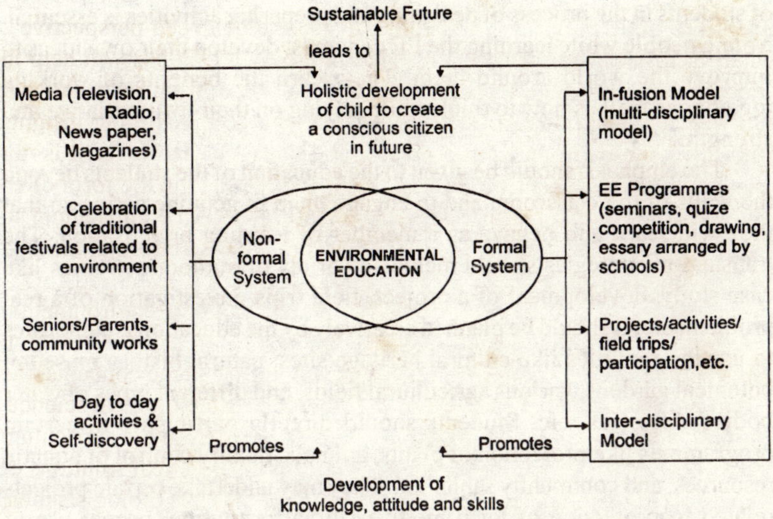

Fig. 2.4: Ways and Means of Imparting Enviromental Education

works should be related to different projects, investigation and analysis, like investigation of a degraded ecosystem, project work to restore a wasteland, tree plantation, study of local bio-diversity, etc. Again the practical inputs in the curriculum should be reflected in the physical environment of the school like cleanliness of school premises, maintenance of school garden, making the campus green by plantation, water and sanitation facilities, water harvesting, garbage management, celebration of environment related festivals, programmes, etc.

Although different transactional modes are used at different levels of school education, the pedagogy should have to be based on local contextuality, the indigenous social perception of environment and the cultural traditions (NCERT, 2004). Side by side it should be based also on modern ideas, thinking and exploration of real situation.

Various methods like inquiry, investigation, simulation, research and problem solving, etc. are ideal to develop knowledge about environmental issues and also help exposing students to a variety of contradictory concepts to increase their environmental literacy (Proulx, 2004). All these activities based teaching help in the blending of most useful constructive concepts with critical thinking and skill development. These activities and projects need to include those relevant to different age groups, in different contexts and in different situations. However activities should not presuppose availability of standard equipment and facilities. Rather it should be designed by using locally available materials. The involvement of students in the process of designing and preparing activities is essential. Young people while learning the EE concepts, develop their own ideas to improve the world around them. They learn the benefits of working together as well as how to think while relying on their own initiative and strength.

The emphasis should be given to the education of the students beyond the walls of the classroom and to engage them in genuine action so that they will learn and behave as a member of learning organisation. The transaction strategies should include a variety of outdoor activities like case study, development of a project, field trips, investigation of a real problem, etc. It should be planned creatively by the educational authorities to use the facilities like cultural heritage sites, natural history museum, botanical gardens, various agricultural fields, and different types of water bodies, factories, etc. Students should directly participate in certain programmes like protection of plants, animals, quality control of aquatic resources, and community sanitation. They may undertake certain projects related to protection of local biodiversity, afforestation, proper use of energy resources, protection of local water bodies, sanitation, etc.

This kind of activity based learning often produces economic as well as environmental benefits. For example "greening" activities of the school campus or of a particular public place addresses problems ranging from water conservation to reduction of pesticide level along with food production. These types of programmes popularly known as socially useful productive works (SUPW) try to nurture the environment and side by side help in the future growth of productive members of the society.

It has been said that environmental problems are social problems and to solve these we must use social approaches. The environmental problems we are facing today have been created by humans. The need of social work is imperative, both to help educate those who create problem and those affected by the problem. It will help in the behaviour modification (Fig. 2.5) and expletive attitude of the people. Side by side it may help people to give up their passive behaviour to environmental degradation taking place around them, thus actively involved in enhancing the quality of environment. So it is necessary to take the help of the school children to disseminate environmental awareness in the form of social work (Tompkins, 2005). They can convince the people to understand what they are really doing to damage the environment. This socio-psychological approach will help to create a new system of values, mould the attitude of the people as well as the students so as to become environmentally conscious.

The active participation of parents, family, educational institutions and the entire community are highly essential for the success of

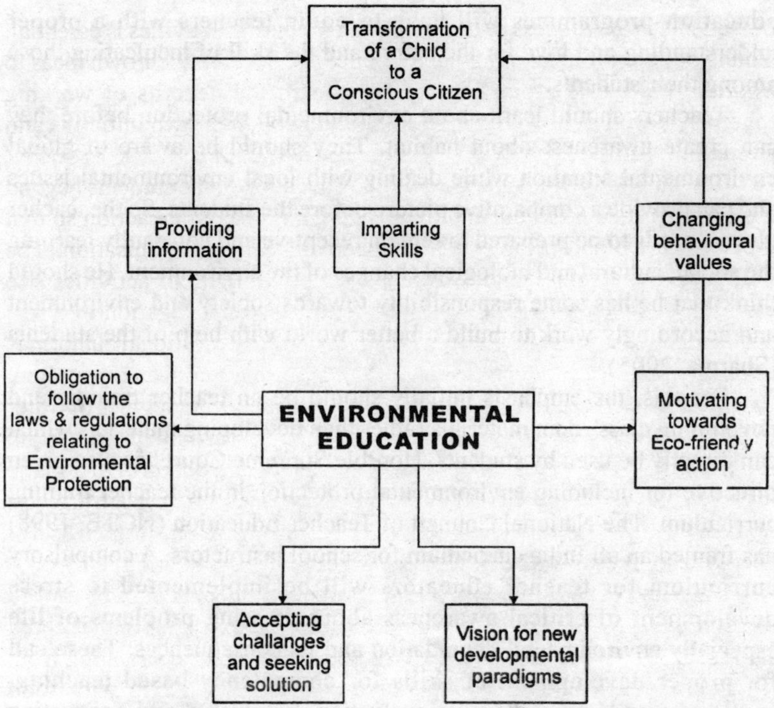

Fig. 2.5: Transformative Role of Environmental Education

Environment Education Programmes. There should be a fair consensus among all the members of the society to interact together for a principal goal that is to enhance the ability of children to become productive members of the society for the development of local as well as global environment. The community based approach like preparation and presentation of street plays for deforestation/afforestation programme, wild life protection, investigation of local polluted water bodies, conservation of fuels, etc. are helpful for action oriented practical value clarification and building up positive attitudes. Thus, the school system must devote certain amount of time to community services and outward activities that seek to produce tangible results.

Teacher Training and Instructional Material

If education has to be an effective tool of change in the general attitude towards the treatment of the environment, teacher education will have to respond to this need effectively at all levels (NCERT, 2004). Teachers being the agents of social change, the content and process of teacher education programmes will have to equip teachers with a proper understanding and love for the nature and the skill of inculcating those among their students.

Teachers should learn about environmental protection before they can create awareness about habitat. They should be aware of global environmental situation while dealing with local environmental issues and can provide a comparative picture before the students. So the teacher always needs to be prepared to remain receptive and constantly learning the social, cultural and biological changes of the environment. He should think that he has some responsibility towards society and environment and accordingly work to build a better world with help of the students (Sharma, 2005).

For this, the emphasis initially should be on teacher training and developing class room materials rather than developing materials which can directly be used by students. Hon'ble Supreme Court has also given directive for including environmental protection in the teacher training curriculum. The National Council of Teacher Education (NCTE, 1998) has framed an all India curriculum for school instructors. A compulsory curriculum for teacher educators will be implemented to stress development of critical awareness about pressing problems of life especially environmental degradation and its consequences. These call for proper development of skills for competency based teaching, continuous and comprehensive evaluation, organising and conducting projects and activities related to local specific conditions and the daily life of learners.

Though some environmental educational materials are being developed by various agencies, they are not available in all the local languages. So materials (Print/non print) which are relevant to the local environmental contexts need to be developed and made accessible to teachers across the country.

In-service education and training through refresher courses, seminars, guidebooks and field exposure are essential to assist practicing teachers to enhance their teaching skills, to infuse environmental education in their teaching (Roux and Ferreira, 2005). These programmes will help them to meet the challenge of attempting to involve themselves and their learners in improving the status of the environment as well as in solving environmental problem. A detailed design of in-service programmes covering various aspects of content and methodology needs to find place in the agenda of District Institutes of Education and Training (DIET), Colleges of Teacher Education (CTEs), Institutes of Advanced Studies in Education (IASES) and State Councils of Educational Research and Training (SCERTs).

The main aim of the environment educators should be to produce and look after certain measurable results. We, the adults were well-informed about environment and its degradation; still, many of us have callus attitude towards nature. Attitudinal change along with updated knowledge/awareness will create future environmental advocates and problem solvers. The teacher should recognise the problems both locally and globally and begin responding effectively in classroom situation to make it an imprint on the child's brain. Once out of school, the child is transformed into a responsible person who has already learnt to function in the real world. For the teachers of environmental sciences, our challenge is to make students fit in the real situation with skills, desires and commitment. This will be helpful for our mother earth and its inhabitants both human and non-human.

Conclusion

At the national level, despite of inculcation of a good amount of information regarding environment, we have not succeeded to generate environmental consciousness among all. An integrated/infused model of environmental education has simply imparted incidental knowledge/awareness responding to the phenomenon related to environment. It has not yet succeeded to create belongingness, an emotional feeling for the nature. The curriculum should reflect this aspect for the betterment of environment and its management. Whether environment education should be a compulsory, separate subject or integrated in science and social science, is a different issue but it must impart value inculcation in the young minds and sensitise them to the environmental problems and concerns. The implementation of environmental education needs to be undertaken in a mission mode to germinate the seeds of positive attitude towards nature care and sensitivity for living creatures in the young minds (Fig. 2.5) leading to a sustainable future.

Environmental education however should not be confined to the classroom alone; teacher and students should extend it through field programmes and Eco-development camps to rural people who are our major producers and stake-holders in managing our natural resources and through pamphlets, booklets and Websites to urban people who are the major consumers and polluters. TV programmes, CDs and DVDs on environmental case studies in local languages can disseminate environmental messages faster to the whole length and breadth of our country. It needs our collective effort and coordination between the MHRD and MoEF, between centre and states, between government department and NGOs, etc.

3

Environmental and Ecological Programmes in Higher Education

J.G. RAY

Environmental educators believe that any good education is in fact environmental (Chhokar, 2000). Ecology is a moral science—a science that should teach humans to improve the sum total of relationships with their fellow beings and surroundings. Ecological studies enable us to change our life style and help us develop an integrated approach to the management of life (Ray, 1999). In fact all the good programmes of higher education also have the same aim. In a discussion on the role of ecological and environmental themes in higher education programmes, it is therefore, inevitable to have a bird's-eye view of the major issues of education system as a whole in the contemporary society.

Ours is a time of very fast transitions in all walks of human life. Major changes in political and economic systems are presently sweeping across the world (Sharma, 1998). Transformations that a society is going through warrant a rejuvenation in the way we teach and what we teach (Gautham, 2000). Lack of job opportunities, chronic parental poverty, aimless education which is neither life oriented nor job oriented, corruption in public life, etc. are challenging the noble concepts of education all over the world. Now the general tendency among the rulers of nations all over the world is to consider higher education as a private merit good. States of the world are trying to put the whole burden of education on the heads of individuals themselves as if the individuals and not the public are the sole benefactors of the process. How can we then make education a perfect and integrated process of development of the brain and the souls of individuals for the sustainable progress of States and the World? (Kale, 2006)

Policies of liberalisation lead to a shrinking of our sympathies and concerns for the underprivileged. The poor are now left to suffer for themselves against the cruel market forces. Environmental educators should definitely note this contradictory situation before trying to introduce programmes to generate concerns and sympathies towards natural systems as a whole in the minds of our people. Environmental concern really stems from concerns for fellow beings and it is definitely an extension of universal goodwill.

Trends in Higher Education—A Postmortem Analysis of the Causes

Most of the countries, especially the underdeveloped have been facing certain paradoxical problems in their national life for the last few decades. Persons of integrity and talent do not enter public life because of the filth and stench, and yet public life cannot be cleansed unless persons of talent and integrity enter it. Another paradox, especially in the Indian context is that of growing indiscipline and mediocrity in the higher educational institutions. Universities and colleges in general, lack leadership of teachers. Most teachers in many of the institutions of underdeveloped world do not possess leadership qualities. They are not able to command respect of their students either by scholarship in their subject areas, or by their personalities. Perhaps, this problem exists in some of the institutions in the developed world as well. Who are to be blamed for this pathetic degeneration of higher educational systems—the teachers or the society that appoint them as their teachers? In fact these two paradoxical problems are interrelated and do require immediate attention by all those who are involved in educating the talented youth towards a better public and environmental consciousness. For environmental education is nothing but a perfect education. It is important to remember at this juncture the famous advice of the great Teacher President of India, Dr. S. Radhakrishnan: "*No society can rise above the level of their teachers.*"

Reasons of Quality Deterioration among Teachers

In countries like India, the major post-independent efforts were to develop more opportunities for higher education. There occurred inflation in higher educational institutions, programmes, and the educated mass in the last few decades. The impact of this inflation is visible on the products—lack of proper knowledge, professional competencies and erosion of value systems are all visible in the majority of the aimless worthless mass who enrol and pass out of these institutions. If we take a closer look at such institutions, what we find is that most of them are still remaining poorly equipped and lack facilities for proper learning. In such over crowded institutions, teachers cannot provide personal guidance. Most of the people who run such institutions—government, majority or minority, caste in the name of charity or business—are not always committed to the sustainable progress of the society and are often mere money mongers having only petty interests. Instead of recruiting the most talented and professionally inspired persons as teachers, they had been seeking the biggest pockets (even if they are mediocre brains). This situation is exactly true in a majority of the government aided private institutions in India where salary is disbursed from the public funds. On the other hand, in government educational institutions of this country, the reservation policies and other petty policies of petty politicians of the states negatively intrude into all levels of teacher selections and thus prevent the most qualified and committed persons becoming teachers. In spite of all the efforts of the University Grants Commission and other agencies of the Government of India, quality maintenance and improvement in higher educational institutions in most of our universities and college remains paralysed. Instead of being the citadels of minds and souls of our people, they have been driven to become shelters of academic mediocrity and choking emptiness.

The unaided private institutions are also not better. They usually seek mediocre persons as teachers who could be satisfied with the minimum salary for maximum job. The academically excellent private institutions, where there could be certain academically bright and committed teachers, are most often inaccessible to the talented youths who are not financially well off to pay the huge admission and tuition fees. Then, do we have the moral right to consider the knowledge the students acquire through such a system as a public merit good to support the delicate needs of the underprivileged as part of the holistic progress of nations? Mediocre faculty and mediocre students cannot generate quality and excellence, which are inevitable in instilling the environmental concerns in the educated elite.

The youth that come out of the higher educational institutions of modern times lack initiative and imagination to solve many of the environmental problems. They usually have no self-confidence and their hearts cannot be moved towards the noble environmental concerns and ecological consciousness. When teaching and learning remain an indifferent and impersonal process, how can we expect students to develop sensitivity towards social and environmental problems, which are the two sides of the same coin? Bernard Shaw once said, "*among all the negative traits that humans possess, indifference is the most inhuman of them all*". The present day education system based on indifferent teaching and learning can unfortunately produce only subhuman or inhuman souls who cannot solve environmental problems however well they are informed of the causes and consequences of the issues. They only make new problems and aggravate the old ones.

Moral deterioration of the educational process brings in cynicism, pessimism, avarice, and rebellious tendency among the youth. The half-filled or half-baked minds of the youth who are irrationally and irresponsibly graded by poorly qualified teachers of our system do not possess the necessary quality and standard to stand united in the interests of sustainable progress of the world. Most often, do we not see students score high marks/grades in the examinations without any comprehensive knowledge in their subject? Therefore, all those who think about environment and ecological training in higher education must be aware of this historical background as well as the present state of affairs in the higher education systems in our country and of the world. First, environmental educators should, therefore, aim at eradicating all the problems of higher educational process. Second, we must try to find out methods to educate our students to become committed and dedicated towards the cause of environmental and ecological problems.

Recent Trends in Higher Education System in Relation to Environmental Education

The present age is an age of informatics. Entertainment media muddy and foul the minds of children and youth with movies that are hell bent on exalting violence, crime, sex and vulgarity. Therefore, the first thing that environment educators should look into is the educational environment itself.

In the field of higher education, the era of acquiring knowledge for knowledge's sake is over (Gnanam, 2000). People are now expecting skills, vocationalisation of education, experimental learning, etc. from higher education. Nevertheless, one of the most important aspects of higher education is the acquisition of culture. Culture is the refinement of feelings and actions. But the culture that we provide in higher educational institutions of modern times enables the pupil only to develop selfishness and a certain indifference to all the social, political and natural systems of the state and the world. Education usually brings in expensive habits which parents cannot afford (Elwin, 1960). We most often teach them the etiquette and customs of foreigners as if they are supposed to live outside. How can then we expect a generation of educated youth with proper environment and social concerns coming out of our institutions? This way the educated naturally get alienated from their environment (Narayan, 1999). The students, when they come out of their institutions, alienate themselves automatically from their parents, home, village, and country and from the world environment. They usually have only materialistic and selfish motives and indifference to all other needs of the society. Higher education, which is supposed to provide a sense of direction to a nation or a community, brings in only confusion and not conviction in the minds of the educated with regard to their total relations and life styles.

A nation's greatest renewable resource is its human resource (Remadevi, 2001). Education is the realisation of perfection already in man. The educated should have the capacity and intellectual curiosity to solve problems of humankind as a whole. The three important goals of higher education are: (a) Produce the human resource required by the society. (b) Promote researches required for industrial development, social progress and survival. (c) Generate knowledge for promoting a better social, political and economic order. A fourth and the most important goal must be added to this which is the environmental goa!, making the environment suitable for human inhabitation forever. Environmental and ecological educational programmes in higher education must ensure that the humans may remain the "roof and crown of creation" forever on our Mother Earth.

Environmental and Ecological Themes in Education

Humans differ from beasts only by rational thinking and education. The highest function of a state is to direct society in such a way, as to effect the greatest good of humankind. The ultimate goal of education is well being of human beings on the basis of sound reasoning. Only an environmental and ecological education can assure the welfare of all forever on the earth. In democratic societies, the emphasis of higher education is to develop the concept of equality and freedom—in attitudes, emotions and interests. Teachers and students in such a system should have the freedom from influences, which prevent their stating the truth as they see or perceive it. A proper higher educational programme should have all the elements of a truly democratic system of education. In addition to that, it must enable us to develop commitment towards sustainable progress and happiness of humans all over the world. This is possible only if people have the required knowledge of the environment and the ecological systems, attitudes (the growth of the affective domain leading to eco-conscious behaviour), and the skills (psychomotor training for environment friendly actions) for dealing with the various aspects of their environmental relations.

Ecological Themes for Cognitive Development

The world today is technologically driven. Discoveries in science in one country have far reaching effects on the life-style of people in other countries (Paroda, 1998). Educational institutions are now focusing on competence and skills rather than the knowledge intensive curricula.

However, all agree that future learners must be flexible generalists—persons equipped with necessary level of knowledge, skills, and values to adjust readily to the inevitable professional changes which they may have to cope with in future. Ecological and environmental awareness and wisdom are the most significant parts of general knowledge that the future technocrats require to excel in any field of specialisation.

Ecology is the integrated study of the complex interrelationships that exist among different kinds of organisms as well as between themselves and their environment. Moreover, it is the study of all sorts of systems originating out of such interrelationships between organisms and their surroundings. Environmental studies prove that no living individual is a perfect or an independent form of life. Instead, the life of all organisms depends on certain unique interrelationships, interaction, and exchanges among the living and the non-living. Ecology reveals that the boundary between the living and the non-living is quite thin, as the exchanges between both are continuous and intensive.

Thus ecology enables us to understand that all organisms on the Earth's surface are nothing but parts of the only perfect living form (organism) popularly known as 'mother nature'; but ecologists designate it as the biosphere. This concept may be extended to visualise that life on the earth has no beginning nor end, and no evolution at all! All such phenomena of birth, death and evolution of individual organisms or species, which we regularly see on the Earth's surface, are nothing but just illusions or temporary transitions on the face of the biosphere.

Environment means the sum total of relationships among the organisms and their surrounding—relationships which are direct and indirect, far and near; between the living and the non-living, all responsible for the sustenance of organisms as specific entities in nature. It means a strong network of relations tightly binds all organisms.

Human being is the only intelligent species capable of comprehending the actual network of relationships in nature and modifying it for its own convenience or benefit. Nevertheless, humans are not as interested in understanding the relationships as they are in modifying it for their convenience. In addition, in this process they ignorantly destroy it. Primitive humans considered all the natural controls as bondage and wanted to break away from them. They could not understand the significance and intricacies of natural balance. Their quest to conquer nature led to massive destruction of forests, revolutionary methods of agriculture, unscrupulous mining of geological resources and criminal release of sewage and sludge and other industrial waste substances (chemicals, solids, liquids & gases) of diverse kinds into nature. Different kinds of industrial developments disregarding their catastrophic influence on environment lead to non-ecological, non-sustainable progress, which is better to be designated as 'regress' in the eyes of ecology. Unaware of the safety provided by the rigid environment relations set by nature, humans have made such mistakes.

Advancement of ecological thoughts has awakened humanity to the possibility of a happy, healthy and sustainable existence if measures are taken to maintain the natural balance. However, at present such a process is not easy. Humans have already forgotten the concept of simple living practices advocated by men of wisdom in the past. Modern humans find themselves in an unprecedented situation. They have to find solutions for all the mistakes of their predecessors and at the same time, they should cautiously proceed to safeguard their own interests as well as that of posterity.

Nature at present is in a highly modified state, which is quite different from its original state untouched by human greed and power. Therefore, at this moment we cannot leave nature-to-nature's processes hoping for a better future. Instead, we have to manage it properly, i.e. ecologically. Human economy, politics, social interests, trades, etc. should be adjusted in tune with sound environmental relationships. Science and technology should have the same goal.

Success of science lies in its ability to provide practical solutions to human sufferings. Therefore, all the educated should learn ecological principles and must understand the Herculean task ahead of them—the task of solving human beings' relations with the environment as well as with their own kind. The ecologically educated have a diplomatic duty to coordinate all human efforts for sustainable progress at a global level. Only a proper ecological knowledge would enable people to work towards eradication of social, racial, economic, political and religious disparities and conflicts of all kinds from the face of the world. Then alone we can expect that a war free, peaceful, conflict-free, happy new world would be ushered into our mother Earth which has been showing signs of death in many of its living systems. Ecological knowledge alone can help human beings to grow out of their 'wells' to a level of international/global citizenship. Environmental education provides a foundation for a new international order (Pandey, 2000).

Environmental knowledge is not only essential for all branches of science but is also an inevitable part of all of them. It is a science, which helps us to understand how everything or every human activity is related to its immediate or distant surroundings in the past, present or future. It is better not to be considered as a branch of science but it must be understood as a super science that embraces all sciences. Therefore, it is important for all humans all over the world. Anything or any human activity can be an object of study for environmental science. It may even be considered as a new method of study that all sciences should follow.

Ecology on the other hand is a science, which is partly abstract and partly concrete. The basis of ecological philosophy (ecosophy) is that life does exist at higher levels—above the level of individual organisms (Ray, 2001). The object of study in ecology is not a living thing but a living state—a system of life.

All the youth in all the different higher educational streams should have the above said style of a cognitive thinking with regard to the environment around. The curricula of all the degree programmes should therefore, contain relevant data on ecological concepts and details of structure and function of diverse natural systems—populations, communities, and ecosystems. This will definitely enable them to have necessary knowledge of interrelations, which humans have to keep in mind to manage and work for sustainable progress on the earth's surface. In addition to that, they require information on problems of pollution and processes of solution for all the different kinds of pollutions.

Concepts of cleanliness, human rights, art appreciation, gender issues, child care, value education, population education, sex education and health education must become part of every department of universities and colleges all over the world. These are all crucial issues related to the holistic concept of environmental education. Science and technology students need to understand the impact of their findings on society and social issues and vice versa. Students must learn that consumerism among the affluent and the example that it sets, and population growth are the two driving forces of environmental stress (Menon, 1997).

In India, religious fundamentalism has begun to raise its demonical head and the people are persuaded to become religious bigots and develop hatred and enmity towards the people of other faiths. Therefore, we must provide proper knowledge to all our youth as was taught by Swami Vivekananda. This is an important part of training that our youth require for a holistic development of their mind and intellect. Swami Vivekananda considered religion not as a mere empty ritual. According to him, it is the way we greet our fellow beings and the friendship we show to others. The approach of locating the divinity that lies within us and searching for it in others must be a life long mission—a mission which will make our life exciting, useful and noble and help us to make India and the world a heaven. Our educated youth of all disciplines should not miss this wisdom as is found in our Upanishads and the teachings of Swami Vivekananda. Indian philosophy as advocated by our great Rishis and Vedic masters can help our youth to develop cognitive thinking based on environmental and social concerns. Therefore, definite programmes on cultural heritage of India and other neighboring countries should be included in the curricula of undergraduate and postgraduate courses of all disciplines. Nation's unique cultural and traditional identity and value system should not be lost in the sweep of globalisation (Pandey, 1998). Environmental education is really a learning, which must transform people to lead an eco-centric and bio-centric mode of life on the earth. Environmental consciousness and eco-friendly behaviour can be expected from people only if they develop a philosophy of life based on truth and principles. Knowledge of ecological concepts and rational thinking about the cause and consequences of human actions on earth are essential for changing thinking habits of people to an eco-friendly one.

How to Develop the Affective Domain toward Eco-centric Behaviour

Being interested in materialistic relations alone would not help humans to become ecological in action and to solve their problems of survival forever. Humans will have to find out the true principles of peaceful coexistence. Ancient humans called such a search religious, spiritual, etc. Religion and spirituality have a very great role to play in developing ecological attitude among the educated youth. The Rishis of ancient India always viewed science and religion as two sides of the same coin. All the Vedic and religious preachers of ancient India—Sri Buddha, Sri Sankara, Sri Rama Krishna, Swami Vivekananda, and Mahatma Gandhi enriched the world a lot by their ideas and life. Their teachings are helpful in making excellent the interrelations of humans among themselves and their surroundings.

Gandhian concepts of politics and economics can help our youth develop both the cognitive and the affective intelligence in Ecology and Environmental Sciences. Our ancestors had placed value on nobler aspects of life and were not materialists. They had great respect towards the noble minds who renounced their wealth and sacrificed their lives for the benefit of humanity. However regrettably, in modern times our educated youth have begun to adore wealth and power (Natarajan, 2001). Bill Gates perhaps is more honorable a man than our Mahatma for the majority of the educated elite in modern India! This is a dangerous attitude in people, which is working against ecological goals. As enlightened persons, teachers have the moral duty to pass unbiased judgments and impartial criticisms of social events and trends so that students develop correct attitudes towards all the issues of environmental and social concern. Professors should practice the simplicity in their lives as was practiced by the Mahatma. Then only they can act as role models for the students in higher educational streams.

Higher education should create in pupils the capability to learn on their own from empirical experiences, and to have innovative thinking and perceptions. It should be able to inculcate values in the minds of people. Of all the levels of education, higher education has to play the most important role in value education (Venkataiah, 1998). Intellectuals in this changing world have a major role to play in articulating the voice of the voiceless and speak for the silent majority of the world whose problems of survival are systematically being sidelined by the logic of the state and the market.

Wisdom, the real essence of education, comes from binding knowledge with virtues. Education should not be used to increase wealth as a part of growing selfishness, which creates grave social problems. Environmental educational programmes given by committed teachers with good leadership qualities can help students develop the right attitudes towards all the social and environmental problems which lead to natural disasters.

The five major environmental issues for the whole world are land degradation, biodiversity erosion, air pollution, and destruction of fresh water resources and hazardous waste management. The global biosphere utilisation rate at present is 10 per cent, which should be lowered to 1 per cent in order to keep the balance of nature. Technical changes are dehumanising the world as a whole at a very fast rate. If we want to have a peaceful, affectionate and sane society, we must strive to create a culture of non-violence in all organisations and institutions. Non violence must become part of the ethics of all the educated people all over the world. Ethics and morals are seen as the basic code of decent behaviour of individuals (Homan, 1992)

Non violence is a power, which can be enjoyed equally by all—rich, poor, weak and strong. The concept of non-violence includes elements such as peace, equality, fearlessness, humility, love, self-control, truth, and tolerance. Mahatma Gandhi taught the world the concept of non-violence and ahimsa by the actual practice of both. The way to peace, according to the Mahatma, leads through self-sacrifice (Rolland Romain, 1924). Peace education helps individuals reach more mature decisions regarding their responsibilities as world citizens. Peace skills include an intelligent openness for involvement in peace in one's own sphere, combined with a sense of responsibility for supra-regional and supra-natural concerns (Hermann, 1992). Principles of peace education can permeate all educational and teaching content aiming at eco-friendly behaviour of people.

Higher education has the major task of preparing leaders of different walks of life—social, political, cultural, scientific, and technological. Intellectual dynamism, resourcefulness, and economic prosperity of any nation are reflected in the personal quality of its leaders framed by university education. Without the ecological outlook and temperament, no leader can direct a society to sustainable progress.

The first University Education Commission was appointed in India in 1948 just after independence. Dr. S. Radhakrishnan was its chairperson. The commission had recommended that in the degree course, lives of great religious leaders like Budha, Confucius, Zoraster, Christ, Ramanujan, Nanak, Muhammed, Kabir, etc. be taught (Ghosh, 1997). The second commission led by Dr. Kothari in 1964-66 felt the need for education on social, moral and spiritual values and generally agreed with the recommendations of Radhakrishnan commission in respect of religious and moral education. The International Education Commission on the development of higher education appointed by the UNESCO in 1972 also emphasised that the aim of higher education is developing the "complete man." Therefore, to have the truly eco-friendly attitude in people we should inculcate the values such as love, compassion, sacrifice, non-violence, etc. in them. Human heart is in desperate search for total involvement in life, which is denied by the compulsions of technological culture. Hence, humans are neither at peace with themselves nor with their social and natural environment. This is an important point to be remembered by all the environmental educators in universities and colleges.

Mahatma Gandhi suggested that the content of teaching curricula and other arrangements must be aimed at serving the needs of the village population that forms majority of the people of India. According to him our regional interests alone need not condition our vision. It should encompass the human society as a whole (Ariyaratne, 1997). The Mahatma was a symbol of simplicity. He valued simplicity because it brought him near to truth. He taught it to us not by just advocating it but by practicing simplicity in all his day-to-day activities. Simplicity alone can enable us and motivate us to share what we have with others who are in need. Gandhian concepts motivate us to have love for humanity and love for all living beings. The world has received the philosophy of Ahimsa from Sri Buddha. Being inspired by the preaching of the Buddha, King Ashoka extended protection to all animals, birds, fishes, etc. and he established hospitals for animals in addition to those for humans. Therefore, a course in our rich cultural heritage must be compulsory for all those who pass through the higher educational establishments in this country in order to assure the development of their cognitive and affective intelligence in relation to the environment. At least all the educated should be compelled to learn the works of the father of our nation. They may be asked to study the philosophy and the works of similar scholars who dedicated themselves for social and environmental causes. This way we will be able to make strong personalities with well-developed emotional intelligence suitable for ecological behaviour and actions. The educated who comes out of our universities and colleges should be able to acquire and internalise values which enable them to feel concerned about the environment and feel motivated and committed to repair, maintain and improve it. Nature camps, club activities, and awareness campaigns alone cannot ensure the proper blossoming of the affective domain of our youth towards holistic environmental consciousness.

The Skills to be imparted through Environmental Education

Environmental education must do what conventional education is not doing: it should equip students to integrate learning from different disciplines. Such an education will help people function as responsible citizens—responsible in decision making and problem solving. The educated should acquire the necessary skills to learn how humans and environment interact, how problems arise and how they might be resolved. Therefore, all the educated should get the skills to identify and investigate environmental problems and to contribute to the resolution of these problems. In order to develop these skills, pupils should get out-door education. These include field trips and demonstrations, investigation of natural systems, simulations, case discussions, and action projects. Such kinds of active studies of the environment and natural systems aiming at psychomotor training of students will definitely help them realise that we can't do just one thing, and that everything we do has numerous impacts, often unpredictable and unwanted.

All the future scientists, engineers, managers and those who are in all other services must develop a skill to ensure efficiency in the use of scarce resources and promote life styles that are affordable for themselves as well as for the coming generations. Indian students should have the training to get convinced that the western models of development and consumerism will very soon surrender to the Gandhian concept of self-reliant local systems at the village level. At the same time, all should get convinced that the stability in the progress of each village system depends on the stability of all the villages all over the world and hence the global interest is above all the private, sectarian, local, regional and national interests. Therefore, educators all over the world should inspire to transfer technical skills, machinery and capital, currently committed to war preparations or traditional industrial and market systems to the production of socially useful eco-friendly items (Cassidy, 1987).

Our great Mahatma had the vision of higher education as a process to acquire the skills of social efficiency so that they are able to live and let others live cooperatively. In modern times, the standard of living is measured by a holistic criteria of the quality of life—not just by GNP but in terms of education, life expectancy, equity, health care, etc. (Sen, 1989). Eco-technological revolution, promoting the blending of the traditional and the modern methods for development will influence the integral management of agronomic systems and help improvement in the scientific approach to relevant national policies (Kasturirangan, 2000). Therefore, we must provide programmes to develop the necessary environment and ecological skills to all the students of all the higher educational streams.

Conclusion

True education widens a man's vision, makes him free from narrow selfish considerations, instills self-confidence and prepares him to face the challenges of the times (Ahmadi, 1997). Time has come for us to critically review and take corrective measures for improving the efficiency of our educational system. Students must be motivated enough to accept all the reforms to instil environmental and ecological programmes in their course of studies. If the programmes included are relevant and catering to real time demand of the students or meet the aspirations of target groups, motivation is inherent (Dave, 1998). If all the educated become properly informed and inspired and have the necessary skill to identify the cause and the consequences of environmental problems and are capable of taking precautions to avoid eco-catastrophes, no doubt the earth will definitely become a sustainable paradise for all.

4

Perspectives of Environmental Education in College and University

S.C. SANTRA

Environmental education is a necessary tool for making appropriate decisions concerning the prevention and solution of environmental problems that may be considered as disequilibrium caused by certain factors in the established relationship between humanity, animals, plants and other organisms and the environment. It has been in the last few decades that the impact of human activities on the environment has become more accelerated and pronounced. Pressures from rapid population growth, uncontrolled and lavish consumption, urbanisation, industrial expansion and advances in science and technology and their applications coupled with huge energy utilisation have caused these accelerated changes leading to serious environmental problems. Humanity is the cause and maker of the current environmental problems. Humanity thus needs to be educated for understanding the cause, getting solution and prevention of these problems. Environmental problems range from local to global. But all such problems have to be addressed from local to regional level or even at global level too. Global environmental problems like ozone depletion, global warming, oceanic pollution, climate changes, etc. call for worldwide action and management based on international conventions as both rich and poor countries face the problem to different degrees.

Pollution of the air, water and land is considered as one of the most widespread and threatening environmental problems of our time. Thus pollution control is essential for environmental protection and it is developing as a lucrative business in numerous countries; but much of pollution problem can be averted through people's awareness and appropriate action for environmental protection. Further environmental education is needed to bring the message of rational use of resources particularly to the consumers.

History and Development

No overview of the history and development of environmental education would be complete without reference to many other "education" and fields of study that have, in some way, contributed to or conflicted with its evolution. Over the last five decades phenomenal changes taken place in the field of "Environmental Education". Some landmark states are given below.

- 1984 : IUCN Conference, Paris—first use of term "Environmental Education".
- 1949 : Founding of IUCN
- 1965 : First use of term "Environmental Education" in UK.
- 1968 : UNESCO Biosphere Conference, Paris.
- 1972 ; UN Conference on the Human Environment, Stockholm, Sweden.
- 1975 : Founding of UNEP and IEEP. UNESCO/UNEP International Workshop on Environmental Education, Belgrade.
- 1977 : UNESCO—First Inter-governmental conference on Environmental Education, Tbilisi, USSR.
- 1980 : World Conservation Strategy (IUCN, UNEP, WWF).
- 1987 : UNESCO/UNEP Educational Congress on Environment Education and Training, Moscow.
  - European Year of the Environment.
  - World Commission on Environment and Development—our Common Future—The Brundtland Report.
- 1988 : European Resolution on Environmental Education.
- 1990 : Publication of National Curriculum Documentation for Environmental Education in England.
- 1991 : Publication on Caring for the Earth: A Strategy for Sustainable Living (IUCN et al.).
- 1992 : UN Conference on Environmental and Development—'The Earth Summit'.
- 1996 : Publication of Government Strategy for Environmental Education in England.

The milestones of the environmental education were initiated in 1970s with major attention in Stockholm, Belgrade and Tbilisi Conference.

Goals of Environmental Education

The first UNESCO-UNEP Conference as held In Tbilisi (1977) suggested the following goal of Environmental Education:

- To foster clear awareness of and concern about economic, social, political and ecological interdependence in urban and rural areas.
- To provide every person with opportunities to acquire the knowledge, values, attitudes, commitment to improve the environment, and
- To create new patterns of behaviour of individuals, groups and society as a whole towards the environment.

For achieving the above stated goals, the materials of education and method of teaching should be framed in such manner that awareness of environmental problems, knowledge about the genesis of the problems, attitudes for action and also people's participation in action programmes may be aroused through education about environment. There are a number of guided principles for curriculum build up process. These are as follows:

- To consider the environment in its totality—natural and built, technological and social;
- To be a continuous lifelong process, beginning at the preschool level and continuing through all formal and non-formal states;
- To examine major environmental issues from local, national, regional and international point of view so that students receive insights into environmental conditions in other geographical areas;
- To focus on current and potential environmental situations while taking into account the historical perspective;
- To promote the value and necessity of local, national and international co-operation in the prevention and solution of environmental problems;
- To explicitly consider environmental aspects in plans for development and growth;
- To enable learners to have a role in planning their learning experiences and provide an opportunity for making decisions, and accepting their consequences;
- To relate environmental sensitivity, knowledge, problem solving skills and values clarification to every age;
- To help learners discover the symptoms and real causes of environmental problems;
- To emphasise the complexity of environmental problems and thus the need to develop critical thinking and problem solving skills;
- To utilise diverse learning environments and a broad array of educational approaches to teaching/learning about the form of the environment with wide stress on practical activities and first hand experience.

Considering the urgency, UNESCO, in co-operation with the United Nations Environmental Programme, launched in 1995 the programme of International Environmental Education Programme (IEEP) for the promotion and development of environmental education for all types and levels of education.

Trends in Environmental Education

For the past four decades there has been rapid change in the approach and targets of environmental education. More and more wider issues have been incorporated in the conventional education pattern due to societal need. The details are given below:

1960s : *Nature Study*: Learning about plants and animals and the physical systems that support them.
Field Work: Led by 'experts' with a particular academic focus-biology, geography, etc.

1970s : *Outdoor/Adventure Education*: Increasing use of the natural environment for first hand experiences.
Field Studies Centers: Growth of field and environmental/outdoor education centers—centers for developing awareness through practical activity and investigation.
Conservation Education: Teaching about conservation issues.
Urban Studies: Study of the built environment, street work.

1980s : *Global Education*: A wider vision of environmental issues.
Development Education: Environmental Education has a political dimension.
Value Education: The Clarifying of values through personal experience.
Action Research: Community problem-solving. pupil-led problem-solving, involving field work.

1990s : *Empowerment*: Communication, capacity-building, problem-solving and action, aimed at the resolution of socio-environmental problems.
Education for a Sustainable Future: Participatory action. Relevant approaches to change behaviour and resolving ecological problems.

2000s : *Community as Partners*? Pupils, students, teachers, NGOs, politicians working together to identify and resolve socio-ecological problems.

There are three important dimensions in education relating to Environment: knowledge and understanding, skills and attitudes. These issues are properly addressed during curriculum build up.

Knowledge and Understanding

As a basis for making informed judgments about the environment, pupils should develop knowledge and understanding of:

- The natural processes which take place in the environment.
- The impact of human activities on the environment.
- Different environment, both past and present.
- Environmental issues such as the greenhouse effect, acid rain, air pollution.
- Local, national and international legislative controls to protect and manage the environment; how policies and decisions are made about the environment.
- The environmental interdependence of individuals, groups, communities and nations.
- How human lives and livelihood are dependent on the environment.
- The conflicts that can arise about environmental issues.
- How the environment has been affected by past decisions and actions.
- The importance of planning, design and aesthetic considerations.
- The importance of effective action to protect and manage the environment.

Skills

- Communication skills
- Numeric skills
- Study skills
- Problem-solving skills
- Personal and social skills
- Information technology skills

Attitudes

Promoting positive attitudes to the environment is essential so that pupils can value it and understand their role in safeguarding it for the future. Encouraging the development of the attitudes and personal qualities below will contribute to this process:

- Appreciation of and care and concern for the environment and for other living things.
- Independence of thought on environmental issues.
- A respect for the beliefs and opinions of others.
- A respect for evidence and rational argument.
- Tolerance and open-mindedness.

Seven areas of knowledge and understanding are identified that may form the basis for the development of worthwhile topics or subject-based interpretation.

These are:

- Climate
- Soils, rocks and minerals
- Water
- Materials and resources, including energy
- Plants and animals
- People and their communities
- Buildings, industrialisation and work

Environmental Curriculum

In general there arc four basic elements to be considered in environmental curriculum build up process. These are as follows:

1. *The Empirical Elements*: This is concerned with those aspects of the environment that lend themselves to objective demonstration, measurement and analysis…the main priority is to ensure that all pupils have as many opportunities as possible of making direct contact with the environment through observation and by measuring, recording, interpreting and discussing what has been observed.

2. *The Synoptic Element*: Pupils need to be made aware of the complex nature of the environment. The aim of synoptic studies is to help pupils realise the complexity of such issues and to introduce them to the inseparable nature of the various components of the environment and to the inter-relations of these. Method is as important as content in achieving this.

3. *The Aesthetic Elements*: Of the many aspects of the environment, perhaps the most important are qualitative rather than quantitative. The aesthetic elements can help a pupil to realise that there is no right or wrong answer in absolute terms to aesthetic questions and that the answer to environmental issues is frequently a compromise.

4. *The Ethical Element*: A programme of environmental education aims at introducing pupils to the idea of personal responsibility for the environment and the concept of stewardship. It trains pupils to ask if the criteria of proposed actions are based on morally justifiable values. These four elements are useful in that they help make the link between the three 'threads' of environmental education and the dimensions of learning. When all of these aspects are fused together, they form an approach to planning teaching and learning tasks that reflects the 'three-fold' structure of environmental education, and the expectations of this, are:

- Education about the environment, which is the basic knowledge and understanding of the environment and our complex relationships with it, reflecting the synoptic element.
- Education in or from the environment, that is using the environment as a resource with emphasis both on planned inquiry and investigations and also on providing opportunities for pupils to engage in first-hand personal experiences within it, reflecting the empirical and aesthetic elements.
- Education for the environment, concerned with values, attitudes and positive actions, reflecting the ethical elements. Thus the environmental education should provide experiences of problem-solving, decision-making and participation, with considerations based on ecological, political, economic, social, aesthetic and ethical aspects. It is also about promoting changes in attitudes and behaviour that will help to solve existing problems relating to the environment and to avoid the generation of new ones. The ultimate aim is for every citizen to have formulated for himself or herself a responsible attitude towards the sustainable development of the Earth, an appreciation of its resources and beauty, and an assumption of an environmental ethic. Furthermore, it has been suggested on a wide global scale that in order to achieve this aim, every educational institution needs adequate arrangements for planning and implementing coherent and progressive programme of work with appropriate teaching and learning tasks.

If one is to adopt an approach to planning based on the three recognised 'threads' of education about, in/from and for the environment, then it will be necessary to analyse their inter-relatedness and recognise that all are essential components of planning at every level of education. In schools, this means at levels ranging from whole institution and year group planning to more specific plans for programmes of study, integrated topics, subject-based curricula, and tasks applicable to a whole class, group of learners or an individual. This terminology can of course be adapted to appropriate levels in any educational setting. So, an integral part of the planning process must be consideration of the inter-relationships that exist among the three threads. Perhaps the best way of achieving this is to analyse the core content of environmental knowledge and understanding that one wishes to address, as well as the desired development of related skills and attitudes. Then, by planning a range of complementary learning processes and ensuring coverage of various curriculum elements (e.g. ensuring some practical problem-solving, investigatory activities, qualitative tasks, personal reflections, consideration of responsibilities, etc.) it will be apparent that the dimensions of concepts (knowledge), skills and attitudes are interlinked with the three core structural components (threads) or overall frame-work of the educative process. Fig. 4.1 represents these various components of environmental education in diagrammatic form. Let us consider some examples of the interrelationships between the components identified:

- The acquisition of knowledge and understanding about the environment will enable pupils not just to hold a store of relevant concepts, facts and figures, but also to critically evaluate issues and situations in the light of informed understanding. Knowledge will also inevitably encourage the appreciation and promotion of desired values and attitudes, especially if that knowledge is gained as a result of addressing real issues and problems that have reference point in the learners own lives.

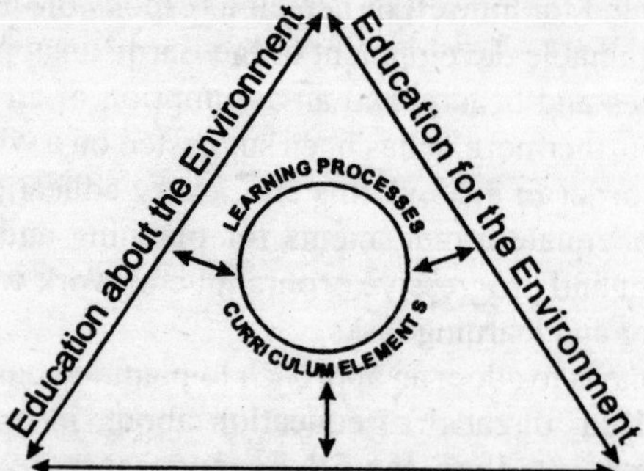

Fig. 4.1: Interrelated Components of Environmental Education

- Personal experiences, investigations and problem-solving in the environment enable reflection and the development of critical awareness and concern. Working in or through the environment leads to the acquisition of a great deal of knowledge and understanding as a result of first-hand experiences, as well as to the refinement of skills such as those needed for investigation, communication, negotiation and problem-solving.
- When pupils are encouraged to explore their personal response to and relationship with the environment and environmental issues, it is likely that this will help them to develop a personal ethic for the world. Knowledge becomes more than 'facts to be

learned'. Learning and reflection 'on behalf of the environment is likely to be of an issue-based, action-oriented, problem-solving nature. Such learning will clearly link with the development of attitudes and values, including elements of and reflections on human understanding and behaviour necessary for the development of sustainable living patterns and caring use of the planet and its resources.

The ultimate goals of environmental teaching and research in college and university level should be the design of survival strategies and the improvement of human well-being.

The environmental education is now taught at college and university levels either as a separate subject or as a component of various interrelated subjects in the West since 1970s. But in the East the process starts somewhat late, i.e. in mid 1980s. Now it was realised as an imperative component of all formal education of Art, Science, Medical, Commerce and Engineering subjects. With the recent Hon'ble Supreme Court judgment, the importance of Environmental Education as an integral component of curriculum at school as well as college level has been realised.

Status of Environmental Education in College and University

In India, over fifty universities offer master level course in Environmental Science/Environmental Engineering as major subject. In addition, at graduate level there is imposition of compulsory environmental studies curriculum already introduced. Though there is wide variation in course content and method of teaching, but the studies on environmental problems, its social and ethical issues, technological solution and community involvement in environment protection, etc. are the major issues of discussion in all sorts of curriculum. Specialised advance course for planner/administrator/management personnels were also introduced in India over a decades or so. However periodic evaluation of status of skill/personality with appropriate attitude for environmental protection of the country needs to be testified.

In addition, College and University will also play a significant role in the countries' non-formal education, i.e. towards "Environmental Awareness Programme". Various voluntary organisations (NGOs) have played a crucial role in linkage of such community based awareness programme implementation. In the last part of the past century the global environmental movement is initiated. It could only be strengthened and meaningful for human welfare through appropriate planning of Environmental Education at all levels.

5

Environment and Sustainable Development

Concept, Model and Principles

DIPAK DE

Environmental issues have served to remind us that development policies need to look beyond the present generation, that we all belong to the same world and that the destinies of all nations are linked. Indeed, it is possible that global environmental issues may reshape relationships among nations. Responding to environmental concerns makes self-interested isolation more difficult and reinforces the need for long-term policies rather than short-term strategies in economic and political relationships.

Environment and Sustainable Development: Concept

Environment is a broad concept encompassing the whole range of diverse surroundings in which we perceive, experience and react to events and changes. It includes the land, water, vegetation, air and the whole gamut of the social order. It also includes the physical and ecological environment. It concerns people's ability to adapt both physically and mentally to the continuing changes in environment. In its natural condition, the environment of any region is in a state of dynamic equilibrium. This is what is called the balance of nature. But when people try to exploit and interfere with nature, this equilibrium is disturbed, in many cases to the detriment of all forms of life. Ultimately, it is the condition of land and water resources and the quality of the air, which we breathe, that determine the health and wealth of a nation.

Over 2000 years ago, the Greek philosopher Aristotle used the spirit of sustainability in defining the term "Oikonomia" the root of the current term economics and contrasting it with an alternate form of development, 'Chrematistics'. Oikonomia is defined by Daly and Coob as "The Management of Household" so as to increase its value to all members of the household over the long run. Much as in the case of sustainable development, oikonomia takes a long run perspective, considers the welfare of the household (or community) as a whole and recognises the necessity of limited accumulation of suppliers if the needs of every one are to be satisfied over the long term. Unfortunately, most of the current economic activities are far from being characterised by the oikonomia. Human kind seems to be much more fascinated by chrematistics, the manipulation of property and wealth so as to maximize short-term monetary exchange value to the owner (taken from TX Annual International Conference of National Environmental Science Academy Proceeding 1996).

During 1950s and 1960s economic growth was considered as one of the important parameters for development while during 1970s environment as another component of the development was considered with emphasis on minimising the negative effects on it. But the higher economic growth and environmental preservation were dealt separately.

Development of human being was guided by enhancing the standard of living of the people whereas sustainability is concerned with the ability of future generation to meet their needs. Maintaining the quality of environment and improving the quality of life are linked up with the present day concept of Development. A search for appropriate technology by using local resources with social and equity justice, participatory decision-making process have become important elements of sustainability.

In the present day, ecology has emerged as a dominant force influencing development-planning efforts. Leibenstain (1957) put forth arguments for a 'big push' to promote development in the developing world. The 'big push' is advocated on the basis of 'theories of circular causation' of poverty. Minimum effort is must to break the vicious circle of poverty. This influenced the planner and the 'big push' got translated into the 'big plan'.

Development is often used interchangeably with the concept of progress, so social process is viewed as the ultimate purpose of development and is a key instrument for the promotion of development. Likewise, in Social Science 'Growth and Development' are two words which have been loosely used in the past. Biologists used these two terms precisely. Growth is increase in weight, height, number or other measured biological parameters while development is coordinated growth of the individual in a way that its genetic potential is fully expressed (Singh 1995)

The meaning of term Development differs from person to person. It is to be considered in total and cannot be categorised into economic, social and political and so on. Thus, the outcome (return against investment) should be appraised in whole than appraising in parts. Most of the interest in planning and development is directed toward and to be focused on economic or material gain. It is assumed that other aspects of the development will automatically be there if material development is achieved. This is being disputed. There are lots of conceptual errors, observed by a group of experts in U.N. Report on problems of social development. The conflicting aspect of development arises from the continued use of those erring concepts. A new shift in concept, which is prefixed with the world 'sustainable', is coming up as an alternative. This shift may be termed as 'sustainable development'. The concept is reviewed chronologically to enrich the field.

The term, 'sustainable development', was coined by World Commission on Environment and Development headed by Gro Harlem Brundtland, in the report *Our Common Future*, London, 1987. The Commission defined sustainable development as 'development that meets the needs of the present without compromising the ability of the future generation to meet their own needs' (Nayak and Kanungo, 1993). It is a concept that can mobilise broader political consensus, one which the international community should build. It is a broad concept of social and economic progress.

The dictionary meaning of sustainability is the amount or degree to which the earth's resources may be exploited without deleterious effects (The Chamber's Dictionary). To sustain means to support life/to provide for the life/to ensure without failing (The New Shorter Oxford English Dictionary).

As quoted by Prasad (1990) in his inaugural address in the 'Third International Conference on Environmental Education' held at Goa, a radically new approach to environment and development is called for, which should be able to anticipate and present or at least minimise damage to the environment with respect to any major development project. The new approach has conceptualised in the term 'sustainable development'. Simply put, this means development, which is in harmony with environmental considerations. The requirements listed by the document *Our Common Future*, of the World Commission on Environment and Development for pursuing sustainable development are:

- A political system that services effective citizen participation in decision making
- An economic system that is able to generate surplus and technical knowledge on a self-reliant sustainability basis
- A social system that provides for solutions for the tensions arising from dis-harmonious development

- A production system that respects the obligation to preserve the ecological base for development
- A technical system that can search continuously for new solutions
- An international system that fosters sustainable patterns of trade and finance
- An administrative system that is flexible and has the capacity for self-correction

According to the World Wildlife Fund (WWF, 1985) sustainable development is the management of human use of the biosphere, taking into account ecological relationships as well as social and economic factors. The capabilities of the living and non-living resource base and long term advantages and disadvantages of alternative actions should be looked into, while maintaining the potentials of a given ecosystem to meet the wants and needs of future generations for food, shelter and other aspects of human civilisation.

IUCN, UNEP and WWF (1991) defined sustainable development as improving the quality of human life while living within the carrying capacity of supporting ecosystems In 1992 Panayotou defined sustainable development as the development that does not result in reduction of the future productive capacity of the economy which depends on the stock of natural capital, human capital and technology, that future generations inherit from the present generation. According to him sustainable development means development at the highest possible rate consistent with leaving the same or an improved endowment of resources and options to the future.

Sustainable development is not a concept that can be implemented through a 'top down' approach. Unlike high technologies which can be acquired, put to use, and maintained without much public participation, any strategy for environmentally sound development needs the awareness, the help and active participation of the citizens. Hence the most important task of environmental education for sustainable development must be to motivate people to get involved in community action and to ensure people's participation in various environmental protection and management projects (Jala, 1989). In general, environment, education and development are the three pillars on which man can sustain his life on earth. Sustained development is simply impossible if environmental degradation is allowed to continue. Environmental education is needed for the wise management and the efficient use of resources (Batanouny, 1989).

Development is sustainable if it consumes resources no faster than they can be generated and a sustainable society is one that satisfies its needs without diminishing the prospects of future generations (Desh Bandhu *et al.*, 1990). UNEP Executive Director Mostafa K. Talba defined sustainable development as development that can be sustainable over the long term by explicitly considering the various environmental factors on which the very process of development is based.

The twin goals of sustainable development are restoration of the past ecological damage and insulation of the society from the damage as a consequence of future development. The latter must entail minimum risk to environment (Khoshoo, 1990). It has been explained by Laflin (1989) in a broader term when he emphasised issues such as participatory decision making and political process, quality of justice, population control, preservation of flora and fauna, efficient use of energy and the quality of life for the present and future generations.

The basic conditions for sustainability are 'participation in the development process that is community driven, community-led and community owned. It depends on conservation of natural resources and their judicial use by the people to preserve and enhance their quality of life. (Manila Declaration 1990)'. Similarly, on the basis of study of several Indian villages, it has been concluded (Agrawal and Narain 1989) that sustainable development can be achieved only by deepening democracy and participation at the village level.

On the nature of sustainability relating to agriculture, Conway (1990) quoted that agricultural sustainability is the ability to maintain productivity, whether of a field or farm or nation, in the face of stress or shock. The stress may be growing salinity, or erosion or debt that is a frequent, sometimes continuous, relatively small predictable force having a large cumulative effect.

The management and conservation of the natural resources base and the orientation of technological and institutional change are organised in such a manner as to ensure the attainment and continued satisfaction of human needs for the present and future generations. Such sustainable development (in the Agril., fisheries and forestry sectors) conserves land, water, plant and animal genetic resources, is environmentally non-degrading, technically appropriate, economically viable and socially acceptable (FAO, 1992).

In addition to covering the essential ecological aspects of sustainable development, this definition also gives equal importance to agronomic, economic and social issues. Optimal resources use and environmental management are combined with increased and sustained production, secure livelihoods, food security, equity, social stability and people's participation in the overall development process. This definition implies fair access to and distribution of production opportunities, economic motivation, equitable distribution of income, development of human resources and optimal use of natural resources.

- Sustainable and equitable development has to be based on ecological principles. Some of the basic assumptions of sustainable development would have to be:
- Human being must learn to live in harmony with nature. All natural things have intrinsic worth. By destroying bio-diversity we reduce our own chance of survival, both physical and metaphysical.
- Quality is important if not more so than quantity. The earth is precious and her supplies are limited hence we must tread carefully and make a conscious effort to minimise our impact on all living and non-living things. Technology is not born in the mind of experts. Technology is a product of human interaction with nature. People know best their own needs and resources and only a decentralised/bio-regional planning approach can result in sustained and low impact appropriate technologies which are creative and meet real human needs (Chatterjee, 1992).

At the practical and operational level sustainable development means ensuring self-sustaining improvements in productivity and quality of life of communities and societies including access to basic needs such as education, health, nutrition, shelter and sanitation, as well as employment and food self sufficiency, ensuring that production processes do not overexploit the carrying and productive capacities of the natural resources base and compromise the quality of the environment, thus limiting the options of the poor, the present and future generations; and ensuring that people have basic human rights and freedoms to participate in the political, economic, social and environmental spheres of their communities and societies (Sing and Titi, 1993).

Sustainable development today means development along the lines of each culture, not development along a common centralised one (Naoss, 1990). In the Diamond Jubilee Symposium organised by Indian Society of Soil Science, Kanwar (1994) mentioned sustainable agriculture as the successful management of resources for agricultural production to satisfy the changing human needs, while maintaining or enhancing the quality of environment and conserving natural resources (TAC, 1988). He also mentioned that there are five important aspects of sustainable agriculture and achievement of all of them is a formidable task. These are:

(i) Meeting the changing needs of today and tomorrow.
(ii) Economic viability at enhanced productivity level.
(iii) Successful management of resources—internal, external, renewable or non-renewable.

(iv) Maintenance, preferably enhancement, of quality of environment.

(v) Conservation of natural resources particularly soil and water, which form the pivot of agriculture.

Jodha *et al.*, (1990) defined sustainability of mountain agriculture as the latter's ability to maintain and enhance its production performance without damaging the long-term production potential. The technical advisory committee of Consultative Group of International Agricultural Research (CGIAR, 1988) states that sustainable agriculture is the successful management of resources for agriculture to satisfy the changing human needs, while maintaining or enhancing the quality of the environment and conserving natural resources. The FAO of United Nations also accepts similar definition.

According to Wright (1995), sustainable Development is 'a process of transformation that increasingly incarnates God's purpose of love for all creation. It meets the essential needs of people but also hopes for improved quality of life. It is a progressive transformation of the situation or problem it addresses'.

For measuring the sustainability qualitatively, we can accept the criteria proposed by Lynan and Herdt (1988), which state that a sustainable system is the one with non-negative trend in a measured output. In other words, a system can be sustainable over a defined period if the outputs do not decrease when inputs are not increased.

From the above discussion, sustainable development can be conceptualised as the process of judicious use and conservation of natural resources for the overall improvement in the quality of life for the present and future generation and not mere short term improvements which may disappear quickly on the termination of any project cycle.

Model of Sustainable Development

Most of the developmental models, either economic or social or any other, should not lack in the 'environmental dimension'. To achieve sustainable development there is a need to incorporate environment as an important component along with other components namely, socio-cultural, economic, technological and political. The dimensions have been presented in diagrammatic form (Fig. 5.1). Shaded portion of the model clearly depicts the position of sustainable development. It is the product of interactions of all components. This model's attention to the development process goes beyond a consideration of the socio-cultural, political, economic, technological and ecological components, stressing the external and internal environment factors.

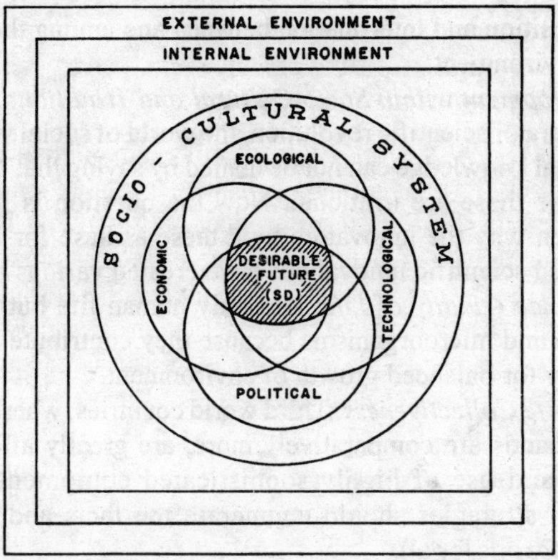

Fig. 5.1: Conceptual Model of Sustainable Development (S.D.)

Principles of Sustainable Development

Harmony between man and nature is prerequisite for sustainable development. It depicts that development of humanity should not be on the cost of environmental health. Thus, whatever the path of development is adopted does not matter but it should always be within such limit that nature allows penetrating beyond that will ultimately cause a threat of survival. Therefore, the code of conduct should be based on 'think of those affected by your use' and 'care while your share'. Both codes of conduct can be followed without any problem when one cares for his need not greed. As per Gandhijee's view "*Earth provides enough to satisfy every man's need but not every man's greed*". To quote the words of former Prime Minister of India, Late Mrs. Indira Gandhi at the Stockholm Conference in 1972 "*Higher standard of living must be achieved without disposing nature of its beauty, freshness and purity, so essential to our lives*".

For the sake of universe and humanity, following are the principles of development with no damage, i.e. Sustainable Development:

1. *Holistic Development*: Considering all the biotic and abiotic material while planning for development. It should have holistic view.

2. *Development within the Boundary of Environment*: Equilibrium among various eco-systems can resist only to certain amount of pressure in the form of natural resource use, ill atmospheric composition, over exploitation of any components and so on. Thus, prior to going for exploitation of natural resources, we should have adequate knowledge

about composition and interrelation between and among the constituent factors of environment.

3. *Development within Socio-Cultural and Traditional Knowledge Base*: In the era of scientific revolution, the world of social values, norms and traditional knowledge can not be denied by saying that it became out dated because these are irrational. Now the question is if these were irrational then why the innovators took these as base for innovations? Why so-called scientific innovations have created various hazards?

4. *Enhance Quality of Life*: Not only human life but life of other living macro and microorganisms because they contribute according to their capacity for balanced growth of environment.

5. *Promote Collectiveness*: Third world countries, where the number of working hands are comparatively more, are greatly affected by the automation and use of highly sophisticated equipments. Thus the development strategies should enumerate the facts and do plan for promotion of work for all.

6. *Needs of the Future Generation*: Development should not be at the expense of forthcoming generation. Here the share fairly and cares need to be materialised. All the benefits and costs incurred in resources use and management must be equitably distributed among poor and affluent, concerned and non-concerned, and among various subgroups and communities. Therefore, this principle leads us towards socially just and equitable distribution of benefits and costs.

7. *Global Diversity*: Conservation based development needs to include deliberate action to protect and maintain the global diversity keeping in view the scale of extinction of various animal and plant species, immediate action should be taken at the earliest.

8. *People's Participation and Empowerment to Manage their Surrounding and Natural Resources*: Development should encourage people's participation and make them capable to manage their resources.

9. *Based on National Policy and Needs*: All developmental efforts should be in tune with the National policies and needs.

10. *Least Energy and Judicious Use of Resources*: Development should consume least energy and should promote judicious use of resources.

Most of the guiding principles indicated above have been formulated on the basis of principles for sustainable living discussed in joint publication of IUCN/UNEP/and WWF (1991) *Caring for the Earth*: A strategy for sustainable living. However, there is a need to follow certain code of conduct for achieving sustainable development. Human being can survive only within a limited ecological boundary and hence degradation in environmental health will certainly lead to catastrophe as far as human being is concerned. Basu (1995) is of view that at the base of practical sustainability there are two issues:

(a) Technology has to be developed so as each transformation process consumes very low energy; hence not only the production system but also the mode of living has to be modified.
(b) Each human being has to accept a code of ethics based on low energy consumption.

Further, he explains that in absence of latter, the previous (i.e. 'a') has no meaning and if one thinks that he/she is merely an accident of cosmos, the latter has no meaning. Hence requisite code of ethics comes only in the case when one thinks that he/she is a part of cosmos and not an accident. This is the place where technology becomes failure and need of asserting spirituality becomes essential if it is to be used for sustainable development. Thus, the sustainability is a living system and the management of living system essentially must be guided by a conscious and logical decision.

Therefore, to achieve sustainable development and higher quality of life, state should reduce and eliminate not only the mode of production and consumption but at the same time promote and emphasise to evolve, appropriate demographic policies and to inculcate ethics of sustainable citizenship among her citizens.

Conclusion

Environment has emerged as a dominant force influencing development-planning efforts. Sustainable development is the process of judicious use and conservation of natural resources for the overall improvement in the quality of life for the present and future generations on long-term basis. It should be based on principles like Development for all which must be within the limits of environment; having respect for quality of life; taking into account the socio-cultural and traditional knowledge base which promote collectiveness, global diversity, people's participation in natural resources management and need for future generations. It should be placed at the top priority while formulating plans for development. Further it should find some place in our educational system.

6

Education for Sustainable Development
Issues and Concerns

M.K. SATAPATHY and D. DASH

Environment is now a typical talk of the day all over the world. In a broad sense, it comprises the whole range of diverse surroundings in which we perceive, experience and react to events and changes. It includes both physical as well as ecological environment such as the land, water, plants, animals and the whole gamut of the social order (Smith, 1992). It concerns people's ability to adapt both physically and mentally to the continuing changes in environment.

From economic standpoint, environment is the asset or capital. Virtually, environmental resources are economic resources, which form the basis of economic growth and development. We derive all raw materials such as food, fodder, fuel, minerals, fossil fuel, medicines, oxygen, energy, etc. from the environment. Not only for survival alone but also for our existence, we are totally dependant on congenial environment, which maintains the life support system (Odum, 1993; Sharma and Chattopadhyay, 2000).

In its natural condition, the environment of any region is in a state of dynamic equilibrium, called as the balance of nature. But when people try to exploit and interfere with nature, this equilibrium is disturbed, in many cases leading to the detrimental of all life forms (Gore, 1992; Ray, 1997; Barrelt and 0dum, 2000).

During the last 50 years, world science has shown tremendous progress and achievements. Scientists have created miracles by stepping on the surface of moon, landing instruments on mars, cloning animals with desired genetic traits, developing high yielding drought and salinity resistant crop varieties, sexing offsprings before birth, producing bio-molecules of human needs in bacteria and plants, producing resistance free superconducting materials, microchips, supercomputers, internet communications and many more.

Along with development the delicate ecosystem of our planet is facing a danger of destruction on a scale as never before in the history of mankind. In the name of development, man has been ruthlessly consuming natural resources and polluting the environment without even scant regard for its carrying capacity. The environmental crisis, the world is facing today is due to people's unlimited desire, ignorance, unethical practices and the materialistic approaches to life. In the quest for the so-called well being, in the desire to dominate and control nature, people have been making uncontrollable assaults on it. Catastrophic events like London Smog of 1952, Mina Mata tragedy of 1953, the Torrey canyon disaster of 1967, the acid rain problems of 1960s, Bhopal gas leak of 1984, Chernobyl nuclear disaster of 1986, forest fire of Indonesia of 1997 and Asian Brown Cloud (ABC) of 1997 got widespread publicity forcing people to change their line of thinking about environment. Improper planning in the name of development has caused enormous harm silently but steadily without giving any apparent warning or danger signal. The time has come to rise together to meet the challenge. This does not mean that there is need to stop all our developmental projects; but the entire concept of economic growth (defined as increasing material consumption) must be rethought, especially as a solution to the growing hosts of interrelated social, economic, environment and developmental issues. There is need for reorientation of certain dominant modes of decision-making, in government and industry and on the behaviour and thinking of the individuals who consume and dispose of the world's goods. Now the challenge is to live sustainably and well but within the material limits of finite planet (Costanza *et al.*, 1997).

The concept of sustainable development, which became well-known through the famous, Brundtland report, entitled *Our Common Future* published in 1987 recognised that natural resources are not inexhaustible and the developmental process should be aimed "to meet the needs of the present generation without compromising the ability of the future generations to meet their own needs". Thus dividends of development must flow continuously through generations for not only alleviating poverty but also upgrading the quality of life. Sustainable development is possible if principles of ecology are followed in planning developmental activities and long-term socio-economic need is kept in view and not just short-term profit. It looks to the upliftment of all citizens of a society to a quality of life which enables them realise their potential, build self-confidence and live life of fulfillment and dignity.

Singh (1998) observes "Our environment has visibly, seriously and irreversibly changed for the worse in our life time and it is we who are the victims. If we do not act today, our children will live in an even worse environment, they will suffer for our errors and omissions". The importance of individual's role in environmental protection and resource conservation has been highlighted in Indian constitution. It states:

> *"It shall be the duty of every citizen, to protect and improve the natural environment, including forests, lakes, rivers, wildlife and to have compassion for living creatures"* (*Article 51A*).

Education is the first and foremost a human right as proclaimed in article 26 of Universal Declaration of Human Rights. It is also the key to building up the skills and capacities in all domains necessary to techno-economic development. Further it is the means whereby people may hope to address some of the most profound problems confronting our societies in the current century.

In the world of tomorrow, education must be concerned with more than simply the transmission of knowledge. It must place a premium on intervention, innovation, anticipation and adaptation. It must foster all forms of behaviour, life styles and values necessary for human survival on a crowded planet (Mayor, 1997). It nurtures the minds of young and old alike broadening our understanding of the linkages that determine our global environment (Yodmani, 1997).

Education makes man flexible, to change and adjust with the new situations (Chaube, 2002). Naturalists are of opinion that "Education is seen from the process of adjustment to environment, it aims at enabling the individual to be in harmony with and well adapted to his surroundings". Education helps set the parameters of future action to help restore our planet and prevent future ecological deterioration (Yodmani, 1997). Thus education should strive to create a nature loving and nature friendly individual having strong emotional ties with nature (Mishra and Airen, 1994). Only such individuals can bring about a change in the developmental paradigm and reverse the self-destructing path of progress. People must realise that any harm done to nature is a harm done to their own selves and future generations too.

Concept of Growth and Development

Growth is measured by the rise of the per capita income or growth rate of industrialisation or increase in the Gross National Product (GNP) whereas development means not only growth, it covers a broad spectrum of people's education, health, nutrition, organisation, discipline and honest labour (Das, 1980). Thus the purpose of development is to enlarge all human choices, not just income. The goals of development in any society are, increased productivity, reduction in social differences, people's participation, efficiency and utilisation of resources (Sathe, 1997). It has two ingredients: productivity and social justice (Joshi and Pushpanadham, 2000).

The first human development report (1990) introduced a new way of measuring human development by combining indicators of life expectancy, educational attainment and income into a composite Human Development Index (HDI)—reflecting economic and non-economic factors as indicators of development (Mishra, 1981).

A report from UNESCO (Goodland *et al.*, 1991) made a distinction between economic growth, which involves getting larger (quantitative growth) and economic development, which involves getting better (qualitative growth) without increasing the total consumption of energy and materials beyond a level that is reasonable and sustainable. During 1950s and 1960s economic growth was considered as one of the important parameters for development while during 1970s, environment as an other component of development was considered (Khor, 2000) with emphasis on minimising the negative effects on it. Thus maintaining the quality of environment and improving the quality of life are linked with the present day concept of development (UNESCO, 1998).

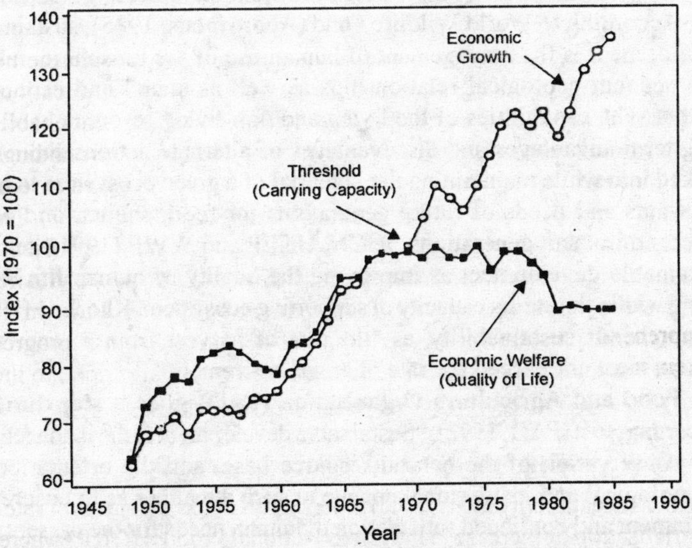

Fig. 6.1: Recent Trends in the Gross National Product (GNP) Index and the Index of Sustainable Economic Welfare (ISEW) with the Threshold Suggested as the Optimum Carrying Capacity (Barrett and Odum, 2000)

Sustainable Development: Meaning and Definition

The notion of sustainable development is considerably old. However, the term itself was introduced to the international community in 1980 by the World Conservation Union (IUCN, 1980). Subsequently the term was introduced in the international diplomatic community in 1987 by the World Commission on Environment and Development (WCED, 1987) headed by Gro Harlem Brundtland, the then Prime Minister of Norway in its report '*Our Common Future*'.

To sustain means "to hold", to keep in existence, to ensure without failing, to support, to maintain, to supply with necessities, to prevent from falling below a given threshold or vitality. The dictionary meaning of sustainability is the amount or degree to which the earth's resources may be exploited without deleterious effects (The Chamber's Dictionary).

However, Sustainable Development has been defined variously by different workers and institutions. WCED (1987) defined Sustainable Development (SD) as "development that meets the needs of the present without compromising the ability of future generations to meet their own needs. This means that the present resource base is the base for the survival of the future generations too. So the nature has entrusted us with a hard task of preserving the environment while exploiting and passing on to the next generation as we have borrowed from our elders.

According to World Wildlife Fund (Anonymous, 1985), sustainable development is the management of human use of the biosphere, taking into account ecological relationships as well as social and economic factors. The capabilities of the living and non-living resource base and long term advantages and disadvantages of alternate actions should be looked into while maintaining the potential of a given ecosystem to meet the wants and needs of future generations for food, shelter, and other aspects of human generations. IUCN, UNEP and WWF (1991) defined sustainable development as improving the quality of human life while living within the caring capacity of supporting ecosystem. Khoshoo (1998) comprehends sustainability, as "the rate of harvest from a renewable system must not exceed the rate of annual increment".

Food and Agriculture Organisation (FAO) goes a step further: According to it (FAO, 1992), "Sustainable development is the management and conservation of the natural resource base, and the orientation of technological and institutional change in such a manner as to ensure the attainment and continued satisfaction of human needs for the present and future generations. Such sustainable development (in agriculture, forestry, and fisheries sectors) conserves land, water, plant and animal reservoirs, is environmentally non-degrading, technically appropriate, economically viable and socially acceptable".

As a whole, sustainable development stresses everything that we can to do to save the planet (Nair, 1994; Elliot, 1994; Brown, 2000). It is the development that responds to the current needs of today's citizens and of the society at large without compromising and hindering the resources required to fulfil the development of tomorrow's citizens (Sequoia, 1997).

Hopkins (1998) observed sustainability as the integration of environmental, economic and social considerations in the development that optimises human and natural welfare and integrity for the present and future generations. Further, it tries to maintain a dynamic equilibrium in which exploitation of the resources, direction of investment, and institutional changes are made consistent with the future as well as present needs (Gupta, 1998). Doctrine of carrying capacity-based development calls for ecological economy, wherein the use of renewable resources would only be at the rate not greater than the generation of resources and the use of exhaustible resources would not exceed the rate at which they are substituted by renewable resources (Himesh, 2001).

Sustainable Development: Issues and Dimensions

A study of the development pattern shows that the present economic system has evolved on a mistaken notion that natural resources are abundant, population is still not so high and ecosystem re-generability is higher than degradability (Oberai, 1997). Further it is also due to lack of strong S&T base in developing counties. However, analysis of the sustainable development concept shows that none of the forgoing assumptions is correct and the root cause for all these ills is the rising population and lack of S&T infrastructure in the developing world and over consumption and wrong use of S&T in the industrial world (Khoshoo, 1998).

Due to overpopulation (Tewari, 2000; Mittal, 2001), our environmental assets (soil, land, air, water, forests, biodiversity, fisheries, etc.) are indeed highly stressed (Schuyier, 1983). Poor destroys the environment on account of his needs, while the rich destroys environment out of greed. Both poverty and increase in population in less developed countries and increase in affluence of developed countries resulting into over-consumption of all kinds of resources result into environmental problems (Agarwal, 1997, 1998). About 27 per cent of the world's population in the developed countries uses 75 per cent of the world's resources. It is the life style of the rich that consumes more of the resources. A child born in a rich country is a much greater burden on the earth due to greater consumption than a child in a poor country. The World Watch Institute (WWI) in its annual report observes that the United States still consumes three times as much grain per person as China and five times as much as India. US per capita carbon dioxide emissions are six times the Chinese level and 20 times the Indian level. If China and India were to consume resources and produce pollution at the current US per capita level, it would require two planet earths, just to sustain the two economies. Chiappo (1978) considers: "The cause of the ecological problem is not essentially hunger, the cause is over consumption, wastage and short sightedness, profit seeking, plundering of the natural world and economic injustice".

For us, to bring the masses out of the present morale of poverty is one of the most important scientific, technological, economic and environmental challenges facing the country. The welfare of villages with development based on ecological and economic principles and gender equality together with access to education, health care, livelihoods, credit and decision-making are critical to the success of such eco-development. It must also lead to empowerment of people through participatory management and decentralised governance (Reddy and Rajanikanth, 1998). Such growth and development will generate employment opportunities and widen the range of choices and opportunities for the people.

Sustainable development has three major dimensions (Fig. 6.2), economical, environmental and social each of which is a function of a whole constellation of many factors as everything on earth is interconnected, interrelated and interdependent. A combination of ecological security, economic security, equity and social justice are going to be the bedrocks (Swaminathan, 2000) of future developmental process. More importance is to be given to conservation technologies (eco-technologies) rather than to consumptive ones by blending traditional wisdom and practices with frontier sciences (Swaminathan, 2001).

The concept of sustainable development does not see environmental protection and economic growth as mutually exclusive and conflicting objectives (Das Gupta, 2000). It underlines the need to tailor the objective of development based on carrying capacity of the environment (Ikham and Shishodia, 1988). Thus it is necessary to merge environment and economics in decision-making (UNESCO 1986) and pay vigorous attention to resource management and the environment (Clausen, 1982; Parashar, 1996). Sustainable development requires that the interrelationships between population, resources and environment and development be fully recognised and brought into harmonious, dynamic balance. (Westing, 1996).

Sustainable deveiopment is not only production centered. All the development programmes should be not only technically feasible and economically viable but also environmentally and socially acceptable (Parashar, 1996; Khan, 1996). The key to development is participation, organisation, education and empowerment of people (Disinger, 1990). Sustainable development must be appropriate not only to the environment

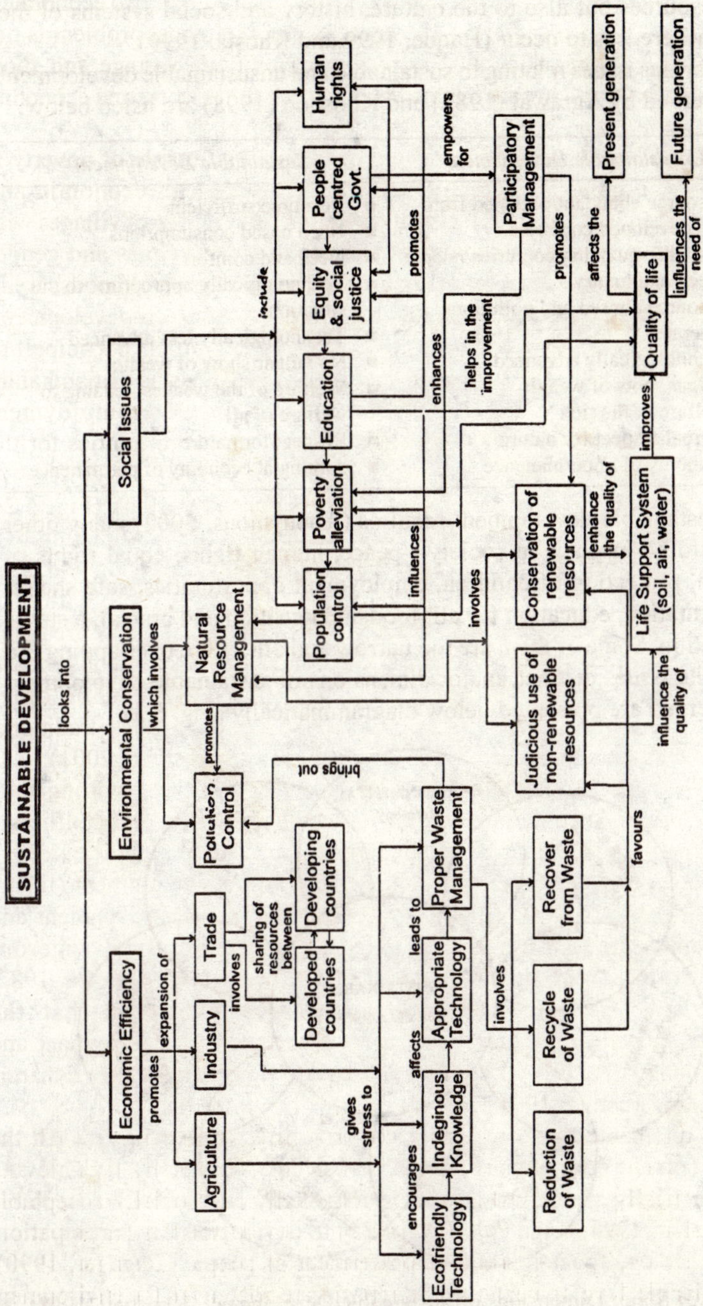

Fig. 6.2: Concept Map of Sustainable Development

and resources but also to the culture, history and social systems of the place where it is to occur (Haque, 1999 and Khosia, 1999).

Various issues relating to sustainable and unsustainable development as observed by Agrawal (1982) and Khoshoo (1998) are listed below:

Unsustainable Development	*Sustainable Development*
■ Resource abundant/obtained from less developed countries	■ Resource sufficient
■ Resource-guzzling countries/people	■ Need based consumptions
■ Greed and luxury	■ Need and comfort
■ Resource abused and pollution generated	■ Technologically appropriate to the situations
■ Technologically advanced	■ Technologically less advanced
■ Vulgar show of wealth	■ No vulgar show of wealth
■ Welfare of the rich	■ Welfare of the weakest leading to welfare of all
■ No real respect for nature	■ Respect for nature
■ Economy of impermanence	■ Aiming at economy of permanence

Sustainable development requires (Anonymous, 2002) many other things to be in place in society—peace, human rights, equal rights of women, protection of children, employment opportunities, safe shelter and sanitation, education for all, food and nutrition and crucial, a stable population. Some of them are too narrow and others are overlapping. To make the issues distinct, major dimensions of sustainable development as observed are presented below diagrammatically (Fig. 6.3).

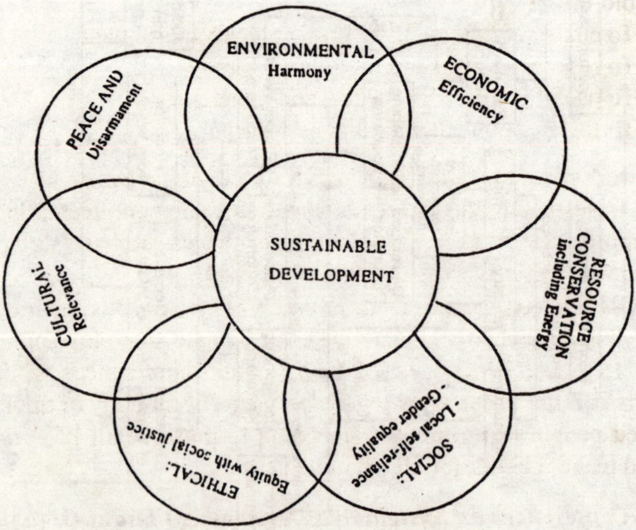

Fig. 6.3: Major Dimensions of Sustainable Development (Khoshoo, 1998)

Looking into different dimensions, Srivastava (2001) defines sustainable development as the development that not only generates economic growth but also distributes its benefit equally, that protects the environment rather than destroying it, that empowers people rather than marginalising them. It is development that gives priority to the poor, enlarging their choices and opportunities and providing for their participation in decisions that affect their lives. In short-true sustainable development is that development that is pro-people, pro-nature, pro-job, pro-women and one, which does not threaten future generations.

What needs to be realised is that sustainable development is both a goal and a process. Its attainment requires a fundamental shift in attitudes, values and behaviours by both individuals and governments alike (Starke, 1990; Narain, 1998).

Principles of Sustainable Development

The Major Principles of sustainable development are:

- To integrate development programmes and conservation strategies through ecological and economic integration.
- To ensure socio-economic security
- To consult public in development programmes
- To respect and care for all life forms
- To respect the carrying capacity of nature & conserve bio-diversity
- To enable communities to protect local environment.
- To respect cultural and religious diversity
- To promote tolerance, peace, and democracy
- To foster global alliance and networking

The work programme for sustainability recognises that environment is central to sustainability, science is key to development, technologies provide appropriate solutions and government needs strategies and plan policies to work towards sustainable development.

The UN held conferences on different areas in the 1990s and they all have pulled ideas and policies into the central organising philosophy of sustainable development. A list of such summits/conferences is given below. These conferences drew together a magnificent body of thinking that helped people learn how we are going to preserve all life on the planet and make it better for all who live here.

Summits/Conferences on Sustainable Development Issues Organised by UN

1. *Education for All Conference* (Jomtien, March, 1990)

- Promised to provide free access to bring education for all by the year 2000

2. *World Summit for Children* (New York, September, 1990)
   - To promote the well-being of children
3. *Earth Summit* (Rio de Janeiro, June, 1992)
   - UN Conference on Environment and Development—Biggest of the UN Summits and parent to Agenda 21
4. *World Conference on Human Rights* (Vienna, June, 1993)
   - Protection of Human Rights is the birth right of all human beings
5. *Small Islands Developing States Conference* (Barbados, 1994)
   Islands form a network to preserve and repair their fragile eco-system. Secure technical assistance for sustainable development programmes.
6. *International Conference on Natural Disaster Reduction* (Yo Kohama, May, 1994)
   Need for new International partnership to enhance preparedness, coordinate relief efforts and help some lives
7. *International Conference on Population and Development* (Cairo, September, 1994)
   Twenty year plan of action to empower and educate individual women to plan, and space their births rather than reach arbitrary population targets.
8. *World Summit for Social Development* (Copenhagen, March, 1995)
   Developed a plan to eradicate poverty, create full employment, justice, tolerance, accelerated economic growth for Africa and 'People centered development of all'.
9. *World Conference on Women* (Beijing, July, 1995)
   Action planned for elimination of all forms of discrimination against women in work, education, in decision-making, health and law.
10. *Habitat II Conference* (Istanbul, June, 1996)
    Proposed for adequate shelter for all in sustainable human settlements in an urbanising world
11. *World Food Summit* (Italy, Nov. 1996)
    Called for sustainable progress to eliminate hunger and malnutrition and "provide all people, at all times, physical and economic access to sufficient, safe and nutritious food.
12. *Millennium Young People's Congress* (Honolulu, October, 1999)
    Established youth priorities for the new millennium. Education was top priority

13. *World Conference (II) Education for All* (Dakar, Senegal, April, 2000) For universal primary education for all by 2015
14. *Millennium Summit,* (New York, September, 2000)
    World leaders discussed and planned to meet major challenges of the new millennium and to redefine the UN's role. Heads of states set a series of targets for global action against poverty by 2015 (Goal 7—Ensure environmental sustainability).
15. *World Summit on Sustainable Development*, (Johannesburg, 2002)
    WSSD besides assessing the progress, calls for vision and ambitious way of thinking about education to promote SD.

The Universal Declaration of Human Responsibilities of the Inter Action Council (IAC, 1997) in two of 'its Principles States

Article 7: Every person is infinitely precious and must be protected unconditionally. The animals and the natural environment also demand protection. All people have a responsibility to protect the air, water and soil of the earth for the sake of present inhabitants and future generations.

Article 9: All people, given the necessary tools, have a responsibility to make serious efforts to overcome poverty, malnutrition, ignorance and inequality. They should promote SD all over the world in order to assure dignity, freedom, security, justice for all people (Westing, 1999). To spread awareness and promote activities UN has declared 2004-15 as the Decade on Education for Sustainable Development (DESD).

Education for Sustainable Development: Issues and Concerns

Education provides the instruments for liberation from ignorance and oppression (Sathe, 1997). Besides sharpening the eye of knowledge, it develops awareness (Alam, 1998) and makes mind logical. Further it is a very important input in human resource development (UNDP, 1993). The relationship between environment and development can be established (Saxena, 1996) as part of education, as it increases economic growth; attacks poverty improves income distribution and reduces inequality (Tilak, 1986). Education is of prime importance in the planned development of a nation. Skills in education include the resource to think clearly, ability to process information, capability to communicate effectively, rational decision-making, competences to understand environment, effective utilisation of resources, technical skills and training for multiplier effect (Pati, 2000).

The concern for environment and its conservation has been reflected in the National Policy on Education (1986) document (MHRD, 1986) which notes:

"There is a paramount need to create a consciousness in the environment. It must permeate all ages and all sections of the society beginning with the child. Environmental consciousness should inform teaching in schools and colleges. This aspect will be integrated in the entire educational process"

Further National Curriculum Framework (NCERT, 2000) also laid high emphasis on health, environment and energy issues.

An individual is the starting point of environmental degradation. If an individual believes in need and not in greed, and in comfort and not in luxury and ponders about what is enough for a comfortable life style, most of the problems can be solved (MacNeill, 1996). A sustainable community can spring from interdependence among well-informed individuals. Thus sustainable life styles of the individuals can lead to sustainable communities to sustainable nations and then to a sustainable world.

Education is an input as well as dynamic force besides promoting knowledge; understanding and disseminating information can help changing attitude by giving stress on ethics and morality (Mishra and Dhaka, 2001). It should be emphasised that man is an integral part of nature and is subjected to its forces. It must find ways and means to live in harmony with nature and be educated about the importance of interdependence of man and nature. The aim is to have welfare of the weakest (*Antodaya*), which in the ultimate sense leads to welfare of all (*Sarvodaya*). The basic philosophy is to live and let live and through fragility (more than less) and fraternity (getting association with others) to achieve sustainability (Khoshoo, 1998). Thus there is urgent need to inculcate action and values that leads to sustainable development.

A Possible Paradigm: Education for Sustainable Development

According to Parashar (1996) the new concept of education of environmentally sustainable development (EESD) could be introduced in the education system, which paves the way for the protection of the environment keeping in view the developmental needs of the society through science and technology (Fig. 6.4). This would mean educating people to awareness, decision making and at a later stage implementing.

The first and foremost need for sustainability is elimination of poverty (Alam, 1998). As it is accepted by all that illiteracy breeds poverty and population growth (Ramaswamy, 1996; Singh, 1998), literacy is an important component for sustainable development. Atchia (1988) observes that any action plan for the future, which does no involve the education of children and youth of today, is doomed, for the future belongs to them.

It is observed (Srivastava, 1994) that educational institutions have to take the lead in stimulating and guiding the sustainable use of natural

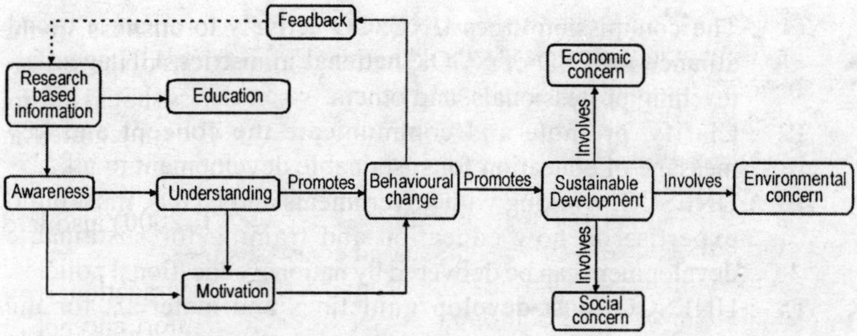

Fig. 6.4: A possible Paradigm: Education for Sustainable Development

resources. Environmental education for sustainable development needs to be introduced at all levels of education, school, college, university as well as in all forms of informal education (Ray, 1999). School has an important role in environmental education as teachers have considerable influence over the children (CEE, 1994). Concepts relating to sustainable development can be taught in many ways as part of standard curricula or in specific programmes, indoor or outdoor, by teachers or resource persons.

National Curriculum Framework for school education (NCERT, 2000) considers energy and environmental issues as frontline curriculum and suggests including the process and patterns of man-environment interaction and the issues related to environment, natural resources and sustainable development at secondary level. It is suggested that environmental education curriculum for sustainable development should include skills, concepts and facts as already exist in the school curriculum but in the context of local specific environment. Issue based curriculum with emphasis on learning the skills of gathering, recording and analysing information (NCERT, 2005) for the purpose of decision-making and social action shall go a long way in solving problems. It will help children equipped to make decisions and participate in community action on issues relevant to their lives when they leave schools (Mishra, 2001). So there is a shift from content and learning outcome to the nature of learning experience and environment.

Agenda 21 of Rio declaration (1992), especially Chapter 36, stressed on "Education, Awareness and Training" the critical importance of public understanding as fundamental to any progress to be made. It asked governments to "reorient their education systems towards sustainable development" but failed to explain how. In 1996, the UN Commission for sustainable development tried to fill this gap by drafting a work plan with 21 tasks for Education for Sustainable Development (ESD). The important tasks (T) are listed below:

T1 : The commission urges UNESCO actively to create a broad alliance for ESD of NGOs, national ministries, UN agendas, teaching professionals, and others.

T2 : Clarify, promote and communicate the concept and key message of education for sustainable development to all.

T3 : UNESCO, working with governments and NGOs, must build expertise on how education and training for sustainable development can be delivered by national educational policies.

T5 : UNESCO must develop guidelines and materials for the reorientation of teacher training towards sustainable development.

T6 : The commission urges institutes of higher education to address sustainable development issues.

T9 : The UN and UNESCO must develop and promote education and training intended to change consumption and production patterns, and introduce indicators for sustainable consumption.

T13 : Governments must work in partnership with youth to provide skills and training to prepare youth for sustainable livelihoods.

T14 : Encourage and strengthen international and regional alliances of educational and training institutions and professional bodies to promote information and exchange of best practices on ESD.

T15 : Governments should encourage and strengthen grassroots networks for ESD with schools, parents, private and public institutions and NGOs.

T16 : Governments must raise public awareness of the social, economic and environmental cost of unsustainable production and consumption patterns.

The importance of education was again highlighted at the special session of the General Assembly (23-27 June, 1997), convened to review the implementation of Agenda 21 and the progress since Rio. The resulting resolution adopted by the session emphasised that a "fundamental prerequisite for sustainable development is an adequately financed and effective education systems at all levels, particularly at the primary and secondary levels, that is accessible to all and that augments both human capacity and well-being". The resolution continues.." Even in countries with strong educational systems, there is need to reorient education, awareness and training to increase widespread public understanding, critical analysis and support for sustainable development. Education for a sustainable future should engage a wide spectrum of institutions and sectors…and should include the preparation of sustainable development education plans and programmes (Hopkins, 1997). The core themes or education for sustainability should include life long education.

interdisciplinary education, partnership, multicultural education and empowerment (Yodmani, 1997).

It is observed (Mishra, 2000) that in order to attain the goal of sustainable development education should be drastically restructured with emphasis on local context. Further, the school curriculum should be framed with the overall objective of promoting human development for sustainability of life on earth in general and human species in particular. It should cover knowledge, competencies and values and attitudes as elucidated in the *Learning: The treasure within*. Learning to live together encompassing the shared resources, mutual trust, respect and tolerance, concern for others and such other things should form the core of educational objective. Though already existing, they need to be underscored along with inculcation of skills of problem solving, decision making, life-long learning, and working together.

In the educational process, key characteristics of ESD are listed below:

Table 6.1: Key Characteristics of ESD

Ontology	*Idealist*
Epistemology	Participatory
Theory of Learning	Participative
Function of Education	Developmental
Focus	Appropriate and context
Emphasis	Towards transformative learning experience
Reflects	Intrinsic and transformative roles
Pedagogy	Constructivitism/Transformative
Desired change	Contextually appropriate

ESD needs that there should be a shift in the focus and approach to education. More emphasis should be on the learning through experience. As observed by Sterling (2005), the details are listed below:

Integration of Sustainability within Education Implies Shift

From	*To*
Passive learner	Active learner
Transmissible learning	Discovery learning
Teacher centered approach	Learner centered approach
Individual learning	Group learning
Learning by theory	Learning by experience
Behaviourist	Constructivist
Behaviour change	Capacity building
Focus on content orientation	Focus on real issues
Cognitive development	Emphasis on cognitive, affective and Psychomotor skills
Institutional learning	Learning from outside world

Conclusion

The promotion of sustainable development is a hard task and it is not possible for the government agencies to cope with the problem alone. While it is highly essential for constant monitoring, evaluation and periodic updating of our data by research and analysis, at the same time, it is necessary to disseminate the information for the awareness, understanding and motivation of the people. When local people share their knowledge, it facilitates the planning process by taking care of the people's felt needs and involvement leading to sustainability of the development programmes (Reddy and Rajanikantha, 1998). In international research, education has been found to increase agricultural productivity, enhance the status of women, improve child health, reduce fertility, enhance environmental protection, and increase industrial production which has implications for sustainable development (Heyn, 1997). Studies (Birdshall *et al.,* 1995, World Bank, 1997) in some countries in East Asia has established that education has increased choice and economic growth which in turn has helped in increasing the demand for education. As such development is the goal of all civilised societies. Development does not come to people. People move towards development through awareness and assertion. Education is a necessary condition for development. Education accelerates, strengthens and sustains the process of development.

7

Education for Sustainable Development in the Context of Teacher Education Programme

M.K. SATAPATHY and D. DASH

Today, people all over the world face grave environmental problems. The continuing depletion of natural resources, deforestation, extinction of many plant and animal species, rise in global temperature, environmental pollution, thinning of life saving ozone layer, etc. are some of the few examples. These problems are further being compounded with population explosion, food crisis, hunger, malnutrition, poverty, insanitation and unbridled consumerism which together have caused serious strains on the essential life-support systems of our planet.

Threats to peace and security of nations from environmental breakdown are today greater than any other foreseeable military threat from conventional arms (Rao, 1999). They are increasing at a frightening pace; local, even regional conflicts based on environmental disruption, water and other natural resource scarcity, energy consumption, could well become endemic in the world of the future. These environmental threats now facing us could have so much momentum that unless steps are taken to reverse them, they may soon overwhelm our ability to respond (Baliga, 1996), even threatening all living beings including man himself with disaster or extinction (Parashar, 1996). The recent Tsunami disaster because of relentless destruction of mangroves and coral reefs bear testimony to it (Shiva, 2005).

The environmental and natural resources directly affect the standard of living or quality of life of the people. The welfare of the individual ultimately depends upon the viability of life supporting system (Das, 1980). False illusion of abundance has led to excessive consumption and damage of the ecosystems in the past and still continues.

> *"God makes all things good; man meddles with them and they Become evil".*

This is what Rousseau reacted against man's destructive nature to spoil things gifted by nature.

Our environment has visibly, seriously, irreversibly changed for the worse in our life time, and it is we who are the victims. If we do not act today, our children will live in an even worse environment; they will suffer for our errors and omissions. Education in general and the teacher education in particular have a special role to play in sustainable development. Teacher's knowledge, and understanding of environment and developmental issues and level of commitment, attitude and devotion determine the future society and its development. World Commission on Environment and Development (WCED, 1987) in its report *Our Common Future* defined Sustainable Development as the development that meets the needs of the present generation without compromising the ability of the future generation to meet their own needs.

The objective of sustainable development is to provide the well-being of the present and the future generations and to maintain a healthy environment and life-support system. The sustainable development framework entails thinking far into the future and how our present actions might affect our ability to live a wholesome and fulfilling life. One can look at sustainable development on a global, regional, national, state, local and even individual scale. The World Watch Institute (WWI) in its annual publication *State of the World 2006* specially focuses on the dramatic rise of the two Asian nations (India and China) with about 40 per cent of world population and says the choice of development they make in the next few years would lead the world either towards a future—a path of development or of acceleration towards a collusion course with world's ecosystems and resources. Sustainable development does not imply absolute limits on economic growth (CEE, 1994) but takes into account the limitations imposed by the availability of resources, present state of technology, the ability of the biosphere to absorb the effects of human activities and social values. It is said (Schuyler, 1983): "A point has been reached in history when we must shape our actions throughout the world with a more prudent care for their environmental consequences. Through ignorance or indifference we can do massive and irreversible harm to the earthy environment on which our life and well-being depend". It is said (Shiva, 1991): Earth has tried to give that "development" that ignores ecological limits which can only lead to unimaginable destruction.

Though physical environment determines the extent of opportunities, but how far man's activities are encouraged depends on the quality of manpower, cultural environment, government attitude and behaviour of people towards economic, social and technological changes (Sharma, 1997). When environment and development concerns are merged, a better set of goals evolve. This includes a better quality of life, satisfaction of basic human needs, sustainability of development, respect for the biosphere and concern for the needs of future generations.

As knowledge and understanding are essential for action, education can make man aware, conscious and knowledgeable about environmental problems and developmental issues. Education can help man to understand the underlying causes, the manifestations and impact of these problems so that he may act in a concerted manner not only to alleviate and solve the existing problems but also to prevent their recurrence.

Education in its traditional forms is not sufficient to meet the immense challenges posed by the phenomenon of unsustainable living. People are increasingly aware of the dangers they face and the need for the informed action. New educational approaches are required to achieve necessary changes in life styles and to be successful in combating waste in developing a new ecological vision and in fostering a sense of global solidarity (Mayer, 1997). Educational initiatives are needed at every level of society to change cultural attitudes, beliefs, as well as practices. Teacher as a professional and as an intellectual can not remain indifferent to those events that are taking place in the contemporary society.

Teachers: The Agents of Change

The world conference on higher education (UNESCO, 1998) proclaimed that education is a fundamental pillar of democracy, human rights, sustainable development and peace. The solution of the existing problems of the century will be determined by the vision of the future society and this role is assigned to education in general. In Brundtland report (WCED, 1987) the Chairman's foreword states:

> "*But first and foremost our message is directed towards people, whose well-being is the ultimate goal of all environment and development policies. In particular, the commission is addressing the young. The world's teachers will have a crucial role to play in bringing this report to them*".

Teachers are the most critical agents of change responsible for growth, development and progress of societies and communities (Mangle, 2002). Enlightened, emancipated and empowered teachers lead communities and nations in their march towards better and higher quality of life (NCTE, 1998). As such, their role as teachers is very crucial to achieve the objectives of sustainable development. They play important role (Rajput, 1997) in moulding the behaviour of children (future citizens of the country) in the classroom formally and people in the society informally to promote desired quality for sustainable development. They not only disseminate knowledge but also create and generate new knowledge. As they have very important role, their quantum of knowledge and understanding of environment and developmental issues and level of commitment and devotions determine the future society and its development. Recently following the Hon'ble Supreme Court's directive, NCTE has observed that environmental education as a compulsory curriculum for Teacher's education will be implemented to stress development of critical awareness about pressing problem of life, especially environmental degradation, its consequences and methods to curtail it.

From Environmental Education to the Notion of Education for Sustainable Development

There is mention of environment and its importance in many ancient literatures, However, the beginning of environmental education (EE) can be traced back to educational thinkers such as Froebel, Montessori, Steiner and Dewey who had put emphasis on the learner and learning environment, on learning by doing and participation and on differential learning needs and styles. With increase in the knowledge of science and technology and initiation of industrial activities in the last part of the nineteenth century, there has been increasing awareness to protect air, water, land, forests and aquatic resources.

In true sense of the term, the origin of environmental education concept goes back to 1899 when Scottish Professor of Botany Patrick Geddes, known as the father of modern environmental education, founded in Edinbury (England) an unique educational establishment, the Outlook Tower, to improve upon the existing environment and education. He was the first to make the vital link, fundmental to environmental education, that the quality of environment and education were closely interdependent and a child brought into the realities of his environment would not only learn better but would also develop a creative attitude towards the environment. Such beginning was strengthened by subsequent global catastrophic events such as London Smog of 1952, Mina Mata tragedy of 1953 and the Torray Canyon disaster of 1967, etc. that forced people to become conscious about the state of global environment and how to preserve it.

The first UN sponsored conference on Human Environment was held at Stockholm (1972) in order to assess the damage done to environment and find ways and means of preventing it. In its Principle 19, it gave emphasis on the need of environmental education (EE) (Bhel, 1993;Ghanta and Bhaskar Rao, 1998, Ramesh, 1998). Subsequently UNEP in collaboration with UNESCO launched UNESCO-UNEP International Environmental Education programme which stressed on the environmental awareness among general public including politicians, planners, administrators and educationist (Srivastava, 1995). The framework for environmental education was formulated in October, 1975 in the International Environmental Education workshop held at Belgrade popularly known 'Belgrade Charter'. Subsequently in October, 1977 the Intergovernmental Conference on Environmental Education organized in October, 1977 at Tibilisi, USSR outlined the structure of environmental education that formed the prototype for environmental education programme world wide (UNESCO, 1978).

Environmental education has two intimately linked goals (Chopra and Kadekoli, 2001; Reddy, 2002)—education towards protection and improvement of the environment and education as an instrument of development for improving the quality of life of human communities. Further EE is considered as education about environment, education for environment and education in the environment (Palmer, 1993). As such EE (NCERT, 2004) is a process aimed at developing a world population that is aware of and concerned about the total environment and its associated problems and which has the knowledge, attitude, motivation, commitments and skills to work individually and collectively towards the solutions of current problems as well as the prevention of new ones. The Tbilisi conference of 1977 (UNESCO-UNEP, 1978) recommended that environmental education should consider the environment in its totality, natural and man made (technological and social aspects), be a continuous life long process, beginning at the pre-school level and continuing through all formal and non-formal stages and be inter disciplinary in approach, drawing on the specific content of each discipline in making it possible holistic and balanced perspective. Further it laid emphasis on creating new patterns of behaviour of individuals, groups and society as a whole towards the environment.

Realising the increased magnitude of human impact on the environment and the consequent deterioration of the latter, United Nations General Assembly set up the World Commission on Environment and Development (WCED) headed by Dr. Gro Harlem Brundtland, the then Prime Minister of Norway to examine critically the environmental and developmental progress on the planet and to ensure that human progress is sustained by development which does not deplete the environmental resources of future generations. The commission in its report *Our Common Future* published in 1987 defined Sustainable Development as the Development that meets the need of the present generation without compromising the ability of future generation to meet their own needs and drew the linkages between environmental problems and socio-economic issues emphasising the improvement of quality of life.

The report clearly states that there is need to change present practices if people to ensure their long term survival. Sustainable development stresses the need to view environmental protection and economic growth (In terms of growth per capita real income over time) as mutually compatible (Balgot, 1990) and not necessarily conflicting objectives. Interestingly, WCED (1987) suggested that "Human survival and well-being could depend on success in elevating sustainable development to a global ethic".

United Nations Conference on Environment and Development (UNCED, 1992) popularly know as 'Earth Summit' held at Rio-de-Janeiro in 1992 endorsed the concept of Sustainable Development (Swaminathan, 1997; Khoshoo, 1998) and the global environmental concern came into sharp focus in this conference. It stressed (Annonymous, 1992)" Reorienting education towards sustainable development. Education is critical for promoting sustainable development and improving the capacity of people to address environment and developmental issues. In its agenda 21 (chapter 36), it considered "Education, awareness and training" as the critical factors of public understanding—fundamental to any progress to be made.

In 1997, UN Commission on Sustainable Development (CSD) Earth Summit plus 5 stressed on the importance of Education and drafted a work plan with 21 tasks for education for sustainable development. The 2nd task speaks "clarify, promote and communicate the concept and key message of education for sustainable development to all. "In International gatherings such as UNESCO-ACEID Conference (UNESCO, 1998), Johannesburg meet (Engfeldt, 2002), International Conference at CEE, Ahamedabad (2005), etc. educational dimension of sustainable development have been highlighted. The Millennium Young people's Congress (MYPC) held at Honolulu, Hawaii in 1993 made education its top priority. The delegates observed "we believe that if every young person is educated about environmental problems, human rights, tolerance, democracy, health and sustainable development, all our other problems will vanish over time". Interestingly to send the message of sustainable development to hook and corner, UNO has declared (2004-15) as the Decade on Education for Sustainable Development (DESD). Hence environmental education for the 1990s has become Sustainable Development Education. (Atchia, 1990, Mishra, 2000). The education for sustainable development is not the same as environmental education. The environmental education has been traditionally concerned with the quality of environment and less concerned with social, economic, and political aspects of change. But ESD besides ecological (environmental) dimension, looks into economic and social issues (Disinger, 1990) with the ultimate objective of improving the quality of life of people living on the planet (Anonymous. 2002). As such there is a shift from awareness and understanding to involvement, participation and problem solving. It is interesting to note that the Millennium Declaration (2000) by heads of states of 189 countries in the form of Millennium Development Goals stressed on eight dimensions all of which have implications for environmental sustainability (Sweetman, 2005). Further the declaration in its target 9 stressed countries to integrate the principles of sustainable development into country policies and programmes (Kiss, 2004). The core themes of education for sustainability include life-long education, education for all, interdisciplinary education, value education, partnership, multicultural education, health education, women education and empowerment (Yodmani, 1997). After the Rio Earth Summit, besides EE various terminologies such as Education for Sustainable Development (ESD), Education for Sustainability (EFS), Education for a Sustainable Future (ESF) and Sustainability Education (SE) have emerged (Sterling, 2005). However ESD is regarded (Hesselink *et al.*, 2000) as the new generation EE.

Sustainable Development Education: Case Study among Pre-Service and In-Service Teachers

Very limited study has been conducted on sustainable development education. A study conducted among 243 pre-service and 207 in-service secondary school teachers with diverse background from Orissa on their knowledge on sustainable development issues (Mishra, 2002) reflected interesting results.

In general, school teachers (pre-service as well as in-service) were found to have moderate level of knowledge on sustainable development. Pre-service teachers understood sustainable development issues better than in-service teachers as reflected from their total scores (Table 7.1). Science teachers (both among pre-service as well as in-service teacher categories) understood concepts and facts relating to sustainable development better than arts teachers. Further, among pre-service school teachers (Table 7.2) all science teachers irrespective of their sex (male/female) and socio-economic background had scores of more than 65 per cent reflecting their very good knowledge on sustainable development issues. Male teachers had better knowledge than their female counter parts. Among in-service teachers, leaving aside science female low socio-economic category teachers, all science teachers irrespective of sex and socio-economic background had good knowledge on sustainable development. Female low socio-economic category in-service teachers had the lowest scores of less than 50 per cent—reflecting their poor knowledge.

Table 7.1: Mean Percent Score on Knowledge in Different Dimensions of Sustainable Development among Pre-Service Secondary School Teachers of Orissa

Pre-service Teacher Category	*Percent Score*				
	Economic Efficiency	*Environmental Harmony*	*Resource Conservation*	*Local Self-reliance*	*Equity and Social Justice*
SML_0	66.07^{a}	76.63^{a}	70.26^{ab}	72.73^{abc}	62.07^{ab}
SML_1	62.73^{ab}	72.73^{ab}	64.70^{abcd}	77.16^{a}	67.20^{a}
SML_2	66.10^{a}	77.77^{a}	75.20^{a}	77.20^{a}	67.87^{a}
SFL_0	70.83^{a}	70.80^{ab}	68.10^{abc}	70.00^{a-d}	61.60^{ab}
SFL_1	68.83^{a}	74.13^{ab}	72.90^{ab}	73.00^{ab}	66.76^{a}
SFL_2	63.20^{ab}	76.30^{a}	68.56^{abc}	66.30^{ab}	59.60^{ab}
AML_0	61.00^{ab}	60.33^{bcd}	50.90^{e}	58.33^{b-e}	47.33^{cd}
AML_1	60.40^{ab}	65.93^{abc}	60.16^{cde}	54.87^{cde}	60.33^{ab}
AML_2	63.73^{ab}	67.63^{ab}	56.46^{cde}	68.17^{a-d}	59.86^{ab}
AFL_0	45.83^{b}	50.33^{d}	49.17^{e}	52.53^{de}	42.20^{d}
AFL_1	55.00^{b}	53.83^{cd}	51.37^{e}	47.00^{e}	55.30^{bc}
AFL_2	56.33^{b}	50.33^{d}	53.17^{de}	55.00^{cde}	53.50^{bc}

In each column, mean followed by a common letter are not significantly different at 5 per cent level by DMRT.

S = Science teacher, A = Arts teacher, M = Male and F = Female

L_0 = Low socio-economic category, L_1 = Middle socio-economic category and L_2 = High socio-economic category.

Table 7.2: Mean Percent Score on Knowledge in Different Dimensions of Sustainable Development among In-Service Secondary School Teachers of Orissa, India

In-service Teacher Category	*Percent Score*				
	Economic Efficiency	*Environmental Harmony*	*Resource Conservation*	*Local Self-reliance*	*Equity and Social Justice*
SML_1	69.43^{ab}	69.97^{ab}	62.87^{ab}	69.30^{a}	60.23^{abc}
SML_0	71.00^{ab}	68.33^{abc}	62.40^{ab}	67.67^{a}	67.83^{a}
SML_2	72.17^{a}	75.00^{a}	70.47^{a}	67.76^{ab}	65.97^{ab}
SFL_0	61.20^{ab}	68.97^{abc}	56.23^{abc}	54.53^{abc}	55.63^{a-d}
SFL_1	63.33^{ab}	73.17^{a}	58.17^{ab}	61.67^{abc}	60.40^{abc}
SFL_2	72.00^{a}	70.67^{ab}	64.13^{ab}	61.33^{abc}	58.50^{abc}
AML_0	50.83^{ab}	57.50^{bcd}	41.54^{c}	56.67^{abc}	50.37^{bcd}
AML_1	52.00^{ab}	63.33^{a-d}	48.27^{bc}	56.00^{abc}	47.83^{cd}
AML_2	56.96^{ab}	68.10^{abc}	54.37^{abc}	60.33^{abc}	60.87^{abc}
AFL_0	48.90^{b}	50.13^{d}	39.87^{c}	45.56^{abc}	39.70^{d}
AFL_1	51.23^{ab}	51.23^{d}	45.17^{bc}	52.33^{abc}	48.70^{cd}
AFL_2	48.00^{b}	54.67^{cd}	47.63^{bc}	46.67^{bc}	48.83^{cd}

In each column, mean followed by a common letter are not significantly different at 5 per cent level by DMRT.

S = Science teacher, A = Arts teacher, M = Male and F = Female

L_0 = Low socio-economic category, L_1 = Middle socio-economic category and L_2 = High socio-economic category.

From studies on selected five dimensions (economic efficiency, environmental harmony, resource conservation, local self reliance, equity and social justice) of sustainable development, it was observed (Mishra, 2002) that pre-service secondary school teachers had good knowledge on dimension of environmental harmony and local self reliance and moderate level knowledge on other three dimensions (Fig. 7.1). Among in-service teachers, good level of knowledge was found on local self reliance, and moderate level on others except resource conservation in which they had poor knowledge. A good level of knowledge in the area of environmental harmony was observed in both pre-as well as in-service teachers. In other dimensions—such as resource conservation, economic efficiency, and equity and social justice, both pre-service as well as in-service teachers had moderate level of knowledge (leaving resource conservation for in-service teachers). Both among pre-service and in-service teachers, science teachers had better knowledge than arts teachers. In each dimension, male teachers had more knowledge than female teachers and arts female teacher had the lowest level of knowledge in each dimension (Table 7.1). Further in each dimension high socio-economic groups were more knowledgeable than middle that in turn were better than low socio-economic category. Science male teachers of high socio-economic category had the highest knowledge in each dimension and the arts female teachers of low socio-economic category had the lowest level of knowledge.

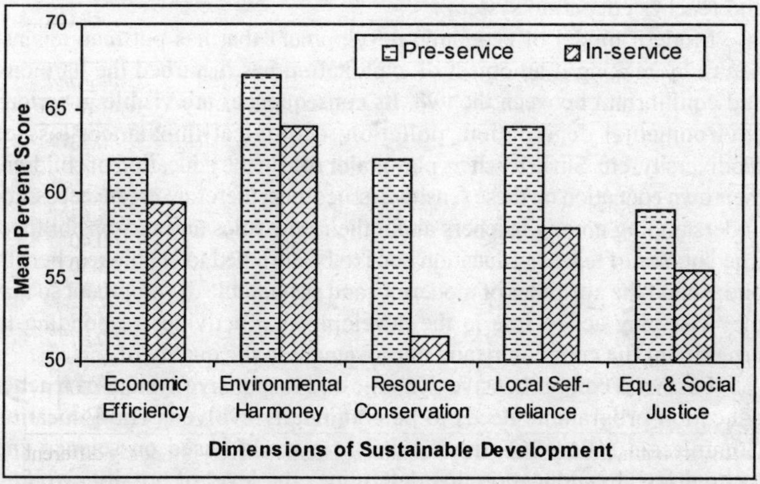

Fig. 7.1: Mean Percent Score in Knowledge on Different Dimensions of Sustainable Development of Pre-service and In-service Secondary School Teachers of Orissa

The pre-as well as in-service teachers were found to be deficient in concepts/issues like indicators of economic development, productivity, eco-technology, waste recycling, carrying capacity, biodegradation, geo-bio-chemical cycling, global climate change, environmental conservation, conventional agricultural practices, biological pest control, indigenous technology, etc. As sustainable development is an interdisciplinary area, many of the issues/concepts related to economics geography, biology, forestry, environmental sciences, etc. are not understood by many pre-service as well as in-service teachers. Das (2003) has observed from his study on teachers perception that most of the teachers realise the importance of greenhouse effect, global warming, deforestation but have very little knowledge of interdependence of all forms of life on earth for existence. It necessitates the development of a specific curriculum.

Toward Establishment of the Curriculum: Education for Sustainable Development

Education is an effective means of social reconstruction and to a great extent it offers solutions to the problems a society is faced with (Sathe, 1997). These problems could be economic, social, cultural, ecological and educational. As teachers are the torch bearers in creating social cohesion, national integration and a learning society, the quality of education is a direct consequence and outcome of the quality of teachers and teacher education system.

Modern model of economic development that has put man against nature by making it an object of exploitation has disturbed the harmony and equilibrium between the two. Its consequences are visible in serious environmental degradation, pollution, ecological imbalance; loss of biodiversity, etc. Since teachers play major role in the education of children, their own education on these sensitive issues must therefore create necessary understanding among teachers about their new roles and responsibilities. The courses of teacher education need to be enriched to enable teachers to understand the attributes of modernity and sustainable development so that they can play active role in the developmental activities responding to progress of the community and improvement in the quality of life.

Further a comprehensive dynamic and responsive system of teacher education programme needs to be continually evolved. The Education Commission (1964-66) stressed that in a world based on science and technology, it is education that determines the level of possible welfare and security of the people and that a sound peogramme of professional education of teachers is essential for the qualitative improvement of education.

Some quality dimensions for developing Sustainable Development Education curriculum for teachers could be:

- Consider the Environment related issues in totality, natural and man made—economic, ecological, social, political and cultural aspects
- Build a sense of global connectedness. We have in common the air, water and soil and the impact of growth or destruction in any place will sooner or later be felt around the world. Emphasise on conservation of life-support system—land, forest and water.
- Be interdisciplinary in its approach, drawing specific content of each discipline in making possible a holistic and balanced perspective
- Stress on continuous life long process from pre-service level and continue that in all formal and non-formal areas
- Emphasise the improvement of quality of life of people irrespective of their socio-economical status
- Promote interrelationship among people, economic development and ecological consequences. What is good for environment is also good for economy and environmental protection can not be considered in isolation.
- Explicitly consider environmental issues in economic development and growth
- Examine environmental issues from local, national and international perspective. Practice eco-development and maximise the use of locally available resources.
- Consider equality, social justice and empowerment dimensions from socio-economic point of view. Promote equity within and between generations. Making appropriate decisions in satisfying one's needs and wants is both personally and environmentally important.
- Promote values such as respect for nature, sharing of resources, reduction in the use of natural resources, recycle of resources, reuse of wastes, living together, etc. with local examples.
- Emphasise the complexity of economic problems and need to develop critical thinking and problem solving skills.
- Emphasise active participation of learners (student-teachers) and utilise diverse learning environments with due stress on first hand experiences
- Stress on renewable and ensure wise use of non-renewable resources, appropriate use of alternate (green) technology.
- Choosing of indigenous technology and life styles which are in

harmony with the environment fostering long term benefits for present and future generations.

- Protect endangered species and wilderness for the sake of survival, aesthetics and recreation Consider the natural resources as components to conserve in order to realise that they will return more in the long run if we do not over exploit them now.
- Ensure that environmental assets are appropriately valued. Introduce the concept of environmental accounting (Chidambaram, 2005) in terms of what one takes from earth in all forms of human activity.

Brundtland report concluded that the main concepts which must be associated with sustainability are the idea of limitations and the meeting of basic human needs, a priority over satisfying endless wants.

IUCN (1980) observes that three objectives that are paramount to the future well-being of the species and the planet are needed to be taught to the teachers. These are:

- maintaining ecological process and life support system,
- preserving genetic diversity and
- ensuring sustainable utilisation of species and ecosystems.

To realize this, the curriculum of teacher education needs to provide the basic knowledge and conceptual understanding of ESD in order to develop relevant skills and attitudes in student teachers and the existing cadre of teachers. This callS for proper development of skills for competency based teaching, continuous and comprehensive evaluation, organising and conducting projects and activities related to local specific conditions and the daily life of learners.

The basic strategies required to strengthen both pre-service and in-service teacher education programmes include:

- Reviewing and modifying the existing pre-service and in-service education programme in order to make ESD an integral part and provide both theoretical and practical inputs.
- Orienting teachers and student teachers with planning, designing and conducting of projects, activities, and case studies in local contexts.
- Exposing student-teachers to different kinds of community projects already in operation in the locality.
- Developing skills to establish closer school-community contacts and
- Using co-scholastic activities in other subjects as a medium of teaching ESD.

Methods and Approaches

Education for sustainable development is not mainly a passive transfer of knowledge. Simply deciding the content does not help in achieving the objectives of the curriculum. Teachers have to be convinced of the need for an environment education orientation to teaching. Teachers have not only to understand the content and contexts of what needs to be taught but also how to facilitate the teaching learning process. Teacher's decision about teaching-learning strategies determine the real curriculum (Sharma, 2005). The teacher becomes the real constructor of curriculum while translating the guidelines into curricular activities. Education for sustainable development believes a shift from content and predetermined learning outcomes towards the nature of the learning experience (Sterling, 2005). It stresses on action oriented approach with emphasis on active, hands-on discovery method with emphasis on learning by doing, exploring, problems solving, etc. While preparing a prospective teacher, socio-economic and cultural background of the community constituting the catchments area is to be realised. Teaching about the environment is most effective if it incorporates projects/activities (NCERT, 2005) that seek to produce tangible results. Looking into the needs activities such as water harvests, vermi composing, tree plantation, recycling of wastes, plantation of useful plants can be organised. Transactional modalities have to be essentially activity oriented, project based and participatory in nature. "Practise what you preach and teaching by example" are after all, just elements of good teaching practice.

Environmental problems being social problems, social approach/ community service (Ediger, 2005) should be used in order to solve those. In teacher education programme, social work is imperative both to help educate those creating the problems and those affected by the problems.

For teaching sustainable development issues, information communication technology (ICT) should be exploited to bring the environmental crises, issues, developments and possible control measures into the minds of prospective teachers.

In such education programmes, in-built mechanism should be there like identification of support material, skills in preparation of indigenous and low cost material, judicious choice and utilisation of material for enhancing the learning and use of community resources for education. Street plays can be organised for prospective teachers to sensitise the community in the ways in which community resources could be utilised and also to motivate the community

Saxena (2000) observed that the traditional methodology which is used for science and technology education is not likely to be suitable for teaching sustainable development issues. Approaches such as visit to actual site and its study, project method, experiments and survey are more suitable methods. As such the current teaching strategy is to be modified (Jackson, 2001) to begin with the local and concrete and then, as children grow older, move to more remote and abstract subjects should be taught.

Schaefer (1989) and Atchia (1990) observed that science and science education (in particular biology) provide the conceptual framework for practically managing the biosphere (forest, soil, air, water, biological diversity, etc.) as well as the techno sphere (human habit, industry, transportation, etc.) for sustainable and environmentally sound development. As a pre-requisite of quality improvement of teacher education, it is essential to provide opportunities to teachers and teacher educators to acquaint themselves with the changes that have been acquired due to scientific and technological developments which has unique role (Arora and Panda, 2000), (Khosla, 1999) in promoting sustainable development. It is interesting to note that science education in the US has undergone reform providing an excellent opportunity to use sustainable agriculture as the basic theme in teaching science (Raman *et al.*, 2000).

Professional development of teachers begins with pre-service and gets renewed through in-service programmes (NCTE, 1998). There are elements of 'change' and continuity in teacher education system which necessitates renewal and up-gradation of skills and competencies. The in-service programmes are to be organised to sustain the "survival competencies" acquired by teachers years ago during their pre-service education. For effective orientation of teachers in the area of sustainable development it is necessary to have coordination among university departments, department of science and technology, pollution control board, department of environment and forest, etc. Ministry of environment and forest (MoEF, 1998) observed that for in-service training support from Centre for Environmental Education, Ahmedabad and Chennai may be sought as they are generating resource materials and educational packages on nature and natural resource conservation.

It is highly necessary to have effective networking among resource institutions, schools and teacher training colleges to promote sustainable development message. In such education programmes, in-built mechanism should be there like identification of support material, skills in preparation of indigenous and low cost materials, judicious choice and utilisation of material for enhancing the learning and use of community resources for education. Interestingly some attempt has been made by NCERT (2001) in form of training module to promote learning looking into the local needs. Further environmental education resource centers need to be built around each teacher training institute involving local NGO and couple of schools in the locality.

Conclusion

Millennium Development Goal (MDG) target 9 calls to integrate the principles of sustainable development into country policies and programmes and reverse loss of environmental resources, but still countries are learning how to achieve the goals. As teachers are the key to the whole education system, it is only through the initiative and innovativeness of the teachers that such programme can be carried. Teachers only look into the needs of future generation through children to whom they teach and mould their character. As such their academic needs in terms of training and in-service programmes are to be looked into on priority basis so as to promote the cause of sustainable development (Roux and Ferreira, 2005).

8

Equity, Environmental Conservation and Sustainable Development

B.P. SAHU and P. GHILDAYAL

The Idea of Development

Development is a multidimensional concept and is defined as planned institutional change so as to bring about a better fit between human needs and resources of a country. It is affected by multiple variables like socio-economic, political, cultural, ethical, scientific and technological advancement. However it may be mentioned that development of any society is an ongoing process and it always reflects the priorities of the planners, policy makers and organisers of socio-economic, political and cultural lives of people. The concept of development has its origin in western thought. Following the end of the colonial era around the middle of the twentieth century, the newly independent countries comprising the third world faced the *Herculean task* of reconstruction and development. Although the idea of progress and development figures in earlier sociological writing, the growth of development theory is a post 2nd world war phenomenon. In such a situation the concept of development understandably gained momentum. To be specific, it was in the 1950s that the term development first came into general use and since then it has been subjected to a searching review and a paradigm shift. Further impetus to the dogma of development was given by United States with the idea of development decades beginning with the sixties. It was first used to differentiate between underdeveloped, developing and developed societies on the criteria of GNP rate and the degree of industrialisation. However, of late it has been realised that improvement in the well-being of individuals and bestowing benefits to all are the motto of development. Although initially development was conceived as economic growth, it has undergone several revisions thereafter (Sharma, 1986). The following conceptions of development have appeared so far: (a) Development as economic growth; (b) Development as growth with equity; (c)

Development as provision of basic needs; and (d) Development as improvement of physical-cum-civic quality of life. Economic growth thus came to be regarded as economic growth plus structural change. Widely, development also means various non-economic aspects of social change. At present sociologists prefer the concept of social development by which they mean 'a normative integrative upgrading of social order leading to enrichment of socio-cultural life of people.

In the early stages, development was influenced by the "Harrod Domar model "and following that model, economists attempted defining development as economic growth, as measured by the GNP or per capita income in the fifties and sixties. But, thereafter it came under severe criticism because of its rough methods of estimating GNP as well as its neglect of the dimension of distribution and the parameters of human development index. To cope with this critique, development was redefined as growth with equity. Equity implied the equality of income and employment as measured in terms of income differentials with reference to regions, rural-urban communities, work organisations, ranks within an organisation, gender stratification, etc. However, in course of time, this concept of development got identified with the left camp and was viewed with doubts due to its presumed totalitarian and oppressive overtones. Hence, it was realised that economic development does not necessarily ensure a better quality of life. As a result, there occurred a sort of paradigmatic shift (Reddy and Kumar, 2002) in the concept of development—a shift from economy to provision for the basic needs, such as food, clean water, health, shelter and education. Representing an advance over the earlier conceptions, this assumption of development as the improvement in people's life chances, has come under criticism for its preoccupation with the physical quality of life. Keeping in view this corrective, development is now conceived as an improvement of physical—cum-civic quality of life, with stress on human freedom and civil rights. These factors have led to big gaps between the elites and the masses not only in developing but also in developed countries.

However, in real terms, citizens in most developing countries associate some identifiable changes with development, such as construction of sky scrapers, ultra modern airports and huge dams, even though majority of the people continue to live a life of poverty, deprivation, ill health, illiteracy and unemployment. The first priority of development in the poor countries, therefore, should be the betterment of the economic life of the people through fulfillment of the basic needs of the large majority. Although development is equated with economic development, particularly with large scale industrialisation, the rate of growth of national income and increase in per capita output of material goods, no unanimity is visualised. One group of development experts recommend the pursuit of private profits which they presume would maximise public welfare, whereas another team of experts counsel to undertake a planned economy with the state assuming the dominant interventionist role. Nevertheless, all the experts opine in common that acquisition of more and more material goods is the ultimate objective of development.

Development and Environment

Economists and decision makers all over the world tend to look at the growth of GNP, while formulating policies. Considering GNP as a development indicator is incomplete (Sharma, 1986), if environmental considerations are not accounted in an economy. Initially development and environment are often seen as antagonistic attributes albeit their complementary links. The socio-economic development and resource planners very often stumble at ecological backlashing when they overlook the environment friendly method of development. On the one hand, we find environmentalists crying hoarse over the technocratic inclination of man for engineering ecological imbalance and environmental degradation and on the other we find those who believe that there is more money in destroying the environment than in conserving it. Gains from such development activities are ephemeral. Both the protagonists of ecological causes and development issues should try to find a sensible balance that leads to the principle of optimality. A symbiotic relationship between environment and development is the need of the people. The level of 'environmental damage' and its economic impact has to be considered in every country (Muralidharan, 1997), both developed and less developed, while framing development goals. The environment around us consists of the atmosphere, water, plants and animals. If the balance of any of these is disturbed, the changes are bound to affect us in one way or the other. Today world is passing through great environmental imbalance; the effect of this problem is before our eyes in every field.

Environmental problems in the developing countries in general, and India in particular, can be classified into two broad categories: (a) those arising from conditions of poverty and under development; (b) those arising as negative effects of the very process of development. The first category has to deal with the impact on health, and the effect on our natural resources like land, soil, water, forest, wild life, etc, a result of poverty and inadequate availability of the means to fulfill basic human needs (food, fuel, shelter, employment, etc.) for a major chunk of our population The second category deals with unintended side effects of efforts to achieve rapid economic growth and development. The latter category falls on distortions imposed on national resources from poorly planned development projects and programme as well as from lack of attention to long term concerns by commercial and vested interests.

Now several questions arise. Are development and environmental conservation opposing or contradictory notions? Does increment in one lead to reduction/depletion in the other? Is environmental stability or ecological balance feasible, without altering the prevailing economic and political equations between and among the developed and developing countries (Dalby, 2003)? Does the positive interface between society and environment need more basic changes in our social outlook and economic agenda, within and across national frontiers? The answer to all these questions lie perhaps in the approach of sustainable development (Gill, 2005). In general, renewable resources like water, forests, and fisheries can be made use of to the extent of their ability to renew themselves through natural growth. Sustainable economic development implies that the environmental capital stock should be held constant over time (Rao *et al.*, 2003). Ecological limits are to be ascertained beyond which the exploitation of natural resources would not be sustainable. The utilisation of non-renewable resources like minerals, petroleum and natural gas has to be done with necessary measures for safeguarding the ecology and environment.

Every developing country needs the strategy of conservation and development because the development process has jeopardised our basic life system. We have vast areas of wasteland, desert areas and flood affected areas. Our major river systems are threatened by the effluents discharged from thousands of industrial units and urban centres. The polluted riverine water is the major source of microbial infections and epidemics. At least 228 outbreaks have so far been notified due to pollution by industries causing a tremendous loss of human life owing to the outbreak of gastroenteritis, typhoid, infections, hepatitis and dysentery. That apart, municipal waste and the domestic sewage of all types of refuse ranging from night soil to human excreta, kitchen wastes, bathroom washings, detergents, agricultural wastes including fertilisers, pesticides, weedicides, fungicides, sediments from land erosion and floods, petroleum compounds, and acid mines discharge are the other major threats to riverine water. The result of these threats is the decrease in dissolved oxygen level and reduction of aquatic life in polluted rivers.

We have a very high rate of growth of human and live stock population creating rapidly growing demand for food, fuel and fodder, and our forests are getting denuded and degraded. Human beings in the pursuit of controlling and exploiting nature from time immemorial have really made themselves controlled by nature instead. Natural hazards are the other most important factors responsible for large scale destruction and degradation of environment, besides all man made nuisances. Natural hazards, such as earthquakes, famines, droughts, floods, landslides, high winds, fires, volcanic eruptions, etc. account for total loss of life and resources amounting to a gigantic figure of 1,37,586 million US dollars. Today some 250 million people are affected worldwide in an ever mounting spiral of disasters. Again, such catastrophic disasters have a rising trend mainly because of faulty human interventions (Jain, 2002) in the form of over exploitation of environment and eco-system beyond the safe limit and absence of proactive measures to contain the loss due to natural hazards.

For the effective and efficient management of environmental resources, and for determining the principles, practices and methodologies, sustainable development spells out the following six major tasks:

(a) Stabilisation of population growth
(b) Integrated land use and water management
(c) Conservation of biological diversity
(d) Sustainable energy and resource utilisation of (a) biomass, (b) fuel and (c) mineral resources
(e) Pollution control
(f) Improvement of human habitats

Development economists have adopted the term sustainability in an attempt to clarify the desired balance between economic growths on one hand and environmental preservation on the other. Although sustainable development has been defined variously, simply speaking it means development that meets the needs of the present generation without compromising the ability of future generation to meet their own needs (WCED, 1987). The concept originally proposed by the world commission on environment and development in 1987 gained prominence after the United Nations Conference on Environment and Development in 1992. It culminated in the establishment of the United Nation's Commission on Sustainable Development (CSD). Since the establishment of the CSD, very little progress has been made in operational concept of sustainable development. This is because according to some observers; there can be no operational definition for sustainable development with the modern worldview. When a concept can not be operationally defined, its realisation becomes difficult (Jain, 2002). Nevertheless, the definition of sustainable economic growth and development in quantifiable terms as upward trend of environmentally adjusted domestic product assumes that the allowances made for environment depletion and degradation can be invested.

Considerable concern began to be expressed in the developed

countries of the world especially towards the end of the 1960s, about the impact that economic growth had on their environment. One of the consequences of the growing concern was the 1972 UN World conference on environment in Stockholm. But at this conference the developing countries stated that, in their ranking of objectives, development was given greater priority than environment. Slowing economic growth in the interests of protecting the environment might appear to be a worthy cause to the richer countries but was not high on the agenda of the developing countries.

Even in advanced countries it was never clear that environmental protection was high on the agenda for the majority of the population, as distinct from the more affluent members of society. They were more concerned with the improvements in their living standards that technological advancement brought to them, for example, washing machines, televisions and automobiles. As far as the less affluent members of the population are concerned, they work with inadequate housing or dirty, noisy, and dangerous conditions. With regard to growth versus the environment, one may ask, if it is possible to reduce environmental destruction by not increasing the incomes of the poor, is it then possible to achieve growth without further damage to the environment. Evidences from worldwide indicate that the worst perpetrators of environmental destruction are the billion richest and the billion poorest people on earth. It follows that increasing the income status of the poorest group would provide an environmental backroll. However, as the income and consumption levels of everyone in the economy rise, there is likely to be net increase in environmental destruction. Therefore keeping environmental degradation at a minimum is no small task (Reddy, 2002).

On the other side there are clear differences in opinion between economists and scientists. These differences in view point arise in part from ambiguities in and disagreement about the real meaning of sustainability in terms of differing assumptions, perceptions and knowledge about: (a) the importance of environmental conditions and processes in supporting the biogeochemical cycles, (b) the sensitivity of these cycles to disruptive human activities. Sustainability is currently one of the most important issues pertaining to environment and development. Development in terms of economic growth has been thought to have resulted in degradation of environment due to the output of pollution, waste and depletion of natural resources. Many conventional economists have considered that there is no limit to growth while others have realised the outcome of uncontrolled development on the environment and exploitation of the limited available resources. Although, the physical systems of planet earth have the capacity to sustain the life supporting processes for a long period of time through various bio-geochemical cycles, interruption in these processes by human development activities could cause impairment of the environment and depletion of resources.

Equity vs. Inequality and Sustainable Development

The concept of unequal division of the world springs out of the words like North-South, Developed, Developing, Industrialised, Industrialising, Production, consumption, Global environment, local ecology, sustained development, eco-friendly technology, Top (rich)—Bottom (poor), etc. These words are appearing more and more in the discourses related to environment and employing a special semiotic field in the pragmatics of environmental discourses.

In spite of the fact that like a sphere, our globe does not have any direction, it is inherent in the cultural tradition to draw the earth with the north on top implying the idea that the countries at the north are developed and industrialised. Eventually its rich top millions of population have the right to consume more than the bottom billions of the 'developing' 'industrialising' countries of the 'south'. Although it is visualised from the historical point of view that the aforesaid concepts justify the act of bringing the south under colonialism by the north, it appears well nigh impossible to divide the earth into north and south, because geographically the two regions cannot be divided sharply. Hence, in terms of resources and population, the consumption of the average American citizen, for example, which is 50 times more than that of an average Indian, must have an environment effect on other geographical regions. So the natural result is that the poor of the south live on the dreaded environment caused by the north's wasteful over-use of natural resources.

During any environmental discourse, the developed countries hoist the problem of increasing population on the developing countries, while the earth can support a projected population of 20 billion with its existing resources. Due to the decline of mortality rate and with increase in life expectancy, the population of the developing countries is facing an immense growth rate mainly due to the adoption of 'western knowledge' in health and medicine. Without appreciating such growth rate, it can be deduced that the fertility rate is bound to "appear high' due to the low mortality rate. The imbalance in the use of natural resources and the population, as well as the problem that the rich 20 per cent of the world resources cause, are never addressed. Whereas the traditional cultural values of the developing nations control the material life as well as the rate of consumption, the industrialised countries encourage more and more consumption. For example a child in United States consumes the resources of 125 children in developing countries. The developed countries control the resources, with the help of arms, to maintain the unabated consumption. The cost of year round basic needs of the entire population of the developing nations can be sustained by unexpected two weeks' expenditure of the developed countries. While the world wide protest and struggle have been intensified against warfare and arms race the World Bank is approaching the developing countries with the sole aim of providing funds through loan to enable them to develop towards the direction dictated by the west. Such development not only generates resources for the industrialised countries but traps them in the immense debt chain that can hardly be loosened. In the recent past, it was a common reading in the print media that the Indian textiles were denied entry in the market of the developed countries like Germany and the United States on the flimsy ground that the Indian textile industries are using a dye that causes environmental pollution or that the manufactured items are inflammable. Although developing the non-industrialised countries by transferring technology through diplomatic relations and denying the entry of their products into global market is considered just one aspect of the problem, yet assent has been given to the GATT treaty by the developed countries.

The west treats the developed countries as the sink of its garbage (Dalbey, 2003). For example, applied energy services of Arlington, Virginia, USA, carefully calculated the emission of 387,000 tones of carbon by its power plant founded in Connecticut in its forty year life span. The company entered a contract with the environmental activists of the United States to plant trees in Guatemala worth two million US dollars. This exercise of not planting trees in USA but in Guatemala has been described by UNEP magazine as questionable and "an interesting scheme to attempt to reverse the balance of the green house effect of its power-house emissions". Similarly, Netherlands had earmarked half a million US dollars to plant 250,000 hectares of land in Bolivia for the simple reason that planting the same amount of tress in Netherlands costs 12 times more in comparison to developed countries. A study on the use of external resources by the developed countries like Netherlands can outwit any environmentalist. Even though the developing countries have won political sovereignty, they now continue to exist under the environmental colonialism of the developed countries. The sincerity of global institutions, such as the World Bank, in emancipating the environment from the hazards can also be questioned. Because of its extensive political clout with the developing countries and NGOs of the North, the World Bank funds and selects the environmental projects. The NGOs of the South who had their links with the NGOs of the North are only able to get funds from the bank for environmental projects that are likely to generate resources for the industries of the developed countries. It has been evident from the clarion call for boycotting tropical timber to keep the tropical forest reserve intact that has faced strong opposition from the G-77 nations in successive forums. Thus, the entire world is divided into two unequal halves, one half paying the cost of the other half for their better living.

Development should not be, as traditionally understood, simple industrialisation, creation of job, constructions or a steady movement of people from agriculture to industry eroding fields and forests. It should maintain a dynamic balance between population, resources and environment. For environmental processes we have to use the resources from environment to improve our lives. We often damage our environment by having too much or over-consumption that leads to waste which pollutes the nature. To strengthen the economy, pressure should not be put on the environment. This is the principle of sustainable economy. Optimum consumption of resources is highly essential instead of over-consumption or minimum consumption as it is economically viable. Also more importance is to be given to conservation technologies or eco-technologies rather than consumptive ones by blending traditional wisdom and practices with frontier sciences (Swaminathan, 2001).

Equity relates to fair play in all actions that are undertaken. Equity is relevant (Dash, 22005) (i) between nations, (ii) among nations—rich nations, poor nations, developed and developing nations (iii) within countries—between regions, social classes, genders, and (iv) between economics and ecology and science and technology.

Sustainable development requires many things (Anonymous, 2002) to be in place in society like peace, non-violence, human rights, equal rights of women, protection of children, education for all, etc. It is the development that not only generates economic growth but also distributes its benefits equally, that conserves the environment rather than destroying it, that empowers people rather than marginalising them. It gives priority to the poor, enlarging their choices and opportunity and providing for their participation in decision making that affects their lives (Srivastav, 2001). In short true sustainable development is that development which is pro-people, pro-nature, pro-job, pro-women and one that does not threaten future generations.

Environmental Conservation and Sustainable Development: Role of Education

There has been huge increase in the range and amount of human activity since the turn of the century which makes increasingly large demands upon raw materials, energy resources and human resources. Agriculture, forestry, energy production, and human population increase have their own socio-economic repercussions. These have been considered, to a great extent, responsible for alteration in the earth's eco-system resulting in global warming, ozone depletion, and loss of bio-diversity which are but a few of the alterations that transcend national boundaries and must be viewed from a global perspective.

Between 6,000 to 18,000 years ago, a global warming of 50°C was responsible for tremendous shifts in the earth's vegetation. Recent scientific data reveal a warming trend of 30°C in the present century alone. Its consequences are imaginable when compared to the previous 50°C warming in 12,000 years. An unprecedented increase in the green-house gases, like carbon dioxide, chlorofluorocarbons, methane, etc. which are considered a major factor in global warming phenomenon, have disastrous short term consequences such as reduction of sea-ice, rise in sea levels, regional vegetation changes, etc., and the long term damages are incalculable (Futuresco, 1992). Although the issue is complex, the green-house effect' appears to constrain the extension of an economic approach to social organisation. The exact consequences of the heating of the earth's surface are still open to debate but there has to be mutual agreement as to what the general trend is. The estimated rise in temperature caused by a doubling in carbon dioxide equilibrium concentrations is much greater than any alterations which have arisen through historical cyclic fluctuations. The effects are thought to be smaller at the equator and much greater at the higher latitudes, altering thermal gradients, changing precipitation patterns, modifying climatic zones and thus changing agricultural viability. Global warming will probably involve a number of complex, inter-connected factors. With an issue like global warming, an observation that thousands of hectares of rain forest can be seen burning everyday from space satellites may be an indicator that such production of carbon dioxide causes global warming. The discovery of high levels of carbon dioxide in factory or traffic emissions does not disqualify forest burning as a factor. We must unravel the multifaceted network of human activities. The advice of the national curriculum council that environmental education is the subject of considerable debate, and there is no clear consensus about how many of the issues are correct in its caution and echoes.

Long considered to be an inexhaustible resource, the earth's forest and notably the tropical rain forests, are being rapidly depleted and degraded due to a variety of human interactions like agriculture, logging, ranching, fuel-wood gathering, etc. Tropical rain forests which covered 30 per cent of earth's landmass in 1950 came down to 12 per cent in

1975. The consequent loss of soil fertility, elimination of thousands of animals and plant species, climate variability resulting in droughts or floods, increase in green house gases, etc., have played a key role in the massive displacements with dramatic consequences. Environmental education incorporates within its field different types of resources, such as soil resources, plant resources, wild life resources, mineral resources, energy resources; water resources, problems of resource deterioration, ways and means of conserving natural resources, ways and means of preventing environmental degradation like crop rotation system, afforestation, use of alternative energy resources such as solar, tidal, wind and geothermal energy and recycling of wastes, etc. In May 1988 the resolution of the Ministers of Education of the Council of the European Community stated that: "the objective of environmental education is to increase the public awareness of the problems in this field, as well as possible solutions, and to lay the foundations for a fully informed and active participation of the individual in the protection of the environment and the productive and rational use of natural resources.

The size and growth rate of population has positive relationship with environmental problems. Human population growth is estimated to be one of the most important factors in increasing environmental stress, depletion of materials and energy resources. An eco-system has only a certain "carrying capacity ", i.e. the capacity to sustain exploitation of its resources without damaging its regenerative capacity, and humans depend upon the eco-system resources for survival which is vital to harmonise human population growth with the environmental reality, i.e. the carrying capacity of the concerned eco-system. Overpopulation in any part of the world puts tremendous pressure on the natural environment due to over-exploitation. In the like manner, the growth of human population directly or indirectly affects the quality of life due to the impossibility of the expansion of land and other resources. An analysis of the population growth rate of the world is given below:

Table A

Period	*World Population (In crores)*	*Growth in Population (In crores)*	*Years Needed for Additional 100 Crores*
1650-1800 AD	100	100	–
1800-1930 AD	200	100	130
1930-1960 AD	300	100	30
1960-1975 AD	400	100	15
1975-1987 AD	500	100	12
1987-1997 AD	600	100	11

Source: U.N. population data sheet.

The resources-man ratio is increasing day by day, leading to overexploitation of the natural environment. Hence, The environmentalists always keep a vigilant eye on the growth rate of population and any debate or discussion in the field of environmental education leads to planned population on account of the fact that population explosion happens to be one of the major causes of environmental problems. Large demographic changes are to be expected in the industrial countries caused by their ageing populations and falling birth rates. Automation and increasing productivity may generate sufficient national product to maintain living standard with a reduced workforce, but a sustainable burden will be placed upon pension and health care system. In addition to that adjustment will have to be made to educational system as the success of family planning attitudes works its way through the population. Differences between countries in the opportunities for individuals to succeed could cause population movements. The population of rich countries will have to prepare itself to accept the reality of the need for cooperation to reduce the significant economic disparity. Human activity which alters agricultural potential and removes fertile land for other purposes, such as mineral extraction or transport, may be linked in its effects with a rising world population. Technically, one may be able to grow sufficient food to support a population of twenty billion, but this is to discount huge demands on energy which would be needed to supply sufficient fresh water to support the enterprise.

As regards energy consumption, since 1990 world consumption of fossil fuels has increased nearly four times as fast as world population. The major sources of fossil fuel-petrol natural gas and coal are expected to last about 200 years. However it is not only the depletion of these non-renewable energy sources that is cause for concern, but the generation of harmful by products due to their excessive utilisation which results in smog, acid precipitation, petrol spills, or global warming. Environmental education reminds us the fact that resources on our planet, the earth, are only limited and we do not have a second planet to plunder. A positive attitude needs to be developed towards environment and we should try to live with nature rather than exploiting and destroying our natural resources and also disrupting the ecological balance.

The entire land on earth accounts for 13 billion hectares, out of which 33 per cent is classified as "wasteland" 31 per cent as forest, 25 per cent as rangeland and only 11 per cent is cultivated. The last three categories supply a large portion of the resources utilised by human beings for their survival. Since the beginning of humanity, control and use of this land has been an essential aspect of human beings. The rapid growth, both of human population and its consumption, has not only increased the variety of its uses but also the severity of the impact of the usage resulting in what is termed as land degradation and due to which the actual amount of land which can be utilised is shrinking. Estimation, made in 1948, reveals that 35 per cent of the earth's land surface is in peril and that approximately 6 million hectares of land are being destroyed annually. The primary reasons of land degradation may be attributed to overgrazing, over cultivation, salinisation and deforestation leading to soil erosion, floods, loss of vegetation, drought, desertification, and poverty. However, if these global issues are approached in a manner so as to produce educational outcomes related to changing human behaviour, changes could lead to a resolution, partly, if not wholly, of the issues.

The environment influences human health and quality of its living life. Apart from the genetic factors, the other determinants of environment, such as water supply, urban environment, quality, climate and the pattern of human contacts are involved in the process. Causation of diseases, such as the communicable diseases, degenerative diseases and neo-plastic diseases are associated with the pattern of human contacts involved. The major diseases which haunt the developing countries are Diphtheria, Whooping Cough, Tetanus, Measles, Poliomyelitis and Tuberculosis. Of course, diseases and death in developing countries may also be attributed to malnutrition and prevalence of various superstitions so much so that even physical description and disabilities on the part of the human infants are construed to have been caused due to pollution and malnourished mother. Environmental education issues throw warning to people in this regard.

The role of human beings in the causation of most of the environmental problems (Anonymous, 2003) is well established. Their attitudes and values have become instrumental in shaping the environment and essentially causing the present day problems. Today, unhealthy competition for materialistic pleasure in developing countries puts too much demand on environment and multiplies the human needs, ultimately leading towards resource exploitation. The need of the hour is to consider the future consequences for living in harmony with the environment and to evolve a balanced way of thinking, acting and feeling towards the environment. Hence, the scope of environmental education encompasses human ethics, attitude, and value decision making analysis of ecological, economic, social and technical aspects.

Education now has come to mean a lot more than mere instruction. It is viewed as the total process by which society perpetuates itself. Professor J. Paul Leonard, in his article *Education for Democracy* considered education as a form of social policy that evolves, reflects and interacts with the changing social climate and aspirations of people. As the most efficient instrument of social reconstruction, it is the maker of new society committed to a particular set of values, demanding conformity to a particular set of norms, assigning responsibility, in particular role-sets, and exercising control of particular set of facilities. Education as a social system must effectively function within and for the efficiency of a larger social system.

All the above exigencies necessitate environmental education which is conceived of as a process dealing with man's relationship with his natural and man-made surroundings, and includes the relation of population, pollution, resource allocation and depletion, conservation, transportation, technology and urban and rural planning to the total human environment. It is the process of recognising values and clarifying concept, in order to develop skills and attitudes necessary to understand and appreciate the inter-relatedness among man, his culture and his bio-physical surroundings. Environmental education also entails practice in decision making and self-formulating of a code of behaviour about issues concerning environmental quality.

Environmental education is a way of implementing the goal of environmental protection. Environmental education is not a separate branch of science or subject of study. It should be carried out according to the principle of life long integral education, (UNESCO, 1974). "It involves teaching about value judgments and the ability to think clearly about complex problems—about the environment—which are political, economical and philosophical and technical" (Anonymous, 1971). Environmental education aims at creating awareness and understanding of the evolving social and physical environment as a whole, its natural, man made, cultural, spiritual resources, together with the rational use and conservation of natural resources for development (Anonymous, 1968). In order to enable people to enjoy good health and a high quality of life, it is vital to prevent harmful effects on human health or damage to the environment caused by pollution of air, water and soil, noise, vibration, noxious smells, etc. caused by firms and individuals. The environment includes animals and plants and their ecological system which are closely related to the livelihood of people (Anonymous, 1969). In a nutshell, it can be stated that environmental education is a continuous process for creating environmental awareness among the people as a result of which they will be able to solve the problems relating to environment.

Environment education aims at: (i) Creating awareness among the students about the environment and its problems; (ii) enabling the student to cognize the environment and its interrelationship with human beings; (iii) enabling the learners to acquire basic knowledge about the environment; (iv) creating favourable attitude among students towards the environment; (v) developing skills among students with a view to solving environmental problems; (vi) developing skills among the students for evaluating environmental conservation measures and educational programmes; (vii) creating a sense of responsibility towards the environment and making the students feel the urgency for ensuring appropriate actions to solve environmental problems.

In 1977, the Tbilisi Conference further elaborated the goal of environmental education as: (a) Fostering clear awareness of and concern about economic, social, political, and ecological interdependence in urban and rural areas; (b) providing every person with opportunities to acquire the knowledge, values, attitudes, commitment and skills needed to protect and improve the environment; (c) creating new patterns of behaviour of individuals, groups and society as a whole towards the environment. The Tbilisi conference has also set the following guiding principles of environmental education: (1) To consider the environment in its totality, viz. economic, political, social, technological, cultural, historical, moral and aesthetic. (2) It should be a continuous process. (3) It should be a lifelong process beginning from pre-school level to death. (4) To help learners discover the real cause of environmental problems. (5) The environmental education should utilise diverse learning environments and a broad array of educational approaches to teaching-learning about the environment with due stress on practical activities and first hand experience. (6) It should develop critical thinking and problem-solving skills in the students. (7) It should stress the complexity of environmental problems. (8) The learners should play a role in planning their own learning experience with others. (9) Opportunities should be provided to the students/learners for making independent decisions and to face their consequences; (10) The inter-disciplinary approach should be followed. (11) The historical perspective should be taken into consideration while dealing with present environmental situation. (12) The holistic approach should be adopted. (13) The local environmental issues should be examined along with national and international ones so that students receive insights into environmental conditions in other geographical areas. (14) The environmental education should explicitly consider environmental aspects in plans for development and growth. (15) The environmental education should relate environmental sensitivity, knowledge, problem-solving skills and value clarifications at an early age but with special emphasis on environmental sensitivity to the learner's own community.

The main function of environmental education is to create a healthy environment. Identifying the people for whom it is required, Dr. Pritchard has categorised different groups of people to whom it helps in a variety of ways for creating healthy environment: (i) It is helpful to the geographers, biologists, geologists, agricultural and forest scientists, foresters and farmers who attempt to make a career in the earth and life sciences. (ii) The planners, designers of land, architects, civil engineers dealing with the design, construction and control of projects affecting the environment are amply benefited. (iii) It enables the physicists, chemists and technologists to carry on research having regard for environmental balance. (iv) It assists statesmen, public servants and other leaders to formulate policies keeping in view the far-reaching consequences of environmental degradation. (v) It is helpful to those who in future will bear the task of interpreting knowledge to young people as educationists. (vi) It also helps those people who have sufficient interest to form a collective voice, without any direct professional involvement, which will influence other members of the above categories.

The scope of environmental education implies the area it covers. Some of the basic, most significant, current issues involved in environmental education are: (a) global warming, (b) tropical deforestation, (c) human population, (d) energy consumption, (e) global land use and (f) health and life style of man.

Education has always played a stellar role in creating healthy attitudes and skills and disseminating knowledge. Therefore, the Stockholm conference on human environment in 1972 emphasised the need for environment oriented education. For a country like India it should not be constructed as a new discipline, rather a new dimension in education system. This type of consciousness towards physical environment is not, by any means, something recent. In primitive days, man tried to observe nature and discover the mysteries hidden behind its occurrences. The snow-clad peaks of the Himalayas, the gigantic rivers and boundless seas, no doubt, had an effect on the Indo-Aryans who lived in harmony with nature. We even worshipped the sun, fire, water and sky with simple or complex rites from the most ancient to Aryan history. In the pre-Vedic age, those powers of nature had been personified. We had always looked upon ourselves as a part of nature and subject to its law. This is amply clear from our ancient texts, our customs, the way the villagers live, and the way Indian tribal people live in the forests. The bulk of our old literature, both oral and written, over thousands of years clearly brings out this relationship between man and nature.

For a country like India, a new dimension in education system has emerged from 1970s as a series of important events which took place during this period, justifying it to be called the decade of environmental education. The roots of environmental education prior to that can be traced back to the school system of different countries under various names such as 'Nature Study', 'Local Study', 'Field Study', 'Rural Study', 'Out-door Education', and 'Conservation Education', etc. In those days, environmental education formed a part of other subjects in formal and non-formal education and was not a separate one. Different aspects of environment found their place in different subjects, viz. Biology, Geography, Economics, etc. Along with gradual increase in man's intervention in the environment, the thinkers realised the changes therein. The concept of environmental education has been undergoing changes ever since the world at large started waking up to the significance of the role played by the environment in human life and vice-versa. But for a long period of time, the environment—mostly understood as nature—continued to be perceived as part of the heavenly order, something immutable and permanent, within which humanity could have no more than a totally submissive relationship. The earth's environment has transformed more rapidly in the past generation than at any other comparable time in history, one of the primary sources of these dynamics being precipitated by human interaction with the biosphere.

Nowadays it has become a *Herculean* task to cultivate favourable attitude among people towards protection of natural resources, so much so that the people who are responsible for the protection of resources, spoil it for vested interests. Erosion of values makes them to speak something and perform just the reverse. This warrants framing of environmental laws to be observed to such an extent that man refrains from indiscriminate exploitation of natural resources. The fear of punishment may result in the transformation of life style and ultimately the human values and attitudes. Environmental laws are vast, decidedly exciting and glamorous. They are vast because of the various subjects and projects that lie within their ambit. They are mostly undefined in the sense of its rules. They are exciting in the newness of some of their techniques. They are glamorous in the publicity which they often receive.

Education about the environment, its climate, geology, water resources, living system and human activities can only provide a common framework within which the moral values debate takes place. One can not teach about the environment without ascribing values to the existence and desirability of certain kinds of environment. The learners may debate how to ensure the best immediate and future use of the environment. They may consider possible solutions to environmental problems taking into account conflicting interests and making informed choices.

The resolution of the Ministers of Education at the Council of the European Community suggested some principles which might enrich environmental education:

- the environment as the common heritage of mankind;

- the common duty of maintaining, protecting and improving the quality of the environment, as a contribution to the protection of human health and the safeguarding of the ecological balance;
- the need for a prudent and rational utilisation of resources;
- The way in which each individual can, by his own behaviour, particularly as a consumer, contribute to the protection of the environment.

For effective implementation of environmental education the Supreme Court of India had made environmental studies a compulsory subject up to the senior secondary level in schools in the year 2003. A two Judge bench of Justice N. Santos Hegde and Justice B.P. Singh asked the National Council for Educational Research and Training, the nodal agency, to monitor how environmental education up to class XII could be implemented. In April 2004, the apex court approved the model syllabus that NCERT came up with. For this, NCERT had consulted more than 500 institutions, state governments, the Central Pollution Control Board, individual experts and NGOs. For students of Classes I to VIII, the subject will be part of the Social Science syllabus. Students of Classes IX to XII will study it as an additional subject. The apex court has asked NCERT to seek opinion of the states on the model syllabus, before proceeding to implement it. On another front, the University Grants Commission has made environmental studies a compulsory subject for all under graduate students. As such education on population and environmental issues will improve if the linkages among population size, consumption and environmental quality are examined and discussed with classrooms (Raman, 2000).

Today environmental studies have become part of our students' lives. Environmental education emphasises natural resource conservation, pollution problems, flora and fauna and biodiversity. Such issues must be conveyed from the primary level itself, because attitudes cannot be changed after secondary education Therefore the educational system should be capable of sustaining this change in the right spirit. Environment as a separate, compulsory subject must lead to increased awareness and interest amongst students and society. This is a subject very close to the heart and soul of individuals. Without environmental education no country can be ecologically safe. The course content of the subject would have to be constantly upgraded. But unfortunately our education system till now has not shown such agility. Over a period of time, the course content must not become dogmatic in nature. There is also a need to adapt the course curriculum locally, especially the school curriculum. Teaching environment should be viewed as a multidisciplinary activity. Teachers must be drawn from physical science as well as social science. As sustainable development is important for mankind; the future citizens should be well aware of their environment and this can only be possible with the right shift in educational policy. It depends more on sincerity in the part of different schools, teachers and policy makers. The aim of teaching environment should not be only for acquiring knowledge and pass the examination but also to make our lives meaningful and future life of the people sustainable.

9

Need and Importance of Value Education for Environmental Conservation and Sustainable Development

M.K. SATAPATHY and D. DASH

Environment is the sum total of all conditions and influences that affect the development and life of organisms including human being. From ancient times, man has been serious minded about environment (*prakrit*) and its basic philosophy has been "one of harmony with nature." Apart from the *Vedic* and *Upanishadic* concepts of human dependence on nature which are partly religious and spiritual, partly aesthetic and ethical, there was a more explicit effort to understand nature and relate it to human well-being by Buddhists, Jains, Hindus and Moguls. Further our ancient literature is full of prayers/worships addressed to nature. Gods have been identified with nature, wild animals, and men. *Dya*, *Marut*, *Agni*, *Varun*, *Mitra*, *Prithvi*, and *Usha* are the incarnations of nature. Nature is an embodiment of *Satyam*, *Shivam* and *Sundaram* (Truth, Beauty, and Goddness). The five elements—fire, water, air, earth, and space—have been considered to be the basic building blocks of this universe and there is a thread of unity running through the world. Deterioration in any one element inevitably affects the other four elements. If the deterioration is for short term, it repairs itself and reverts to the origional state but if the deterioration continues, the whole system including other life forms is thrown out of gear. It therefore goes without saying that the very existence, survival and progress of man on earth depends on the quality of environment (Kaur *et al.*, 2003).

Human beings interact with environment in three ways, as space for living, as a bank of resources such as food, water, materials and energy and as sink for waste disposal. As the most enlightened species, *Homo sapiens,* man has paramount responsibility to preserve the environment and improve it qualitatively not only for himself but also for the future generations. However, unfortunately with development in science and technology, man has been dominating nature, shaping the environment to suit itself using everything around him without scant regard whatsoever for the natural scheme of interdependent ecological regimes. In course, human race has changed itself from a simple minded fruit gatherer who worshiped nature to a callous, self-centered destroyer of nature by adding stress and strain, unhealthy competitions, intensive consumerism, dishonesty and unethical practices. In the name of development, man has been ruthlessly consuming natural resources and polluting the environment (Siva, 1991), without scant regard for its assimilative power and carrying capacity (Barrell and Odum, 2000). The environmental crisis the world is facing today is due to overpopulation, hunger, poverty, people's unlimited desire, ignorance, and materialistic approaches to life (Nagchaudhuri, 1983). However in the last two decades, millions of people in the world over have started realising that much of what god created, man is now destroying (Joshi, 2003), not only earth's basic life supporting capital of forests, animal species and soils but also its fresh water and oceans and even the ozone shield which protects all life forms from the sun's more deadly rays. Now we are threatening ourselves with climate change—a rapid rise in global temperature and sea levels—greater perhaps—in the next forty to sixty years than in the 10,000 years since the last ice age (Brown, 1997).

These environmental threats that now facing us could have so much momentum that are unless steps are taken to reverse them, they may soon overwhelm our ability to respond (Baliga, 1996), even threatening all living beings including man himself with disaster or extinction (Parasher, 1996).

Sustainable Development: The Concept

It is understood that "Our environment has visibly, seriously and irreversibly changed for the worse in our life time and it is we who are the victims. If we do not act today, our children will live in an even worse environment, they will suffer for our errors and omissions". (Singh, 1998). Thus now the time has come to live sustainably and well but within the material limits of finite planet (Costanza *et al*., 1997). This concept of sustainable development became popular through the famous Bruntland report entitled "*Our Common Future*" published in 1987. It recognised that natural resources are not inexhaustible and the development process should be aimed to meet the needs of the present generation without compromising the ability of the future generations to meet their own needs (WECD, 1987). The dividends of development must flow continuously through generations for not only alleviating poverty but also upgrading the quality of life (IUCN, UNEP, WWF,

1991). Sustainable development is possible if principles of ecology are followed in planning developmental activities, and long term socio-economic need is kept in view and not just short-term profits. As a whole it realises that economic development can not be achieved at the cost of environment and life support system.

Education for Sustainable Development

Education is first and foremost a human right as proclaimed in article 26 of Universal Declaration of Human Rights. It is also the key to building up the skills and capacities in all domains necessary to techno-economic development. Further it is the means whereby people may hope to address some of the most profound problems confronting our societies in the current century and the new millennium. Further, education helps to foster all forms of behaviour, life styles and values necessary for human survival on a crowded planet (Mayor, 1997).

Education is a pre-requisite for development. It promotes awareness, sharpens the eye of knowledge and makes mind logical (Alam, 1998). Further it attacks poverty, increases economic growth, improves income distribution and reduces inequality. Literacy as the backbone of education (Seth, 1997) acts as the cause and effect of development. Literacy as a qualitative attribute of the population, is one of the most important indicators of the socio-economic and political development of a society It strengthens and sustains the process of development.

The concern for environment and its conservation has been reflected in the National Policy on Education-1986 document (MHRD, 1986). The UN conference on environment and development popularly known as Earth Summit (Anonymous, 1992) in its Agenda 21 and Chapter 36 gave importance to "Education, awareness and training "the critical factors of public understanding, fundamental to any progress to be made. It stressed reorienting education towards sustainable development. Education is critical for promoting sustainable development and improving the capacity of people to address environmental and developmental issues. To be effective, it must deal with both the physical, biological and socio-economic environment and hence development.

In 1994, the UN commission for sustainable development realising the importance of education drafted a work plan with 21 tasks on education for sustainable development (ESD) (Anonymous, 2002). The second task is: "clarify, promote and communicate the concept and key message of education for sustainable development to all".

The achievement of environmental goals through education, awareness and training described in Principle 10 of Rio declaration (Anonymous, 1992) states:

> "*Environmental issues are best handled with the participation of all concerned citizens, at the relevant level. At the national level, each individual shall have appropriate access.... Participation by making information widely available*".

Again in 1997, UN commission on SD (CSD) earth summit plus 5 stressed on the importance of environmental education at all levels for a sustainable future which was also highlighted in the third UNESCO-ACEID International Conference held in Thailand during 1-4 December, 1997 (UNESCO, 1998) and recently concluded Johannesburg meet (Engfeldt, 2002). As a whole sustainable development stresses everything that one can do to save the planet (Kauri *et al*., 2003).

Value Education and Development

Values are the salient features of individual behaviour in the society. These are so deeply embedded (Vijayalaxmi, 2002) in human actions and thoughts that one should make an effort to implement it. High values lead to objective, fair, correct decisions and actions and ensure the welfare of all concerned. In almost all societies values are transmitted through parents, grandparents, teachers, religion and the arts, be it literature, music, dance, films, etc. Lack of value education has been an important factor (Westing, 1996; Khandal, 2003) in the global scenario of growing violence, terrorism, pollution and ecological imbalance.

National policy on Education (NPE, 1986) states that value education should be based on heritage, national goals and cultivation of social and moral values. Acharya Rama Murthi Committee (1990) reviewing NPE (1986) states that the child be committed not only to the world of knowledge and skills but also to the values associated with it. Hence value development in education should include development of proper attitude, feelings and behaviour patterns across all curricular experiences.

As knowledge influences the attitude that turns into action, it is essential that a good knowledge base be made about nature at the early childhood level. It would lead to protection and preservation of the environment leading to economic prosperity in the long run. In the name of comfort, prosperity, and economic development man should not forget about mother earth and its protection. The process has to begin from home. Mother is the best teacher and home is the first school for learning. Next comes educational and religious institutions. School system has a very important responsibility (Rajput, 2003) in value education, value nurturance, and value development. Once the process is initiated in schools, impact can be realised in family, community, and society to achieve an attitudinal transformation for resource management.

Literacy scale for community should not limit to simple 3R's, Reading, Writing, and Arithmetic only. On the contrary it should include environmental literacy that looks into resource awareness and judicious use of resources—thus helping in the improvement of one's life style based on the knowledge and understanding of his/her environment. Various issues relating to value education are discussed below.

Respect for Nature

Traditional people recognised that the relationships among humans, plants, animals and all life forms are sacred. They lived within a community that nurtured relationship and created bonds between people and the natural world. They learn and realise that diversity is the pre-condition for stability. Human being is a part of the vast web of interconnected species and systems that fit together in intricate ways enabling the whole system to continue. There is one earth and one humanity. Man must know that nature is not for man but man is a component of nature.

In ancient literature, natural elements like air, water, earth fire etc. are considered as *Devas* giving all good things of life. Nature is considered as "Bountiful Nature" and earth as "Mother Earth". One can use nature and mother earth for his need, for his survival, for his sustenance but he must not waste, spoil, exploit or destroy for his greed and selfish ends. To strengthen this attitude various animals such as lion, tiger, elephants; birds like owl, peacock, crow, etc. are worshiped and protected.

Sacred Groove is a bright example of nature protection. As an age old tradition sacred groove represents a patch of forest or land dedicated to gods and goddesses and none is permitted to destroy it in terms of cutting plants or killing animals. Though the number of sacred grooves are coming down because of modernisation and economic growth, these banks of genetic diversity maintained by local community have still helped to preserve animal and plant species which otherwise would have disappeared. As such one should be sensitive to flora and fauna while traveling to countryside. To build the love for nature in the young minds, children may be encouraged to be member of nature clubs and people for animal society and attend nature camps wherever possible. Futher they should boycott circuses where animals are known to be treated badly

Care and Share

The resources on the surface of earth are very limited. It may be soil, water, forest, wild life, etc. With fast growing population, the resources are getting depleted. So there is urgent need that we should not only take care of the existing resources but also share it among rich and poor, developed and developing countries for its sustainable use. For example the developed countries consume 80 per cent of the world's commercial energy, 85 per cent paper and 50 per cent of the fat content of the food. Poor countries like India having 18 per cent of the world population has only 2 per cent of land resources to meet the basic needs. Further, developed countries face the problem of increased per capita waste generation and industrial pollution. As environmental problems created by one country are not limited and often cross national boundries and affect the people, economy and ecology of other countries, developed countries should extent their help, support and cheap technology to developing countries as those (developing countries) with high population density and intensive land use do not have necessary infrastructure and technologies to waste treatment and disposal. Similarly there should be sharing of resources between rich and poor in a society. To promote caring habit, children may be asked to put water and food for animals/birds in seasons where sustenance is scarce on the ground.

Participation in Traditional Rituals

The tradition of sanctifying various trees and plants dates back to vedic period. Though wood as a fuel was a basic need and trees in general were treated with care and respect, some trees like the Peepal, Banyan and Neem commanded more respect than others. The Tulsi (Basil) plant is grown in every household in the centre of the yard and is ritually watered. The rituals served an important purpose—they made people aware of the environment and its importance and thus indirectly helped to preserve and nurture it.

We need to make the effort to find out and understand the basic principles behind the rituals, traditions and customs that are essential elements of ancient civilisations. The worshiping of trees, bushes rivers, and ponds, animals and birds just emphasise their importance for human survival. Religion was used largely to ensure community participation in all those practices that would lead to the maintenance of ecological balance. For instance during the "*Chhath*" festival devotees are required to stand in deep water while paying obeisance to the sun-god. This festival ensures community participation in maintaining ponds and lakes. Thus collective effort to maintain water resources lead to their preservation as reservoirs. As such religion which was an effective social marketing tool, that was used to involve people in environmental management, is lacking presently.

Reduce, Recycle and Reuse

Present consumption of world resources as reflected in recent WWF's earth report statistics is quite alarming. We are currently consuming 20 per cent more natural resources than the earth can produce (Fossil consumption has increased by 700 per cent in the 40 years between 1961 and 2001). Species number—terrestrial, freshwater, and marine, declined by 40 per cent in the 30 years between 1970 and 2000. In North America alone, rate of over-consumption and exploitation of natural resources is double that of Europe's and seven times that of Asia or Africa. The report also warns that future problem on earth will result from spiraling consumption in Asia. It is interesting that Brundtland report observed the main concepts which must be associated with sustainability are the idea of limitations and the meeting of basic human needs, a priority over satisfying endless wants. Thus the environmental philosophy of 3R's (Reduce, Reuse and Recycle) (Fig. 1) besides environmental literacy is highly essential for survival of mankind. (Dash and Satapathy, 2006)

Reduce

It is understood that the resources of earth are limited and they are declining rapidly. Industrialisation which is considered very important for economic development is responsible for depletion of natural resources on one hand and causing pollution on the other (Pandey and Kaushik, 2004). With expanding human population there is rise in needs and demands but the main reason that prompts individuals to destroy and harm the environment is greed and selfishness. Once Mahatma Gandhi observed "*Nature has enough for our need but not any body's greed*". The culture of consumerism has led man to exploit nature for his/her own benefit and comfort so it is high time that we should reduce our consumption of resources. One can use nature (Priority) for his need, for his survival, for his sustenance but he must not waste, spoil, exploit, destroy for his greed and selfish ends. In daily life reduction in the use of natural resources and wastes generated is very essential as every ecosystem has a carrying capacity (Barrell and Odum, 2000). Reduction in the use of water, wood, forest products, minerals, fossil fuels, etc. is very essential as these resources are finite and not renewable. Promotion of appropriate and alternate technology and renewable sources of energy such as solar, wind, and tidal should be encouraged. In daily life for example everyone should switch off lights and fans at home, offices, and public places to save energy. Children may be discouraged to use firecrackers during Deewali and synthetic colors during Holy to reduce pollution and save environment. During puja and festivals use of synthetic colors and paints for coloring statues is to reduced or stopped as they often pollute river and ocean water and kill organisms in the aquatic ecosystems. Use of plastic bags should be discouraged or minimised as their use often chokes water pipes, drains and causes soil pollution. People may be told to reduce wastage of food and avoid use of luxury items like shampoos, detergents, cosmetics, and other synthetic oil items that affect the soil and aquatic environment besides affecting personal health. People should cut down buying leather and silk items. Use of canned or bottled food should be avoided as it creates more waste in the environment especially in public places and places of tourist interest. In energy use people should change to compact fluroscent light (CFC) bulb and can reduce energy consumption by one fourth. It is necessary to switch off the car engine in traffic jam in order to reduce petrol/diesel consumption. Further vehicle owners should change petrol and diesel engines into environment friendly CNG. Besides pollution of air, water, and soil many other unthoughtful activities (for example production of CFC) has resulted into global warming besides depletion of ozone layer.

It is interesting to note that with development of modern science and technology, cultivation of GM plants (genetically modified crop plants) (Govil, 2003) has slowed down pesticide use resulting in reduction of soil pollution. Of course it is often opposed by green activists. Further, the expansion of organic farming has reduced the use of chemical fertilizers responsible for loss of fertility and ground water pollution (Swaminathan, 2000).

Recycle

Presently land and resources are being exploited without restraint and wastes are discharged freely into the environment (Water and air) assuming that they have unlimited assimilative and carrying capacity. So there should not only be reduction in the use of resources but it is equally important to limit the generation of both hazardous and non-hazardous wastes and utilise recycle methods as far as possible. Recycling refers to the process by which material once used and discarded is used again to substitute for virgin material. To reduce stress on the natural resources and carry out economic development within the carrying capacity of the ecosystem, recycle of waste is highly essential as its accumulation often causes pollution and damage to the ecosystem. Further, if managed properly, it reduces the amount of energy needed to make new products. It reduces the requirement for virgin material and it generates employment. Wastes should not be burnt. Before use, wastes should be segregated into bio-degradable and non bio-degradable forms. Both should be recycled in appropriate manner. For example to recycle animal excreta, domestic and municipal wastes as plant nutrients, it should be made into compost. Plastic bags and containers should be recycled for other uses. Waste water from thrills and factories should be recycled for irrigation purpose. Municipal corporations can take up appropriate responsibility for waste recycling.

Reuse

Besides recycling, reuse of wastes, damaged and torn items is very essential from economic and ecological point of view. For example night soil and garbage should be used for generating bio-gas to save fuel wood. News papers and printed papers can be reutilised for preparing packets and packing materials. Slates made of clay can be used in place of note books leading to saving of forests. Scrape irons, wood items, glass, china clay materials, etc. from damaged buildings can be reused for secondary purpose in construction and industry. Instead of foil and plastic people can use whenever possible reusable containers. Wastes lands can be used for housing purpose. Unused and barren areas should be used for planting trees to meet the food-fodder and fuel requirement of the local community. Agro wastes can be reused for ply woods. Buildings are to be designed in such a way that besides reuse of kitchen waste water for gardening they should ensure conservation of water by providing facilities for collection and storage of roof-top rain water for future use. Use of battery recharging set is to be encouraged.

With development of science and technology many waste products are being utilised now. For example fly ash which is a by product of coal fired electricity generation plants, besides pollution, cause health hazards. Now it is utilised for making bricks besides in construction of roads, bridges, etc. Further, through bio-tech methods, fly ash dumping sites are being brought under reclamation employing *Mycorrhiza.* Mine dumps are brought under eco-restoration through biotechnological process. It is not only environmental friendly but also economically viable

What Can We Do

For sustenance of life and sustainable economic development every individual, rich or poor, young or old has to contribute in his or her own capacity. Besides community members, teachers and parents have important role to play. Some of the possible programmes/activities through which values can be taught include:

- *Design and Development of Exhibits on Sustainable Issues*: For promoting values relating to reduction in the use of resources and conservation, materials made of plastics, metals, etc. as an alternate to wood may be exhibited. Generation of bio-gas through use of plant and animal wastes may be demonstrated. Bricks made of fly ash coming from thermal plants may be displayed. Economy of rain water harvesting should be demonstrated in the school complex.

- *Development of Audio and Video Programmes Both for Teachers and Students*: To generate thinking and change of attitude of learners video programmes relating to conservation of water, the rational use of LPG for cooking purposes, soil conservation, social forestry, water pollution, energy from wastes may be shown to the students and teachers.
- *Demonstration of Specific Activities in Schools*: Use of different wastes materials produced from domestic sources for compost preparation can be demonstrated in the schools. Further use of vermicomposting as a technology for speedy composting may be used. Further organic farming for production of crops and vegetables in school complex can be carried out in the school complex. Advantages regarding turning off the tap while brushing teeth, use of bucket bath instead of a shower may be demonstrated to children. It may be shown that a leaking tap with 10 drops per minute wastes comes out 3000 liters of water a year. Childen may be advised to use left over water in their bottles on return to home in watering potted plants instead of throwing it outside. They may be demonstrated how thawing out frozen food before cooking consumes less energy than frozen food
- *Project Work*: Through project work children may be explained about the impact of joint family system in reducing resource conservation. Children can be asked to find out how waste papers, wooden items, glass and plastic bottles can be reused for different purposes. Children can find out how waste water coming from toilets can be reused for irrigation purposes. The idea of burning wastes to minimise its volume should be given up. Segregation of wastes into bio-degradable and non bio-degradable components can be carried out by students. Advantages of using pressure cooker in energy conservation may be demonstrated to students in the form of project. Children may be discouraged to kill animals for dissection purpose in the classroom.

Conclusion

It needs to be realised that sustainable development is both a goal as well as a process. Its attainment requires a fundamental shift in attitudes, values and behaviour by both individuals and governments alike (Narain, 1986).

An individual is the starting point of environmental degradation. If an individual behaves in need and not in greed, and in comfort and not in luxury, and ponders about what is enough for a comfortable life style, most of the problems can be solved (McNeill, 1996). A sustainable community can spring from interdependence between well informed individuals. The sustainable life styles of the individuals can lead to sustainable communities, to sustainable nations and then to a sustainable world.

Education being a dynamic force, besides promoting knowledge, understanding and disseminating information can help changing attitudes by giving stress on ethics and morality (Mishra and Dharka, 2001). Real education enables one to utilise the knowledge, one has acquired to meet the challenges of life and to make all human beings happy as far as possible. Therefore value education should be introduced at the pre-primary and primary stages highlighting the 3R's relating to the problems of the future especially those related to food, water, energy, environment, pollution, health, and population. Because the children of today are the adults of tomorrow and whatever they are taught as young students will mould them.

It should be emphasised that man is an integral part of nature and must find ways and means to live in harmony with nature and be educated about the importance of interdependence of man and nature. It is observed (Uhl and Anderson, 2001) that teachers should be taught to understand a set of five core principles like respecting life and natural process, living with limits, valuing the local, accounting for full costs, and sharing of power. Such ecological literacy is as fundamental to living fully and wisely as the capacity to read and write. The curriculum should guarantee ecological literacy reducing alienation from natural world and increasing connection to natural world.

10

Biodiversity and its Conservation Strategies for Sustainable Development

A.S. DIXIT and M.K. SATAPATHY

Biodiversity is a key barometer of the planet's health.
Its preservation is not a luxury but a necessity.

Variation is the law of nature. It occurs every where and every moment. Biodiversity is the variety of forms the different plants, animals and microorganisms. It also includes the genes they contain and the ecosystem they form. It deals essentially with dynamic processes and increases when new genetic variation is produced and decreases on the loss of genetic variation or species extinction. Thus, it is a concept laying emphasis on interrelated nature of the living world with its processes. The biological variations in nature over time and space form the basis of evolutionary process.

Bio-diversity is an irreplaceable resource; its extinction is for ever. At present there is no way to recreate extinct plants and animals whatsoever way it is attempted. Biodiversity is essential for human survival and economic well being and for the ecosystem function and stability. As such there is not only a need to formulate meaningful programmes for its conservation and sustainable utilisation, but also to demystify this subject and make people knowledgeable about its tremendous implication for human survival. The conservation and sustainable utilisation of this resource has to be central to all developmental planning, because economy of most of the countries is dependent on agriculture, animal husbandry, fisheries, forestry, medicinal and the likes of these.

Biodiversity exist on the earth in eight broad realms with 193 biogeographical provinces that include ecosystems. The ecosystems consist of communities of living species in an ecological region. Biodiversity can be described on the basis of three levels of biological organisation, which are hierarchically related (Botkin and Keller, 1995). These include:

Ecosystem Diversity

In an ecosystem, there may be different landforms, each of which supports different and specific vegetation (Table 1). Ecosystem diversity in contrast to genetic and specific diversity is difficult to measure since the boundaries of the communities, which constitute the various sub-ecosystems, are elusive. Ecosystem diversity could best be understood if one studies the communities in various ecological niches within the given ecosystem. Each community is associated with definite species complexes. These complexes are related to composition and structure of the biodiversity.

Forest System: The forest systems differ from one another on the basis of climate, soil and water regions. It constitutes variety of trees, herbs, shrubs, climbers, etc. Forest floor has variety of small animals and plants. The ground is covered with leaf litters that contain immense fungi and bacteria. Each type of forest has its own community of insects, reptiles, amphibians, birds and mammals. The relationship between plants and animals is established through various processes. Some plants depend on insects and birds for pollination. The trees, bearing fruits, are linked to birds and other animals. Such types of interactions are common in a variety of ways in the forest ecosystem and provide stability to them.

Forest cover of our country is about 639, 600 sq. km as per the assessment made by forest survey of India (1995). This represents 19.46 per cent of India's total geographical area. India has different forest types ranging from the tropical net evergreen forest in north east to the tropical thorn forests in the central and western India. The forests of the country provide several essential services to the mankind. They are the sources of a number of food items, fuel, wood, fodder and timber. Other economic uses include provision of raw materials for forest-based industries. Some of the minor forest products include gum, resin, honey, etc. Forests perform important ecological functions such as maintaining delicate ecological and hydrological balances, conserving soil, controlling floods, droughts and pollution. Forests provide habitats for innumerable plants, animals and microorganisms. They are also the source of recreation and religious inspiration.

Grass land System: Grass land comprises the area where rainfall is not sufficient to support a luxuriant growth of trees. They have vegetation types with predominance of grass and grass-like species, herbs, insects, birds reptiles and mammal, etc. These areas are degraded and have become unproductive due to changes in land management in the recent times. In India, total grassland area is about 3.9 per cent or 12 million hectares. It is estimated that Indian grasslands harbor about 1256 species belonging to 245 genera. The grasslands are significant for their highest productive capacity. Grassland ecosystem plays a crucial role in the global biospheric responses to climate change and in augmenting vegetation in forests facing plunder.

Aquatic System: Wetlands are transitional zones that occupy intermediate position between dry and open water. These ecosystem are dominated by the influence of water. They encompass diverse and heterogeneous habitats ranging from rivers, flood plains and rain fed lakes to swamps, estuaries and salt marshes. India, by virtue of its extensive stretch and varied terrain and climate, supports a rich diversity of inland and costal wetland habitats. It is estimated that India has about 4.1 million ha. of wetland. These systems perform a variety of functions that include breeding areas of fish and crustaceans, grazing areas for domestic animals and acting as flood control buffers. They are also homes of a variety of aquatic birds such as ducks, geese, cranes, egrets and fish-dependent birds of pray.

Semi Arid and Desert Systems: The species of this ecosystem are adapted to long dry periods. These xerophytic plants may be of great value to develop new agricultural crop to fight the challenges of global warming due to climate changes. The plants and animals of these zones can withstand great temperature variations.

Species Diversity (Diversity between Species)

It refers to the variety of species within a region. Such diversity could be measured on the basis of number of species in a region. Natural tropical forests have a much greater species diversity than most of the other regions. Biogeographically, India is situated at the tri-junction of three realms namely afro-tropical, Indo-Malayan and paleoarctic realms and therefore has characteristic element in each of them. This assemblage of three distinct realms make the country rich and unique in biological diversity. Based on the available data, India ranks tenth in the number of mammalian species and eleventh in the number of endemic species of higher vertebrates in the world.

Table 10.1: The Composition and Levels of Biodiversity

Ecological diversity	*Genetic diversity*	*Organism diversity*
Biomes	Populations	Kingdoms
Bio-regions	Individuals	Phyla
Landscapes	Chromosomes	Families
Ecosystems	Genes	Genera
Habitats	Nucleotides	Species
		Subspecies
		Populations
		Individuals
Cultural Diversity: Human interaction at all levels		

Genetic Diversity (Diversity within Species)

This variability is among individuals of a species, e.g. each human being differs widely from all others. This diversity is the results of large number of possible combinations of our genes that provide us specific characteristics. This genetic variability is significant to a healthy population of species. Inbreeding may result, if the number of breeding individuals is reduced leading to the extinction of the species. It is ultimate source of diversity at the species and ecosystem level. India possesses a rich genetic diversity. Studies in genetic diversity are not as yet very widespread and sharply focused.

Global Biodiversity

It is estimated that there exists 5-50 million species of living forms on our earth (Singh, 2002) and of these only 1.75 million species have been identified. These include 3,00,000 species of green plants and fungi, 8,00,000 species of insects 40,000 species of vertebrates and 3,60,000 species of micro organisms. Tropical forests, wetlands and coral reefs are 'Bio-rich' areas. The high species diversity in tropics is explained on the basis that in tropics (i) conditions for evolution were optimum and for extinction fewer (ii) species diversity was conserved over geological time because of low rates of extinction prevailing there.

The Indian region (8°-30° N and 60°-97.5° E) having a geographical area of 329 million hectares is quite rich in biodiversity with a sizable percentage of endemic flora and fauna. This richness in biodiversity is due to immense variety of climatic and altitudinal conditions coupled with varied ecological habitats. These vary from humid tropical Western Ghats to the hot desert of Rajasthan, from the cold desert of Latah and the icy mountains of Himalayas to the warm coasts of peninsular India. At present, 175 million species have been recorded so far in the world (Global Biodiversity Assessment, 1995). India's contribution to this record stands at 7 per cent. Surveys conducted so far have inventoried over 49,000 species of plants and 81,000 species of animals, about 30 per cent of which are insects (Table 10.1). As until now, only 70 per cent of the area has been surveyed and it is estimated that the flora and fauna already identified are only a part of what actually occur in India. The list is being constantly added especially in the case of lower plants and invertebrate animals.

Biowealth and Biodiversity Hot Spots

All those areas that support rich biodiversity, because of geological formation and endemic fauna and flora and exhibit exceptional scientific

Table 10.2: Species So Far Described from India

Bacteria	850
Algae	6500
Fungi	14500
Lichens	2000
Bryophytes	2850
Pteridophytes	1100
Gymnosperms	64
Flowering plants	17500
Protista	2577
Other invertebrates	8329
Arthropods	60383
Mollusca	5050
Protochordata	166
Fishes	2546
Amphibia	206
Reptiles	485
Birds	1228
Mammals	372

Source: Gadgil, M. 1999. Resonance 4: 80-90.

interest are called hot spots. Hot spots, that contain outstanding examples of evolutionary processes of speciation and extinctions, are severely threatened by human activities. Mayers (1998) has identified 10 hot spots of tropical forests to which he later added 8 areas at the global level. These areas collectively include 49, 955 endemic species, which consist of 20 per cent of world total plant species. Eastern Himalayas and Western Ghats are the regions in India that are included in hot spots. Mittermpir and Warner (1990) introduced the concept of mega diversity centres using the criteria of species richness. Twelve countries/regions namely Ecuador, Columbia, Mexico, Zaire, Peru, Brazil, India, China, Madagascar, Malaysia, Indonesia and Australia have been classified as Mega biodiversity centres. In India, the botanical hot spots lie in the (i) Western Ghats: particularly the southern Western Ghats known as Malabar has an enormous biodiversity of ancient lineage. (ii) North East India: represents the transition zone in Indian, Indo-Malayan and Indo-Chinese bio-geographic regions as well as the meeting place of Himalayan Mountains with that of peninsular India. Namdapha, Tirap, Dzuko, Tura, Tale Valley and Senchal are some of the hot spots of the zone. (iii) Western Himalayas: is well known for its alpine flora. Gymnosperms are quite dominant. Some hot spots of the region are Pithoragarh, Gorivalley, Karakorum and Ladakh. (iv) Andaman and Nicobar have a rich flora with about 2500 species of flowering plants. Some of the hot spots of this zone are North Andaman, Tabe islands, south recf island, spike island, etc. (v) Sacred forests: these areas are protected by tribals due to some religious sanctity (Rajendra Prasad, 1998) attached to them. They contain a number of endangered, rare, endemic biota of the country. They have been given the names as '*Devaskadu*' in Karnatak, '*La-Kyntok*' in Meghalaya and '*Devarahati*' in Maharastra. (vi) Mangrooves are the salt tolerant forest ecosystem found mainly in tropical and sub-tropical inter-tidal regions. India harbours some of the best mangrove swamps in the world, located in the alluvial deltas of Gaga, Maharani, Guava, Krishna and Calvary rivers and on the Andaman and Nicobar Islands. The total area covered by mangroves in India is 6,700 sq. km. amounting to 7 per cent of the world mangrove with the Sunderland having the largest stretch covering an area of about 4,200 sq. km.

The distribution of biodiversity is not uniform across the globe. The species diversity increases from poles towards tropics. Tropical forests constitute 5.7 per cent of land but possess 50 per cent of the world species. There are some regions, which, though, may not have a high diversity, display a high degree of endemism. About, 16, 04,000 species including monera, protista, fungi, planate and animalia have been described so for in the world. However, it has been estimated that, at least, 179,80,000 species exist in the world, but as a working figure, 1,22,50,000 species are considered to be near reality (WC MC, 1993). The number of already identified species of fungi, bacteria, plants and animals in India is over 1,08,276. Out of these 84 per cent species constitute fungi (21.2%), flowering plants (13.9%) and insects (49.3%). The class insecta alone constitutes nearly half of the biodiversity in India. These species occur on land, fresh and marine water or as simians in mutualistic or parasitic state. Thus India accounts for 8 per cent of the global biodiversity existing in only 2.4 per cent land area of the world (Khoshoo, 1996). There are a total of 12 Biogeographical provinces in India. India is tenth among the plant-rich countries, eleventh in its number of endemic species of higher vertebrates (amphibia, birds and mammals) and tenth in the world as far as its richness in mammals is concerned. India has four hot spots out of eighteen identified in the world. These are North-East India, Eastern Himalaya, Western Ghat and Andaman and Nicobar Islands. Out of these, the two namely Eastern Himalaya and Western Ghats have 5,332 endemic species of higher plants, mammals, reptiles, amphibia and butterflies (WCMC, 1993). Information about some flora and fauna in the country is patchy. Hundreds of new species may be present in the country awaiting discovery. It is estimated that almost one-third of the animal varieties in India have taken refuge in Western Ghats of Kerala alone.

Importance and Values of Biodiversity

Valuing biodiversity is a Herculean task. It is difficult to estimate the total value of biodiversity firstly due to lack of information and uncertainties; secondly, due to variation from location to location, country to country and region to region. Furthermore, the economic value of each species depends upon the economic, ethical, cultural, aesthetic, and social values. Biodiversity is crucial because it (i) provides food, construction materials, raw materials for industries, medicines, etc.; (ii) provides the basic genetic material for all improvements to domesticated plants and animals; (iii) maintains ecosystem function, including evolutionary process; (iv) stores and recycles nutrients essentials for life, e.g. carbon, nitrogen and oxygen; (v) absorbs and break down pollutants, including organic wastes, pesticides, heavy metals; (vi) recharges ground water, protects catchment basins and buffers extreme water conditions and (vii) produces soil and protects it from excessive erosion.

It is the basis for the continuous evolution of species and ecosystem. The value of biodiversity also depends on biotechnological progress. There are some commonly accepted values that provide a clear and broad view of the possible benefits that we gain from biodiversity. Direct Values refers to the those products that are directly harvested and used by the people. Consumptive use values refer to goods such as fuel wood and food from wild plants and animals that are consumed locally and are unlikely to appear in national and international markets. People leading a low lifestyle depend on land and water for a variety of goods like fuel wood, fodder, vegetables, fruits and other plant-based food items like meat, medicines, cordage and building materials, etc. to sustain themselves. Hence, if these are unavailable to them, which is likely, due to environmental degradation, then their standard of living drops dramatically and even their survival is threatened. It has been estimated that 80 per cent of the word's population still relies principally on traditional medicines derived from plants and animals. Biodiversity provides a genetic base (Rana, 1972) to continuous improvement in agriculture, fisheries, medicine, industries and other sectors. Considerable research is being done all over the world into biodiversity products in search of "miracle cures" for some of the deadliest diseases or industrial and other products that could revolutionise human lives. Ecotourism is affected by the diversity of the species and the range of habitats that can be visited, e.g. the number of flowering plants, big and small games. Indirect values refer to environmental process and ecosystem services that provide benefits to the human race without having to be harvested.

Non consumptive use values refer to the environmental services provided by biological community like pollination, carbon fixing, protecting watershed, protecting soil and waste disposal. This also includes the value of satisfaction attained by the society by the fact that rhino, lion, wild ass, bustard, raulwolfia, etc. exist and also moral and religions values attached to plants and animals.

At present it is direct use value of biodiversity, which is highly valued by local people in developing countries because of subsistence nature of economy. People living in poverty and miseries are neither bothered about sustainability nor option, existence or other value of biodiversity. Developed world on the other hand are concerned about option and existence values of biological resources since their approach has shifted from "Quantitative Growth" to Qualitative Development".

The conflict between gene rich developing world and gene poor, developed world, therefore, is because of value biodiversity. In the face of economic and scientific uncertainty the less developed nations can only rely on direct use values of biodiversity but this too leaves some questions unanswered, i.e. (i) What is the economic value of biodiversity vis-a-vis other resources that provide more short term and visible gains? (ii) How much can the poor society afford on conservation? and (iii) even if the society agrees to preserve and protect—who will be the beneficiary in future in view of the "Intellectual Properly Rights".

To most people biodiversity is undeniably of value. A major challenge for the future is development of a new ecological economics (Costanza, 1991) in which the worth of a species, community and ecosystem can be assigned financial value to be set against the gains to be made in industrial and other human projects that may damage them. Many species are recognised as having actual direct value, which yet remains untapped (Miller, 1988). In future wild strains of some species may be exploited for their genetic diversity and quite different species of plants and animals that appropriate for domestication may be found. There are potential benefits of natural enemies to be used as biological control agents for pest species. Most natural enemies of many pest species remain unstudied and often unrecognised. The monetary value of ecotourism, which depends on biodiversity, is becoming ever more considerable. Ecotourists, who visit a country wholly or partly to experience its biological diversity, spend approximately $ 12 billon a year worldwide on their enjoyment of the natural world (Primack, 1993). Many people believe that these are ethical grounds for conservation, arguing that every species is of value in its own right and would be of equal value even if people were not here to appreciate or exploit its. From this perspective even species with no conceivable economic value requires protection.

Threat to Biodiversity

The loss of biodiversity is a global crisis. There is hardly any region on the earth that is not facing ecological catastrophes. Though biological extinction has been a natural phenomenon in geological history, the rate of extinction was about one species per 1000 years. The rate has increased to one every ten years between 1600 and 1950 and presently it may be one in every year. As Gandhiji once said "The mother nature has everything to meet our needs and not to satisfy our greed". Failure to consider this aspect has resulted in the threat to biodiversity as a whole. The problem of biodiversity is essentially one of conflict resolution between mankind and nature.

Direct causes of biodiversity loss are (i) fragmentation or loss of habitat, (ii) overuse of individual species, (iii) ecological invasions resulting from human activities, (iv) pollution, (v) regional climate change.

The indirect causes include (i) patterns of land use, (ii) poverty and civil strife, (iii) population growth, (iv) lack of economic development opportunities in rural areas, (v) patterns of consumption, (vi) use of limited number of varieties, (vii) subsidies for unsustainable use of biodiversity and pricing not reflecting environmental costs, (viii) weak institutions, legislations and regulations and (ix) lack of scientific knowledge.

However, extinction is not the result of a single reason but it is due to the additive effect of a host of causes. Since the biodiversity of earth is one big inter-link, in most of the cases, the loss of one species triggers off the downward slide and consequent loss of many other dependent species.

The destruction of the world's tropical forests, which are disappearing at an alarming rate, is one of today's most urgent global environmental issues. A rich biodiversity is slowly being lost for ever. About 17 million ha. of tropical forests are cleared every year. At least 5-10 per cent of tropical forest species will face extinction in the next 30 years if this trend continues. At present, tropical forests are estimated to contain 50-90 per cent of world's biodiversity. Tropical forest is shrinking at the rate of 0.8 per cent each year. Rain forest, the home to half of the world's life forms, continues to be destroyed at the rate of over 100,000 Km^2 every year. This loss of biodiversity has immediate and long-term effects on human survival.

In the present day world, many species of plants and animals are being destroyed at a rapid rate. The classical example is indiscriminate logging, which destroys not only trees but also other life forms, as forests harbour many animals, and plants that depend on environment for survival. In the past we placed great importance on the selection of species, protecting and promoting the variety with high yields and ignoring other inferior variety causing great loss of biodiversity. This loss is all the more regrettable as we posses now-a-days modern technologies which can utilise the different genetic qualities in a variety of ways. Through modern technology wild diversity can also be incorporated into cultivated crops and contribute to world agricultural development.

Indians biodiversity is one of the most significant in the world. In the last few decades, India has lost at least half of its forests, polluted over 70 per cent of its water bodies, built on or cultivated much of its grasslands, and degraded most of the coasts. Under such circumstances, none can say how many species have already been lost. The country has several problems such as over population, large number of cattleheads, growing demand for land, and water supply. Unplanned developmental works and over exploitation of resources have made its living resources most vulnerable and left our biodiversity exposed to various ecological threats. It can be said that biodiversity stands as a measure of the health of our relationship with the natural world, of how much we care about our forests and our seas as well as the species that live in them.

Broadly speaking there are three main causes of biodiversity loss:

(i) *Development Pressure*: Any path of economic development will sustain itself only when the stock of capital assets remain constant, or rises over time. The capital assets may be in the form of machines, roads, factories, human capital, forests, wildlife, soil quality, etc. But the population growth has two counteracting effects on the environment and development. Firstly, it brings in prospects for development by rising GNP per capita. At the same time, it impedes development by reducing environmental quality leading to biotic impoverishment. Most of the current projects are justified on the basis of discounting that prefers present value over future value. Since the cost and benefits of biodiversity are uncertain and concentrated in future, it is rarely taken into consideration for justifying the project.

(ii) *Market Failure*: The biodiversity market is skewed and does not indicate the real value of biodiversity or its by products. Biological products from the common property or open access resource, are normally zero priced commodities, e.g. fuel wood, grasses, seeds, gum, etc. and are exploited by the stakeholders with unintended destruction. Since the markets do not consider the option and existence value, the higher reflected market price becomes an incentive for habitat destruction.

(iii) *Intervention Failure*: Lack of political will is an important hindrance for the conservation of biodiversity. Intervention by the Government in the economy through subsidies, price controls, physical output targets, exchange control, etc. leads to inefficiency. Environmental quality is affected by excessive utilisation of fertilizers and pesticides leading to increasing level of pollutants in the environment. In addition to this, shortsighted gains, personality clashes, political agenda and lack of coordination on the part of various wings of the government combine to create degradation of habitats and loss of biodiversity.

Threatened Species

The world conservation monitoring centre has recorded that 533 animal species (mostly vertebrates) and 384 plant species (mostly flowering plants) have become extinct since the year 1960. The tropical forests alone are losing roughly 14000-40000 species per year (or 2-5 species per hour). More species have gone extinct from the islands than from the mainland or the oceans and the earth may lose up to 50 per cent of the species by the end of the 21st century if the current rate of loss continues. The number of species considered threatened have been presented in Table 10.3.

Table 10.3: Number of Species Considered 'Threatened' by the World Conservation Monitoring Centre

Threatened	*Endangered*	*Vulnerable*	*Rare*	*Indeterminate*	*Total*
Mammals	177	199	89	68	533
Birds	188	241	257	176	862
Reptiles	47	88	79	43	257
Amphibian	32	32	55	14	133
Fishes	158	226	246	304	934
Invertebrates	582	702	422	941	2649
Plants	3632	5687	11485	5302	26106

The world conservation union (formerly known as International Union for the Conservation of Nature and Natural Resources-(IUCN) has recognised eight Red list categories of species: Extinct, Extinct in wild, Critically Endangered, Endangered, Vulnerable, Lower Risk, Data Deficient, and Not Evaluated. The species which are threatened with extinction are included in Vulnerable, Endangered, or Critically Endangered categories. As per United Nations Environment Programme (UNEP) definition (1995), threatened species are the species that are often genetically impoverished, of low fecundity, dependent on patchy or unpredictable resources, extremely variable in population density, persecuted or otherwise prone to extinction in human dominated landscapes.

The IUCN Red list is a catalogue of taxa that are facing the risk of extinction. The 2000 IUCN Red list, (the most comprehensive Inventory) contains assessments of more than 18,000 species of which 11,046 species (5485 animals and and 5611 plants) are listed as threatened (critically endangered, endangered or vulnerable). Of these 1939 are listed as critically endangered (925 animals and 1014 plants). According to Red list, in India, 44 plant species are critically endangered, 113 endangered and 807 vulnerable. Among animals 18 are critically endangered, 54 endangered and 43 vulnerable.

Need for Biodiversity Conservation

Conserving biodiversity is a slow but critical process not only for maintenance of our quality of life but for genetic resources contained within animal and plant species that form the basis for continued existence. The world is an interdependent whole made up of natural and human communities. The well-being and health of any part depends on well-being and health of the other parts. All life depend on uninterrupted functioning of natural systems that ensure the supply of energy and nutrients, so ecological responsibility among the people is necessary for the survival and securing dignity and equity of the world's communities. The well-being of the future generations is a social responsibility of the present generation. Hence, it is necessary that the present generation limits its consumption of non-renewable resources to the level that is enough to meet the basic needs of the society and ensure that renewable resources are nurtured for their sustainable productivity; otherwise there will be nothing left for the future generations. The human population is continuously increasing which in turn has led to decrease in biodiversity due to increased consumption. If the human population continues to increase, pressure will continue on endangered species and it will be an increasingly greater challenge to maintain the existing biodiversity. The need to save the biodiversity is of utmost importance as it is a keystone to sustainable development. The present biodiversity is the result of a very long and slow process of genetic changes and adaptations, once lost, the diversity of the gene pools can not be restored.

The World Commission on Environment and Development (WCED, 1987) constituted by General Assembly of the United Nations published its reports in 1987 which provided a major boost and endorsement to the need for conserving the world's rich biodiversity, particularly that of the tropical areas. Despite conflicting views among nations, a broad consensus was reached after bitter negotiations, and 170 countries signed the biodiversity convention, which is now ratified by 104 countries (42 articles were adopted). One of the prerequisite tasks as expressed by article 7 of the convention is the identification and monitoring the components of biological diversity. Article 12 calls for research and training and suggests programmes for identification, conservation and sustainable use of biodiversity.

Keeping the conservation of biological diversity in mind, the "Earth Submit" was organised by the United Nations at Rio-de-Janeiro in June,

1992 where a comprehensive programme of action known as the 'Agenda 21' was adopted. The convention on Biological Diversity is one of the most important elements of this agenda. There are several articles, which in some form or the other deal with conservation of Biological diversity in different ecosystems. India is a signatory to convention and therefore has the responsibility for conserving the biodiversity in the country.

Conservation is the science concerned with increasing the probability that the earth's species and communities (or, more generally, its biodiversity) will persist into future. We need to appreciate the scale of problem, understand the threats posed by human activities, and consider how our knowledge of ecology can provide remedies.

Measures for Biodiversity Conservation

A quarter of the earth's total biological diversity amounting to a million species, which might be useful to mankind in one way or the other, is in serious risk of extinction over the next 2-3 decades. The realisation that biodiversity erosion may threaten the very extinction of life has awakened man to take steps to conserve it. Thus it has become imperative to rapidly assess and conserve biodiversity both at regional and global level. Basically, the conservation plan has a holistic approach and encompasses whole spectrum of biota and activities ranging from ecosystem at the macro level (*in-site* conservation) to DNA libraries at the molecular level (*ex-situ* conservation) (Fig. 10.1).

(a) *In-situ Conservation*

Conservation of biodiversity has been possible primarily through *in-situ* conservation, i.e. on site conservation in the natural habitats. Such conservation is relatively inexpensive and takes care of all the species (plants, animals and micro organisms as an interacting system) in a particular habitat. In situ conservation also warrantees the continuation of the ecological processes and organic evolution, thus helping the concerned biota to continuously to evolve in response to newer environmental changes. Local communities need to be involved in the management of biological resources and to benefit from their substance. This can be achieved by integrating rural development with ecosystem conservation. It includes biosphere reserves, national parks, sanctuaries, watershed, sacred grooves, etc. (Fig. 10.1).

(b) *Ex-situ Conservation*

Ex-situ conservation is the conservation of components of biological diversity outside their natural habitat, in facilities such as botanical gardens, zoological gardens and gene banks. Ex-situ conservation of

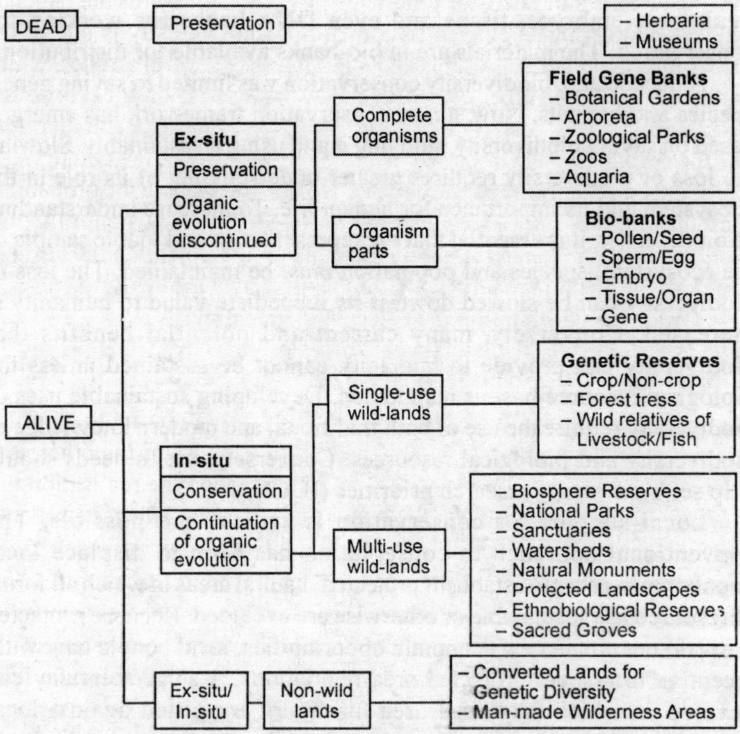

Fig. 10.1: Options of Conservation

genetic material has become a serious concern for the under developed and developing countries. Such countries may be rich in biodiversity but are poor in bio-technological know-how. Once the developed countries with full grip on biotechnological techniques are able to manage *ex-situ* storage of genetic material of a species of potential value, they go for patenting it and monopolies the product and the process as well. Under such circumstance the developing countries are compelled to buy back with exorbitant price their own genetic material. The extent and nature of capability in biotechnology will determine the capability of the country to conserve and sustainably utilise biodiversity (Khoshoo, 1994).

In *in-situ* conservation, the share of the dividend of the biodiversity may be enjoyed by the people where it occurs. Whereas in *ex situ* conservation the state or country importing the biodiversity will tend to enjoy its fruits depriving very often the people who once really owned it. The conservation of cultivated crops and domesticated animals has been primarily possible through *ex-situ* conservation ever since agriculture evolved. There are many ways to achieve it through seed, pollen, sperm, ovule/ova, embryos, tissue and even DNA banks are working for conservation. The materials are in bio-banks available for distribution.

A decade ago, biodiversity conservation was limited to saving genes, species and habitats. Now, a new conservation framework has emerged based on saving biodiversity, studying it and using it sustainably. Slowing the loss of biodiversity requires greater understanding of its role in the ecosystem and its importance for human life. To increase understanding of biodiversity, it is essential that the representative and viable sample of the ecosystem, species and population must be maintained. The loss of biodiversity can be slowed down if its immediate value to humanity is increased. Conversely, many current and potential benefits that biodiversity can provide to humanity cannot be sustained unless the biological resource base is maintained. Developing sustainable uses of biodiversity require the use of both traditional and modern knowledge of biodiversity and biological resources. Conversely, user's needs should help set biodiversity research priorities (IUCN, 1991)

Local support for conservation is critical and possible. The conventional approach to conservation has been to displace local population in order to establish 'protected' natural areas in which all forms of resource use sustainable or otherwise are excluded. Because protected areas do not create new economic opportunities, local people have little incentive to respect protected area regulations. A siege mentality can develop in which protected area managers are pitted against local population, and must rely on patrols and similar mechanisms to limit use of biological resources in the area.

Biodiversity preservation has become an accepted goal for many people. When this goal conflicts with other goals like economic development, it leads to a question, How much biodiversity and at what cost? To find the answer, it is important to think carefully about the values of biodiversity and to separate those based on science from those based on other present or potential values such as ethical, religious or economic values (Mc Neely *et al.,* 1900).

Followings are important for the conservation of biodiversity:

- A clear cut and realistic national policy on conservation and utilisation of biodiversity should be evolved by a National Biodiversity Conservation Board (Khoshoo, 1996) in the best interest of each country.
- Both *in-situ* and ex-situ forms of conservation are important and mutually reinforcing and supportive. FAO is required to be involved in *in-situ* conservation particularly through genetic reserves.
- Realism demand that in the area of biodiversity there will always

be tremendous interdependence between gene-rich/technologically poor and gene-poor/technologically rich countries. With the global climate change, there are likely to be newer challenges, candidate gene will have to be identified to evolve new cultivar, resistant and/tolerant to such changes. The cooperation between North and South must increase for the success of human race. No nation can be self sufficient in biodiversity. There would always be newer demands (Kumar and Sharma, 2001)

- There is considerable interdependence between industrial and developing countries. Biodiversity is a fit case for North-South cooperation. Trainings in terms of knowledge and skill should be imparted by North to South as far as biotechnology is concerned. The two groups of countries, though essentially interdependent, have to recognise their policy on biodiversity, biotechnology and bioproductivity, so as to complement and supplement one another.
- Conservation and management of our natural resources must derive from a set of clear objectives, mechanisms for action and commitment from all stakeholders. Apart from this, halting the process of degradation and species loss requires specialised solutions and understanding of ecological processes.
- There is the need for greater involvement of communities and fair models which decentralise management and conservation roles and responsibilities. Bridges need to be built with NGOs and women groups regarding on-farm conservation and utilisation by involving communities. Such bridges also need to be built between scientific and technical groups working in the area of conservation and utilisation of biodiversity and the local communities and women's groups. The latter have considerable local technical knowledge and wisdom that need to be utilised by the farmers.
- As of now, there are still major lacunae in information resources pertaining to forests, biodiversity, flora and fauna, causative factors for their degradation and major threats. The available data is alarmingly inadequate to provide a lucid picture of the current status and on going losses/gains.

Strategies for the Future

Despite all adversities, one has to adopt viable strategies for the conservation of species as this only will guarantee our future and lead us towards the goal of sustainable society, sustainable economy, sustainable use and sustainable development. The strategy should be aimed at policy makers, all government and non-government organisations, private organisations, individuals and inter-governmental organisations. Interestingly the Article 7, of the 19 principles enunciated by the recently formulated Universal Declaration of Human Responsibilities of the Interaction Council of UN stresses for (Westing, 1999) protection of animals and natural environment. There is need for collaboration at National and International level (such as International Board for Plant Genetic Resources). This will help in achieving the objectives of biodiversity conservation and sustainable development. To conserve the biodiversity, immediate task will be to devise and enforce time bound programme for saving plant and animals species as well as habitats of biological resources. Action plan for conservation must be directed to:

1. Preparation of inventories of biological resources in different parts of the country including the island ecosystem (Pushpangadan & Nair, 2001).
2. Conservation of biodiversity through a network of protected areas including National Parks, Sanctuaries, Biosphere Reserves, Marine Reserves, Gene Banks, Wetlands, coral reefs, etc.
3. Conservation of microorganisms which help in reclamation of waste lands and revival of biological potential of land.
4. Rehabilitation of rural poor/tribals displaced due to creation of protected areas.
5. Protection and sustainable use of genetic resources/germplasm through appropriate laws and practices.
6. Control of over exploitation through different agencies.
7. Protection of domesticated plants and animal species in order to conserve indigenous genetic diversity.
8. Maintenance of corridors between different nature reserves for possible migration of species in response to climate, or any other disturbing factors.
9. Support for protecting traditional skills and knowledge for conservation.
10. Multiplication and breeding of threatened species through modern techniques of tissue culture and biotechnology.
11. Restriction on introduction of exotic species without adequate investigations.

For promotion of biodiversity conservation and sustainable utilisation, all developing countries must not only take to capacity building but also work towards innovation, acquisition and adaptation of relevant biotechnologies, regal aspects, trade secrets, intellectual property rights (IPRs), patents, petty patents, and plant breeders and farmers rights.

India is the second most populous country, and therefore, any plan attempting at conservation must consider socio-economic development with the mounting human pressure threatening the biotic resources of the country. Successful strategies for people's participation in preserving biodiversity are lacking. India has a rich tradition of conservation and with growing inputs from the government, scientists and NGOs should provide leadership in developing appropriate methodologies and strategies for biodiversity assessment and conservation. Furthermore, ours is predominently an agroindustrial country, and hence policy makers should realise and declare biological diversity a national resource, its conservation and sustainable utilisation a national goal and national priority.

11

Women's Education, Environmental Sustainability and National Development

K.K. TIWARI

The inextricable linkage between education of women and the development of a nation has been brilliantly summed up by Dr. Karve, a pioneer for the cause of women, in his words "If you educate a man, you educate an individual, if you educate a woman, you educate the whole family" Contemporary experiences in the world are establishing a strong link between education and development, particularly in the case of developing countries (Pareek, 1982), as education is vital to human resource development. Women comprise half the world's population and their role in development can not, therefore, be overlooked. The International Women's year in 1975 served as a catalyst in many developing countries for an examination of the actual role of women in society. Simultaneously there was a search for policies and activities, which could improve women's actual participation in national development. Investment in education and training for women is expected to fetch high returns. Even if we keep in mind the social implications as reported in Word Development Report 1991, "failing to raise women's level of education closer to men's detracts from the social benefits of raising men's."

Women's development is directly related to national development (Basu, 1979). A large number of programmes have been initiated by both government and non-government organisations for women's development (Shah, 1947). These emphasise providing equal opportunities to women by removing gender bias, empowering women and creating self-reliance. It stresses adoption of a holistic approach to women's development encompassing health, education and employment. Programmes connected with women's development received impetus with the report of the committee on the status of women in India in 1974, which focused on direct specific action for women to enable them to overcome their problems based on their involvement and participation in the process of development (Tiwari, 1998). In 1976, the government of India prepared a national plan of action for women, which along with the guidelines of UN's world plan of action for women emphasised employment, education and health for women. In 1980, at the mid point of the decade, the Copenhagen World Conference adopted the programme of action for the second half of the United Nations Decade for Women.: Equality, Development and Peace, which further elaborated on the existing obstacles and on the international consensus on measures to be taken for the advancement of women. The programme of action was endorsed by the general assembly in 1980 in its resolution 35/136.

Also in 1980, the general assembly, in its resolution 35/56 adopted the International Development Strategy for the Third United Nations Development Decade and reaffirmed the recommendations of the Copenhagen World Conference. The strategy for providing importance to the participation of women in the development process, as both agents and beneficiaries, called for appropriate measures to be taken in order to bring about profound social and economic changes and to eliminate the structural imbalances that compounded and perpetuated women's disadvantages in society. The strategies contained in the World Plan of Action and in the Programme of Action were important contributions towards enlarging the perspective for the future of women. In recent years the National Perspective Plan (NPP) for women 1988-2000 A.D., adopted by the Government of India is also aimed at streamlining women's issues in policies and programmes and giving women at least one third share in the decision making bodies from Panchayats to Parliament.

This should not make anyone think that the status of women in society or their role in public life was not thought of earlier. The "Sub-Committee on Women's Role in Planned Economy", constituted by the National Planning Committee of the Congress Party, formed in 1939 observed: "We do not wish to turn woman into a cheap imitation of man or to render her useless for the great tasks of motherhood and nation building. But in demanding equal status and opportunity, we desire to achieve for women the possibility of development under favourable circumstances of education and opportunity...we would like to displace the picture so deeply impressed upon the racial imagination of man striding forward to conquer new worlds, woman following wearily behind with a baby in her arms. The picture which we now envisage is that of man and woman, comrades of the road, going forward together."

Independent India in her commitment to user in a just society as embodied in the constitution accepted the principle of equality and included in article 15 the specific constitutional provision prohibiting discrimination on the ground of sex. At the same time it has empowered the state to make special provisions for women and children. Equality of opportunity in public employment of all citizens without regard to sex, equality before the law and equal protection of the law are guaranteed by articles 14 and 16 of the constitution. Several legal enactments and administrative decisions were made by the government to make the constitutional commitments effective. Later on, the government set up a committee to enquire into the status of women in India with broad terms of reference. The committee examined women's status from various angles including socio-cultural setting, law, rights and opportunities for economic participation, education, political participation, etc. However, the experience of women in many areas of life continues to be disturbing.

An Overview of Educational Status of Women in India

In pre-independent India the formal system of education was created essentially with the objective of utilising the educated for serving the British administration. In the initial years, women had little or no access to formal education especially in rural areas. It was so partly because of the traditional prejudices against their formal education and partly because society at that time could not conceive their role as government servants. In subsequent decades, as the formal system of education began to spread (Baby, 1969) the role of education as a liberating force came to be recognised and increasingly felt. Thus began the advocacy of the access of girls and women to the formal system of education. But it received little response. Only few girls belonging to urban upper and middle class families entered the formal system of education in the late 19th century. The low participation of women in education at that time is evident from the fact that female literacy just after independence was a mere 7.9 per cent compared to the male literacy rate of 24.9 per cent (Census of India, 1951).

The First Five Year Plan (1951-66) advocated the need for adopting special measures for overcoming the barriers to women's education (Govt. of India, 1959). Educational facilities were provided for girls by way of elementary education, secondary education, university education, technical education and adult education (Asthana, 1974). During the Second Five-Year Plan (1956-61) the emphasis continued on the overall expansion of educational facilities for women (Govt. of India, 1995). The Government of India set up a national committee on women's education in 1958. The committee after reviewing the education of women in India since 1900, made special recommendations to bring women into the fold of formal education (Govt. of India, 2000). Following the recommendations of the national committee on women's education, the

Government of India constituted the national council for women's education in India in 1959. As a result, during the Third Five-Year Plan (1961-66) *Bal Sevika* training programmes, condensed school courses and vocational training for adult women were launched (Asthana, 1974). Apart from this incentives such as free text books and scholarships were provided for girls.

The trend continued in the Forth Five-Year Plan (1969-74) as well. In 1971 a committee was constituted to study the status of women in India. The committee recommended provision of primary schools within walking distance, sustained propaganda by women officials, non-officials, social and political workers in order to bring every girl into school, particularly in rural and backward areas. Other important measures recommended were special incentives for areas where enrolment of girls is low and a system of part time education for girls who can not attend schools on full time basis. Even so, disparities continued in the utilisation of these facilities by boys and girls at various educational levels (Govt. of India, 2000). Therefore, in the Fifth Five Year Plan (1974-79) it was decided to step up enrolment and retention of girls and cut down on wastage by providing text books free of cost, mid-day meals, free uniforms and attendance scholarships. One of the reasons for the low enrolment of girls was the shortage of women teachers (NCERT, 1984). Scholarships were therefore given to girls who enrolled in the teachers training course.

Based on the recommendations of the Committee on the Status of Women in India women's education was included as a major programme under women and development during the Sixth Five-Year Plan (1980-85). Adult education centres for women were set up during this period to provide education in health, nutrition and family welfare. The adult education programmes aimed not only at making people literate but also at modification of the contents so as to highlight the role played by women in the family and community. It was envisaged to provide creches so that girls would not have to stay out of school to look after their siblings, appoint women teachers in rural areas, and provide girls hostels and step up the adult education programmes. To break away from the stereotype of domestic science courses for women it was decided to concentrate on science courses to increase participation of women in science and technology. Steps to eliminate gender bias in school curricula were taken in Seventh Five-Year Plan (1985-90) also. Elementary education was made free for girls.

The National Policy on Education (NPE), 1986, emphasised female literacy. Provision was to be made (NIEPA, 1990) for measures to increase the enrolment and retention of girls, their participation in vocational, technical and professional education and in non-traditional occupations.

It suggested that centres be organised for imparting vocational training and steps be taken for retention of literacy skills and for application of this learning in their daily life. Courses for women would also include banking and credit, entrepreneurship, etc. The NPE also recommended that women's issues should be incorporated in courses of study in various disciplines, educational institutions be involved in programmes of adult education, legal literacy, use of mass communication to disseminate information on issues of relevance to women, besides providing information and training support for socio-economic programmes for women.

Female Literacy

The role of education in human resource development for nation building and development can hardly be over-emphasised. However, our achievements in this respect in the last fifty four years are not encouraging. This is evident from the Tables 11.1 and 11.2. Our literacy levels for both males and females have grown from what they were at the beginning of the century. The percentage of literate males has gone up from 9.83 to 73.00, and females from 0.60 to 50.00. In Table 11.1 the literacy percentage up to 1941 is for undivided India and the entire population including the population in the age group of 0 to 4 has been taken into account except in 1981, 1991 and 1997, where the population in the age group, 0 to 6 has been excluded for the purpose of calculation of literacy percentage...

Table 11.1: Literacy Percentage 1901 to 1997

Year	*Males*	*Females*	*Persons*
1901	9.83	0.60	5.35
1911	10.56	1.05	5.92
1921	12.21	1.81	7.16
1931	15.39	2.93	9.50
1941	24.90	7.30	16.10
1951	24.95	7.93	16.67
1961	34.44	12.95	24.02
1971	39.45	18.69	29.45
1981	56.50	29.85	43.67
1991	64.13	39.29	52.21
1997	73.00	50.00	62.00

Source: Census of India, paper of 1 of 1981 prove. population totals, page-43 census of India, paper 2 of 1992, final population total excluding J&K 53rd Round NSSO, December, 1997.

In spite of the increase in educational facilities female literacy continues to lag woefully behind the male literacy rate. This is reflected in Table 11.2 that shows the literacy rates of different sections of the population.

Table 11.2: Sex Wise/Rural-Urban Literacy Rates—1951 to 1997

Year	*Males*	*Females*	*Persons*
1951(a)			
Rural	19.02	4.87	12.10
Urban	45.06	22.33	34.59
Total	24.95	7.93	16.67
1961(b)			
Rural	29.10	8.55	19.10
Urban	57.49	34.51	46.97
Total	34.34	12.95	24.02
1971(c)			
Rural	33.76	13.17	23.74
Urban	61.27	42.14	52.44
Total	39.45	18.69	29.45
1981(d) (7 years and above)			
Rural	49.69	21.77	36.09
Urban	76.83	56.37	67.34
Total	56.50	29.85	43.67
1991(e) (7 years and above)			
Rural	57.87	30.62	44.69
Urban	81.09	64.05	73.08
Total	64.13	39.29	52.12
1997(f) (7 years and above)			
Rural	68.00	43.00	56.00
Urban	88.00	72.00	80.00
Total	73.00	50.00	62.00

Source: From Segovia, 2001, Size of the Higher Education System in India by 2011 A.D.

Female Enrolment

Although there has been a considerable increase in enrolment, females still lag behind in comparison to males at the stage of enrolment and their drop out rate is higher. This is quite evident from the Tables 11.3 and 12.4. The total enrolment at primary stage during the period 1950-51 to 1996-97 increased by 5.57 times, while for the girls the increase is 9 times. At the upper primary stage of education, the increase during this period is more than 13 times, while that of girls, the increase is more than 32 times, which is quite appreciable. At the secondary and Sr. Secondary stage the total increase is 18 times and for girls the increase is 49 times.

Table 11.3: Sex-wise Enrolment by Stages/Classes Since 1951-Second Level

(in million)

Year	*Primary*			*Middle/Upper primary*			*High/Hr. Secondary*		
	Boys	*Girls*	*Total*	*Boys*	*Girls*	*Total*	*Boys*	*Girls*	*Total*
1950-51	13.8	5.4	19.2	2.6	0.5	3.1	1.3	0.2	1.5
1955-56	17.1	7.5	24.6	3.8	1.0	4.8	2.2	0.4	2.6
1960-61	23.6	11.4	35.0	5.1	1.6	6.7	2.7	0.7	3.4
1965-66	32.2	18.3	50.5	7.7	2.8	10.5	4.4	1.3	5.7
1970-71	35.7	21.3	57.0	9.4	3.9	13.3	5.7	1.9	7.6
1975-76	40.6	25.0	65.6	11.0	5.0	16.0	6.5	2.4	8.9
1980-81	45.3	28.5	73.8	13.9	6.8	20.7	7.6	3.4	11.0
1985-86	52.2	35.2	87.4	17.7	9.6	27.1	11.5	5.0	16.5
1990-91	57.0	40.4	97.4	21.5	12.5	34.0	12.8	6.3	19.1
1991-92	58.6	42.3	100.9	22.0	13.6	35.6	13.5	6.9	20.4
1992-93	57.9	41.7	99.6	21.2	12.9	34.1	13.6	6.9	20.4
1993-94*	55.1	41.9	97.0	20.6	13.5	34.1	3.2	7.5	20.5
1994-95*	62.3	46.8	109.1	24.5	15.8	40.3	16.0	8.4	24.4
1995-96*	62.4	47.4	109.8	25.0	16.0	41.0	16.1	8.8	24.9
1996-97*	62.5	47.9	110.4	24.7	16.3	41.0	17.2	9.8	27.0
1997-98*	61.2	47.5	108.7	23.7	15.8	39.5	17.08	10.16	27.24

* Provisional.

Source: From Segovia, 2001, Size of Higher Education System in India by 2011 A.D.

Rate of drop out has been defined as percentage of the number of children to total enrolment dropping out of the school educational system in a particular year. There are a number of methods for estimating these rates. The results arrived at by convectional method have been indicated in Table 11.4.

Table 11.4: Drop Out Rates at Primary and Middle Stages

	1960-61	*1970-71*	*1980-81*	*1990-91*	*1992-93*	*1997-98**
Class-IV						
Boys	61.7	64.5	56.2	40.1	43.83	38.23
Girls	70.9	70.9	62.5	46.0	46.67	41.34
Total	64.9	67.0	58.7	42.6	45.01	39.58
Class-VIII						
Boys	75.0	74.6	68.0	59.1	58.23	50.72
Girls	85.0	83.4	79.4	65.1	65.21	58.61
Total	78.3	77.9	72.7	60.9	61.10	54.14

* Provisional.

Source: From Segovia, 2001, Size of higher education in India by 2011 AD.

Factors Contributing to Educational Backwardness of Women

The role of education in human resource development for nation building and development can hardly be over-emphasised. However, our achievements in this respect in the last fifty four years are not encouraging. Education, and particularly higher education, is beyond the reach of many, but when it comes to women the social attitude towards women's status and role acts as an inhibiting factor (Jain, 1975). The dominant idea, which persists amidst the Indian society including among women is that woman's first place is the home. A highly respected person like Dr. S. Radhakrishan has gone on record to say that 'home making was the greatest profession' for women. These ideas not only influence sex-typing in the curriculum courses, attitude and behaviour of teachers, but also narrow the boundaries of women's own vision about themselves and their lives. These have allowed many biases against women to enter the textbooks. A conscious effort to identify these biases and eliminate them has been made only recently. The pioneering work of the National Council of Educational Research and Training in this respect can not be ignored.

However, these measures should not be expected to radically alter Indian women's literacy or educational status immediately. While the National Policy on Education (1986) in its section titled Education for Women's Equality' states the objective to use education as 'an agent of basic change in the status of women,' factors like increasing privatisation and the rising cost of education have already started pushing out women. The masses will take advantage of education only when it is within their reach in every sense. The experience of Kottayam town in Kerala, where a hundred per cent literacy was attained in a short period by people's involvement, is a good lesson for others. Such effort can be made use of not only to spread literacy, but also to educate women in nutrition and health, maternity and child care, family planning, economic activity, and law and media, etc.

Nutrition and Health Care

In our country, where a sizeable section of the population do not have regular work, or steady income, or social security, and where a large number fall below the poverty line, it should not be surprising if many among them fall short of the necessary nutrition and health care levels. In the case of woman in particular, her productive function lends great importance to the issues of nutrition and health care. During pregnancy a woman is required to consume at least 2500 calories per day. But an average Indian woman consumes barely 1400 calories. The short falls are found to be more marked during lactation. Poverty and the absence of sufficient economic means contribute to short fall in nutrition in general, but women experience this all the more because of the gender discrimination (Dash, 2005) and the above mentioned perception of the man-made social system. Giving men and boys better shares of food in terms of quantity and quality is a deeply entrenched idea among a large section of our women. In poorer homes where the girls and women bring equal or more income (in cash or in kind) compared to men, they take less than equal not to speak of sufficient food even during pregnancy and lactation. The same girl who experiences discrimination at a tender age even in respect of food is burdened with domestic work and responsibility in helping the mother, taking care of the young, etc. No doubt all normal and desirable urges, zest and joy about life get crippled in her at that early age itself. She grows up without receiving adequate nutrition or health care and also without knowing that something is being denied to her or that it is her right to have it.

Describing the health situation of women, the national perspective plan document for women 1988-2000 A.D., points out that major disparities in health care prevail among women (people) of rural and urban, developed and remote, backward, hilly or desert areas and also among those belonging to different socio-economic groups. Other factors they list include social attitudes and prejudices, inadequate health care facilities, inefficient use of resources available for health care of women, ignorance, and absence or inadequacy of essential non-health facilities which effect health such as potable water, sanitation, female education, food supply, etc.

Maternity and Child Care

These factors are closely related to women's health and status. The committee on the status of women in India (CSWI) noted that the maternal mortality rate was high enough to raise the overall female death rates and accounted for the unfavourable sex ratio. Many of the studies have pointed out that much of pregnancy loss and pre-natal mortality result from premature births and malnutrition. Frequent pregnancies resulting in protein malnutrition and nutritional anemia cause a large proportion of maternal deaths. As mentioned earlier, the NPP document states that a woman in the sub-continent runs a life-time risk of 1 in 18 of dying from pregnancy related causes. Anemia, hemorrhage, toxemia, sepsis, and abortion are some of the major causes of maternal deaths.

Childcare is a major responsibility and cause of concern for women. In our country it is mainly a private affair and the class differences in our society are reflected in this as in most other aspects of life. Even women from well to do households face problems in the absence of crèches and similar facilities to suit their convenience and to their satisfaction. Women have started feeling the pinch of the disappearance of the joint family system without the creation of an alternate support system. Many middle class women, who are employed, try to cope with the situation by employing young women from the lower class. But this cannot be considered to be a perfect arrangement, as the young women are not trained for this task.

The situation is depressing when it comes to poorer households. Even in establishments, which are legally required to provide crèches, only a very small number of them do so, and even there the ladies of the poorer sections are not able to utilise the facility. The case of those women who work in the unorganised sector, often as household producers or as landless agricultural labour is even worse. It is with the help of a wide network of elders-parents of wife or husband, disabled husband, old or invalid uncles, aunts, unmarried sisters, elder children, other relatives and neighbours-that most of these women manage to take care of children.

Family Planning

While the emphasis on the implementation of the family planning programme (now popularly known as the family welfare programme) is crucial in the context of the development of the nation and the quality of life (Dash, 2005) of the people, it is often observed that various measures for attaining the targets are thrust upon more on women than men. The programe is aimed at rapid reduction of birth rate but it neither shows adequate concern for the health of women nor for medical practices currently prevalent in the country. The massive propaganda, particularly through television that 'all methods are safe' is something to be considered carefully. It is hard to believe that such standard advice can be given to women and men who belong to different cultures, socio-economic backgrounds, and living levels, with varying levels of food intake, education, etc.

More research should be done in this area and the public should be informed of the results. Research is also necessary on the traditional methods of controlling or spacing pregnancy, which our own women have been using. The emphasis on sterilisation and other methods of controlling or spacing pregnancies, the practice of making women the targets of policies and the possible effects of these on mothers and nursing mothers have been noticed by researchers who have sounded notes of caution regarding insensitive and indiscriminate policies and methods.

Economic Activity

It has been found that by and large women are working most of the time they are awake, yet that is not generally seen or recognised as work.

Women themselves do not get counted as workers. However, one can appreciate the role of women and their economic activity better if one considers what women in general do and not merely what women workers do (Ambannavar, 1978). Class and caste differences, variations in climate and crop production, land distribution, general economic level of the household, openings available in the area, presence or absence of adult earning males in the family, availability of some help in sharing the domestic work and responsibility, demands from the domestic front, and various other factors influence a woman's decision and ability to seek work (Bardhan, 1978) outside the home. Since education and skill decide the level at which one can enter the labour market, most women are engaged in low skilled and low waged work.

In the organised sector, teaching and medicine are two areas, which first absorbed women, and they continue to be areas where the maximum numbers of women are employed (Ahmed, 1979) even now. Women have entered the administrative and other services, and many professions, including those areas, which need high levels of scientific and technological skills. But it is pertinent to note that the number of these women is insignificantly small even when compared to the number of women who have had the benefit of education. The observation made in the NPP is significant in this regard. It states, 'the organised sector in India (which consist of public sector and non-agricultural private sector establishments) absorbs less than one eight of the actual work force of the country. Of this, the share of women as of 1978 was 12.4 per cent. The number of women job seekers through employment exchanges rose from 11.25 lakhs in 1975 to 50.98 lakhs in 1986. The percentage of placements on the other hand increased from 1975 to 1982, but defined in the subsequent years, i.e. 1983-1986.

However, the majority of women are to be found in the vast rural and urban unorganised sector (Awasthy, 1982). According to an estimate by the National Commission on Self-Employed Women, 94 per cent of the total female work force operates within this highly exploited sector. Employment in this sector is characterised by intermittent work and irregular income, low pay, long hours of work, low skills, absence of security and abysmal state of facilities like health, maternity and child-care (Saradamani, 1988). They include agricultural workers, all those who are engaged in traditional arts and crafts including handloom, bidi, coir, and other newly emerging works.

A more realistic estimate of the status of women can be made, if we examine the domestic sphere, which is believed to be the women's world and their prime concern. Except for a very small minority, all women who go out of home to work, bear the responsibility for the household work as well. They are treated as supplementary and secondary earners and this affects the wages they get even for the same work they do along with men. Educated and professional women are not free from the adverse effect of this bias. Poor women, with insufficient household income, stretch their day to bring in some additional income by collecting grass, fuel, cow-dung, etc. in addition to cooking, cleaning, caring for the children and elderly, drawing water, etc. We have plenty of empirical evidences to show that their income is crucial to the sustenance of the family, the female-headed households are increasing in number, and that intra-household disparities between women and men persist as regards the access to food, clothing, health care, employment and education. The removal of these constraints alone would make women independent and equal partners in national development.

Law and Media

The two other important factors with great potential for liberating women from many of their bindings, are the law and media. In addition to the constitutional guarantees, a series of legislations have been passed, for instance, the changes in personal laws, criminal laws, and labour laws, amendments to the Dowry Prohibition Act, Rape Law, Equal Remuneration Act, Prevention of Immoral Traffic Act, and the Indecent Representation of Women (Prohibition), Act. From repots about dowry deaths, rapes and atrocities on women, it is obvious that implementation of these legislations is ineffective or faulty. In spite of the level of education and awareness of these legislations on the part of the women themselves, they are not in a position at present to take advantage of the legislations.

The cinema, advertisements and stories in some glossy and cheap, widely read magasines often play a negative role in their portrayal of women. However, the portrayal of women as self-confident forward looking individuals with social consciousness and concern, and the recent portrayals on television about the worth of women's work and the need to give special care to the girl child are welcome developments. We have to remember that our country is big; and development that has so for taken place is uneven.

Women Education and Sustainable Development

Looking from the hunting gathering stage of human evolution, it is observed that women are closely linked to the environment (Mishra, 2005). Women are primarily responsible for the gathering of fire wood, collection of fodder, wild food and the growing of subsistence crops for survival. Besides fire—wood, collection of water and caring for animals are also some major activities of women. All these are disturbed by environmental degradation. Sustainable human development implies enhancement of gender equity and promotion of participation of women in the main stream. Various national and international studies as well as different women's environmental movements inspired the fact that by bringing women more actively in environmental decision making at all levels and thus to the center-stage of sustainable development, we will be successful in future both in the sector of economy and ecology. For this goal women have to cover a long path of education, training and empowerment.

Several studies and survey in recent years have indicated that women express more concern for the environment than do men (Dash, 2005; Jaggi *et al.*, 2005). Women are approximately equally concerned about economic and environmental crises, whereas men are twice as concerned about economy and women are more concerned about toxic wastes and overuse of technology than men. It is women who have been teaching humankind for centuries to love, to conserve, to be compassionate. Through the ages, it is felt that the most active and vibrant contribution to preserve the environment comes from socially and economically deprived sections. Women can be very active participartants in the defense of the environment and can stop or even reverse the degradation of our natural resources. Their involvement in the organisation and conservation of heritage sites, biosphere reserves, natural parks and community banks will enhance the effectiveness of the conservation movement. As environmental educators and motivators for change, women are key agents in the processes leading to a more sustainable and healthy development of the planet.

Women's education promotes women empowerment, which in turn restricts violence, brings peace and allows their participation (Heyzer, 2005) in development. In International research (UNESCO 1977), education has been found to increase agricultural productivity, enhance the status of women, improve child health, reduce fertility, increase industrial productivity and enhance environmental protection. All the four international conferences on women and development have stressed that education has vital role in the nurturance of women's competence and creativity, as well as promoting sustainable development. Women's education should not be seen only as a right (Dash, 2005) but also the duty of individuals and of the society. Thus providing education to women and giving access to further knowledge and new information, society in turn gains from women's educated and informed decisions, since society in turn also depends on women's contribution in all areas of work and life. There is growing evidence that women in several countries around the world are taking central roles (Jaggi *et al.*, 2005) in the environmental movements. Further there is increasing belief that development policies that do not involve women and men alike will not be successful in the long run.

Socio-Economic Problems of Women: Issues Ahead

In fact, it has been observed rather unfortunately though, that certain changes which were expected and desired, and which were regarded as a natural sequence of the process of 'development' have not actually taken place, especially in certain areas concerning women. Instead, this 'so called' development has resulted in great deal of tension in various socio-economic spheres of our lives. This is partly because of our 'inability' to adjust to the new changes and partly because of the lack of clarity in our purpose or goal. Hence it has become necessary today, to pause for a little while in this quest for 'development' and examine as to what exactly are we looking for or what are the needs of the women in this changing situation and how best we can achieve them. Bearing these points in mind, an attempt has been made in this section to point out some of the lags prevailing in the different aspects of women's social and economic life due to the uneven process of development.

Socio-Economic Problems of Women Belonging to Lower Strata

It is in this category we find the highest proportion of women workers. They are mostly agricultural labourers in the rural areas or coolies and casual labourers in urban construction sites, or employed in petty and menial services. The women in these strata are compelled to work in order to make both ends meet. Due to economic compulsions it is not possible for them to conform to any 'rigid' social values or norms. Men and women have to work together in fields or construction sites. They lead an 'open life' because they can not have the luxury of 'privacy. Some of the most common problems facing the women in this stratum may be as the low and unequal wages paid to the women in this category even when they are doing more or less similar type of work as the men do and the evil of excessive drinking which is very common among men in this category but also prevalent among women to some extent. Women in this category are often subjected to the double burden of earning as well as caring for the children with no financial security, large size of families, lack of facilities for the care of children, extremely low levels of literacy, unhygienic living conditions, lack of basic medical facilities, lack of minimum facilities of privacy which every woman is entitled to, etc.

Educational Measures Needed to Resolve These Basic Problems

It has been found that various legislations passed by government concerning some of these problems have not proved effective. Whether it is the Minimum Wages Act, Child Marriages Act or prohibition they have remained mostly on paper. What are required are dedicated and committed social and educational workers, who are genuinely interested in improving the condition of these women. They can play a key role in educating the women in this category to realise their simple and basic needs. The work can be done in the following manner:

1. For example, the importance of the role of women in agriculture has never been recognised. Though they participate in all the activities of agricultural production, provide the basic requirements of their family and in addition bear and rear children, yet their contribution is mostly ignored; it is never valued in terms of money. In the case of women who work as labourers, they are mostly exploited and paid a paltry sum as wages. These women should not only be made aware of the Minimum Wages Act but the voluntary organisations should take keen interest to see that the land lords and contractors conform to this Act.
2. There is also a need for 'legal literacy' by which women are made aware of their legal rights and it should be possible for women to hold land titles, especially in case of women who have wayward, undependable husbands. At present, even when a woman is bearing the entire economic burden of the family, she is not treated as a head of the household. Every voluntary organisation should have a legal advisory cell which can render such services to the needy women.
3. Drinking is a widespread social problem among the lower classes and many families are ruined due to this social evil. Much of the quarrelling and wife beating in these families arise due to the men forcibly taking away what the women have earned. The families which have such addicts habituated to excessive drinking should be identified. Attempts should be made to see that liquor shops are not located near their residential areas. Some kind of healthy entertainment in which these people are interested should be provided in the locality during the evening hours to keep the men away from liquor shops.
4. Functional literacy classes should be organised for the women during their leisure hours giving some basic lessons in child care, health and nutrition, related, of course, to the type of diet they are accustomed to in the different regions. The education should be mainly oriented towards time-saving devices in doing their routine work, or less strenuous ways of doing certain traditional tasks.

5. Crèches should be organised in the slum locality or villages to take care of the small children when the woman goes for work. This will also enable the older girls to go to school.
6. Family planning programme is very essential in this category. Frequent child-birth coupled with inadequate and unbalanced diet affects the health adversely of the women of the lower classes. But here again the husband and wife need to be approached and persuaded.

These are simple measures and not perhaps entirely new. But the need of hour is a positive desire to help and improve the conditions of our less fortunate sisters and a more organised and systematic way of going about it. Sporadic attempts do not yield the required results. There must be a determined and co-ordinate effort by the different voluntary organisations to improve the socio-economic condition of these classes.

Socio-Economic Problems of Women Belonging to Middle Classes

In this category, the problems are more 'social' than economic and naturally more complex. While some kind of economic development has been affecting our middle class women, some of the concomitant social changes expected with it (Barnabus, 1966) have not come about. This has resulted in a great deal of tension and conflict. An attempt has been made here to list some of these areas of 'cultural lag, or uneven levels of development giving rise to social tensions.

1. Neither the men nor the women themselves are clear as to what should be the status of women in present day society. There is a great deal of conflict as to whether women should be purely traditional, or more traditional and a little modern. To be modern means to be educated, efficient and relatively more rational in one's attitudes.
2. Total disregard towards women as equal partners in life and in decision-making.
3. Over emphasis on the status of male or role of a son.
4. Lack of due recognition to the duties and responsibilities of daughters particularly in families with 'daughters only.'
5. Too much emphasis on marriage as the end all of a woman's life and existence.
6. Conservative attitudes in arranging of marriages.
7. The evil of excessive dowry.
8. Dual responsibilities of a middle class working woman who has to struggle double hard to maintain efficiency at the place of work as well as the home.

9. Lack of adequate protection to women in various walks of life.
10. Some misconceived ideas of women's equality egged on by western concepts and ideas. These are only a few of the several problems facing the middle class women.

Some Educational Measures Needed to Resolve These Problems

Regarding the status of women, there is still a good deal of conflict. Education of women has not been given due importance in our country. Here, education does not merely mean a degree. It is the ability to judge and imbibe what is good in the changes taking place due to modernisation. Parents, however, think twice in giving education to girls and some kind of education is given half-heartedly. Some of educational measures needed for this category of women are as follows:

1. It would do well for a girl from the middle class family to know something about biology, nutrition, hygiene, first-aid, some knowledge about banking, insurance, marketing, preparing a monthly budget to manage the household finances which is becoming increasingly a skill these days. In addition, some training in child psychology and human relationships would be useful, as life around us is becoming more complex due to rapid economic growth.
2. Lavish expenditure and unnecessary show and pomp in marriages should be discouraged. That money could be utilised by the couple for more useful purposes.
3. Adequate protection should be given to women to safe-guard their self respect and morality. Any violation of these, particularly in places of work, by the employers, teachers, or officials should be dealt with severely.
4. Due recognition to the women's valuable contribution in all the developmental activities, congenial work environment and the rights to be treated with respect and dignity in all walks of life.

Training of Women

Apart from providing facilities for education of women, it is also important to train them so as to equip them with the economic power, decision making, self confidence, enhanced skills, ability to think critically, ability to participate in the development process, ability to unify and take collective action, etc. Women contribute substantially to the economic resources of a family both by way of services rendered and wages earned. Yet development projects are meant mainly for men, and only social welfare schemes cater mainly to women. There is however, an increasing realisation of the fact that women play an active role and have to be involved in any development scheme. Training of women is thus important so as to increase their involvement in the development process and enhance their skill and make them equal partners in national development.

The major objectives of training for women should be to equip them with better skills and enhance their knowledge so as to prepare them to face new challenges due to technological development and assert themselves as persons.

Training Areas

There are various policies and programmers like TRYSEM and DWCRA, which provide scope for training of women. Here we will take a look at some of the areas in which it would be useful to train them. There may be four major areas:

(a) *Health, Nutrition and Child care*: Training in these areas can be addressed to update knowledge and skills in the areas of child care, nutrition, hygiene and house keeping.

(b) *Agriculture*: Rural women work extensively in agriculture. Mechanisation of agriculture creates a need for a different sets of skills. Thus it would be useful to train women in such areas which can ensure employment opportunities instead of retrenchment.

(c) *Cottage Industries*: Women play an important role in cottage industries such as toy making, weaving and basket making. Training in rural crafts is essential for women for self-employment and for securing better economic gains.

(d) *Other Areas*: There is a need to allow women to break out of stereotyped roles. For instance, women can be encouraged to enroll for courses in TV and radio repairing, animal husbandry, operation of agricultural machinery, etc. and not confine themselves to food preservation or tailoring and embroidery alone.

Agencies Involved in Training

Some important agencies imparting training to rural women are:

Central board of social welfare, state boards of social welfare, literacy house, *krishi vigyan Kendra*, *Mahila mandals*, *and* various voluntary organisations.

Training is given to women by voluntary organisations and cooperative societies for opening small production units. Some of the areas in which programmes have been successful are: handloom and handicrafts, and training cum-production units, e.g. cane and bamboo articles, mat weaving, carpet weaving, etc.

Mahila mandals provide an opportunity to rural women to learn from each other and from resource persons appointed by the government in areas such as child care, environment, hygiene and nutrition. Other relevant areas which can be incorporated are legal literacy, adult education, information on procedures to be followed for seeking financial assistance for projects, and dissemination of information on various rights of women and policies framed for them periodically. *Mahila mandals* need to be reoriented so that they do not reinforce the image of women as leisured housewives, mothers and non-workers.

Krishi Vigyan Kendra is an innovative scheme implemented by Indian Council of Agricultural Research. Besides training in agriculture, women receive training in such areas as nutrition, hygiene, kitchen gardening poultry keeping, home management, child care, rural sanitation, etc.

There are various training programmes to train the field level workers and functionaries like Mushy Services, Mid-wives, Gram Services, Bal Services and craft instructors to operate welfare programmers and projects for women in rural areas.

Several voluntary organisations in the country are also engaged in education and training of rural women. However there is still much to be done. Let us list in simple terms recommendations for giving an impetus to women's education and training.

1. Steps must be taken to ensure universalisation of elementary education and minimisation of drops-out rate and stagnation.
2. Equal opportunities for women should be provided at all educational levels.
3. There should, at the same time, be provisions for vocational education, non-formal education and training in skill development.
4. Removing the gender bias in curriculum and providing family life education for all.
5. School timings should suit the local conditions.
6. Support structures such as crèches and *balwadis* should be provided.
7. Educational facilities and incentives should be provided for SC and ST girls
8. In view of the constraints faced by women, provision of open learning system, part time education programmes and coordination of school/college hours with the agricultural cycles would go a long way in stepping up enrolment and retention.

9. Women's issues and concerns information and training in new technology could form the core of Adult Education Programme.
10. The emphasis should be on improving conditions for assimilation by enabling women to participate in the educational process rather than just opening more educational institutions.
11. A group motivated woman can become a focal point for mobilisation of education.
12. Using mass media and folk art forms to the fullest extent in bringing to light the need for sustained efforts towards empowerment of women.

Conclusion

Women's development is directly related to national development. Programmes connected with women's development received impetus with the report of the committee on the status of women in India in 1974, which focused on direct specific action for women to enable them to overcome their problems based on their involvement and participation in the process of development. The National Perspective Plan (NPP) for Women 1988-2000 A.D. adopted by the Government of India is also aimed at streamlining women's issues in policies and programmes and giving women at least one third share in the decision making bodies from panchayats to parliament.

The first five-year plan advocated the need for adopting special measures for overcoming the barriers to women's education. During the second Five Year Plan the emphasis continued on the over all expansion of educational facilities for women. In the Third Five Year Plan, *Bal Seiko* training programmers, condensed school courses and vocational training for adult women were launched. During the Fourth Five Year Plan a committee was constituted to study the status of women in India. In the Fifth Five Year Plan it was decided to step up enrolment and retention of girls in the institution. Women's education was included as a major programme under 'Woman and Development During the Sixth Five Year Plan. Steps to eliminate general bias in school curriculum and free elementary education to girls were taken in Seventh Five Year Plan. The NPE (1986) emphasised female literacy.

In-spite of the increase in education facilities female literacy continues to lag woefully behind the male literacy. Although there has been a considerable increase in enrolment, females still lag behind at the stage of enrolment and their drop-out rate is higher. Some of the reasons for this may be: marriage of the girls at early age, reluctance to send girls out of the house after puberty, lack of relevant school curriculum, shortage of women teachers, lack of school buildings and hostels and requirements of girls to help out in the forms/family occupations or household chores or responsibility of looking after younger siblings, etc.

Giving men and boys better shares of food in terms of quantity and quality is a deeply entrenched idea among a large section of our women. Major disparity in health care prevails among women of rural and urban developed and remote, backward, hilly or desert areas and also among those belonging to different socio-economic groups. Many of the studies have pointed out that much of pregnancy loss and pre-natal mortality result from premature births and malnutrition. Child-care is a major responsibility and cause of concern for women. Quite often it has been observed that various measures for attaining the targets of family planning are thrust upon women. It has been found that by and large women are working most of the time they are awake, yet that is not generally recorded as economic activity. The two other important factors with great potential for liberating women from many of their bindings are the law and media.

Women belonging to the lower strata of society are mostly agricultural labourers in the rural areas or coolies and casual labourers in urban construction sites, or employed in petty and menial services. It has been found that various legislations passed by government concerning some of the basic problems of women belonging to this category have not proved effective. Dedicated and committed social and educational workers can play a key role in educating the women in this category to realise their simple and basic needs. Problems of women belonging to middle classes are more 'social' than economic and naturally more complex. While some kind of economic development has been affecting our middle class women, some of the concomitant social changes expected with it have not come about. Adequate protection should be given to women belonging to this category to safe guard their self-respect and morality.

Women play a vital role in economic activities, agriculture and at home. It is quite essential to provide appropriate training to women for human resource development and to enable them to live as equal and independent partners. The training must equip them with better skills, knowledge and information in relevant areas. The government and voluntary agencies are actively involved in imparting training to women. However, we have still a long way to go in education and training of women.

12

Environment, Biodiversity, Conservation and Sustainable Development in the Perspective of Education

N.C. DATTA

> *Who verily knows and who can here declare it,*
> *Whence it was born and whence comes this creation?*
> *The Gods are later than this world's production.*
> *Who then knows whence it first came into being?* THE RIGVEDA

Environment is now a typical talk of the day all over the world. Environmental issues have attracted considerable attention of the commoners and the elites, policy makers, politicians and planners, proponents of development and its opponents as well. Nearly three four decades back very few persons cared to bother for environment excepting some conscientious environmentalists, ecologists and ardent transcendentalist naturalists who could foresee the dismal future of mankind in the event of unjudicious human intervention in the spontaneity of nature and natural laws. However, it is now believed that the decline of some of the earlier civilisations was due to environmental crisis caused by man's myopic outlook, utter indifference and lack of proper knowledge about the conservation and management of environment. According to one view, in Mesopotamia large scale irrigation led to the increasing salinisation of fertile agricultural land and this was one of the factors which ultimately brought about the decline of the legendary Mesopotamian civilisation. Probably the debacle of the Egyptian and Indus Valley civilisation was due to some kinds of environmental impoverishment amongst other causes. Recently it has been observed that the productivity of crops in irrigated region gradually declines with the passage of time due to slow salinisation of soil.

What is Environment?

Environment, according to common man's perception, means just surroundings—a nontechnical term, which does not communicate the depth and dimension of the term in a technical sense. From ecological standpoint environment comprises two basic components: habitat diversity (abiotic part) and biodiversity (the biotic part). Habitat diversity includes the physical space (eg. lithosphere, hydrosphere and atmosphere) and the factors (eg. temperature, light, pH. humidity, energy, chemicals, etc.) which regulate the ecosystem processes. Biosphere is the berth on the planet earth where biota of all kinds occur and their life processes take place. Biodiversity comprises diverse kinds of biota from microbes to man.

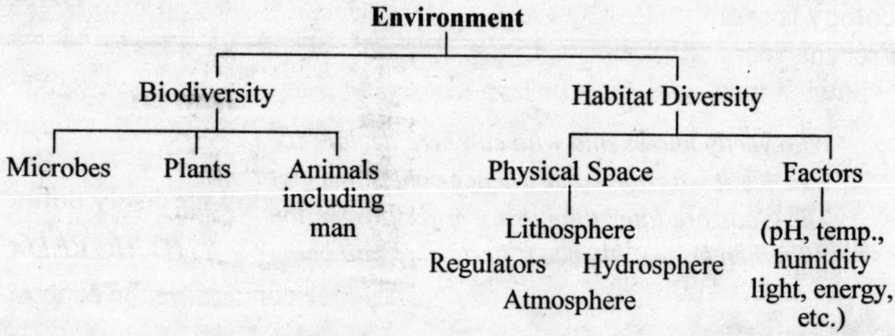

From economic standpoint environment is our asset or capital. Virtually environmental resources are economic resources which form the basis of economic growth and development. We derive all raw materials such as food, fodder, fuel, fossil fuel, minerals, medicines, oxygen, energy, etc. from environment. Other than solar energy we receive nothing from outside our planet. Not only for survival but also for our very existence we are totally dependent on congenial environment which maintains the life support system.

Calendar of Cosmological and Other Events

Nothing is more fascinating as a mystery than the beginning of universe. Equally fascinating are the birth of earth, origin and evolution of life and origin of man. There are many myths and folklores in all the religious scriptures of the world regarding the origin of earth, life and man. However, whether time is eternal or it has a beginning is a big question. It is too difficult to obtain a unanimously acceptable answer to this question. Stephen Hawking (1988), one of the most brilliant and scientific minds since Einstein, has elegantly highlighted the history of time in his *magnum opus*, "A brief history of time". However, a tentative calendar of cosmological and other events is furnished below:

Origin of universe	:	15 billion years ago (after a Big Bang)
Origin of earth	:	4.6 billion years ago
Origin of life	:	3.6 billion years ago
Origin of man	:	250,000 years ago
Age of civilisation	:	10,000 years.

According to St. Augustine the creation of the universe took place 5,000 B.C. following the "Book of Genesis". The 17th century Archbishop Ussher had estimated by careful calculation that the earth was less than six thousand years old and, moreover, that God had specially created man on October 4, 4004 B.C., at 9 a.m. (Knowles, 1949).

Ecology Defined

Ecology is rapidly emerging as an exciting and indispensable enterprise in recent years. Although ecology is as old as biology but for reasons unknown its progress has been tardy. Probably Hanns Reiter first combined the Greek words *oikos* meaning "home", and *logos* "the study of" to form the term ecology in 1865 (Kormondy, 2000). A year later in 1866 Ernst Haeckel also used the term ecology. In 1870 Haeckel precisely defined ecology as stated below:

> By ecology we mean the body of knowledge concerning the economy of nature—the investigation of the total relations of the animal both to its inorganic and to its organic environment; including above all, its friendly and inimical relation with those animals and plants with which it comes directly or indirectly into contact—in a word, ecology is the study of all the complex interrelations referred to by Darwin as the conditions of the struggle for existence.

With the above definition in the background ecology started to grow steadily. In this context some more terms tangential to ecology may be mentioned. French zoologist Isodore Geoffroy St. Hilaire introduced the term *ethology* for the "study of the relations of the organisms within the family and society in the aggregate and in the community". St. George Jackson Mivart coined the term *hexicology* to depict the study of the relations existing between the organisms and their environment and also the relations among the organisms themselves (Kormondy, 2000). *Sociology* is also akin to ecology which according to Kendeigh (1974) encompasses the ecology and ethology of mankind. By their own merits both ethology and sociology are now developed as distinct disciplines.

Ecosystem Epitomised

It is well known that ecology started as 'Natural History' which provides an account of the broad observations on the life and living of organisms in the perspective of environment. At the beginning floral and faunal exploration with special emphasis on taxonomy formed the corpus and core of ecology. Very often biotic components and abiotic parameters of the environment were studied in segregation and the relationships existing between them remained unexplored. This is an inherent weakness in classical ecology. But with the enunciation and introduction of ecosystem concept (Tansley, 1935) the science of ecology was rejuvenated in having a unifying concept—a holistic approach to the problems of man and his environment.

It seems that the term ecosystem needs elucidation. Ecosystem is an idiomatic and abbreviated expression comprising two vocables, 'ecological' and 'system'. The meaning of 'ecological' is obvious but the term 'system' needs clarification. The term system may be interpreted as *a set of different elements or components, or compartments, or units, or events or even phenomena joined in regular interaction or interdependence.* The connectedness of the components constituting a system essentially exhibits an "orderly working totality" and this outlook is philosophically known as holism. In this context it may be specified that energy is the driving force of an ecosystem and chemical substances (matter) are its structural components. Keeping the above contention in view *ecosystem may be defined as a conceptual scheme/framework where biotic and abiotic components of environment are bound together forming a system which facilitates the flow of energy and cycling of matter.*

The entire planet earth may be conceived as an ecosystem. But such an enormously huge ecosystem is almost beyond our comprehension. For convenience of study smaller units of global ecosystem which may be a pond, a lake, a wetland, a grassland, a forest or even a particular sea shore may be selected. Although as such an ecosystem is an abstract idea in the sense of being a notional framework but a given ecosystem such as a pond is a concrete one.

However, *Noosystem*, a new term coined by Barrett (1985), which integrates biological, physical and socio-economic parameters within a framework of holism, is gaining ground because the role of social science in the concept of ecosystem was either ignored or overlooked.

Emergence of Modern Ecology

Modern ecology by and large is a product of the last four decades. Ecology has now gained a rank of synthetic science, multidisciplinary in nature and boundless in its concern due to immense input from various areas of human knowledge. Although basically ecology is biological in its marrow but it has now become a social science, a basic component of liberal education for commonner to elite (Datta, 1990). Southwick (1976) made a very revealing statement that deserves due consideration. He states, "Rarely has an academic subject become such a major issue in the public consciousness as ecology in the late 1960s and early 1970s. Within a few years ecology progressed from a rather quiet and obscure branch of biology to a subject of national and international concern. Education, business, politics, law, agriculture, engineering, medicine, public health, and even international affairs were all affected by the sudden upsurge of ecological and environmental concern".

In accordance with above argument a comprehensive and a radical definition of ecology in keeping with the modern trends of the subject is the need of the time. Datta (1990) defined ecology as "*a branch of science or rather a discipline of human knowledge dealing with the strategies of survival of man and biosphere in space and time*".

Environmental Science

In recent years the term environmental science is widely used and has become very popular too. Although there is some kind of overlapping between ecology and environmental science which is obvious but the latter puts more emphasis on relevant parts of other sciences like physics, chemistry, geology, geography, anthropology, etc. to explore and explain environmental relationships.

Environmental Studies

This term is also a recent coinage. It includes ecology, environmental science, economics, ethics, sociology, and other branches of humanities so that an overview of human relationships with environment can be obtained. Interestingly, it may be noted that 'economics' and 'ecology' are derived from the same Greek root '*oikos*' meaning home. According to E.P. Odum (1971), economics deals with financial housekeeping and ecology with environmental housekeeping. Furthermore, he also significantly mentioned following H.T. Odum (1971) that energy can be thought of as the "currency" of ecology. Of course, it is well known that money circulates whereas the flow of energy is unidirectional.

Aspect of Ecodegradation

> *"And I brought you into a plentiful country" says prophet Jeremiah, "to eat the fruit thereof, and the goodness thereof, but when ye entered, ye defiled my land and made mine heritage an abomination".*

Probably the validity of the above statement leaves no scope for any evidence to be shown, since after second world war we have become much scared about ecodegradation to a considerable extent. There is an apprehension that our environment is now under serious threat so much so that it has become a global enigma (Datta, 2000a). It is well known that ecodegradation/pollution is a man made event and has been defined as undesirable changes in the quality of our environment which comprises soil, water and air. It has also become apparent that ecodegradation is the result of unjudicious development—the development which does not take care of its harmful byproducts. Such byproducts very often disrupt the subtle life support system causing serious ecologic and socio-economic backlashes. Perhaps pollution may be considered as the function of population as well as development. Because more the population, the more development is needed and therefore, more adverse changes are likely to take place in the environment.

According to Datta (1990), the present day environmental problems may be the sequel of the following facts:

1. Rapid increase of human population
2. Excessive consumption of matter and energy
3. Degradation of environment due to:
    (i) Increasing industrialisation allowing the discharge of toxic industrial effluents and emissions in the environment without proper treatment.
    (ii) Growing urbanisation, which adversely changes the existing land use pattern and which produces huge solid as well as liquid wastes.
    (iii) Enormous deforestation which removes the green cover, enhances soil erosion and induces climate change.
    (iv) Excessive loss of top soil by various human activities including deforestation. Topsoil is the fertile soil where all kinds of crops grow (our civilisation is known as topsoil civilisation).
    (v) Indiscriminate use of non-biodegradable biocides of all kinds.
    (vi) Overuse of chemical fertilizers which makes soil obsolete in course of time.
    (vii) Profuse emission of green house gases which will cause global warming and depletion of ozone layer.
    (viii) Relentless release of toxic synthetic chemicals (xenobiotics).
    (ix) Profuse use of non-biodegradable synthetic materials like plastic.
    (x) Excessive oil spill in the ocean.
    (xi) Frequent emission of radioactive substances.

(xii) Recurrent acid rain.
(xiii) Increasing trend of eutrophication.

4. Lack of due public awareness about environment and education for the management of environment.

It is obvious that all the above facts and phenomena have already caused and will be causing colossal deteriorative changes in the structure and function of all kinds of ecosystem. Obviously many such changes are injurious to man and biosphere. It seems that our environment at least in some areas is under the spell of sub-lethal toxicity. Only time will tell the after-effects of sub-lethal toxicity. It is well established that sub-lethal toxicity apparently does not show the signs of degradation but ultimately it will show damaging syndrome which will be detrimental to man and biodiversity.

Global Awareness about Environment

In recent years, say for the last half century, man has become very much concerned and scared about environment and its degradation. A chronology of global events concerning environmental awareness is furnished below:

1948 UN Charter: International Union for the Protection of Nature (IUPN) established.
1956 Man's role in changing the face of the Earth. An international symposium held at Chicago.
1957 The IUPN becomes the International Union for the Conservation of Nature and Natural Resources (IUCN).
1958 Law of the Sea. The first UN Conference on the law of the Sea approves draft conventions.
1959 Antarctic Treaty.
1961 Establishment of World Wildlife Fund (Worldwide Fund for Nature).
1962 'Silent Spring' by Rachel Carson published.
1964 International Council of Scientific Unions (ICSU) established the International Biological Programme (IBP).
1966 IUCN Red Data Book first published.
1968 UNESCO Biosphere conference.
1969 Friends of the Earth (FOE) founded.
1970 The US National Environmental Policy Act (NEPA) requires preparation of Environment Impact Assessment (EIA).
1971 Man and the Biosphere Programme (MAB) of UNESCO launched. Greenpeace International founded.

1972 UN Stockholm Conference on the Human Environment. Concept of a global environment monitoring systems (GEMS) endorsed by the Stockholm conference. United Nations Environment Programme (UNEP) established. 'Blueprint for Survival' sponsored by the journal Ecologist, *Limits to Growth* (Meadows *et al.*, 1972) published.

1974 UNEP Regional Seas Programme established.

1975 Convention on International Trade in Endangered Species of Wild Fauna and Flora (CITES).

1976 The Scientific Committee on Problems of Environment (SCOPE) reports to the International Council of Scientific Unions (ICSU) on global trends in the Biosphere most urgently requiring international and interdisciplinary scientific effort.

1979 UN Conference on desertification.
World Climate Conference Organised by the World Meteorological Organisation recognises the 'greenhouse effect'.

1980 World Conservation Strategy (IUCN) launched. IUCN Conservation Monitoring Centre (now the World Conservation Centre) established. The global 2000 report submitted to U.S. President Carter.

1982 UN Nairobi Conference, ten years after the Stockholm Conference.
World Charter for Nature adopted by UN.
The World Environment 1972-1982 is published.

1983 The World Commission on Environment and Development (WCED) established and Gro Harlem Brundtland appointed as Chairman.

1984 The Resourceful Earth. A response to Global 2000 is published.

1985 Vienna Convention for the protection of the ozone layer.

1987 Our Common Future published by WCED
Montreal Protocol on substances that deplete ozone layer.

1988 Oslo Conference on Sustainable Development—to get away from the tyranny of the immediate.

1989 The 'Green Summit' in Paris of G 7 (Canada, USA, France, Italy, Japan, UK and West Germany)
Urgent need to safeguard the environment is emphasised. IUCN publishes 'From strategy to Action' a response to *Our Common Future*. Saving the Ozone Conference in London (UK and UNEP).

	Basle Treaty on International Transport and Disposal of hazardous wastes.
	Non-aligned Movement (NAM) conference at Belgrade.
	Proposal for Planet Protection Fund.
	Langkawi (Kualalampur) declaration on environment.
	Hague declaration on ozone depletion and global warming.
1990	Tokyo Conference: A youth Perspective on Sustainable Development—The role of economics and education.
1992	United Nations Conference on Environment and Development (UNCED). It is also known as Earth Summit or Rio Conference. Major environmental issues discussed are: Deforestation, Biodiversity loss, Climate change etc.
1997	Kyoto Conference on global warming.

In this context it is worthwhile to mention that the Silent Spring authored by Rachel Carson (1962), a valiant science communicator, is said to be "The most important chronicle of this century (i.e. the 20th century) for the human race". This small book has not only awakened the world but also warned us of the devastating dangers caused by pesticides and other toxic substances released by man in the environment. The meaningful comment of Margaret Mead on this book also deserves special mention. She wrote, "Not war, but a plethora of man made things...is threatening to strangle us, suffocate us, and bury us, in the debris and by-products of our technologically inventive and irresponsible age". Robert Van den Bosch (1978) in his book, *The Pesticide Conspiracy* clearly disclosed the ugly connivance of the big money moguls of the pesticide industry and their "bought-and-paid for entomologists and toxicologists". These people promoted the sale of pesticides without mentioning the possible environmental hazards that might be caused by indiscriminate use of those harm-causing chemicals. Paul R. Ehrlich (1978) in the preface of the same book wrote, "Pesticides were big business in 1962 and are still big business and pesticides are an ideal product; like heroin they promise paradise and deliver addiction". It may be pointed out that xenobiotics (Gr. *'Xenon'*—a stranger and *'bios'*—life) are chemical compounds foreign to the body, such as drugs, food additives and environmental pollutants etc. Most of the agrochemicals and petrochemicals are environmental pollutants and xenobiotic in nature. It is known that at present there are more than 200,000 such compounds and that about 150×10^6 tonnes of xenobiotic compounds are produced annually which contaminate our water, soil and air. Obviously it will create massive adverse changes in the quality of environment.

Datta (1996) wrote that "in recent years we are using huge amount of plastic and other synthetic wrapping and packing material which are non-biodegradable. According to one estimate 1,19,48,775 kg. of plastic has been imported to India during 1992 and 1993 in addition to the quantity produced in India. We are indiscriminately dumping those here and there. I have every reason to believe that in no time our entire planet earth will be wrapped by plastic materials. You can easily imagine the ecological consequences of this activity. Very soon it will be a matter of not only great but also grave concern needing an instant strategy to overcome this malady".

Crux of the Earth Summit

Earth Summit at Rio de Janeiro, Brazil is a unique event in the history of mankind. The UNCED document comprises five separate agreements. These are:

1. The Convention on climate change.
2. The Convention on Biological Diversity.
3. The Rio Declaration.
4. The Forest Principle.
5. Agenda 21.

Agenda 21 is a 500 pages document or rather a comprehensive master plan of action for protection and management of environment which will be conducive to sustainable development. There are 40 chapters organised into 4 sections which will address the problems of social and economic development, natural resources, fragile ecosystems, byproducts of industrial production, finance and means of implementation. The opening remarks of the Agenda 21 outline the fundamental perceptions and the goal of the exercise. It states, "Humanity stands at definite moment in history. We are confronted with a perpetuation of disparities between and within nations, a worsening of poverty, hunger, ill health and illiteracy, and the continuing deterioration of the ecosystem on which we depend for our well-being". However, it is expected that if Agenda 21 is pragmatically followed sustainable development will be achieved. But the stern reality is that the dominating developed countries will have to sincerely foster an attitude of altruism shunning extreme consumerism and sharing sparable resources of all kinds. Developed countries should also extend cooperation in all possible ways and at the same time developing countries must also come forward to accept and implement the program in keeping with the need and aspiration of their people.

Ecodegradation and Biodiversity

Biodiversity is the product of time and the precious possession of our earth. It has already been stated that nearly 3.6 billion years back life originated on earth. Biodiversity, as mentioned before, includes all species of biota from microbes to man. It may also be defined as "global composite of genes, species and ecosystems". According to United Nations Environmental Programme (UNEP) there are about 30 million species on our planet of which according to Freedman (1995), about 1.7 million organisms have been identified and designated with a binomial name. According to some estimates there may be 30-50 million species and even more. Indeed lots of animated discussions leading even to unresolved confrontations have taken place at the Earth Summit at Rio, Brazil in 1992.

In this context it may be mentioned that biodiversity in essence also includes genetic diversity which accounts for the variety of genetic information possessed by the members of the same species.

Biodiversity is invaluable for many reasons. Not only it has academic and applied value, but also it has social, cultural and aesthetic values or intrinsic values. Datta (1990) stated, "Every species in an ecosystem has got its own role and importance and some are seemingly pantomime. Man is incapable of creating a species. Therefore, what man cannot create, he does not have any right to annihilate. Extermination of any species is a loss forever". Realising the aftermath of increasing loss of biodiversity Gro Harlem Brundtland (Chairman, World Commission on Environment and Development) said, "The library of life is on fire and we must put it out". Virtually, real threat to our civilisation is not pollution but loss of biodiversity. Pollution can be prevented, abated and polluted habitat can be reclaimed and restored but a species once lost is a loss forever. The following chart will provide an idea of academic concern and applied value of biodiversity.

Concern and Value of Biodiversity

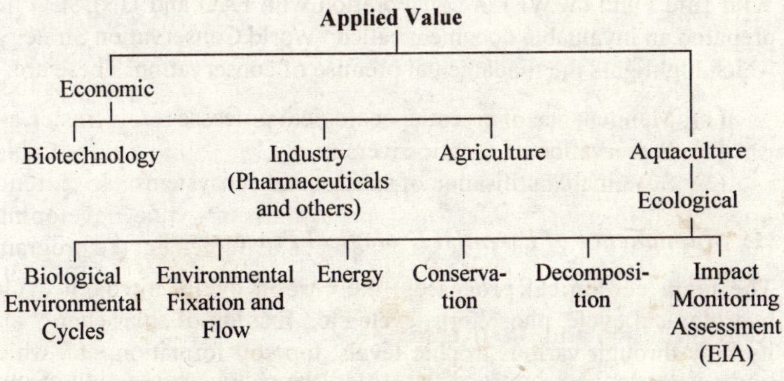

Ecology of Conservation—The Concept and the Practice

In recent years conservation has become a key concept in ecology and is considered as a segment of human welfare ecology. It may be defined as the practice of management of earth's resources in such a manner that it will continue to exist for future use. Conservation is an antonym of over consumption of resources which leads to their ultimate exhaustion. Eminent ecologist E.P. Odum (1971) appropriately suggested two fundamental aims of conservation: "(1) to insure the preservation of a quality environment that considers esthetic and recreational as well as product needs and (2) to insure a continuous yield of useful plants, animals and materials by establishing a balanced cycle of harvest and renewal".

But with the exponential growth of population man has not only been rapaciously exploiting resources but also degrading the quality of resources rendering those useless. Natural resources are untold—this conviction is just a myth. Customarily natural resources are considered under two categories: *renewable* and *non-renewable*. Renewable resources are primarily living or biotic resources and others such as soil, water, nitrogen, oxygen, etc. which move in the environment in a cyclic manner and such phenomena are called biogeochemical cycles. Biotic resources have the ability to reproduce and thus they renew themselves. Non-renewable resources are finite and once totally used, these are gone forever. Minerals and fossil fuels are examples of non-renewable resources. The kernel of conservation comprises preservation, maintenance, sustainable utilisation, restoration, and improvement of natural environment.

International Union for Conservation of Nature and Natural Resources (IUCN) with the advice, cooperation and financial assistance of United Nations Environmental Programme (UNEP) and the World Wild Life Fund (WWF) in collaboration with FAO and UNESCO has prepared an invaluable document called "World Conservation Strategy" which highlights the fundamental premise of conservation. These are:

(1) Maintenance of essential ecological processes
(2) Preservation of genetic diversity
(3) Sustainable utilisation of species and ecosystems

(1) *Maintanence of Essential Ecological Processes*

The main ecological processes like carbon cycle, nitrogen cycle, hydrological cycle, phosphorus cycle etc., fixation of solar energy and its flow through various trophic levels, top soil formation, etc. which spontaneously occur in nature should be allowed to continue without any impediment. Green plants synthesise carbohydrate with the help of solar energy, CO_2 and H_2O. It has been estimated that the total amount of radiant energy received by earth is about 13×10^{23} calorie/year and the organic matter produced is about 10^{17} grams (about 1 billion tons) in a year. This production is the capital on which rest of the living world survives. Evidently by removing the greens we not only disturb O_2-CO_2 balance, climate, soil formation but also vitiate the vital machinery that entraps solar energy. These ecological processes are indispensable in keeping the biosphere alive.

(2) *Preservation of Genetic Diversity*

Genetic diversity and biodiversity are our biological wealth. These provide our food, fodder, fuel, fibre, medicine, etc. Many species of plants and animals in the wilderness may serve as panacea for many dreadful diseases. In this context it can be mentioned that the rosy periwinkle, an angiospermic plant of Madagascar, has been found to possess potential anticancer properties. Undoubtedly, there are many such plants as well as animals, which may be having therapeutic values. Therefore, for obvious reasons genetic and biodiversity should be preserved.

(3) *Sustainable Utilisation of Species and Ecosystems*

Sustainable utilisation of species and ecosystems is obligatory for future provision of the society. It is not an one-time use but continued use over time. Therefore, we should not extravagantly use resources since ecologic and socio-economic consequences of unjudicious exploitation will tell upon the well-being of the posterity. It is also explicit that since the question of conservation also concerns the forthcoming generations therefore, it has got an altruistic component which deserve due respect of the mankind.

Sustainable Development

In 1983 Gro Harlem Brundtland, Prime Minister of Norway, was made Chairman of the World Commission on Environment and Development (WCED) by United Nations to look into the critical problems of environment and development, to suggest environmental strategies for achieving sustainable development and to foster international cooperation and participation of the nations. The report of the WCED was published as a book entitled, *Our Common Future* in 1987.

Sustainable development was the 'leitmotif' of the Brundtland Report. Development is said to be sustainable when it "meets the needs of the present without comprising the ability of future generations to meet their own needs". But what is development? It needs to be defined precisely so as to understand its concern, depth and dimension. Development is desired to fulfill the material, moral and aesthetic aspirations of mankind and his society so that optimum well-being of mankind is achieved. Development, unlike economic growth, is a qualitative concept and sustainability is a doctrine indicating the notion of up keeping and perpetuation of the dividend of development available to its beneficiaries over time. Sustainability from holistic point of view should be realised from economic, environmental and socio-cultural milieu.

On the basis of degree of development, countries of the world are broadly classified as (1) *developed countries*, (2) *developing countries* and (3) *underdeveloped* countries. USA, UK, Germany, France, Canada, Italy, Japan are considered as developed countries. India, Pakistan, Bangladesh and Egypt are branded as developing countries. There are a number of countries in Latin America, Africa, and Asia where poverty prevails and the people are utterly deprived of the basic amenities of life. Such countries are graded as underdeveloped countries. Developing and underdeveloped countries are confronted with the problems of overgrowth of human population, overload of debt, poverty, poor health condition and a number of other obstinate problems. Alleviation of poverty is an uphill task and maintenance of congenial environment is also not an easy job. It has been postulated that development can hardly subsist on deteriorating environmental resource base. Perhaps that is why environment and development have been clubbed together by WCED. The problem of population especially those of the developing countries, should not loose our sight. Because the benefit of development will be eaten away by the population added every year and therefore the living standard of the existing population will hardly be improved. Hence the purpose of development will be defeated. Rapid population growth with resource limitation will cause poverty. It is obvious that as population growth retards, developing countries can afford to divert more resources for the cause of education, health care, job creation, social security and other developmental programmes that may improve quality of life. In order to make sustainable development effective and useful the following maxims as formulated by WCED in *Our Common Future* (1987) may be accepted in principle and practiced sincerely.

1. A political system that secures effective citizen participation in decision making.
2. An economic system that is able to generate surpluses and technical knowledge on self-reliant and sustained bases.
3. A social system that provides for solutions for the tensions arising from disharmonious development.

4. A production system that respects the obligation to preserve the ecological base for development.
5. A technological system that can search continuously for new solutions.
6. An international system that fosters sustainable patterns of trade and finance and
7. An administrative system that is flexible and has the capacity for self-correction.

In continuation of the above seven maxims I have (Data, 1993) already suggested the following three phraseologies which will be complementary to the above.

1. An education system that stimulates the sense of sincerity to promote purposefulness.
2. A cultural system that creates an attitude to cope with narrow regions and orthodox religionist.
3. An ethical system that upholds the dignity of mankind.

Education—The First and the Last Word

For the last quarter century ecology has been receiving requisite attention of the people all over the world. Although ecology developed as a branch of biology but it did not find its due recognition in the sphere of formal education. Krebs (1985) stated, "Until the 1960s ecology was not considered an important science". However, because of the omnipotence of the principles of ecology for the sustainable existence of biosphere in general and mankind in particular, *ecology as well as environmental science may now be considered as the science of survival*. After the first UN Conference on Human Environment at Stockholm in 1972 all environmental issues including environmental education have come to limelight. UNESCO has also formulated the guiding principles of environmental education and reiterated that importance of environmental education can neither be overlooked nor ignored in the interest of man.

Botkin *et al.*, (1980) submitted a valuable report entitled *No Limits to Learning: Bridging the Human Gap* to the Club of Rome. According to this report most education lays emphasis on an individual learning or "micro learning" as they call it. Micro learning may make an individual knowledgeable enough to satisfy his thirst for knowledge but it will be of less value to the society at large. Without "macro learning" or "collective" or "societal learning" neither awareness of any kind can be created nor society can derive any benefit out of it. The said report provoked some pertinent questions. How can "we create awareness and understanding of regional and global predicaments among people who have had little or no schooling?" Only the highly educated few have the knowledge of global predicaments. Therefore, environmental macro learning will be an important tool in understanding and deciphering many global environmental issues. In this context it may be mentioned that one of the forty chapters of the Agenda 21 discusses the importance and indispensability of environmental education, public awareness and training. Environmental literacy is an important social goal (Freedman, 1995).

Although 'macro learning' is preferable to 'micro learning' for effective environmental protection, Datta (2000b) gave due importance also to micro learning. According to him an individual is the smallest unit in a human society. A farsighted individual being aware of the impending danger of ecodegradation may come forward to motivate others so as to generate mass awareness which will flow through community, society, nation and finally to the nations of the globe. Mass awareness will lead to mass movement against environmental malady. Environmental education programme should be comprehensive so as to give a fair idea of the structure and function of natural ecosystems. Ecosystem's sensitivity, fragility, resistance to obviate undesirable change and the power of resilience which means the ability of any system to recover from disturbance must be given due consideration. All means of mass communication should be exercised so as to make environmental education comprehensive and meaningful.

Information technology especially electronic media has come in a very big way which can serve mankind significantly. Traditional printing media should also be made attractive and informative to the people who may not avail the advantage of electronic media.

All modes of education such as formal, informal and nonformal should be given due attention so that all the strata of human society get the privilege of getting themselves duly educated. After all "environment is our refuge, resource and capital and we can not afford to degrade it" (Datta, 2000b).

It is indeed gratifying to note that very recently in India Environmental Studies has been introduced as a compulsory subject in degree course to all the students of science, humanities and commerce faculties.

Conclusion

Datta (1996) emphasised that in order to deal with the present day ecological crisis a new philosophy of life should be developed, which will not only give due weight age to the ecological principles and to the concept of environmental management but also will not deter development. The older philosophy, i.e. the Judaic Christian philosophy proclaimed that Nature existed for man, to be used by him and exploited for his own good. "Go ye forth, multiply and subdue nature"—this was the slogan. Perhaps the backbreaking consequences of exponential growth of human population, tending to reach the upper limit of the carrying capacity of the planet earth, are probably known to everybody specially the citizens of highly populous developing countries. The Baconian creed emphasized that scientific and technological knowledge means control and power over nature. But to what extent we can overpower nature and with what consequences, are to be judged unbiasedly and with far sight. However, an antagonistic philosophy has also been enunciated by Leopold (1949), Osborn (1948) and Vogt (1948) who advocated that "man was out of balance with his environment and would soon pay the consequences". They also asserted that "only strict attention of the principles of ecology and the view that man was part of a sensitive and intricate eco-system could rescue us from a programme of self destruction". Another remark of Osborn (1948) becomes relevant in the present context. He wrote, "Man must recognise the necessity of cooperating with nature. He must temper his demands and use and conserve the natural living resources of this earth in a manner that alone can provide for the continuation of civilisation".

Evidently, two contradictory philosophies are in front of us, one of optimism and the other of pessimism. The former assures us of the "fabulous future" and the other warns us that we are engaged in a "programme of self defeat". We are to ascertain which one is right. I believe that the controversy will continue but truth will emerge in due course. However, I like to quote a revealing statement of Eugene Pleasant Odom, a celebrated ecologist (1971) who wrote, "It is man the geological agent, not so much as man the animal, that is too much under the influence of positive feedback, and, therefore, must be subjected to negative feedback. Nature, with our intelligent help, can cope with man's physiological needs and wastes, but she has no homeostatic mechanisms to cope with bulldozers, concrete, and the kind of agro-industrial air, water, and soil pollution that will be hard to contain as long as the human population itself remains out of control". Still I have got great faith in man and infine I quote from my Presidential Address (Datta, 1990) which may be relevant here: "Since mankind is potentially resourceful in having originality, ingenuity, imaginations, intelligence and techno scientific power, the ample evidences of which will be found in the history of mankind himself at least during last 30 centuries, therefore, so long as the rational outlook of man towards the application of his ever renewable attribute remains, the future of mankind can never be so bleak".

Perhaps it is also necessary to remember that the problems of environment are not exclusively ecological, rather these are enmeshed with socio-economic, educational, administrative, legal, philosophical, psychological and ethical issues. Hence, it is difficult to find any linearity, the absence of which makes the enterprise enigmatic.

13

Understanding Microbes for Biosphere Sustainability

R.N. BISOYI

A century ago, Australian zoologist Eduard Suess coined the idea of Biosphere so as to understand the dynamics of life processes on earth. Biosphere is restricted to a thin zone of about 14 miles thick that envelopes air, water and land of earth. Microorganisms contribute indispensably in maintaining the life cycles on earth. Microorganisms invisibly exist in the interface of most habitats in atmosphere, hydrosphere and lithosphere due to the ubiquity, diverse metabolic capabilities and high enzymatic activities, which play a major role in cycling of various elements in nature besides contributing to ameliorate the degraded environment.

Currently there has been substantial international concern over the increased rates of man made interferences due to improper disposal, misuse and release of toxic organic and inorganic compounds into the biosphere which has resulted in widespread pollution of soil, ground water and marine environments. Challenge for the coming decade lies in the fact that the ongoing environment is unstable and degrading by which the balance between intensive and extensive use technologies to increase economic development is precarious. Sustainable development has been accepted as a concept that must be central to all future human endeavors. This concept has two basic objectives:

(i) Ecological sustainability.
(ii) Economic development.

Besides, both issues must be addressed simultaneously.

Experience from the past decades has shown that mismatch between resource characteristic and economic development has disturbed the ecological balance in the biosphere. Hence increasing attention is being directed at the development and implementation of innovative technology for cleaning up contamination (Hopper, 1989). Under such backdrop, microbial resources offer wide opportunities to mankind to augment sustainable development in the biosphere which not only could maintain ecological sustainability but also could be used for economic development.

Innumerable physical, chemical, and biological processes occur simultaneously in a very complex manner in the biosphere, which has maintained different life processes since million years without much change. Hence, attempts have been made to highlight the role of microbes in sustaining life processes in the nature, which support and invisibly maintain life. Further, all microbial transformations occur in the soil micro-habitat and proper maintenance of microbial habitat facilitates efficient nutrient transformations (Bisoyi, 2002).

Hence, this chapter attempts to discuss various basic issues of sustainable development threatened by mankind in maintaining proper habitat and clean environment and the potential role of microbes facilitating life systems in a conceptual manner. The basic issue and its possible remedial addressal through microbes and other beneficial roles of microbes in a concise form has been highlighted so as to highlight the potentialities of microbial resources in a major role in maintaining different life systems of biosphere. This chapter seeks to highlight the basic issues of life system of the biosphere and restricts to the role of microbes in maintaining its self-sustaining systems.

Role of Microbes in Maintaining Ecological Sustainability

Microbes profoundly affect the geology of earth by assisting chemical transformation like biosynthesis, biodegradation and oxido-reductive bio-transformations. All living organisms participate in the biogeochemical cyclings of materials through microorganisms with their diverse metabolic capabilities and high enzymatic activities (Jorgensen, 1989).

Biogeochemical Cyclings

Biogeochemical cycling of essential nutrient elements of earth occurs both within ecosystem as well as on a global basis. The bio-genic elements other than carbon, hydrogen and oxygen are often referred as mineral nutrients and their cycles as mineral cycles (Deevey, 1970). Mineral nutrients including N, S, and P are usually taken up by autotrophs and phototrophic heterotrophs in the form of mineral salts. Biogenic elements like N, S, Fe, Mn get cycled in the biosphere through autoreductive reaction and P, Ca, Si cycles through dissolution and incorporation to organic matter, balanced by mineralisation and sedimentation. All the elements are required to maintain life in the biosphere and deficiency or excess delivery of one or more elements disturb the ecological balance with unforeseen consequences. On the other hand, microbes continue to maintain all the biogeochemical cycles which assist to have equilibrium in the biosphere; these cycles are discussed as follows:

(i) *Carbon Cycle*: Microorganisms convert carbon dioxide to organic matter through photosynthetic or chemotropic activities and increase the organic material in the biosphere through the food web. Organic carbon formed by primary producers is transferred to grazers and predators. Decomposers and respiration of grazers and predators return carbon dioxide to primary producers. In most terrestrial, aquatic environments, the predominant primary producers are microbes, which fix carbon dioxide.

Currently due to high industrialisation and increased burning of fossil fuels CO_2 reservoir has increased in the biosphere, which has caused global warming due to the greenhouse effect. It has been observed that between 1860 and 1980, atmospheric CO_2 rose by 70 ppm, which from 270 ppm in a pre-industrial period increased to 340 (Houghton *et al.*, 1983). Additional carbon dioxide was contributed by forest biomass and soil humus due to forest clearing for agricultural land. Further human activities like drilling of oil and natural gas, land filling of solid waste, large scale cattle raising, wetland rice cultivation, etc. contributed to the release of methane into the atmosphere which also hastens greenhouse affect. Microbes being the largest primary producers, fix CO_2 in the biosphere and through respiration, it is released back. However, other miner roles are as follows:

Microbes for abetting green house effect: Scientists have tried to develop alternative technology for reducing atmospheric CO_2 theoretically, since microbes could remove enough of this greenhouse gas from atmosphere. An experiment was conducted in the equatorial Pacific Ocean wherein iron mineral was artificially applied to the deep sea, which increased phytoplankton productivity (Kerr, 1994). This indicated potentialities of microbes in mobing extra CO_2. Although large-scale experimentation in the tropical oceans did not give predictable answers so as to control greenhouse effect successfully but certainly it gives a clue on role of microbes in controlling excess carbon dioxide by fixation of carbon dioxide.

(ii) *Hydrogen Cycle*: The largest global reservoir of hydrogen in the biosphere is water. Water retained in crystal lattices of rock is not cycled activity. Hydrogen is produced by fossil fuels and biomass burning. Hydrogen is also produced in the atmosphere by the photochemical decomposition of methane. The gravitational pull of earth is not strong to prevent loss of hydrogen from upper atmosphere which affects hydrogen cycling.

Microbes for hydrogen retention: Microbes like *Pseudomonas, Paracoccus*, and *Xanthobacter* are capable of fixing carbon-dioxide in presence of hydrogen through enzymatic activities. This microbial activity reduces the escape of hydrogen from the atmosphere, which indicates the role of microbes in partially retaining hydrogen.

(iii) *Oxygen Cycle*: Photosynthesis derived oxygen not only transforms our oxygen but also oxidizes large quantities of minerals such as ferrous iron and sulphides. Atmospheric oxygen produced in photosynthesis is removed from atmosphere by respiration.

The burning of fossil fuels has an effect on atmospheric oxygen as well as CO_2 concentration. However, concerns have been expressed about potential exhaustion of atmospheric oxygen by human activity. It is estimated that the burning of all known fossil reserves would reduce the oxygen supply by 3 per cent (Broeker, 1970). However, these concerns are groundless because oxygen reserve is about 21 per cent in the atmosphere. In the absence of oxygen, microbes recycle organic carbon through fermentative and methanogenic processes. All living organisms participate in cycling of Hydrogen-Oxygen. However microbes dominate both the production and catabolic processes which reveal the role of microbes in cycling of oxygen in the biosphere.

(iv) *Nitrogen Cycle*: Nitrogen present in the atmosphere gets recycled mainly by the microbes. Higher plants present in the biosphere cannot consume atmospheric nitrogen directly which is to be fixed and incorporated in chemical forms and this fixation of nitrogen is carried out by microbes called as diazotrophs which possess the genetic code for the synthesis of enzyme nitrogenase which catalyses the atmospheric nitrogen fixation. This is known as biological nitrogen fixation which occurs through symbiotically and free livingly. The symbiotic N_2 fixing systems fix nitrogen through bacteria (*Rhizobium, Bradyrhizobium, Azorhizobium, Sinorhizobilim, Mesorilizobium*) with host leguminous plants, Cyanobacteria symbiotically associated with bryophytes, pteridophytes, gymnosperms, *Frankia* symbiotic associated with forestry plants. Besides *Azospirillum*, *Herbaspirilllim* function asymbiotically, aerobically through *Azotobacter, Azomonas, Arthobacter*, *Beijeinekia, Derxia* besides large number of Cyanobacteria as well as anaerobically through *Clostridium, Chromatium, Desulfovibrio*, *Methanobacterium, Rhodobacter* and a vast number of microbes (Evans *et al.*, 1991).

The gamut of total nitrogen recycled in the biosphere is estimated to be about 1050 million metric tones. Of these, the diazotrophs account for only 140 million metric tones. Non-biological agents like lightening or fire contribute 40 million metric tones. The balance of 870 million metric tones of nitrogen in the form of organic matter come from dead plants, animals and sediments of earth which are recycled by microbes through mineralisation processes:

(a) *Ammonification*: During the course of organic matter decomposition the complex organic nitrogen is rendered by microorganisms into ammonia and nitrate, which is assimilated by plants for nutrition. The bacteria which facilitate in ammonification are *Pseudomonas*, *Bacillus*, *Clostridium*, *Micrococcus* and fungus *Alternaria*, *Aspergillus*, *Mucor*, Penicillium, *Ruinous* besides *actinomycetes*.

(b) *Nitrification*: The process of oxidation of ammonia to nitrite and nitrite to nitrate is called as Nitrification, which is a microbial process wherein, the bacteria oxidise ammonia to nitrite are *Nitrosomonas*, *Nitrosococcus*, *Nitrospira* and the bacteria oxidising nitrite to nitrate are *Nitrobacter*, *Nitrospira* and *Nitrococcus* and fungus like *Aspergillus flavas* etc.

(c) *Denitrification*: Again, the nitrogen added to soil is being converted back into free nitrogen to the atmosphere through the microbes. This pathway of microbial reduction of nitrate to molecular nitrogen through conquentinal changes from nitrate, nitrite, nitric oxide, nitrous oxide, atmospheric nitrogen, which liberates freely, is called as denitrification. These microbial activities occur through microbes like *Pseudomonas*, *Bacillus*, *Paracoccus* as well as occasionally by *Thiobacillus denitrificans*, *Chromobacterium*, etc.

(v) *Phosphorus Cycle*: Phosphorus is the most important constituent of all living organisms. The major storehouse of it is rock deposits and the plant and animals. Phosphorus is in different compounds in the form of phytine, nucleic acids, coenzymes; etc., and these compounds present inside the living bodies are transformed through various biological processes by the microorganisms by alternation of solubility of inorganic mineralisation of compounds or through immobilisation means or through oxygen reduction of inorganic phosphorus compounds (Tiessen and Stewart, 1985). This transformation or solubilisation processes are done by microbes like *Pseudomonas*, *Bacillus*, *Flavobacterium*, *Micrococcus*, *Penicilium*, *Aspergillus,* etc. Soil contains large amount of organic phosphorus, which is not available to plants unless it is microbiologically converted into inorganic form through mineralisation. Besides the bacteria, mycorrhizal fungi play an important role in making phosphorus available from soil reservoir to host plants.

(vi) *Sulphur Cycle*: Sulphur is an essential nutrient for sustaining life in the biosphere. It is most abundant at low concentrations in the soil. Although sulphur enters in the form of plant residues, animal waste, but is metabolised through microbes in form of decomposition of organic sulphur compounds. Immobilisation or assimilation or oxidation of inorganic ions occur in the form of such as sulphides, thiosulfate, and elemental sulphur. Plants derive sulphur from the soil in the form of sulphate. The microbes responsible for sulphur transformations are *Thiobacillus thiooxidans*, *T. thioparus*, T. ferrooxidans, *T. denitrificans* as well as other microbes like *Arthrobacter*, *Bacillus*, *Flavobacterium* and *Pseudomonas*. They generate thiosulfate from elemental sulphur (Nelson, 1990). As such, microbes play a key role in sulphur cycle in the biosphere.

(vii) *Iron Cycle*: Iron is the fourth most abundant element in the earth's crust, but only a small portion of iron is available for geochemical cycling (Ehrich, 1995). The cycling of iron consists largely of oxidation-reduction reactions that reduce ferric iron (Fe^{3+}) to ferrous iron (Fe^{2+}) and oxidize ferrous iron (Fe^{2+}) to ferric iron (Fe^{3+}). These ferric and ferrous ions have different solubility properties and microbes assist in the cycling of iron. Flooding of soil, which creates anaerobic conditions favours accumulation of ferrous iron. In aerobic habitats, most of the iron exists in the ferric state. Microbial growth is often limited by the availability of iron. Most bacteria have the ability to produce and secrete molecules called as siderophores (Greek for iron bearers). Many of the bacteria like Pseudomonas have sidorophores, which transform iron. The bacteria like *Thiobacillus ferrooxidans*, contribute oxidation of ferrous to ferric under acidic conditions. Under non-acidic conditions the bacteria like *Pedomicrobium,. Hyphomicrobium* also take part in iron exchanges. These activities of iron oxidizing bacteria lead to substantial iron deposits. Since oxygenic photosynthesis changes into oxidizing one, most iron in the biosphere is kept in the oxidized (ferric state). In water logged soils and aquatic sediments, ferric iron act as an electron sink to be reduced to ferrous (Lovley, 1993). This shows the importance of microorganisms in recycling of iron in the biosphere.

(viii) *Manganese Cycle*: Manganese is an essential trace element for all organisms. It is also cycled by microorganisms between its oxidized and reduced states like iron in the biosphere (Ehrlich, 1995). In an aquatic habitat manganic oxide precipitates into sediments where reductive reactions produce manganous carbonate. Some monogamous ions are released into toxic water where oxidation occurs resulting in precipitation of manganese oxide. These reactions assist in the formation of manganese nodules in many aquatic habitats (Nealson and Saffarini, 1994). The bacteria responsible for manganese transformation are *Gallionella, Metallogenium*, *Leptothrix*, *Bacillus*, *Pseudomonas* and *Arthrobacter.*

(ix) *Calcium Cycle*: Calcium is one of the major elements present in the earth, which is essential to all living organisms. From geochemical point of view, biological precipitation and dissolution in the form of carbonate ($CaCO_3$) and Bicarbonate ($Ca(HCO_3)_2$) respectively are very important (Ehrlich, 1995). During the process of ammonification, nitrate reduction and sulphate reduction carbonates are formed. The coral reefs present inside tropical water are due to the calcium deposition made by blue green algae. These microbial activities indicate the role played by microbes in recycling of calcium in the biosphere.

(x) *Silicon Cycle*: Silicon is the second most abundant element in earth which occurs mostly as silicon dioxide and silicates. The biological recycling through microorganisms is very much restricted to diatoms and Radiolaria which are estimated to be 6.7 billion metric tons annually. The residence time of the dissolved silica in surface ocean water through biological precipitation is estimated to be around 400 years (Treguer et al., 1995). Diatoms play most important role in recycling of silica in the biosphere.

Biogeochemical cycles interact with each other extensively. Individual minerals are oxidized or reduced by microorganisms only at specific redox potentials. This leads to zonations in soil, aquatic environments where minerals accumulate in specific chemical forms and specific microbial populations proliferate, which assist to recycle the elements needed for the life systems so as to assist in maintaining the ecological sustainability of the biosphere.

Microbes for Economic and Sustained Development

Microbial resources contribute substantially for the economic well-being of resource management, general public health and environmental quality. Present day biosphere is threatened in maintenance of fertile agriculture soils, ensuring supply of healthful drinking water besides means for disposal of liquid and solid waste materials which are long standing problems of human society caused due to fast economic development, needs solutions which are economically and environmentally sustainable. Current day technology relies on the application of microbes to address the issues of human problems in agriculture, resource recovery, public health and pollution control so as to find a long standing economic growth so as to derive sustainable development without damaging the biosphere.

(i) *Microbes for Maintenance of Sustainable Agriculture*: Current day global agriculture has witnessed tremendous growth, which has changed from traditional agriculture to corporate enterprise with an objective to increase unit area productivity which is challenged due to over dependence on fossil-based high doses of chemical fertilizers, low fertilizer use efficiency, degradation of soil health and fertility, high crop nutrient removal from soil coupled with low replenishment, yield stagnation despite increased use of chemical fertilizers and environmental hazards of ground water contamination, heavy metal pollution, eutrophication, ozone layer depletion and so on. On the other hand using microbes crop nutrition demand could be met with sustained crop yield besides maintaining soil health and fertility as well as facilitating to restoration the degraded soil (Singh and Bisoyi, 1992).

The biological nitrogen fixation by free living nitrogen fixing bacteria, Cyanobacteria as well as their symbiotic nitrogen fixation are well known which contribute as high as 300 kg. N/ha/year to as low as 2.5 kg. N/ha year (Bums and Hardy, 1975). These capabilities of microbes to fix atmospheric nitrogen or solubilising/mobilising phosphate or release crop nutrients biologically has led to bio-fertilizer industries in developed and developing countries in the globe wherein crop specific *Rhizobium* for different legumes (pulses), oil yielding crops like soyabean, groundnut, fodder legumes (Clover), *Azospirillum*, *Azotobacter* for cereals, sorghum, vegetables, plantation crops, floriculture, cotton, sugarcane as well as phosphate solubilising microorganisms are used for all crops. These microbes with high count are industrially produced and used for sustainable agriculture and environmental quality.

(ii) *Microbes for Protection of Crops*: Modern day agriculture is faced with the problems of high crop loss due to increased pests that needed use of pesticides which in turn adversely affect the homeostasis of crop ecosystem. In order to address this issue, microbes that play a major role to fight pests and diseases are used. Many of the microbes have insecticidal properties such as I) bacteria like *Bacillus licheniforemis*, *Pseudomons fluorescens*. *Bacillus thuringiensis*; viruses like Nuclear Polyhedrosis Viruses (N.P.V.), Cytoplasmic Polyhedrosis Viruses (C.P.V.) and some fungi like *Aspergillus, Ochraceus,* etc. (Deacon, 1983). *Bacillus thuringiensis* (BT) is the most widely used microbial pesticide in the globe. In most countries it has risen as a big industry which has succeeded commercially. These reveal the potentialities of microbes as a means of biological control for safe and effective application in integrated pest management programmers so as to maintain environmental quality.

(iii) *Microbes for Treatment of Solid Wastes*: One of the major problems faced by mankind is disposal of solid wastes. Vast amount of solid wastes produced require safe disposal. Urban solid waste production in the United States, a single country in the globe is estimated to be about 150 million tons per year. Part of this material is inert, composed of glass; plastic and so on but the rest is decomposable solid organic waste such as kitchen scraps, paper and other garbage. In traditional operations, the most organic solid waste is composted and recycled to the land as manure fertilizer. This preparation of manure is dependent on microbial activities.

The simplest way to handle solid waste disposal at the lowest cost is in landfills wherein solid waste both organic and inorganic is deposited in low lying lands. Anaerobic and facultative microbes attack the organic compounds in the waste, that in turn forms the manure for the crops.

Composting: Compared to land filling process, composting has environmental advantages wherein fast decomposition with retension of crop nutrients in the manure is prepared (Diaz, *et al.*, 1993). Composting is accelerated by static piles (Windrows), aerated piles or continuous feed reactors. Oxygen concentration in the compost is usually five times lower than air. The composting process is initiated by mesophilic heterotrophs, as the temperature rises, these are replaced by thermophilic forms of bacteria like *Bacillus stearotheimophilus.* Important fungi which help composting are *Aspergillus fumigatus*, *Mucur pusillus,* etc. Mechanised composting is done by most developed countries and many developing countries to mitigate garbage disposal and production of quality compost for its use as soil conditioner.

(iv) *Microbes Used for Treatment of Liquid Wastes:* Mankind is faced with problems of disposing liquid waste, which needs scientific management so as to maintain environmental quality. Liquid wastes are produced everyday by human activities (domestic sewage) and by various agricultural and industrial operations, which disturbs the homeostasis of aquatic communities and cause deterioration of water quality. Liquid wastes are created by a variety of sewage treatment processes, which reduce the oxygen demand and remove nutrients, causing eutrophication. Sewage treatment involves physical removal of solid (primary treatment) wastes, biological decomposition of organic compounds (secondary treatment). Microbes like *Beggiotoa*, *Nocardia*, *Sphaerotilus, Desaltoxibrio, Zooglea, Micrococcus, Arthobacter, Bacillus, Cephalosporium, etc.* are used during primary, secondary and tertiary treatments (Hawkes, 1977). Chemical, physical or biological removal of other heavy metals, nitrogen and phosphates (tertiary treatment) and disinfection to remove pathogenic microorganisms is carried out. A variety of bioreacters are used for secondary treatment of liquid wastes. Anaerobic conditions within a bioreacter permit denitrification and removal of nitrogen compounds. Sludge collected during primary treatment is further decomposed in anaerobic digesters with the formation of a stable solid product that can be used as soil conditioner. Methane could be used as a useful byproduct. Bacteria, algae and plants can be used in tertiary treatment to remove phosphates and heavy metals. Microbes are used in sewage treatments of Trickling Filter System, Rotating Biological contactor, Submerged Aerobic Filters, Fluidized Bed reactors, Oxidation of Lagoons, activated sludge processes as well as Anaerobic Digesters.

These activities indicate the role of microbes in treatment of liquid waste to maintain water quality and form the organic manure for use in agriculture besides acting as aids in sustainable water recycling of earth.

(v) *Bioremediation*: The most challenging issue faced by present mankind is disposal of many xenobiotic compounds, which differ from natural organics, solvents, pesticides but which are resistant to biodegradation. The technology uses the microbes for removal of pollutants. For effective bioremediation, the pollutant must be subjected to microbial attack (metabolic transformations). The metabolic products must be safe and the process must not cause ecological side effects. Environmental conditions must permit into growth of the microorganism for bioremediation or the extraction of the pollutant from the environment. It can be biodegraded ex-situ in bioreactors. Bioremediation is a cost effective means to maintain environmental quality.

(vi) *Microbial Degradation of Xenobiotics*: Xenobiotics such as pesticides are toxic elements which interfere with microbial reactions of target organisms. Synthetic pesticides adversely affect the soil microflora. The microorganisms metabolise pesticides and herbicides like *Clostridium progenies* from the chemical YBHC to 1,2,3,5—tetrachlorobenzene, *Pseudomonas putida* from the chemical y-BHC to Y-BTC and a-BHC, *Proteus vulgaris* from the chemical DDT to I, I-dichloro-2-2 bis (P-chlorophenyl), ethane (TDE or DDD), *Trichoderma viride* from the chemical Malathion to dyfoxon are known. These microbes enzymatically metabolise as substrates or as electron acceptors, catabolises wherein insecticides serve as energy source or detoxify as a resistance. Further, non-enzymatic processes like photosynthetic break down, change of pH, production of organic and inorganic reactants and cofactors also contribute in biodegradation.

The insecticidal metabolism occurs through hydrolysing processes and reductive systems as well as through oxidation seeding with microorganisms called bio-augmentation is effective for the bioremediation of xenobiotic compounds with multiple chlorine constituents. Recombinant DNA technology has been used to genetically engineered bacteria with specific biodegradative metabolic capacities (JohnsoneLal 1985).

(vii) *Biodegration of Petroleum Hydrocarbons*: The uses of bioremediation are expanding. The leakage of gasoline from underground storage tanks into soils and ground water are being treated by bioremediation. Marine oil spills are treated by bioremediation involving oleophlic fertilizer EAP 22 which produces harmless CO_2 and H_2O reducing environmental damages. Bioremediation is also used for the treatment of various air pollutants. Biofilters, biotrickling filters and bioscrubbers are used to remove odour-causing compounds from the air near sewage treatment. These bioreactors have biofilms of microorganisms that remove over 99 per cent of volatile pollutants from the air. Toxic compounds such as toluene, hydrogen sulphide, chloro and nitrobenzenes can also be removed in this manner. These activities revealed the role played by microbes in remedifying the nature (Atlas, 1981).

(viii) *Microbes used as a Resource for Recovery of Metals*: The metabolic potentialities of microbes are being used in the recovery of metals from low-grade ores. *Thiobacillus* and other iron and sulphur oxidising bacteria are used in mining operations to increase the recovery of copper and uranium. Bioleaching with *Thiobacilli* and related iron oxidizing bacteria contribute significantly in commercial recovery of copper (Tuovinen, 1990). This recovery process is based on transformation of iron sulphide associated with mineral resource by microbial oxidation. The insoluble metal sulphide is transformed to water soluble metal sulphate which is lost from the mineral deposit and recovers (Tuovinen, 1990).

(ix) *Microbes for recovery of petroleum*: The metabolic ability of microbes is used to improve the recovery of petroleum from the environment. Microbially enhanced oil recovery (MEOR) contributes to improve petroleum recovery from existing old wells. Xanthan gums produced by *Xanthomonas campestris* are used as surfactants to increase the yield of petroleum from oil bearing formations. Biosurfactants are also used to release oil from tar sands (Moses and Springham, 1982).

(x) *Microbes used as biofuels*: The foremost problem faced by modem civilisation is energy, which is mostly dependent on fossil fuels. In order to address this problem, microbes can be used to produce various gaseous and liquid fuels. Many communities use gasohol as an efficient fuel. Gasohol (gasoline to ethanol 9:1) is routinely used (NRC, 1979). Similarly ethanol is produced by microbial fermentations using carbohydrate substrates largely. Brazil is successfully using ethanol produced from fermented sugarcane (Jackson, 1976). Many waste treatment plants use methane produced by methanogenic bacteria and use methane gas to generate electricity (NAS, 1977). Hydrogen production is being developed through bacteria or Cyanobacteria as a potential automotive fuel that would alleviate global warming caused due to carbon-dioxide production, use of bacteria like *Desulfovibrio gigas* (Cammack, 1995) as well as Cyanobacterium, *Anabaena variabilis* (Reddy *et al.,* 1996) are also known. These studies indicate high potentialities of microbes to accelerate economic development with stable maintenance of biosphere.

(xi) *Microbes for Production of Biomass*: One of the foremost problems faced by mankind is to supply food to its ever increasing human population so as to meet nutrition demand. Microbes play an important role. Biomass is renewable resource which could be produced using microbes for human and animal consumption as food or feed (Rose, 1979). Microbial biomass is a potentially attractive food additive because it contains a large percentage of high grade protein. Traditional uses of microbial biomass for human food are limited to yeast, mushrooms and certain algae. Expanded future of microbial biomass for human food or animal feed requires suitable and inexpensive substrates that will make the process economical and provide a nutritious product acceptable to the consumers. The use of waste materials for single-cell protein production seems attractive (Litchfield, 1979) Algae and Cyanobacteria have additional benefits to be used as single cell protein since only inorganic nutrients and sunlight are required for their production. Cyanobacterium, *Spirulinia* forms large blooms in Lake of Chad, Africa where the local population use it as traditional food or feed supplement. The historic record indicates that *Spirulinia* was traditional food of Mexico at the time of Spanish conquest (Ciferri, 1983). *Spirulina maxima* is commercially produced at Lake Texcoco, Mexico at the rate of 2 metric tons per day which contains 60-70 per cent of high grade protein. These studies indicate the use of microbial resources to supply food and feed to the ever-increasing human population.

Conclusion

These studies indicate the vast potentialities of microbes in maintaining ecological sustainability of the biosphere through biogeochemical cycles as well as fascinating and economically important areas of environment management with sustained development so as to retain its ever continuing life processes. Although some new problems have emerged due to the use of modern technology but simultaneously new microbes are being identified/developed so as to address these issues through current advances of biotechnology. It has been argued by Gaia's theory of Earth that the Earth is a living organism like us and the basis of life is the microorganisms and man cannot influence them (Syriac, 2002) The basic issues faced currently by mankind and its possible redressal through use of microbes are known but its effective realisation is challenging which are beyond the limitation of human mankind so as to maintain homeostasis in the biosphere However, human mankind could prevent further deterioration of biosphere certainly through formal and non-formal education by creation of awareness so as to allow microbes to congenially grow in nature. Thus, microbes would continue to play a very potential role in sustainable global development that supports human population, fosters economic development and maintain environmental quality in the biosphere.

Summary

Sustainable development involves economic development as well as ecological sustainability Biosphere is a complex system where innumerable lifc processes occur and human beings dwell along with inhospitable activities that emerged due to industrial development. Microbes invisibly exist in most of habitats in the biosphere. Further, microbes are endowed with diverse metabolic capabilities, which maintain different life systems in the biosphere. The article has dealt with the role of microbes in cycling of carbon, hydrogen, oxygen, nitrogen, phosphorus, sulfur, iron, manganese, calcium, and silicon in terms of maintaining ecological sustainability of the biosphere. Further, the role of microbes as resource management for agricultural sustainability, bioremediation of waste management, pollution control, recovery of metals, and potential use as bio-fuels and biomass usage as supplement of human food are discussed conceptually.

14

Role of Mass Media in Promoting Environmental Conservation and Sustainable Development

B.N. NEELIMA

Sustainable development is a form, or theory, of environmental sustainability (Dobson, 1998). Environmental sustainability is a condition in which one develops without taking away the right of the future generations to enjoy the bounties of nature. Sustainable development implies that the ecosystem can be manipulated, exploited or distributed without loss of integrity. Sustainability implies compatibility with natural resource base limitations and biospherical waste assimilation carrying capacity, requiring "bioeconomic equilibria" (Clark, 1976). This raises the use and maintenance of sufficient biodiversity to ensure the resilience of the ecosystem to provide resources for human use. Sustainable development today, is an indispensable organ of developmental policy due to the overuse of natural resources by a burgeoning population. Most of the routine natural resources are for what they dc, not for what they are (Solow, 1992). It is this perspective in the human nature that is leading to the unabated depletion of natural resources, a case for serious concern and concerted action. What is required today is understanding the instrumental value of nature as an ethical keystone for sustainability. There are limits to sustainability and it is dangerous to stretch it beyond its parameters. Michael Jacobs and David Pearce have pointed out the result of undermining the value of natural resources: "On the weak sustainability interpretation of sustainable development there is no place for the environment.... the environment is simply another form of capital" (Pearce, 1993).

Sustainable development assumes a vary important place in our life today due to the unprecedented rush for economic development set off all over. The worst affected is the natural resource base which is depleting in alarming proportions. The unabated abuse of the environment has reached preposterous levels and the extinction of the human race along with its co-inhabitants on this planet is no longer a distant possibility. The danger lies, in part, in the gradualness of environmental effects, a gradualness that lulls us into calling the unacceptable normal (Gore, 1992). The multiple tragedies of pollution of land, water and air, loss of several species of flora and fauna, loss of forest cover, fall in the level of ground water, global warming are all threatening the ultimate destruction of man's "nest". In this scenario of reckless habitat destruction, Communication could play a vital role in disseminating knowledge to the key segments in the population, who would halt this process of environmental destruction that threatens global security.

The argument for sustainable development that we maintain is that the next generation must have access to the same resource base as the previous generation. A sustainable economy should therefore serve the needs of justice. The three types of justice involved here are (Sundaram, 1993):

- Justice to people within a generation (intra-generational)
- Justice to people within generations (inter generational)
- Justice to nature.

Knowledge for Environmental Management

The environment is a very important component of economic development of a state. A state in its initial development may overuse its natural resource base in order to obtain maximum level of progress. However, long-term goals of development should not be sacrificed at the cost of immediate gains. Conserving the environment is a part and parcel of development and this fact needs to be borne in mind while embarking on any venture. Sound development policies can support sustained development strategies by protecting the environment while promoting economic growth.

The key aspects of integrating environmental conservation with development are as follows:

1. Formulating a relevant and effective policy for minimising undesirable effects of human intervention in the environment.
2. Providing a comprehensive resource base for researchers and policy makers regarding the environment.
3. Disseminating environmental knowledge from the resource base to the public and raising awareness among people regarding the environmental aspects of development.
4. Influencing public opinion in favour of optimum use of natural resources.

Most of the times, conservationists and/or development planners are faced with the problem of lack of environmental variables in a particular locale. Data on environmental variables are usually insufficient and vague. Knowledge takes time to evolve, disseminate and cause a behavioural change. It can also be lost in the hub of technological development. For example, many of the traditional practices that existed were eco-friendly have been lost over time, putting the knowledge of such traditional conservation methods in the garbage bin of time.

The Role of Communication

Communication plays a predominant role in disseminating the acquired knowledge about the environment to all those who are directly or indirectly linked to the conservation process. It plays an appreciable role in informing, persuading and motivating individuals, groups and the society into desirable patterns of environmental behaviour.

The most widely accepted interpretation of the word communication is that it is a dynamic process; a transaction that affects both the sender and the receiver; it is a personal, symbolic process requiring a shared code or code of abstractions. Other definitions suggest that communication includes all activities in which the source intentionally transmits stimuli to evoke a response. Miller and Steinberg (1975) stated:

> "We have chosen to restrict our discussion of 'communication' to intentional symbolic transactions: those in which at least one of the parties transmits a message to another with the purpose of modifying the other's behaviour (such as getting him to do or not to do something or to believe or not to believe something). By our definition, intent to communicate and intent to influence are synonymous. If there is no intent there is no message."

Schramm (1964) notes: "When we communicate we re trying to establish commonness with someone. We are trying to share information, an idea or an attitude. The essence of 'Communication' is getting the sender and the receiver tuned together for a particular message".

The main objective of communication in this regard is to communicate positive nuances about the environment and the available knowledge pertaining to it. There is need to communicate the potential hazards of faulty practices and decision making that leads to slow but sure degradation of the environment. The principal aim is to motivate people to adopt practices that are conservationist in nature and in tune with ecological harmony. Attitudinal changes towards certain practices (e.g., not using covers/bags that are non-biodegradable) need to be followed by a substantial change in behaviour. Thus the principal aim of communication is to influence behaviour. Cartwright (1949) points out a series of processes that must be initiated to bring about a behavioural change in a person:

1. Creating a particular cognitive structure.
2. Creating a particular behavioural (action) structure. In other words, behaviour is determined by the beliefs, opinions, and facts a person possesses, by the needs, goals and values he has; and by the monetary control held over his behaviour by given features of his cognitive and motivational structure. To influence behaviour from outside requires the ability to influence these determinants in a particular way.

Moore (1986) presenting a comprehensive discussion of development communication process notes that access to messages provides a basis for knowledge and socialisation and participation. Environmental communication is an extension of the development communication process, and the communication programme so designed should be in tune with the projected goals.

The main objective of environmental communication is to assist people, both citizens and decision makers, to make sound decisions on the use of natural resources. A substantial and effective communications component must be employed and carefully integrated. The people must first be aware of the problem; the problem must be relevant to heir personal aspirations and concerns; they must pursue the course of action that seems practical and worthwhile and must be willing to act. The following is a short list of objectives that effective environmental communication programmes must achieve.

1. Understanding the environment and the processes that affect it by identifying the cause of environmental degradation and the action needed to minimise it.
2. To empower people with knowledge and skills that will enable them to take responsibility to conserve and protect the environment.
3. To cause a qualitative change in pubic regulation and private decision-making.
4. Involving communities and civil society in environmental management with particular attention to publication of environmental information, the role of traditional knowledge and appropriate informal regulation by local organisations.

Planning and implementing environmental communication activities is however not a simple process, mainly due to the multi-faceted developments in communication and allied fields. The global communication atmosphere has undergone rapid transformation in the past few decades, with the new technological revolution bringing about sweeping changes in the communication scenario. The new satellite technology and Internet have opened up new vistas for communication effectively, economically and rapidly. However, communicating effectively is becoming more and more difficult today because:

1. People are already loaded with information.
2. It is not easy to link up a message with the interests and concerns of a heterogeneous mass audience, and
3. Changing deeply rooted beliefs is often impossible.

Planning for communication must take into consideration factors like educational approaches and their relative effectiveness, resource available, geographical coverage, target group to be reached, social and cultural milieu of the target population, messages to be communicated, monitoring, evaluation, etc. It is not an easy task to back upon a predestined approach to communication especially if the audience happens to be a heterogeneous group, varying in their socio-economic cultural status, attitudes and levels of knowledge. In such cases, where information needs to reach an audience spread over a wide geographical area, the mass media prove to be an effective choice. Today the mass media are an overbearing influence on the lives of people all over the world. The mass media is not only an instrument for entertainment but also has a very important educational value. The mass media can be effectively used to supplement and support the efforts for the cause of environmental education.

Need for Communication Support for Environmnetal Education

Communication media offer a tremendous potential in making people aware of their environment and the associated problems, in all walks of life. The elements of media have reached millions of people with messages concerning the environment and have helped to place environmental preservation and improvement among top national and international concerns. They are also most effective in teaching the out of school population. Media can foster environmental awareness and encourage people's participation in the conservation issues. It has the potential to create community forums on environmental issues. Media can therefore set the pace for better understanding of our environment.

"The goals of environmental education programmes on media should be to provide the learner with direct experience in the real environment, so that he may develop an awareness and appreciation of the factors and the inter-relationships operating in the environment, leading to an ecological understanding of man's oneness with his environment and how he both affects it and is affected by it. Programmes should encourage the learner to test values of society as well as his own, so that he may ultimately select those values in which he believes and which are relevant to him in dealing with the environment. He must be free to investigate and choose among them. Based on his knowledge and beliefs, the learner should be guided to make rational decisions leading to constructive action on environmental problems. Environmental education programmes should seek to develop a commitment both towards the environment and towards learning that will last beyond the years of schooling and will form life long concern" (Hawkins and Vinton, 1973).

The public broadcasting center set up in the United States in the 1970s, for the purpose of increasing environmental awareness among people states its objectives as follows:

- To respond to the national mandate, to raise the level of knowledge and understanding of the environmental status and to present viable alternatives.
- To create an innovative system of environmental education and reach large and diversified audience quickly, at the primary, secondary, higher and the continuing education levels.
- To increase perception of the environment as a totality, to communicate understanding and recognition of the parts, and to stimulate action necessary for man to move towards what he perceives to be a more desirable condition of life.

Such non-governmental organisations devoted to the cause of promoting environmental education is the need of the hour.

Mass Media and Environmental Education

An intricate web of messages and information woven by the mass media threatens to overpower the traditional learning methods, often accomplishing the task. Education is no longer a watertight compartment closed in on its integral components but is rather a fluid concept, affecting and being affected by the variegated media. The elements of media are not mere vehicles of communication; they often go one step further by conditioning thought and determining behaviour. Apart from the power of the messages they convey, media gain a tremendous momentum owing to their emotional content, informal setting, and ability to create a blend of education and entertainment, and the refreshing effect that they impart to education. While the schools have been reduced to isolated hillocks in the sea of media information, it is time to use an effective mix of both to achieve an unprecedented velocity in converting an information poor people to a more educated, aware and liberated literates. This is especially true of the developing countries, where learning through a formal education system is a luxury. The comenious concept of school as adopted today remains a closed concentration of individuals for learning in a systematic manner, often within the boundaries of a rigid syllabus and limited to the confines of the instructor's experience. The media messages in contrast, are available to anyone, anywhere, encompassing a wide range of topics and enriched by the participation of a number of resource persons. Since learning takes place everywhere, the environment and the process of learning are wedded to each other. Awareness requires education and the awareness of environmental deficiencies requires environmental education. It is a two way process, education can provide the impetus for improving the environment, and an improved environment can provide enhanced learning opportunities.

"Environmental education is an integrated process that deals with man's interrelationships with the natural and man made surroundings, including the relation of population growth, pollution, resource allocation, and depletion, conservation technology and urban and rural planning to the total human environment. Environmental education is the study of factors influencing the ecosystems, mental and physical health, living and working conditions decaying cities and population. Environmental education is intended to promote among citizens the awareness and understanding of the environment, our relationships to it, and is concerned with responsible action necessary to assure our survival to improve the quality of life" (United States Senate report on Environmental Education Act).

The doomsday ecologists point out that overpopulation, vanishing wildlife, overgrazed ranges turning to deserts, forests to barren lands, erosion, pollution and a host of other issues, only point to the impending disaster that we have triggered off. It is awareness, reason and rational action that offer a viable alternative to the continued misuse of the environment—a case for environmental education. The solution to the above issues surely rests with the welfare governments in each state, which must implement the national environmental policy with more vigour. But the government ultimately depends upon aware citizens to indicate the direction and implementation of public policy. Environmental protection has not yet received due attention from citizens and a public policy on it will only be implemented successfully if the citizens take up the issue in all its intensity. The solution to the present day environmental problems does not lie with the government or with the scientists, but with a well-educated citizenry. It is only an aware citizenry who can play a vital role in environmental preservation. The immediate issue is to replace short-term attitudes to environment, which see it as a commodity to be exploited, with attitudes that look to sustainable, rather than maximal level of progress and development. The route to these long-term attitudes invariably lies with education. Environmental education must encourage people to aim their activities at improving the environment.

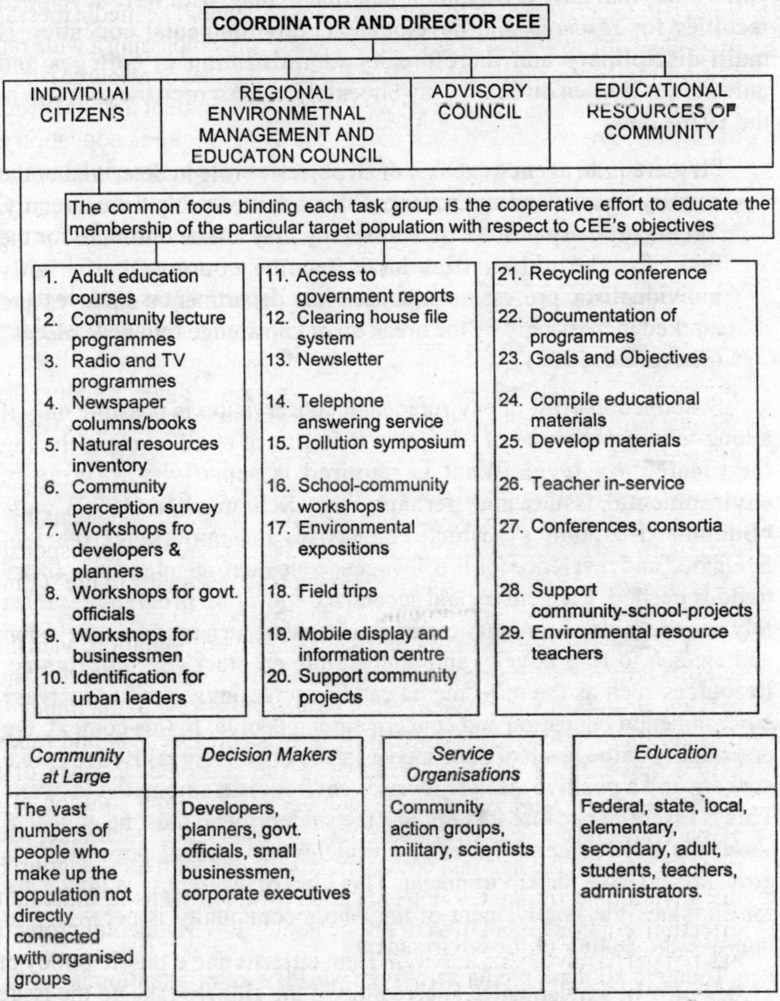

Fig. 14.1: Centre For Environmental Education Model

The two very important reasons for involving members in a community in environmental education programme is because many of the adults in a community are involved in making decisions involving the environment and also the students have to be taught about the importance of conserving the environment. The following model (Gessel, 1976) presents a hypothetical situation of a Centre for Environmental Education (CEE) that can be implemented in most of the regions.

With regard to education of the community, it is the colleges and the universities that have a very important role to play, with well-developed faculties for research and development. Environmental education is multi-disciplinary and therefore its administration in colleges and universities is often difficult. Clay Shoenfeld underscored the problem in the 1970s thus:

> "If there is an agency capable of an objective role in determining the country's basic land and water problems, it is possibly the university. Yet the ordinary posture of a university may not be optimum for the task, for the universities have become composed of highly individualistic professors organised into departmental enclaves and marked increasingly by the break up of knowledge into little pieces" (Shoenfeld, 1971).

Sustained interest in environmental conservation is possible only if a long-term programme of education is instituted at all levels including the elementary level. What is required is sensitivity training in environmental issues and perhaps what Schumacher (1973) calls "Buddhist Economics", which emphasises the importance of right livelihood and reverence for life. In higher education, an inter-disciplinary trend is needed. Elementary and secondary education programmes must rely on other aids of communication and teaching such as radio, television and cinema to ring novelty and interest into an otherwise dull routine. Resources such as the mass media can be increasingly used to increase environmental education and concern among people. In this context, the potentiality of the reach of mass media can be effectively utilised to evoke concern and a positive attitude towards environment among the viewers. This is essential because it is not just the students who must be educated about the environment. We cannot wait for our student population to grow up and save the environment. This kind of awareness is important for all, since the involvement of the whole community is necessary to improve the quality of the environment.

Today in all mass media across the world, a lot of attention is being paid to issues of sustainable development. Ecological degeneration, population growth, faulty development issues that harm the environment, use of renewable and non-renewable resources, energy consumption by the burgeoning population, all are being dealt with extensively. An important constraint in media reporting of issues of sustainable development is that they deal with the matters in a regional perspective.

Regional issues in environmental degradation receive prime importance, relegating the more comprehensive national issues into the background. The media must understand that environmental issues don't respect regional boundaries. In fact, most of the issues have an international implication. Also there is no specialisation in environmental affairs in the media. Specialised reporters with an in-depth knowledge of environmental issues are lacking in most media. Also the coverage of sustainable development issues is pushed back by issues of political importance in most of the developing countries, where political instability still remains a leading national issue. The purpose of media support to environmental conservation is thus lost in this myriad sea of uncertainty.

Environmental journalism is still in its infancy in most countries. The media still have a lack luster interest in environmental issues in comparison to its coverage of stories of human interest. There has also been no consistent effort made by any major newspaper so far to adopt and pursue an environmental campaign. Environment reporters lack the necessary training and background to write more responsible and informative stories. Those with a skill for such reporting do not get a chance to develop as the environmental beat is only transitory and after a while they are allotted another beat. Therefore most of the environmental affairs covered by the print media are rather piece meal of a more comprehensive situation.

Most of the environmental issues in India that have received wide media coverage are offshoots of industrial, commercial or political operations. People's movements for conserving the environment have a proud place of success in India due to the involvement of numerous NGOs and environmental activists in the movement and the increasing media coverage available thereon. This has been the case from the Chipko in the Himalayas to Apiko, Narmada Bachao Andolan over the construction of the Sardar Sarovar Dam, and the Silent Valley in Kerala. The debate over the Narmada Bachao Andolan received wide coverage by the press and the electronic media due to excessive political involvement. Those issues of environmental conservation that do not involve much political involvement are not vehemently pursued or analysed by the media. Particularly the print media pay a very little attention to issues of sustainable development. Lack of specialised correspondents in dealing with environmental issues also leads to ignoring of regional environmental issues. Those issues that do catch the attention of the media are frequently such that involve immediate conflict between states or involves a judicial decision. Media in most of the developing countries tend to highlight conflict over cooperation in environmental issues. Public curiosity and knowledge of environmental issues is rather limited in developing countries as media often tends to belittle issues by playing them down in the light of the more important issues of conflict and human interest. As a result, the public remain uninterested, uninformed and non-reactive.

Policy Implications

To bring about a change in the present situation of dismal environmental reporting, the following measures can be adopted:

1. Developing and supporting organisations that are dedicated to promoting environmental awareness in the country through effective media coverage of issues.
2. Such organisations need to train journalists in environmental reporting as a specialised part of development journalism.
3. Establishing specialised environmental reporting agencies that will turn out environmental reports and supply the same to dailies.
4. A special issue on environment or an environment page needs to be included in the major dailies.
5. Environmental cartoons also can be included as a daily feature.
6. A number of television talk shows, quiz programmes, discussions on major environmental issues affecting various regions of the country and the world need to be introduced.

15

Ecological Concerns and Environment-friendly Agriculture

SHIVADHAR SINGH

About ten thousand years ago when the agricultural revolution began with the domestication of animals and crop plants, it was mainly aimed to support the life of people who were dependent on hunting of animals in the past. Once discovered, agriculture spread rapidly because it provided a larger and more stable food supply than did hunting and gathering. Agriculture thus supported ten to hundred times more people per unit land area than hunting. It led to increase in human population and finally required people to settle in permanent village rather than continue the nomadic and scattered life they had in the past (Singh, 2001).

The agriculture in the past was totally practised for the sustenance, not for economic gain. It was basically dependent on the use of organic matter in the form of manures and recycled in the fields from where produced, thus it never posed any kind of environmental problem or destruction. Along with crop plants, people also reared different kinds of domestic animals which provided them not only various animal foods such as milk, meat, eggs but also power for operating various farm activities such as ploughing and tillage of lands, threshing of crops, lifting of water from well, chaffing of fodder and transport of farm goods. Thus cultivation of various crop species, forestry and rearing of domestic animals at farm had led to the integrated farming system which provided almost all kind of crop and animal foods to the people and animal power to drive various farm activities without causing any damage to the environment. Our traditional agriculture was highly safe, scientific and sustainable as it was based on environmental sustainability and safety rather than economic growth and productivity. Such environment-friendly agriculture continued for several thousand years since its inception, and the agricultural produce was mainly consumed by the people who lived there in the villages. Long ago when almost all the people and their domestic animals who lived in the villages consumed all the agricultural produce whatever produced at their cultivated lands, thus organic wastes were being recycled in crop fields. Hence whatever nutrients required by the plants for their production were absorbed and again returned to the same fields following their decomposition in the form of organic manures. Our traditional system of agriculture was based on the organic manures and thus never led to the problem of environmental pollution or degradation as the nutrients supplied to the crops in the form of organic manures were produced naturally. At the beginning of agriculture whole land was covered with the forest and wild lives. Men started agriculture only by clearing the forest and used the land for cultivation of crops and animals which they domesticated over the period. Earlier agriculture was generally extensive in nature, but to increase the food production for gradually increasing human population, men converted more and more forest area into agricultural lands, thus demographic increase in human population was directly associated with the extent of deforestation. The traditional agriculture which flourished continuously until middle of 20th century (before industrial era) was totally based on organic source of farm inputs such as manures, biopesticides, etc. Though the productivity of traditional agriculture was low and unstable, but it was highly sustainable, that is why the old methods of agriculture could last for about ten thousand years without posing any threat to our environment. Our traditional agriculture though was highly sustainable from the view point of environment, but due to its heavy dependence on nature, crops used to suffer frequently from natural calamities such as drought, floods, disease and pests attack, which led to the victimisation of people and animals, depended on crop production. In fact various natural calamities helped in controlling the human and animal population in the man-made agro-ecosystem. With the development in human civilisation and technological advancement in almost all spheres over time, especially the medical facilities and greater food production resulting from the production and consumption of chemical fertilisers and development of irrigation facilities, helped supporting the lives of large number of human populations through reducing their death rate. Even after the use of chemical fertilisers and irrigation facilities, the agricultural production could not be increased significantly until the development of modern semi-tall high yielding cultivars of cereals especially wheat and rice (late 60s of 20th century), as the crop cultivars used in the past (before green revolution) were tall and lodging susceptible which did not show any response to better crop management especially nitrogenous fertilisers (Swaminathan, 1996). Thus the agriculture before green revolution was extensive as the productivity per unit land area could not be improved even through better crop management and thus the food demand of growing population was met through expanding the arable land by deforestation. Such agricultural system designated as low input sustainable agriculture (LISA) was most prevalent every where and is still followed in many areas except some states which have adopted and developed productivity technology of green revolution (Punjab, Haryana, West U.P., and some parts of Tamil Nadu and A.P.).

With the advent of green revolution, which was mainly attributed to gene revolution (transformation of traditional tall lodging susceptible cultivars into semi tall lodging tolerant ones) especially in wheat, rice, sorghum and pearl millet, and simultaneous development of irrigation facilities and increase in production and availability of chemical fertilizers and pesticides, the crop production (wheat and rice) enhanced significantly in the north and southern parts of India, which led to greater availability of food grains and thus helped increasing human population. Initially, when the improved semi tall high yielding wheat and rice cultivars responded to heavy dose of chemical fertilizers and synthetic pesticides, farmers and even the government emphasised to increase the production of food grains through increasing their productivity by using chemical fertilizers and pesticides without considering their negative environmental impact, because at that time economic growth and benefit to the farmers were only taken into consideration. Thus our traditional integrated farming system based on low input sustainable agriculture lasting for several thousand years without posing any severe environmental problems was mainly attributed to the integration of several crop species alogwith domestic farm animals, production technologies, nutrient water and pest management, has been turned into intensive agro-chemical based over resource exploitation and high input unsustainable agriculture (Swaminathan, 1996). The green revolution which is presently designated as greed revolution has finally led to several environmental problems such as soil erosion, soil, water and air pollution, depletion of ground water, salinization and massive loss of biodiversity which in turn may devastate the agro-ecosystem in the quest of mismatched development. Finally our chemical input based intensive agriculture which caused several environmental problems mainly resulted from excessive, unscientific and imbalanced use of agro-chemicals and abuse of land, ground water and forest. The productivity improvement technologies associated with green revolution which helped in catering the food demand of global population and saved the hues areas of forest from denudation is thus best described as forest saving agriculture on positive side, but on negative side the improper use of chemical fertilizers and pesticides is worsening the quality of foods and river and ground waters. Agriculture thus brings both favourable and unfavourable consequences to mankind and to the natural environments.

Recently, when our environment is said to be on the verge of devastation, emphasis is now being given to harmonise agriculture more with the natural ecosystem. This trend probably derives from the people's realisation that too much economic efficiency oriented agriculture has caused massive deterioration of biosphere and both natural and agro-ecosystem. Reflecting on excessive use of chemicals fertilizers and pesticides, people are now stressing the introduction of low input sustainable agriculture (LISA) which is in the harmony and friendly with our environment, and could sustain the life for ever without posing any environmental cost (Udagawa, 1991). Now people are proposing several kinds of environmental based agriculture, viz., environment-friendly agriculture or eco-friendly agriculture, ecological farming or organic farming, low input sustainable agriculture and integrated intensive farming system, etc. By and large all these farming or agriculture systems convey similar meanings and feelings of agriculture without environmental cost or deterioration which is based on environmental sustainability rather than economic growth and efficiency (Dahama, 1994). In simple words agriculture is to be in harmony with the environment to ensure ecological balance in the nature. But truly speaking the exploding human population has been responsible for all kinds of environmental and social degradation, as most of the developmental processes are driven to meet their nutritional and social requirements. Perhaps the best solution to overcome the environmental problems led by agriculture is to control the growth of undesirable human population, which is indeed easier to do than to boost the food production further. Decline in population will automatically turn the chemical input based agriculture into echo-friendly agriculture.

Environmental Cost of Modern Intensive Agriculture

With the advent of green revolution, which was mainly aimed to increase food production through enhancing the crop productivity, farmers all over the world, especially in developed countries and in some parts of developing countries like India (Punjab, Haryana) have almost abandoned traditional means of low input sustainable agriculture which was based on organic and integrated farming systems, and adopted the monoculture specialised and high chemical input unsustainable agriculture, that finally led to severe environmental damage and degradation (Singh, 1996;

Dahama, 1999). The chemical input intensive agriculture became profound since the development of semi tall high yielding varieties of wheat, rice, sorghum, pearl millet, etc., which unlike traditional tall cultivars showed greater response to chemical fertilizers and pesticides, and enhanced the global food production through their greater productivity under high input management. If the yield improvement associated with green revolution in wheat, rice and other crops had not taken place in India, we would have required another 70 million hectares agricultural land mainly converted from forest to produce the same we now to harvest (Swaminathan, 1996). Thus, the productivity oriented intensive agriculture could be best described as forest land saving agriculture which is a positive aspect of green revolution, for which it must be appreciated. But at the same time the excessive, unscientific and imbalanced use of agro-chemicals and over exploitation of natural resources, i.e., soil, surface and ground water, and crop and animal diversity for higher crop and animal production has led to ecological imbalance and environmental problems for which it must be abused as well.

As a consequence of adoption of high yielding varieties and hybrids of crops and animal, and production technologies (chemical fertilizers and pesticides) by the farmers, the agricultural production (food grain, vegetables, fruits, milk and egg) of our country and the world has enhanced remarkably. The total food grain production of India has increased from 50 million tons in 1950 to the level of 205 million tons in year 2000. The production of wheat alone has increased from 6 million tons at the time of independence to 75 million tons today (12 folds increase) which has mainly resulted from the chemical based intensive agriculture (Singh, 1995; Swaminathan, 1996). Despite spectacular increase in food grain production, there is a growing concern about the global environment among the agricultural scientists, environmentalists and politicians as well, and it has been felt all over the world that such environmental destructive chemical based agriculture should be discouraged and prohibited. Recently the National Academy of Sciences of USA published a report on agriculture, which has strongly recommended the adoption of organic based low input integrated farming system, as the modern high input intensive agriculture has caused several environmental problems such as (I) environmental pollution because it advocates extensive use of synthetic chemical fertilizers, pesticides and other agro-chemicals, (II) the agricultural products from this chemical farming are not safe for human consumption and (III) the chemical based farming is not safe in the long run and is not sustainable as it does not provide environmental safety (Singh *et al.*, 1994). Some of the negative impacts of chemical based intensive farming are briefly discussed here.

Soil Degradation

In our traditional agriculture, lot of organic manures are used to maintain and enrich the soil fertility. The organic matters following their microbial decomposition not only provide the nutrients to crop plants for their growth, but also supply basic food materials to soil microorganism and thus improve the physical properties of soils such as water infiltration, cation exchange capacity, water holding capacity, etc. which directly and indirectly improve the soil health and finally impart sustainability to the crop production (Singh, 2001). Since the advent of green revolution which is basically dependent on the use of agro-chemicals, frequent irrigation and farm mechanisation for rapid and higher crop productivity, the use of organic and green manures has been depleted due to decline in farm animal population, and burning of organic residues in the fields. Excessive, imbalanced and indiscriminate use of chemical fertilizers and pesticides, frequent irrigation of fields with ground water and river canal contaminated with industrial effluents have been responsible for deterioration of soil health (Dahama, 1994). Million of soil biota including arthropods, mites, fungi, bacteria, nematodes inhabit the soil and keep it an alive media for agricultural purpose through biological nitrogen fixation, solubilising fixed soil phosphorus and help in decomposition of organic matters into plant nutrients and organic colloids (humus) have been severely destroyed by excessive use of agro-chemicals, which in turn depleted the fertility and productivity of arable lands (Singh *et al.*, 1994; Singh, 1995; Singh, 2001). Thus unscientific and imbalanced use of chemical fertilizers and pesticides, tendency of farmers to abandon the use of various forms of organic manures and canal irrigation have led to soil degradation in form of soil acidification, salinisation, accumulation of heavy metals and deficit in essential macro and micro nutrients in large area of intensive crop cultivation (Singh, 2001). Inadequate replenishment of plant nutrients over the years has resulted in nutrient imbalance in the soil which impaired the applied nutrient utilisation efficiency and finally reduced the farmers' income. Chemical based intensive agriculture also induced soil erosion through the process of soil disintegration, which is easily broken and carried out by water and wind forces. On the other hand, the use of organic manures in our traditional farming helped in the binding of soil particles and thus was responsible for soil aggregation and conservation. An annual global loss of fertile crop land due to soil degradation is estimated to be 6-7 million hectares every year (FAO). In India alone about 60-70 per cent area of arable land (mainly in green revolution belt) suffers from soil erosion, salinisation and water logging problems (Singh *et al*, 1994). Based on the experiments in USA and other parts, it has been proved that the magnitude of top soil erosion from chemicaly fertilized fields was significantly more than those of fields fertilized with organic manures. China is perhaps the only country in the world which is leading towards high crop productivity with sustainability because agriculture in China is based on the integration of both indigenous organic and modern chemical farming system. It could be a leader and model nation for global sustainable agriculture.

Water and Air Pollution

Apart from soil contamination and degradation, the other environmental components namely water and air have also been contaminated and polluted severely by the excessive and unscientific use of chemical fertilizers and pesticides. Frequent irrigation of crops near the cities using municipal sewage water and crops irrigated with polluted water of river or reservoir causes ground water contamination. Use of municipal and industrial effluents contaminated with heavy metals and other toxic substances in the crops also pollute the water bodies such as river, ponds, ground water and finally the sea and ocean. Excessive use of dairy waste, farm yard manures and compost produced from imported cattle feeds also causes soil and water pollution in the countries like Japan and Netherlands (Udagawa, 1991). Application of excessive dose of heavy metal and non-heavy metal containing pesticides such as Agro son, Ceresin, Mercuric chloride, Cuprastar, Phytolon, BHC, DDT, Aldine, etc. in the crops especially in vegetables and cereals have contributed to water and air pollution significantly (Dahama, 1994). A substantial amount of nitrogen from the nitrogenous fertilizers could escape to the atmosphere as ammonia through volatilisation from soil surface, nitrous oxide or elemental nitrogen through denitrification and eventually as nitrate by leaching in the ground water (Singh, 2001). Thus, crops such as cotton, tobacco, sugarcane, plantation crops, and vegetables which require high dose and frequent application of nitrogenous fertilizers and synthetic pesticides are more responsible for water and air pollution. Due to high cost of phosphatic fertilizers, farmers generally apply higher dose of comparatively cheaper and easily available nitrogenous fertilizer, Urea, which in the deficiency of P and K is not utilised properly by the crops and is finally leached out to the ground water as nitrate nitrogen (a chemical water pollutant). Studies conducted in U.K., Germany, Japan, and Punjab (India) showed that most of drinking water supplied to the inhabitants is contaminated with NO_3 beyond permissible level which is harmful for health, especially children (Singh *et al.*, 1994). Except green revolution belts of India, where the consumption rate of chemical fertilizers is beyond 150kg/ha, other parts of our country in fact do not have the problem of ground water pollution with NO_3 nitrogen.

Green House Effect: Intensive agriculture is also responsible indirectly for green house effects, as lot of green house gases such as CO_2, CH_4 and N_2O are produced during various activities of intensive agriculture (Udagawa, 1991b). Intensive agriculture which improves the biomass production and crop productivity would certainly enhance the emission of green house gases, including carbon dioxide, methane and nitrous oxide. In particular, it is estimated that roughly half of anthropogenic methane emission comes from farming activities such as organic manuring, flooding of paddy fields, etc. Similarly a substantial amount of carbon dioxide is emitted from various agricultural activities including manuring, fertilization, biomass burning and its decomposition especially in the highly farm mechanised areas where most of the crop stubble and residues are burnt and buried. Crop fertilization with high dose of nitrogen leads to emission of nitrous oxide during the process of nitrification in wheat and upland crops, and during denitrificaton process in irrigated rice fields. About 30 per cent of anthropogenic methane is emitted from paddy fields, and 20 per cent from ruminant animals. The methane emission from these agricultural sources is greater than that from industrial sources. Thus, the intensive agriculture characterised by high level of chemical fertilization, frequent irrigation and mechanisation could possibly enhance the rate of green house gas emission especially CO_2, CH_4 and N_2O from agricultural sources and thus increase their level in the atmosphere, which in turn may contribute significantly to the global warming through green house effects (Udagawa, 1991b).

Ground Water Depletion

Intensive agriculture in various parts of the country especially where the crop are irrigated frequently by the ground water has created the severe problem of ground water depletion. Due to excessive use of ground water for crop irrigation especially in the areas of moderate and low rainfall, the water tables have gone down as the lifted amount of water is gradually increasing with low recharging capacity of ground water (Singh, 2001). Mismatch cropping during off season, particularly cultivation of rice during summer in several parts of India, has created a big problem of water scarcity in those areas. The water table of some places has gone down very much and people from those areas are unable to lift water due to lack of deep bored pumps and are finally migrating to other areas. Due to low rainfall and poor soil conservation practices, recharging of ground water has been depleted on one hand, and lifting of ground water for irrigation of crops on the other hand have finally led to the problem of ground water depletion which could be rectified only by preventing the excessive use of ground water and better watershed management in those areas. Thus, afforestation of such areas with better soil conservation practices and discouraging the mismatch cropping and over exploitation of ground water could possibly be helpful in restoring the ground water level.

Biotic-Environment Contamination

Excessive and imbalanced use of agro-chemicals such as chemical fertilizers, synthetic pesticides and growth regulators and cattle feed additives in green and white revolutions areas have not only contaminated the physical environmental components namely water, soil and air, but also the biotic components such as crops, farm animals, birds, fishes and finally the human beings through various food chain integrity. Nitrate nitrogen from chemical nitrogenous fertilizers and several harmful pesticide residues beyond the requirement of crops move to soils and various water bodies, e.g., ground water, ponds, river, reservoir and sea. The amount of agro-chemicals absorbed by the crop plants persist in the grains, seeds, roots, tubers, fruits, leaves, straw, fodder, concentrate and cakes, which finally contaminate the various consumers such as domestic and non-domestic animals (cattle, buffaloes, dogs, horse, camel, fouls, fishes, birds, scavengers and finally the human beings) directly and indirectly through diverse food chains and food webs exist in our agro-ecosystem (Dahama, 1999). Such chemical contamination for longer time may lead to several health problems among the consumers at various trophic levels. Thus, the modern intensive agriculture based on chemical inputs and economic growth efficiency has finally led to the chemical pollution of both abiotic and biotic environmental components which is a severe indication of distress of life on this beautiful and bountiful space ship, the Earth planet.

Increased Incidence of Disease and Insect Pests

High chemical input, intensive agriculture though has enhanced crop productivity and production to a great extent, but the same especially high N fertilization has also intensified the crop vulnerability and susceptibility to disease and insect pests. Application of higher dose of nitrogen enhances the foliage and vegetative growth of crops, which, in turn, causes greater humidity in crop canopy and succulence in plant tissues and finally leads to severe incidence of disease and insect pests. Thus in order to control such pest attack, farmers use the synthetic chemical pesticides frequently, which protect the crop at the cost of agro-ecosystem. Monoculture on large scale with limited number of high yielding crop cultivars, having almost common pedigrees have caused genetic vulnerability and finally led to severe crop damage by insects and pathogens (Singh, 1995). Substantial use of chemical N fertilizers, pesticides and monoculture interactively have contributed to the emergence of more virulent biotypes and races of the prevalent insects and pathogens and of new insect pest and disease emergence. There are several examples of insect pest and disease outbreak such as Brown plant hopper, Green leaf hopper, Sheath blight, Tungro virus, Grassy stunt disease of rice which once upon a time were endemic and sporadic, have now become epidemic and causing severe damage to the rice crop regularly (Singh, 1995).

Loss of Biodiversity

Chemical input driven modern agriculture which is based on economic growth rather than ecosystem has been responsible for the massive loss of biodiversity on the Earth planet. Excess dose of agro-chemical application as fertilizers and pesticides, mechanisation, monoculture, and adoption of limited number of high yielding crop varieties and hybrids, poor crop and farm-animal diversification under modern intensive agriculture have all together led to the massive genetic and species erosion or loss of precious crop and non-crop plants and animal species from their natural habitats and thus are responsible for disintegration of agro-ecosystem which is indispensable for sustaining the life on the Earth (Singh, 1995; Swaminathan, 1996). Several traditional precious crop and animal genetic resources including cereals, pulses, oilseeds, vegetables, fruits, fibres, fodder, medicinal plants; cattle, buffaloes, goats, camels, sheeps; and microorganism which directly and indirectly not only provide us foods, health, taste, job security but also impart environmental security and finally the life security through their various usefulness and participation in the build up of our ecosystem are presently said to be threatened by the anthropogenic activities associated with the modern chemical input agriculture (Babu *et al.*, 1993; Dahama, 1999). Thus modern agriculture in the name of development has devastated our environment through loss of biodiversity. Massive depletion in the population of several indigenous cattle and goat and fowl breeds, a potential scavenging bird, vulture, several organic matter decomposers (soil biota) and aromatic and scented traditional rice and other crops land races especially minor millets and amaranthus and several kinds of indigenous vegetables especially gourds, and fruit and medicinal plants species have been the recent examples of massive loss of biodiversity, which must be conserved on the farms through their judicious use and improving their productivity.

Reduced Crop and Animal Diversification

In the quest of more food production and farm income, the farmers have now shifted from their integrated farming and cropping system to specialised or mono-farming and mono-culture, which are not based on the integrated use of crops and livestocks for various foods and energy. The integrated farming and cropping system was based on the principles of agro-ecosystem management through the use of various farm products for foods, fodder, fiber, fuel and manures to meet the nutritional requirement of crops, farm animals and human beings dependent on agriculture without any competition. The integrated farming and cropping systems adopted in our traditional agriculture provided greater opportunity of cultivating several kinds of crops, viz., cereals, pulses, oilseeds, fodder, fibers, fruits, vegetables and rearing various livestocks on the farm to cater to the food, nutritional and energy demands through various sources, which reduced their dependency on one or two crops and animals as well as risk of loss due to natural calamities. However the present agriculture based on limited number of crops and animals and their few varieties have reduced crop and animal diversification which may be highly prone to the natural calamities such as drought, floods, cyclones, and disease and insect outbreaks. Farm mechanisation, ensured irrigation and easy availability of chemical fertilizers and pesticides have in fact accelerated and promoted the modern mono-culture and specialised agriculture. Thus, modern intensive agriculture which reduced crop and animal diversification is not at all a good sign for sustainable agriculture as this is highly dependent on synthetic chemical farm inputs and invites greater risk to the growers under adverse climatic and epidemic conditions.

Poor Food Quality

Another negative impact of high productivity agriculture has been noticed in terms of poor food quality. Adoption of high yielding crop varieties and hybrids of crops and animals with intensive chemical inputs, i.e., chemical fertilizers, pesticides and other synthetic agro-chemicals for higher production of food grain, oilseeds, vegetables, fruits, spices, fibres, milk, meat, eggs, etc. to meet the demand of ever increasing human population have led to the depletion in the quality of various farm produce in term of their hygiene, taste and nutritive values. The productivity and production of various agricultural products have increased substantially at the cost of environmental safety and food quality. The taste and quality of various foods derived from our traditional varieties of different crops (cereals, pulses, oilseeds, vegetables and fruits) and breeds of farm animals (cow, buffaloes, goats, fowls) were much better than the food products of modern high yielding crop and animal varieties/hybrids, although their productivity was certainly low. Indeed, whatever breakthroughs have been made in terms of higher crop and animal productivity through green and white revolutions they have always been at the cost of their safety and quality.

How Safe, Scientific and Sustainable was our Traditional Agriculture

Our centuries old traditional agriculture was much safer, scientific and sustainable than our so called modern intensive agriculture, as our traditional agriculture was based on the principles of integration, cooperation and non-competition between different kinds of crops and animals on the farms. The integration between crops and animals, and between different crop and different animal species was so strong and harmonious that food and energy requirement of diverse kinds of farm animals and human beings were met from different crop species grown without any competition. The various crop species were grown in the integrated ways not only to provide varieties of food materials such as cereals, millets, pulses, oilseeds, fodders, fibers, vegetables, fruits, etc. to the human beings, but were also responsible for meeting the feeds and fodder requirements of milk, meat, eggs and energy imparting animals (cattle, buffaloes, goats, camel, sheep, fowls etc.). The combination of crops and animals on farm provided an opportunity to use the animal power to drive the various farm operations such as ploughing, irrigation, threshing and transportation, etc. by feeding them straw, green fodder, concentrates, cakes and other crop by-products, which are not utilised by the human beings. Thus both the human beings who consume the economic portion of crops such as grains, seeds, leaf, fruits, and the animals who consume the non edible parts by human beings i.e., straw, fodder, cakes, etc., live together without any competition for food, and meet the requirement of each other. Various crop combinations and their integration through mixed, inter, multistoried cropping and crop rotation system involving legumes as a crop and green manures not only provide varieties of crops to meet human requirements, but also enrich the soil fertility through biological nitrogen fixation (Singh *et al*., 1994; Dahama, 1999). The straw, grain and cakes consumed by different farm animals and human beings are converted into excreta after digestion and finally converted into nutrients in the form of organic manures by decomposers (micro-organism) in the soils. The integrated farming system adopted by the traditional agriculturists has been responsible for the sustainability of agriculture since thousands of years because it was based on the principles of ecosystem management and integration of various crops, animals and human beings without competing each other for food, shelter and energy. Thus, the basic requirement of each biotic component in an agro-ecosystem was met by each other without posing any environmental problem. Another scientific basis of sustainability of our traditional agriculture was in-situ or on-site recycling of organic waste which enables the crop to grow without any nutrient deficiency as almost all the forms of foods, fibre and fodder were finally decomposed by the micro-organism in the agricultural fields and subsequently supply nutrients to the crops grown over there in the fields. Thus, our traditional agriculture was more safe because it did not cause any environmental damage, more scientific because it improved the soil fertility by improving their physical and chemical properties, and more sustainable because it was based on ecosystem management and integration of different crop and animal species without any competition.

Basic Concepts of Environment-friendly Agriculture

The basic concepts of environment-friendly agriculture which is more or less also designated as eco-friendly agriculture, ecological farming, organic farming, sustainable agriculture, low input sustainable agriculture and integrated intensive farming system is rooted/based on the principles of optimum crop and animal productivity and production without environmental degradation or deterioration. All the proposed farming systems may be slightly differing in their definition, philosophy and concepts but all of them convey almost similar meaning and feelings of "agriculture in harmony with surrounding environments" and consider the agriculture production site as an agro ecosystem, not the agro-industry and based on environmental sustainability rather than economic growth efficiency (Sheriff and Menon, 1994; Swaminathan, 1996; Dahama, 1999). The environment-friendly or eco-friendly agriculture does not allow any anthropogenic agricultural activities beyond the limit of ecological threshold, thus it is mainly aimed to achieve optimum agricultural production without posing any severe problem to our environment. This objective could possibly be acquired by blending or synergising the ecological prudence and technologies (ecotechnologies) of the past with the best in frontier technologies, particularly biotechnology, information technology, space technology, renewable energy technologies and management technologies (Swaminathan, 1996). Our old traditional agriculture was based on organic farming systems which manifested in low crop and anima! productivity but high environmental sustainability because it was dependent on the use of organic inputs evolved naturally at the farm, and animal power and waste to operate various farm activities and maintaining soil fertility and ecological balance. Due to green and white revolution, the traditional concepts of organic farming has turned into chemical inputs and mechanisation based agriculture to enhance the crop and animal food production to meet the food and energy demand of exploding human population.

Recently, emphasis has been given to the significance of harmonising agriculture more with agro-environment. This trend probably derives from the realisation of people that green revolution associated productivity technology based on economic growth, chemical inputs and over exploitation of natural resources has led to deterioration or pollution of natural environments (Udagawa, 1991). Reflecting on excessive, unscientific and imbalanced dose use of chemical inputs, agricultural scientists, environmentalists and policy makers are now advocating the introduction of low input sustainable agriculture, ecological farming, eco-friendly agriculture and integrated intensive farming system, which is mainly based on the principles of integration of both organic and inorganic farming systems so as to acquire the target of agricultural production without causing severe environmental problems. Presently we neither totally adopt the true organic farming system as it is not at all possible to arrange the required dose of organic manures (15-20 tons/ha/year) and biopesticides for whole cultivated lands, nor totally abandon the use of chemical inputs. Those who advocate going back to the old methods of farming ignore the fact that just a century ago when the population of undivided India was 281 million, famine claimed 30 million lives between 1870-1900 (Swaminathan, 1996). The famine eradication strategy and achieving self-sufficiency in food production are the most important and significant achievement of post-independent India (Honorable president of India). The first and foremost need of eco-friendly agriculture is to change the mindset of the growers from economic growth efficiency to environmental safety as well. Thus the requirement of a low input sustainable or environment-friendly agriculture is presently being advocated to maintain the soil health and ecological balance, keeping the environment clean and safe and providing stability to the food production level without polluting our environments (soil, water and air) (Swaminathan, 1996; Udagawa, 1991; Dahama, 1999). The basic concept of environment-friendly agriculture lies between modern chemical and mechanical inputs, and organic biological inputs; in other words it is the blending of both old and new methods and techniques of agriculture in order to complement the effects of each other for ensuring optimum agricultural productivity and environmental safety. In this system, the crop animal productivity may reduce as the results of impaired inputs of fertilizers and pesticides and use of heavy machines in agriculture, but the extent of reduction in yield could be overcome by reducing the cost of production, which will be greater than decrease in farm income. Consequently, a positive and balanced outcome may be attained (Udagawa, 1991). Dr. Norman E. Borlaug, the Nobel Laureate agricultural scientist has been advocating the judicious balanced use of chemical fertilizers, pesticides, mechanisation and new frontiers of agricultural research to enhance the food production for ever increasing population, but at the same time he emphasizes the necessity of organic farming which can offset the negative impact of intensive agriculture. In real perspective, environment-friendly agriculture is a new approach of farming system highly based on the ancient arts of Indian and Asian agricultural practices which is relevant even in this modern era of chemical and mechanical dominated agriculture. The philosophy of eco-friendly agriculture is based on judicious and scientific use of natural-biological processes and resources for not only immediate gain but for their conservation for posterity as well so as to enable the agriculture to support and sustain life on the earth (Shroff and Menon, 1994). Thus eco-friendly or environment-friendly agriculture may be defined as under

Environment-friendly agriculture which is also known as eco-friendly agriculture may be defined as the agricultural production system which avoids the excessive, unscientific and imbalanced use of synthetic chemical fertilizers, pesticides, growth regulators and livestock feed additives; and to the maximum extent this systems rely upon the use of natural resources such as organic manures, crop residues, green manures, biofertilizers, animal waste, farm yard manures, compost, legume based crop rotation, natural mineral bearing rocks, biopesticides, and mechanical cultivation, integrated cropping and farming systems and judicious exploitation of natural input resources to maintain soil fertility and productivity, to manage the crop pest and to meet the domestic and non-domestic food, shelter and commercial requirement in various forms such as cereals, millets, pulses, oilseeds, vegetables, fruits, fibers, fodder, milk, meat, eggs, etc. without posing severe environmental problems. The eco-friendly agriculture is primarily based on the principles of integration and non-competitive cooperation between crops and livestock resources, and their diversification for nutrition and energy, and minimise the use of agrochemical and maximise the use of natural resources as input and energy so as to achieve the target of agricultural production in harmony with the environment, which support the life on the earth. The ecofriendly agriculture may be defined as the combination of both traditional organic farming and modern chemical farming systems and emphasise the importance of both economic growth as well as environmental safety.

In fact any alternate farming system except human population control can not lead to the philosophy of environment-friendly agriculture. Finally efforts at personal as well as government levels should be made to decline the human population rather than to increase further the food production; otherwise there is no end of food production, which would certainly lead to environmental degradation and damage to severe and irreparable level.

Principles and Practices of Environment-friendly Agriculture

Our agriculture has sustained since several thousand years mainly due to adoption of eco-friendly agriculture. Until the middle of 20th century, agriculture all over the world was based on the principles of eco-friendly organic farming system, which ensured crop and animal food production as well as environmental safety to the human beings and other forms of domestic and non-domestic animals. Since the commencement of green and industrial revolutions, people in some agricultural advanced countries and some states of a developing country like India (Punjab, Haryana, Western U.P.) abandoned the traditional means of agriculture and stressed the need of more food production and economic growth through chemical inputs without environmental consideration, which led to environmental degradation and ecological imbalance (Swaminathan, 1996). When the green revolution has turned into greed revolution and started posing several environmental problems, the agricultural scientists, environmentalists and policy makers are now proposing to practices eco-friendly agriculture with slight modification of allowing the judicious use of chemical inputs and mechanisation with all means of traditional organic farming so that both the economic growth and environmental sustainability could be attained together (Udagawa, 1991; Dahama, 1999). Followings are the fundamental principles of environment agriculture.

1. Organisation of crop and livestock production and management of farm input resources in such a way that they harmonise rather than conflict with each other.
2. Use and development of appropriate technologies based upon an understanding of biological systems rather than physico-chemical system.
3. Attaining the food and environmental security and sustainability along with food quality and safety.
4. Integration and diversification of crop and livestock to maintain soil fertility, crop and animal productivity and diversity without posing major environmental problems.
5. Optimising crop and animal food production through maximum application of natural organic inputs and judicious use of synthetic inorganic inputs too.
6. Shifting the dependency from conventional to non-conventional form of energy for various farm operations.

Strategies for Environment-friendly Agriculture

The present proposed form of environment-friendly agriculture is not in fact similar to the traditional means of organic farming system which was responsible for sustaining our agriculture since its inception/ several years. This is a new form of sustainable agriculture which follows both the principles and practices of traditional organic farming and present inorganic farming systems on the ground of economic growth and environmental safety as well, because we can neither completely adopt the organic farming system which is characterised by low productivity with sustainability nor can completely abandon the inorganic farming system which is highly productive but unsustainable. Thus, by combining the principles and benefits of both the farming systems in judicious and appropriate ways, we can possibly evolve a new system or form of agriculture which may be highly productive and sustainable too. China is perhaps the only country which has been able to blend the traditional methods of agriculture with the new frontier research and has already proved the concept of new form of eco-friendly agriculture with high productivity and sustainability. The strategies and measures to achieve the goals of eco-friendly agriculture are briefly discussed as under.

Integrated Farming System

Integrated farming system is perhaps the first and foremost basis of environment-friendly agriculture and is indispensable for achieving the goals of the same. In this farming system, more than one agricultural enterprises such as cropping, animal, dairy, poultry, pig, sheep, goat and fish farming, and bee keeping, etc. are performed together at the same farm to meet the demand of various kinds of crop and animal foods such as cereals, millets, pulses, oilseeds, vegetables, fruits, fibers, milk, meat, eggs, honey, etc.; to maintain soil health, to provide farm income throughout the year; better utilisation of natural and agronomic farm resources; to minimise the risk of crop and animal loss by natural calamities and finally to ensure environmental security. Integration of various kinds of crops and livestocks on the farm not only provide an opportunity to produce different kinds of food products simultaneously, but also utilise the input resources efficiently without competition by each other forms of plant and animal lives in the same agro-ecosystem. For examples, the grain, seeds, vegetables, fruits, fibers, etc. are utilised by the human beings, while straw and by-products such as cakes, concentrates, molasses and physically, mechanically and insect damaged grains, etc., which can not be consumed by the human beings, are easily consumed by the ruminants (cattle, buffalo, goats, sheeps, camel, etc.) and non-ruminant animals (pigs, poultry, horse, etc.), and finally the digested out put in the form of dung, faeces or excreta could be utilised by each crop as manures and by fishes and earthworm as their feeds. Rearing of farm animals, viz., cattles, buffaloes and camels along with cropping not only provide power to operate various farm activities and various kinds of foods to human beings, but also help in rapid degradation of cellulosic organic waste such as straw into the dung in their rumen stomach which is used later as organic manures. Thus, the cattle rumen acts as a bio-reactor and thus expedite the decomposition of fibrous materials, which would otherwise take months together in compost pits to convert the same into dung manures. Integrated farming system in fact offers more stability to agro-ecosystem by imparting the foods and energy through larger number and kinds of food chain integrity without any competition for foods and energy among the diverse users. Thus integrated farming system provides an ecological balance between producers, consumers and decomposers in the existing agro-ecosystem and could possibly be very effective and helpful in achieving the goals of environment-friendly agriculture.

Integrated Cropping System

Integrated cropping system or diversified cropping is a component of integrated farming system in which more than one kinds of crop species such as cereals, pulses, oilseeds, fodder, fibers, vegetables, sugarcane, fruits, commercial, ornamental and plantation are grown together in an agro-ecosystem either in the form of sole cropping at different plots or mixed cropping, inter-cropping, relay cropping, multistoried cropping, green manuring, crop rotation with leguminous and non-leguminous crops and sequential cropping. Thus integrated cropping system provides more than one kind of crops, greater job opportunities, more income, less risk of crop loss, keep the soil healthy and productive, offers greater crop species diversity and finally provides greater agro-ecosystem stability, productivity and environmental sustainability. The ecological stability and sustainability of integrated cropping system is based on the principles of competitive cooperation between various crops for their inputs and natural resources, and practice of crop rotation with legumes and other non-legume crops improve soil fertility and productivity through biological nitrogen fixation and mobilisation of fixed phosphates. It is also responsible for better soil, water and crop diversity conservation and their efficient utilisation. Integrated cropping system leads to diversification and efficient utilisation of input and natural resources and thus enhances the physical, chemical and biological integrity of crop production ecosystem which is most important component of eco-friendly agriculture (Singh etal., 1994; Singh, 2001).

Integrated Nutrient Supply Management

Integrated nutrient supply management (INSM) is another basic requirement of eco-friendly agriculture where the nutrients demand of crop plants for their optimum growth and productivity is met through various organic sources such as farmyard manures, compost, green manures, biofertilisers, legumes crops, bone-meal and natural rocks as well as inorganic chemical fertilizers in order to utilise the organic resources of nutrients to the maximum extent and to reduce the economic pressure on the farmers by curtailing the dose of chemical fertilizers significantly (Singh *et al*., 1994; Singh, 2001). Thus, the integrated nutrient management offers an opportunity to maintain and improve the soil health by enriching the soil with organic manures which not only provide the nutrients to the crops but also support the life of immense soil micro-organisms and arthropods, improve the soil fertility by enhancing its water holding capacity, cation exchange capacity, aeration to crop roots, water infiltration and reduce the leaching loss of nutrients and finally improve the productivity of soil without causing any environmental problems at on and off sites of crop production. Integrated nutrient management does not mean to completely ban the use of chemical fertilizers, but only restrict their dose to judicious level to ensure environmental sustainability without compromising with crop productivity, their quality and safety. At least 40-50 per cent requirement of chemical fertilizers could be supplied through various forms of organic manures especially green manures (biological nitrogen fixation) and biofertilizers such as *Rhizobium* (symbiotic) in legumes, *Azotobactor* (non-symbiotic) and *Azosperillum* (associatives) in cereals and cotton, and Blue green algae (phototropic) and *Azolla* (aquatic symbiotic) in flooded rice, *Vesicular arbiscular mycorrhiza* (VAM), etc. (Vyas and Vyas, 1994; Pawar *et al*., 2001). Apart from application of various organic manures, use of legumes crops as green fodder, vegetables and pulses in the crop rotation would certainly improve the soil fertility level. In fact all this integrated nutrient supply management existed in our traditional agriculture, presently we have only to supplement this with judicious level of chemical fertilizers to maintain and improve our food production level in the future. Thus INSM synergise the effect of both organic and inorganic forms of nutrients following their application together and finally save the environment from nitrate pollution and enhance the income of farmers by curtailing the dose of chemical fertilizers. The success of environment-friendly agriculture relies heavily on the efficiency of integrated nutrients supply management. The list of various biofertilizers and green manure crops with their associate crops and nitrogen fixation efficiency has been presented in Table 15.1 and 15.2.

Table 15.1: Biological Nitrogen Fixation and Nutrients Absorption and Solubilising Efficiency of Biofertilizers

Biofertilizer	*Biological Activity*	*Crops Benefited*
Rhizobium (symbiotic)	N fixation, 50-300 kg/ha/year under optimum P, Mo level and sunlight	All the leguminous plants including pulses, oilseeds, egetables, fodder and tree
Azotobacter (non-symbiotic)	N. fixation, 20-25 kg/ha/year Under optimum organic matter	Cereals, millets, sugarcane, cotton, vegetables and other Non-leguminous crops
Azospirillum (associative)	N fixation, 10-20 kg/ha/year	Cereals, millets, cotton, sugarcane, vegetables etc.
Blue green algae/ *Cyanobacteria* (phototropic)	N fixation, 25-30 kg/ha/year under bright sunlight	flooded rice crop
Azolla/aquatic fern (symbiotic)	N fixation, 30-90 kg/ha	Flooded rice crop
Vesicular arbiscular oilseeds, mycorrhizae (VAM) (obligate symbionts)	increase the absorption of P, Zn, S, Cu, Fe and water	Cereals, millets, and legumes
Phosphate solubilising Bacteria and fungi (PSM)	Solubilize about 50-60% fixed phosphorus in the soil	almost all the crops

Table 15. 2: Symbiotic Nitrogen Fixation by Some Green Manuring Crops

Crop	*Range of Nitrogen Fixation (kg/ha)*
Sun hemp	60-100
Sesbania	80-100
Alfalfa	100-300
Berseem	120-150
Chickpea	26-63
Pigeon pea	60-200
Cowpea	50-85
Cluster bean	40-200
Clover	100-150
Groundnut	110-150

Integrated Pest Management

The modern high productivity associated farming system, which depends heavily on the use of synthetic pesticides, has already posed several environmental problems in both developed and developing countries (Okada, 1991; Kapoor *et al.*, 1994). Thus the ecosystem poisoning resulted from pesticides compelled the growers, researchers, and environmentalists to propose a new concept of pest control, i.e. known as integrated pest management. This is an idea of integrating all the possible mechanism and methodologies of pest (insects, disease, and weeds) control (physical, mechanical, cultural, biological, genetically and chemical methods) in harmonious ways to hold down the pest below the "economic injury level" (Okada, 1991). This system uses two types of control measure: one aims to reduce the pest population, while the other to protect the crops. Instead of controlling the pest through various traditional methods such as physical (burning of crop residue, light trapping, solar treatment, hot water treatment), mechanical (trenching, beating, netting, bunding), biological (use of predators and parasitoids) and cultural (crop rotation, deep ploughing, trap cropping, flooding), farmers are now accustomed to use indiscriminate and excessive dose of synthetic pesticides to control the crop pests for enhancing the productivity of crops, which not only pollutes the ecosystem, but also killes several kinds of birds and animals which used to control the cop pests naturally through various food webs operating at different trophic levels in the agro-ecosystem. Several insects found to be useful in pollinating the cross pollinated crop plants and thus helpful in improving the crop yield significantly, are being destroyed by the excessive use of pesticides. Thus to combat increasing disease, insects and weed pressure in the intensive cropping system, emphasis should be made to promote and adopt the IPM which involves resistant/tolerant crop cultivars, biological control, crop rotation, appropriate cultural operations and judicious use of pesticides so as to keep optimum production level of crops without environmental damage. Priority should be given to prevent rather than to control the pests. Ploughing the fields or hand weeding before seed formation in weed plants, summer deep ploughing, green manuring, and crop rotation, solar treatments have been found very effective in controlling the weed population in crop fields. Uprooting the deep rooted perennial weeds during occurrence of natural flood is very promising method of their eradication. Besides these non-polluting cultural, physical and mechanical methods, the use of several natural enemies (predators and parasitoids in the form of fungi, bacteria, viruses, insects) against various insects, pathogens and weeds have been reported to be very effective, useful and environment friendly (Okada, 1991; Kapok *et al.*, 1994). Apart from these biological control measures, biodegradable pesticides (biopesticides) and chemical pesticides especially those which are easily degradable and less harmful should also be used judiciously under unavoidable circumstances, as we can not let the crop damage by the pests. Presently emphasis is being given to develop the insect and disease resistant transgenic crop cultivars to combat the situation, but the problem is that such types of genetically resistant cultivars generally do not last for longer duration due to biological changes in the feeding behaviour of biotypes and races of insects and pathogen, respectively. Thus along with continuous breeding and biotechnological programs for developing resistant/tolerant crop cultivars, other non-chemical, especially the cultural, methods should be prioritised and emphasised to manage the pest below the economic injury level. Different bio-agents against various insect pests have been presented in Table 15.3.

Table 15.3: Use of Biotic Agents for Insect and Pathogen ontrol of Cultivated

Crop	*Insect/Pathogen*	*Potential biological control agents*
Rice	Stem borer Leaf folder Aphids, White flies Thrips	*Trichogramma japonicum T. chilonis Chrysoperla carnea*
Maize and Sorghum	Stem borer	*Trichogramma species*
Sugarcane	Pyrilla Borers Top shoot borer	*Boiri ania, Tetrastichus pyrellae Trichogramma chilonis T. japonicum*
Cotton	Aphids, White flies Thrips	*Chrysoperla carnea*
Chickpea Pigeon pea	Pod borer	*Chrysoperla, Chilonus, Bracon* and Nuclear polyhedrosis virus (NPV)
Tomato	Fruit borer	*Chrysoperla, Chilonus, Bracon, Trichogramma* and NPV
Potato	Tuber moth	*Bacillus thuringiensis*
Coconut Crop diseases *flavus*	Rhinoceros beetle Pathogens	*Baculo virus Trichoderma species, Talaromyces, Gliocladium,* and bacterial antagonists such as *Pseudomonas species*

Integrated Energy Management

The success of green, white and blue revolution in India and rest parts of the world have resulted from the integrated approaches of high yielding crop and animal varieties/hybrids, use and availability of agro-chemicals, land reforms, ensured irrigation, mechanisation for various farm operations and better financial supports through nationalised banks. Tractors, threshers, combines, seed drills, have indeed played a crucial role in achieving the targets of green revolution without which the fruits of success would have never been acquired. Thus to perform various agricultural activities, these machines and implements are presently heavily dependent on fossil fuel conventional energy which have their availability and cost limits and priced heavily towards the cost of crop and animal production. However the fact is that several farm operations could be performed by using various forms of non-conventional or renewable energy such as solar, wind, biogas through solar oven, photovoltaic cells, wind mills, wind pump, biogas plant, etc. without paying rccurrent cost, and environmental pollution. The most significant aspects of such forms of energies are that these are never going to be exhausted or finished, and also the establishment of such power plants cost only initially and last for several years without much maintenance charges. As we know that the conventional source of energy, e.g., coal, fossil fuel and radioisotopes are not endless and would be finished after some period, it is better to develop the technologies and establish the power plants which can transform the non-conventional energy into usable forms such as mechanical and electrical energy to run the various farm operations. Although these renewable sources of energy have not yet been exploited for heavy farm activities such as ploughing, threshing, lifting sufficient water for irrigation or transportation, etc., but heavy dependency on the conventional source of energy could certainly be reduced through the integrated approaches of using both forms of energy for several small farm operations and domestic works such as lifting ground water by wind mill pump, solar cells electric motor, biogas engine, cooking by solar oven and biogas, and solar electricity for domestic uses. Thus use of non conventional source of energy has great potential of power generation which could be managed at every village level through cooperative and collective approaches (Fig. 15.1).

Conservation of Natural Resources

Conservation of natural resources (soil, water, air and biodiversity) imparted by nature on this beautiful and bountiful space ship, Earth should be given top priority in the environment-friendly agriculture, because over exploitation of various natural resources may lead to severe environmental damage and ecological imbalance, which must be protected by conserving them on their own sites (in-situ conservation). Excess and imbalances use of chemical fertilizers and pesticides, etc., over exploitation of ground and river water and monoculture with high yielding cultivars, abandon of traditional ways of organic farming system, etc. have all collectively posed a severe threat to our agro-ecosystem, which support our lives on the Earth. To conserve our natural resources for sustainable agriculture, we should now go back to our traditional form of

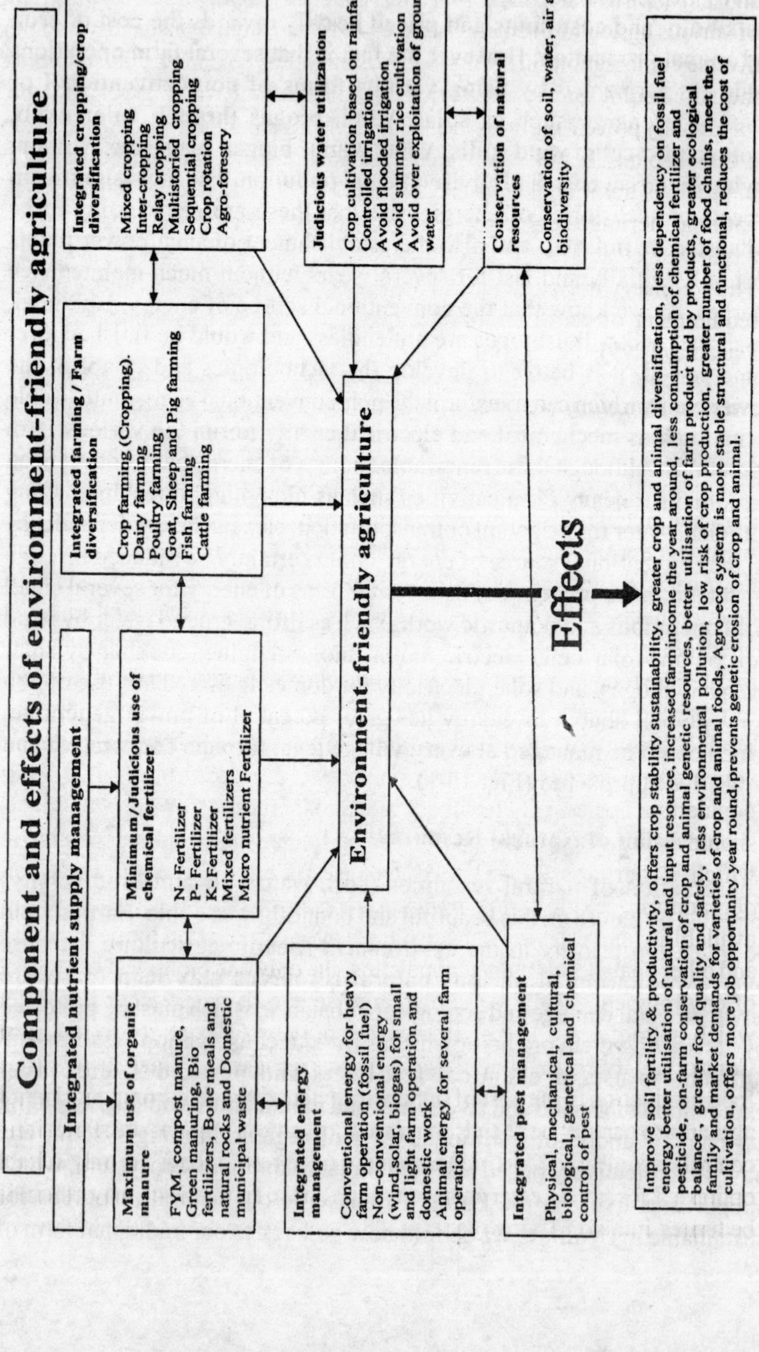

Fig. 15.1: Component and Effects of Environment-Friendly Agriculture

integrated cropping and farming systems, which are based on organic source of inputs and judicious use of natural resources rather than use of chemical and unnatural resources, and over exploitation of natural resour··es. Integration of various agricultural enterprises, i.e., crop and animal husbandry and their diverse combinations in the agro-ecosystem offers an opportunity to improve the soil health and productivity, resume ground water level and most importantly prevent the crop and animal genetic resources from genetic erosion at their habitats. In other words, it encourages on-farm or in-situ conservation of precious traditional crop and animal species and varieties which are our national heritage and meet several specific farm, domestic and social requirements, and finally leads to our food, life and environmental security. Thus conservation of natural resources is prerequisite and essential requirement of eco-friendly/sustainable agriculture (Swaminathan, 1996; Dahama, 1999).

Human Population Control

Population leads to poverty and poverty leads to pollution, thus directly and indirectly exploding human population has been responsible for every kind and magnitude of environmental degradation and problem. In other words excess and undesirable human population (human weeds) is perhaps the greatest pollutants on earth, which nullifies all the economic and social developments made in the past. All the anthropogenic activities including, intensive farming and green and white revolutions have been aimed mainly to cater the food demands of ever increasing population and simultaneously to raise the income of the farmers through agriculture. Thus more food production for more people has resulted in several environmental problems, which could be overcome to a great extent by controlling the human population. I personally feel that instead of increasing food production, we should rather stress more on decreasing the unwanted human production which is perhaps the main root cause of environmental and social degradation. Exploitation of natural resources has limitation of their availability and carrying capacity, their over exploitation to meet the food and other demands of human population, the only one biological component of environment, would certainly cause severe damage to our ecosystem which supports the life of immense biodiversity existing on the earth. Controlling the human population is perhaps easier than increasing further food production at the cost of our environment. Even environment-friendly agriculture can not be the ultimate solution unless population explosion is controlled logically. Thus human demographic restriction is the only suitable option left for saving environment and life on the earth, which may otherwise be turned into non-living planet.

16

Indigenous Technology, Eco-friendly Environment and Sustainable Agriculture

P.S. SIVAKUMAR, M. NEDUNCHEZHIYAN and R.C. RAY

The greatest challenge facing mankind in the 21st century is to produce the basic necessities of food, feed, fibre, fuel and raw materials from dwindling available per capita land. The phenomenal increase in food production in the last few decades has been the direct result of the extensive use of the high yielding varieties, high quality seeds, fertilizers, irrigation and use of plant protection measures. Dependence on these modern agricultural inputs was necessitated because of their quick, spectacular and quantitative response in overall production and productivity (Garforth and Lawrence, 1997). However, over the years of success, adverse effects are coming to light covering major areas such as soil productivity, product quality, environment and sustainability, etc (Lal and Lal, 1988).

Thus, there is a growing concern about the problems and challenges of sustainable development throughout the world. The sustainable development aims to improve human welfare by protecting the scarce resources and minimisation of wastes. It is a process of economic development, which does not hamper the future ability of the environment to provide adequate means of livelihood for the population. Generally many countries have taken economic objectives of development and neglected the ecological objectives in the form of natural resource management, and as a consequence, they are unable to cope up with a sustainable balance. In this context, there is need to understand and apply the eco-friendly technologies to conserve the degrading environment. This review discusses the hazards of modern agriculture and various eco-friendly technologies, which can be implemented for sustainable agricultural development.

Hazards of Modern Agriculture

Loss of Agro-biodiversity

Agricultural biodiversity refers to the varieties and variabilities of animals, plants, and microorganisms on earth that are important to food and agriculture. It comprises:

- the diversity of genetic resources (varieties, breeds, etc.) used directly or indirectly for food and agriculture (including crops, livestock, forestry and fisheries) and for the production of feed, fodder, fibre, fuel and pharmaceuticals,
- the diversity of species that support production (soil biota, pollinators, predators, etc.) and those in the wider environment that support agro-ecosystems (agricultural, pastoral, forest and aquatic), and the diversity of the agro-ecosystems themselves.

Agricultural biodiversity fulfils a number of important roles, including:

- *Providing food and livelihood security*. Dynamic and complex rural livelihoods usually rely on plant and animal diversity, both wild and in different stages of domestication.
- *Ensuring productive and environmental sustainability*. In addition to contributing to environmental sustainability, agricultural biodiversity helps sustain many production systems both in low external input and high input-output agriculture such as soil organic matter decomposition, nutrient cycling, pollination, pest control, yield functions, soil and water conservation, action on climate and water cycling, biodiversity conservation and influences on landscape structure.
- *Supporting development*. Agricultural biodiversity can provide the basis for biotechnology (old and new), natural product development, eco-tourism, and other activities important for well-being and income generation in local, national and global economies.

Indian sub-continent is one of the twelve mega centres of biodiversity in the world (Katyal, 1997) and harbours very rich varieties of flora and fauna. About 25 crop species are reportedly domesticated in the region and it hosts 1800 species of higher plants including 160 major and minor crop species along with 325 of their wild relatives. Native tribes have been exploiting about 1500 wild edible plant species which include 145 species of roots and tubers, 521 of leafy vegetables/grains, 101 of buds and flowers, 647 of fruits and 118 of seeds and nuts. Apart from the above, nearly 9500 plant species of ethano-botanical uses have been reported from the country of which around 7500 are for ethano-medicinal purpose, and 3900 are multi-purpose/edible species (Katyal, 1997; Dandin, 2000). Similarly, a total of 81,000 animal species have been recorded in India which constitute about 6.24 per cent of the fauna species recorded in the world, that include 26 breeds of cattle, 8 of buffaloes, 4 of sheep, 20 of goats, 8 of camels, 14 of horses and 18 of poultry apart from the yak, the mithun, and several species and breeds of birds including geese, ducks, pigeons, and doves (Patil and Kolekar, 2002; Sahai, 1993).

Causes

Deforestation: The rapid loss of forest cover is possibly the most serious environmental threat for biodiversity. In Asian and Latin-American countries, the average annual rate of deforestation was 1.815 million ha, or 5000 $ha^{-1} day^{-1}$ during the period 1976-1980 (Kimmins, 1987). The trend is more or less similar even to day. The main cause of deforestation is shifting cultivation, which supports nearly 30 million people in various parts of the world (Armson, 1977). The shorter cropping cycles of traditional shifting cultivation, and the unorganised and spontaneous encroachment into forestland by low landers reflect the increasing demand for cultivable land among the landless and the unemployed rural poor. Also, destruction of tropical forests and other native vegetation for agricultural production has a role in elevated levels of carbon dioxide and other greenhouse gases (Viro, 1974).

Extensive use of modern varieties: Farmers prefer high-yielding varieties because of easy agronomic practices. Large-scale adoption of these high yielding varieties resulted in the extinction of valuable traditional genotypes. A FAO* study revealed that 75 per cent of the genetic diversity of agricultural crops has been lost in the 20th century (FAO. 1993). Only about 150 plant species are now cultivated, of which just 3, i.e. rice, wheat and maize supply almost 60 per cent of calories derived from plants. In India; once more than 30,000 rice varieties were grown, but now just 10 varieties cover 75 per cent of the whole rice area (FAO, 1993; Fowler and Mooney, 1990).

Degradation of Land Resources

Land degradation is a complex phenomena (Fig. 17.1) driven by a strong interaction among socio-economic and biophysical factors. It is also fuelled by increasing population, fragile economy and dismal farm policies. It finally results in serious imbalance in the cycling of major elements such as C, N, P, S, etc in soil.

In this context, the scenario of land degradation in India is precarious.

Out of 329 million ha geographical area in India, about 145 million ha is cultivated at present, with practically no scope to bring more area under plough as marginal and a part of slope lands are already under cultivation (Singh, 1999). Further, the cropping intensity is only 136 per cent. The per capita cultivable land will reduce to about 0.14 ha in 2025 A.D as compared to about 0.17 ha at present. Annually, 0.8 per cent of agricultural land is being usurped for urbanisation. About 50 per cent of the cultivated land is likely to remain rainfed even after realising irrigation potential fully in the country.

Landslides, soil erosion and topsoil loss are common due to improper land management practices. Sehgal and Abrol (1994) estimated that 57 per cent of land (187.7 M ha) in the country is potentially exposed to various degradation forces of which a dominant fraction is under-water erosion (148.9 M ha; 45%) and the rest about 12 per cent is suffering from wind erosion (13.5 M ha; 4.1%), chemical degradation (13.8 M ha; 4.2%) and physical degradation (11.0 M ha; 3.6%). Soil erosion is directly linked to deterioration of soil health, which in turn affects crop productivity and sustainability. Therefore, soil and water conservation is the need of the hour to reverse the process of land degradation for increasing agricultural production to ensure food security and sustainability.

Depletion of Water Resources

Depletion of water resources is a global phenomenon. Water scarcity due to erratic monsoon and ground water depletion is a major problem in India. Out of the annual rainfall of 400 mham, only 29 per cent (60 m ham) is utilisable (Singh, 1999). The present water use in agriculture is about 85 per cent of the developed water resources and likely to be reduced by 10-15 per cent to meet the increasing demand of drinking water and industrial uses in next couple of years. However, the irrigation efficiency is only 20-50 per cent (Padmanaban, 2001). Rainfed agriculture accounts for over 97 million ha with contribution of only 40 per cent to the national food basket and is subjected to inadequate and erratic rainfall. Studies estimated that the depletion of aquifers would bring down India's potential crop harvest by 25 per cent in the future (Padmanaban, 2001).

Indiscriminate Use of Chemical Inputs

Although chemicals have been extremely beneficial in crop production and protection, their loss in the environment causes severe problems.

1. *Environmental contamination*: A significant (30-40%) amount of nitrogen and pesticides, applied in agriculture are lost to soil to contaminate water, food, fodder, and atmosphere (Guenzi,

1974; Lal and Lal, 1988; Pretty, 1996). The problem due to contamination by residues (pesticides/fertilisers) may appear far removed from the initial point of introduction into the environment. As a consequence, the hazards of pesticide residues have been noticed in drinking water, milk, food grains, fruits and vegetables (Manohari, 2002). Likewise, nitrate accumulation has been reported in ground water (Charjan and Hajre, 2002).

2. *Resistance:* Several pests have developed resistance to commonly used pesticides. The best examples are DDT and HCH against mosquitoes (Tu and Miles, 1976). This resistance has rendered pesticides less effective against certain pests and shortened the useful life of the chemical. Several studies have indicated that over 400 insects and mite pests and more than 70 fungal pathogens have become resistant to one or more pesticides (Edwards and Thompson, 1973).
3. *Misuse of chemical pesticides:* Chemical pesticides were relatively inexpensive and easy to apply. Very often, farmer's resort to higher doses of pesticide applications than might actually be necessary in order to protect the crop resulting in toxic residues (Ray *et al.*, 1992).
4. *Secondary pest outbreaks:* Complete control of one pest by means of pesticides often leads to secondary population outbreaks (Pretty, 1996). In other words, eliminating one pest would upset the ecological balance and another organism, which was previously not harmful, would emerge as a pest.
5. *Non-target organisms:* The broad-spectrum pesticides kill not only pests, but also their natural enemies and non-target soil microflora and fauna. Several beneficial soil microorganisms, i.e. nitrifying (*Nitrosomonas, Nitrobacter*), N_2—fixing (*Rhizobium, Azotobacter, Azospirillum* etc) bacteria and soil fauna, i.e. earthworms are highly susceptible to pesticides and inorganic fertilisers (Guenzi, 1974).
6. *Resurgence:* Using pesticides regularly sometimes leads to a resurgence of the original pest population. This often occurs because the use of pesticides would upset the ecological balance by eliminating both pests and non-target organisms. Thus, any pest, which survives or has re-invaded, would have an excellent opportunity for increasing its numbers, even to a level higher than before the pesticide application because neither their natural enemies nor competitors would be present.

Population Pressure

According to recent United Nations population projections, the world population will grow from 5.7 billion in 1995 to 9.4 billion in 2050, 10.4 billion in 2100, and 10.8 billion by 2150, and will stabilise at slightly under 11 billion around 2200 (Pretty, 1996). The rate of population increase is especially high in many developing and under-developed countries. In these countries, the population factor, combined with rapid industrialisation, poverty, political instability, and large food imports and debt burden, make long-term food security very urgent. In Indian context, the country will have to feed about 1.3 billion mouths by the year 2020, requiring production of 5-6 million tonnes of additional food grains per year. All the non-renewable resources (land, water and fuels) are disappearing at an alarming rate due to unplanned development and over-exploitation. If the population does not stabilise at this stage, even a super green revolution would not be able to satisfy the hunger of the people.

Sustainable Agriculture

Agriculture has come a long way in counteracting Malthusian principles by allying with 'The Margquis of Condorcet', who predicted that country like India and China would be able to meet the food requirement of its people with the same amount of land by scientific progress and farmers' involvement. At present, Indian agriculture is still confronted with three major challenges:

1. To increase food availability to an ever burgeoning population.
2. To achieve this task through an efficient use of our natural resources, causing minimal damage to the environment.
3. To contribute through this developed growth towards the economic, social, and food security of our masses, particularly of women and malnourished children.

Indian Green Revolution

The Green Revolution, undoubtedly, is one of the most striking outcomes of this impact that changed the agricultural scenario of the country. As a result of this silent revolution, the total food grain production rose from a mere 50.8 million tonnes in 1950-51 to 208.9 million tonnes in 1999-2000. This impact was clearly manifested in rice (771 to 2583 $kg.ha^{-1}$), wheat (655 to 2583 $kg.\ ha^{-1}$) and oilseeds (519 to 944 $kg.\ ha^{-1}$).

Rapid growth in rice and wheat production has resulted in substantial increase in the marketable surplus of these crops contributing to food security. The per capita net availability of staple food rose from 158.9 $grams.\ day^{-1}$ (56.9 $kg.year^{-1}$) and 65.7 $grams.day^{-1}$ (24.0 $kg.year^{-1}$) in 1951 to 202.2 (73.8 $kg.year^{-1}$) and 155.9 $grams.day^{-1}$ (56.9 $kg.year^{-1}$) in 1999 in case of rice and wheat, respectively (Malaisamy, 2002). All this production was achieved in 142.82 million ha of net area sown.

The foundation laid by the Green revolution paved the way for an all round development in allied sectors such as yellow revolution (of oilseed crops), white revolution (of milk production) and blue revolution (of fish production).

Sustainable Agriculture

According to CGIAR, sustainable agriculture is the successful management of resources for agriculture to satisfy the changing human needs, while maintaining or enhancing the quality of environment and conserving natural resources (Hazell and Ramasamy, 1991). It encompasses:

- the changing needs
- economic viability at enhanced productivity level
- successful management of resources—internal/external as well as renewable/non-renewable
- maintenance and enhancement of quality of environment
- conservation of natural resources

Eco-friendly Approaches and Technologies

Conservation of agro-biodiversity

Conservation of biodiversity is accomplished in a number of ways. *Ex-situ* methods focus on species conservation in botanic gardens, zoos, gene banks, and captive breeding programmes. *In-situ* methods use conservation areas as "warehouses" of biological information.

Ex-situ Conservation

It is conservation of components of biological diversity outside their natural habitats. *Ex-situ* conservation minimises the further evolutionary processes but ensures safe conservation of existing genetic variability and its sustainable use. The most common example of *ex-situ* conservation approach is seed species, which are preserved for long term in seed gene banks at –20°C. Other approaches, namely cryo-preservation, *in vitro* conservation and DNA storage and field repositories for tree/vegetatively propagated species have been adopted. Now, the DNA banks are becoming popular. India has a large capacity for *ex-situ* conservation of genetic resources in their networks of gene banks. The NBPGR and ICAR have several hundred thousand accessions in their network of gene banks (Kothari, 1999).

A sustainable agriculture, therefore, is any system of food or fibre production that systematically pursues the following goals:

- a more thorough incorporation of natural processes such as nutrient cycling, nitrogen fixation and pest-predator relationships into agricultural production processes;
- a reduction in the use of those off-farm, external and non-renewable inputs with the greatest potential to damage the environment or harm the health of farmers and consumers, and a more targeted use of the remaining inputs used with a view to minimizing variable costs;
- a more equitable access to productive resources and opportunities, and progress towards more socially-just forms of agriculture;
- a greater productive use of local knowledge and practices, including innovative approaches not yet fully understood by scientists or widely adopted by farmers;
- an increase in self-reliance among farmers and rural people;
- an improvement in the match between cropping patterns and the productive potential and environmental constraints of climate and landscape to ensure long-term sustainability of current production levels; and
- profitable and efficient production with an emphasis on integrated farm management, and the conservation of soil, water energy and biological resources

In-situ/plant Habitat Conservation

In-situ conservation means the conservation of ecosystems and natural habitats and the maintenance and recovery of viable populations of species in their natural surroundings. In the case of domesticated or cultivated species, conservation is done in the surroundings where they have developed their distinctive properties. *In-situ* conservation of crop plants involves the conservation on-farm of local crop landraces with the active participation of farmers.

In-situ conservation has the advantage of continuing evolution and adaptation of the material and conserving wider range of diversity. *In-situ* conservation complements *ex-situ* conservation by way of (i) conserving the processes of evolution and adaptation of crops to their environments, (ii) conserving diversity at all levels—the ecosystem, between the species and within species, (iii) improving the livelihood of resource of poor farmers, (iv) maintaining or increasing control and access of farmers over their genetic resources, and (v) integrating farmers into the national plant genetic resources system for conservation.

Soil and Water Conservation

The intensified and exploitive soil use has resulted in soil degradation and decline in productivity. Buringh (1989) estimated about 15-30 per cent decline in world food production over a 25-year period was due to soil degradation. Therefore, prevention of soil degradation through soil and water conservation measures, and restoration of productivity of deteriorated soils are absolutely essential.

Soil Microorganisms

Our interest in biological degradation of soil is directly related with soil microorganisms. Microorganisms play a key role in cycling of nutrients, decomposition of wastes and pollutant compounds in soil. Cycling of nutrient elements by microorganisms facilitates continued production of plant and animal derived food. Hence, any impairment in the nutrient cycles adversely affects soil microorganisms and consequently soil fertility. The most significant nutrient cycles affected are carbon, nitrogen, sulphur and phosphorus.

Cycling of plant carbon appears to be one of the least sensitive features of the soil microbial community. For example, as many as 90 per cent of soil fungi may be capable of utilising cellulose. Elimination of any one particular fungus is unlikely to markedly affect decomposition of cellulose. Moreover, there are numerous bacteria capable of utilising cellulose (*Cellulomonas, Pseudomonas, Vibrio, Bacillus*), which may in part replace the role of fungi in the event of major changes in fungal populations.

Nitrogen (N) Cycle: Nitrogen is among the most important nutrients for living systems and is often the limiting factor in productivity of ecosystems. It is also one of the nutrients most affected by the activities of soil microorganisms. Of the major components of the N cycle (mineralisation, immobilization, etc), nitrification appears to be the most sensitive to environmental perturbances (Schmidt, 1982). Symbiotic nitrogen fixation is a very complicated biological phenomenon, involving numerous coordinated processes that must take place for establishment of effective root nodules or other analogous structures.

Phosphorous (P) Cycle: Phosphorus cycling is important, next to N cycle in agriculture. The contribution of phosphorus solubilising bacteria and mycorrhizal fungi in phosphorus nutrition is discussed in the subsequent section.

Cycling of sulphur iron, manganese and other elements in soil has been reviewed extensively (Alexander, 1977). Iron and manganese undergo red reactions in soil as a function of the availability of oxygen. Reductive processes involving these metals have generally been attributed to indirect action of microorganisms. Sulphur may also be subject to redox reactions in soil. As in the case of iron, and manganese, sulphur (or sulphate) reduction has generally been attributed to microbial activity.

Maintenance of Soil Fertility

The day-by-day decline in the already low soil fertility is the main cause of low productivity of most of the cultivated lands. According to soil test analysis in India, N deficiency is universal, P status is low in 50 per cent and medium in 48 per cent soils (Singh, 1999). Likewise 48 per cent soils are low to medium in available K and its deficiency is rapidly increasing due to intensive cropping and unbalance input of fertilizer. The long-term fertilizer experiments under different agro-climatic regions of the country have shown that K deficiency in future will become a limiting factor for crop production.

Soil and Water Conservation Measures

Soil and water conservation measures refer to proper land and water management on sustained basis, improving the productivity of these resources and reducing the sediment and nutrient losses. All these factors result in the rehabilitation of agro-ecological environment and assume an important place in future strategy of development.

Water erosion: Water erosion is a major source of organic matter decline in soil (Voroney *et al.*, 1981). This is partly due to the fact that although organic C in soil may be protected from degradation by adsorption to clay (Parton *et al.*, 1982), the clay fraction is quite susceptible to water erosion and therefore, will carry organic carbon with it. It can be controlled through agronomical measures such as contour farming, mulching, tillage, strip cropping, mixed cropping, intercropping *etc.*, and mechanical measures like contour bunding, graded bunding, bench terracing on steep slopes and runoff harvesting storage.

Wind erosion: Wind erosion results in removal of topsoil and therefore, a loss of substrates for soil microorganisms. Since soil organic matter is largely associated with the soil surface, it is usually one of the first major soil components lost by erosion (Lucas *et al.*, 1977). Microbial biomass is usually strongly correlated with organic C and/or organic N content. Thus, highly eroded soils would be expected to possess relatively low levels of biomass and heterotrophic activity, as well as slow rates of associated nutrient transformations. Wind erosion in India is most prevalent in western Rajasthan and the adjoining parts of Punjab, Haryana, Malwa and Gujarat.

Wind erosion can be reduced by placing any barrier perpendicular to the direction of wind and reducing the wind velocity near the ground by exerting a drag on the wind and deflecting the wind stream. Windbreaks with tree lining and shelterbelts are effective in reducing wind velocity. Roughening of the soil surface, stubble mulching, tillage to develop cloddy surface and strip cropping are very useful conservation measures for controlling wind erosion.

Integrated Watershed Management

It is universally recognised that conservation of natural resources should be essentially on area basis. The unit of adoption be a natural unit or a draining runoff water to a particular point is called as watershed.

Soil and water conservation programmes on watershed basis in different agro-climatic regions of India have proved economical and enhanced crop productivity (Ram Babu *et al.*, 1997; Samra, 1997; Bhardwaj and Dhyani, 1994). A few instances are cited here to elucidate the success of watershed management in India. An untreated ravine watershed of 8.4 ha at Chhalesar (Agra) generated 4.5 t $ha^{-1}.yr^{-1}$ soil loss but with treatment of check dams and grassed waterways at appropriate places, the soil loss was only 0.4 t. $ha^{-1}.yr^{-1}$ (Tiwari and Bhushan, 1983). Adoption of soil and water conservation measures, *viz.* earthen dams, contour bunds, farm ponds, anicuts, etc. in the Tanwar watershed in arid region of Rajasthan resulted in reduced wind and water erosion, created additional storage (19,500 m^3), reduced the soil loss on sloping cultivated lands (5-6%) and increased the yield of dry land crops, grasses and fruit trees (Singh, 1996).

Integrated Nutrient Management

In the previous sections, we have discussed how indiscriminate uses of fertilisers and pesticides, and physical factors like wind and soil erosions have led to the deterioration of the ecosystems. In this context, integrated nutrient management (INM) has been found promising on a long-term basis for improvement and maintenance of soil fertility leading to sustained crop production.

Need

Independent use of neither the chemical fertilisers nor the organic sources can sustain productivity of soils and crops (Manahari, 2002; Nedunzhiyan, 2001). There should be a proper admixture of organics and inorganics to sustain crop production (Nedunzhiyan, 2001; Stevenson, 1986).

Components

Fertilisers: At present emphasis is on the use of chemically pure high analysis fertilisers such as urea, di-ammonium phosphate and muriate of potash, which are practically devoid of nutrients other than NPK.

Continuous use of the fertilizers coupled with heavy uptake of secondary and micronutrients by exhaustive production systems lead to emergence of multi nutrient deficiencies (Stevenson, 1986). Now deficiencies of secondary nutrients like sulphur and micronutrients like zinc are reported from large areas besides deficiencies of NPK (Wang *et al.*, 2001).

Recyclable Wastes: The quantity of wastes available annually is staggering, amounting to several million tonnes (Krishna Nanda, 2002). Agro-industrial wastes, agricultural crop residues, food processing and municipal solid wastes are by far the largest wastes available, which cause pollution of land, water and atmosphere. At present, these wastes are disposed off by dumping, land filling, spreading and burning. However, composting and vermin-composting can process these solid wastes into organic manure.

Crop residues and oil cakes: Although most of the crop residues and oil cakes with feed value are needed to support huge livestock population, some residues and cakes available in specific locations/situations can be made use of as a source of plant nutrients. Straw incorporation in paddy could serve as an ideal soil building process of rice soils, which maintain the organic C status, supply nutrients and improve the efficiency of applied fertilizers (Rao and Mikkelsen, 1977).

Animal waste and manures: Fresh animal waste, fishmeal, bone meal, livestock dung and urine, etc. could be carefully integrated in the nutrition management of crops depending on its level of availability.

Domestic and industrial wastes: These materials serve as energy source for soil microorganisms, nutrient source for plant growth or as an amendment for soil amelioration when applied to the soil.

Rice husk: A major by-product of the rice milling industry. Unhulled paddy grain constitutes 20-25 per cent of husk. It is a poor source of manure and the nutrient content is very low (0.3-0.4% N, 0.2-0.3% P_2O_5 and 0.3-0.5% K_2O). Rice husk should be incorporated into the wet soil and can also be used as a bedding material for animals.

Bagasse: The most important by-product of sugar industry is bagasse. It is mainly used as fuel in boilers of sugar factories. It can be used as manure raw or after composting. It contains 0.25 and 0.12 per cent P_2O_5.

Pressmud: Pressmud (Filter cake) is a by-product of cane sugar industry. It is soft, spongy, amorphous, dark brown to brownish white material, which contains sugar, fibre, and coagulated colloids, including cane wax, albuminoids, inorganic salts and soil particles. Presently more than 2 million tonnes of pressmud is produced annually in India. The composition of pressmud is however variable depending upon the quality of cane and process of cane juice clarification. It contains about 1.25 per cent N, 2.0 per cent P_2O_5 and 20-25 per cent organic matter. Addition of pressmud is highly useful to acidic soils since it contains high amount of lime (upto 45%).

Molasses: Molasses are the waste and by-product of sugarcane milling industries. They are acidic in nature besides having good reserves of calcium, carbohydrate and plant nutrients. The carbohydrate fraction of molasses consists of 36.4 per cent sucrose, 13.39 per cent invent sugar, 0.63 per cent starch, and 4.69 per cent gums.

Tea wastes: In the tea industry, tea wastes are available during the course of tea production, processing and storage. Tea wastes are used for extraction of caffeine. The decaffeinated tea wastes can be used as manure. Nutrient content of the spent waste are 0.3-0.35 per cent N, 0.4 per cent P_2O_5 and 1.5 per cent K_2O.

Coir waste: It is a waste product from the coir industry and mostly dumped near the roadsides. Coir pith contains high amount of lignin (30%), cellulose (26%) and wide C:N ratio (112:1). To reduce the bulk and C:N ratio, composting is recommended. The composted coir pith contains 1.26 per cent N, 0.06 per cent P 1.20 per cent K with C/N ratio 24:1. The lignin content is reduced to 4.8 per cent due to composting.

Fly ash: A vast quantity of coal is being burnt in thermal power plants for the purpose of power generation. The utilisation of coal in power generation results in production of huge quantities of fly ash. There is, however, good possibility of using fly ash as a soil amendment in the reclamation of alkali soils as it is a potent source of calcium, sulphur and magnesium (Mahalingam, 1973).

Cover Crops and Green Manures

Cover crops and green manure are used to improve soil fertility and/or to break disease cycles. Cover crops have been also an integral part of crop rotational programmes in sustainable agriculture. In Hastings (Florida), summer and fall cover crops have been a feature of potato production program for over 100 years, resulting in weed management, use of residual fertilizers, and conserving soil organic matter (Davis *et al.*, 1996). Cover crops provide several benefits to the agro-ecosystem such as residual fertilisers and moisture, improved C and N content, reduced soil temperature, soil erosion and enhanced weed control. Green manuring provides a significant portion of the following crop's nutritional requirements. In China, over 20 per cent of land under rice production is green manured for this purpose (Sanginga *et al.*, 1992). Desirable traits for green manure species include ease of establishment, high and fast biomass production, effective nodulation with indigenous *rhizobia*, ease of eradication, and inability to host important pests or diseases. The length of the growing season of the green manure species should match the cultural programme of the cropping system. In the Philippines, short-duration cover crops such as mung bean (*Vigna radiata*) and cowpea, contributed 40-80 kg. ha^{-1} N in a 45 day growing cycle, which in turn increased yield of the subsequent rice crop by over 2 t ha^{-1} (Morris *et al.*, 1986). In India, Egyptian clover, *Trifolium alexandrium*, was the green manure that contributed the most towards the yield of the subsequent maize crop, compared to the yield contributions provided by peas (Singh and Lal, 1985). In Maryland trials conducted over two years, *Vicia villosa*, sowed in the spring after fall planting, contained an average of 182 kg.N.ha^{-1} (Teasdale and Abdul-Baki, 1997). Effective green manure species that were evaluated in Africa included *Centrosema pubescens, Mucuna pruriens, Pueraria phaseolodies*, and *Stylosanthes guianensis* which resulted in improved soil bulk density, soil moisture retention, and protection against erosion (Sanginga *et al.*, 1992).

Table 16.1: Impact of Soil and Water Conserving Technologies and Practices in India (Pretty, 1996)

State	*Technology*	*Yield (t^{-1} ha^{-1})*	*Increase in yields (%)*
Gujarat	Soil and water conservation biogas	–	R: 253% S: 117% P.pea: 222% Co: 153%
Tamil Nadu	Contour bunds, percolation tanks, gully checks agroforestry	R:- Gram: 0.4	++ **
Maharashtra	Soil and water conservation	So (dry): 0. 7 So (Irrig): 2.2	350% 176%
Haryana	Soil and water conservation, social fencing	Grass:-	400-600%
Rajasthan	Grass strips, field and contour bunding	So: 0.33-0.46 Mi: 0.72-0.93	210-292% 120-154%

Biofertilisers

Microorganisms employed to enhance availability of nutrients, viz. N (by fixing atmospheric N_2) and P (by solubilising soil P), to the crops are called bio-fertilizers. The various microorganisms having realised/ potential applications as biofertilisers are: bacteria (*Rhizobium* spp., *Azospirillum, Azotobacter*), fungi (Mycorrhizae like *Glomus*), blue-green algae or cyanobacteria (*Anabaena, Nostoc*, etc) and *Azolla* (a fern) containing symbiotic *Anabaena azollae* (Table 16.2).

Table 16.2: A List of Some Important Microorganisms with Practical/ Potential Application as Bio-fertilizers (Kanniyan, 2000)

Organisms	*Activity*	*Association if any*	*Used in Crops*
Rhizobium (*leguminosarum, japonicum, phaseoli* etc.)	N_2-fixation	Symbiotic	Legumes (pulses, oilseeds, forage crops)
Azospirillum	N_2-fixation	Associative	Graminaceous crops like wheat, rice, sugarcane, jowar
Azotobacter	N_2-fixation	Asymbiotic	Wheat, rice, vegetables
Blue-green algae (*Anabaena, Nostoc, Plectonema* etc.)	N_2-fixation	Asymbiotic	Rice
Azolla-Anabaena complex	N_2-fixation	Symbiotic	Rice
Phosphate solubilising bacteria (*Thiobacillus, Bacillus* etc.)	Phosphate solublisation	Asymbiotic	Many crops
Mycorrhiza (*Glomus*)	Phosphate solublisation	Associative	Many crops including pulses

Blue Green Algae and Azolla: Blue green algae (cyanobacteria) are photosynthetic, prokaryotic organisms, which fix N_2 asymbiotically, but some cyanobacteria, i.e. *Anabaena azollae* is known to form symbiotic associations with *Azolla*. Cultures of cyanobacteria like *Nostac, Anabaena, Tolypothrix* can be multiplied by farmers and introduced into wetland rice, which under ideal conditions may fix 25 to 30 kg. N. ha^{-1} per season. *Azolla* and blue green algae serve as important component of INM in wet land rice cropping system (John *et al*., 2001; Kanniyan, 2000).

Rhizobium: Inoculation of appropriate *Rhizobium* strains on legumes like cowpea, greengram, blackgram, groundnut, etc. may help in fixation of substantial quantities of atmospheric nitrogen and should be an integral component of INM for legumes. Fixation of 50-100 kg. N ha^{-1} with 10-35 per cent increase in yield is reported in several studies of cowpea, groundnut, *etc.* (John *et al*., 2001; Kanniyan, 2000).

Free-living N_2-fixing Microorganisms: Azo-culture of free-living nitrogen fixing bacteria *Azotobacter* and associative symbiotic bacteria *Azospirillium* are available for use in cereals, vegetable, etc. (Stewart,

1975). *Azospirillum* is ubiquitous in the rhizosphere of grasses in the field. Usually two species are found *A.lipoferum*, the isolate from the roots of C-4 grasses and *A.brasilense* from C-3 grasses and sugarcane (C-4) in tropical and sub-tropical regions. Apart from fixing 15-20 kg. $N.ha^{-1}$, they may modify the rhizosphere of crops by exudating root growth stimulants.

Phosphorus Solubilising Microorganisms: Tropical soils are deficient in P. Further. most of the P is not available for plant growth. There are some fungi (*Aspergillus awamori, Penicillium degetatum, etc.*) and bacteria (Bacillus *polymyxa, Pseudomonas striata, etc.),* which can solubilise unavailable forms of P to available forms. The cheaper sources of rock phosphates like Mussorrie rock phosphate, Udaipur rock phosphate, *etc.* can be used along with phosphate solubilising microorganisms for providing P to crops.

The mycorhizal fungi, which form symbiotic association with the roots, can help the uptake of P (Powell, 1980). Vesicular Arbuscular Mycorhiza (VAM) fungi colonise roots of several crop plants. The improved seedling growth and vigour of many plants like tobacco, chillies, tomato, cardamon and mango, *etc.* are partly due to improved P uptake (John *et al.*, 2001).

INM on Cropping System Basis

Cropping system rather than an individual crop is the focus of attention in INM. The low levels of utilisation of nutrients supplied through fertilisers and manures call for choosing appropriate combination/ sequence of crops to effectively utilise the nutrients for long-term sustainability like rice-pulse system. Specific attention needs to be given about the residual effect of fertilizers containing P and K so that the application of these nutrients can be phased to get maximum profit. Legume-cereal rotation can give another dimension in practising INM for sustainable crop production.

Mulching

Any material such as straw, plant residues, leaves, loose soils or plastic films placed on the soil surface to reduce evaporation, erosion or to protect plant roots from extremely low or high temperature is called mulch. By doing mulching apart from the above benefits, soil will be enriched with nutrients.

The use of organic mulches is an effective way to utilise locally available resources, returns nutrients to cultivated land, protects fields from soil and nutrient erosion, and smothers weed growth (Kwapata, 1991; Obiefuna, 1991; Tindall *et al.*, 1991.

Living Mulches : The use of living mulches (sod culture) is common in orchards (Shribbs and Skroch, 1986. In a selection study of eight living mulch species, three (*Festuca rubra, Poa pratensis*, and *Trifolium repens*) were identified as having no adverse effects on main crop yields (Nicholson and Wien, 1983), indicating that some species can suppress weeds without decreasing yield of the main crop.

Integrated Pest Management (IPM)

Integrated Pest Management (IPM) is a sustainable approach to managing pests by combining biological, cultural, physical and chemical tools in a way that minimises economic, health and environmental risks. This approach seeks to reduce pest-induced losses by managing the agronomic, biological and socio-economic components and interactions of the entire system. It is now the preferred way of confronting pest problems pre-and post-harvest in agriculture, as well as in forestry and livestock production, and in public health situations. IPM aims to minimise the use of chemical pesticides and to ensure that, where they are necessary, they are used in an appropriate, informed manner without harmful effects on health and the environment.

Components

Botanical Pesticides: As many as 2121 plant species are reported to possess pest management properties, 1005 species of plants exhibiting insecticidal properties, 384 with anti-feedant properties, 297 with repellant properties, 27 with attractant properties and 31 with growth inhibiting properties have been identified (Singh, 2000).

Resistant Crop Varieties : These are bred and selected when available in order to protect against key pests.

Natural Enemies: Predators and parasitoids (birds/animals/insect) are used to regulate the pest population whenever possible. Some examples of beneficial insects used in agriculture is given in Table 16.3.

Microbial Pesticides: A range of microbial pesticides is currently available for controlling large number of insect pests and fungal pathogens. Some examples of each product type are given in Table 16.3. The type of active agents include microorganisms such as virus, bacteria and fungi, as well as more complex organisms such as protozoa and nematodes. Ninety-two per cent of microbial pesticide sales are insecticides containing *Bacillus thuringiensis* as the active agent.

Behaviour Modifying Substances: Pheromone and kairomones are also used to lure and destroy male insects. Pheromone traps are successfully used to keep sweet potato weevil population within acceptable levels.

Table 16.3: Examples of Current Bio-pesticide Products for Control of Insect Pests (Rodgers, 1993)

Active agent	*Product examples*	*Manufacturer*	*Market*
Bacteria	Biobit, Dipel, Delfin	Novo, Abbott, Sandoz	Vegetables, forestry
Bacillus thuringiensis var. *kurstaki*			
B. thuringiensis var. *alzawai*	Certan	Sandoz	Apiculture
B. thuringiensis var. *israelensis*	Acrobe, skeetal, Vectobac	Cyanamid, Novo, Abbott	Mosquito control
B. thuringiensis var. *fenerionis*	Trident	Sandoz, Novo	Vegetables
B. thuringiensis conjugates[a]	Foil, Cutlass, Agree	Ecogen, Ciba-Geigy	Vegetables, forestry
Pseudomonas fluorescens (Bt toxin)[b]	MVP, M. Trak	Mycogen	Vegetables
Bacillus popilliae	Doom	Fairfax	Turf
Serratia entomophila	Invade	Monsanto	Turf
Fungi	Mycogermin. Mycotal	Chr. Hansen, Koppert	Protected horticulture
Verticillium lecanii			
Nematodes		Ecogen. AGC	Protected horticulture
Heterohabditis spp.			
Steinernema spp.	Exhibit, Nemasys	Biosys. AGC	Horticulture, mushrooms
Protozoa	Noto Bait	M&R Durango	Turf
Nosema locustae			
Viruses	Granupom, Madex	Hoechst Andermatt	Fruit trees
Cydia pomonella GV[c]			
Lymantria dispar NPV[d]	Gypcheck	Crop Genetics International	Forestry
Neodiprion sertifier NPV[d]	Monisarmiovirus	Kemira Oy	Forestry
Beneficial Insects	Trichocap	BASF	Maize
Trichogramma spp.			
Encarsia formosa	En-Strip	Koppert	Protected horticulture

Active agent	*Product examples*	*Manufacturer*	*Market*
Phytoseiulus persimilis	Fightmite	Kargro	Protected horticulture
Aphidoletes aphidomyza	Fightaphid	Fargro	Protected horticulture
Chrysopa camea	Laeewing larvae	Better yield insects	Protected horticulture
Dachusa and *Diglyphus*	Leaf miner parasite	Bunting Biological control	Protected horticulture
Cryptolaemus montrouzieri	Mealy bug predators	Bunting Biological control	Protected horticulture

(a) Produced by conjugation of two *B. thuringiensis* variants each containing different toxin genes.
(b) Heat killed cells of *P. fluorescens* containing a *B.thuringiensis* toxin gene Granulosis virus
(c) Nuclear polyhydrosis virus

Other Assorted Cultural Practices: Cultural practices such as flooding, row spacing, plot spacing, using rotations, sanitation and other farm practices that reduce persistent pest problems.

Impacts of IPM Programmes

The IPM approach has been widely demonstrated, tested in various countries. Several studies, both on-farm and off-farm, have revealed the importance of IPM approach in improving both the productivity and profitability especially through reduction of costs of inputs (Table 16.4). However, several studies conducted on the impact of IPM programmes revealed that lack of awareness, inability to exhibit instant and dramatic response like chemical pesticides, limited production capacity and less accessibility resulted in poor adoption of IPM practices by farmers (Singh, 2000; Krishnamoorthy and Veerabhadraiah, 2001;Srivastava *et al*., 1998; Venkatachalam *et al*., 2001).

Table 16.4: Impact of IPM Programmes on Pesticide Use, Crop Yields and Annual Savings (Pretty, 1996)

Country and Crop	*Average Changes in Pesticide use (as % of conventional treatments)*	*Changes in Yields (as % conventional treatments)*	*Annual Savings of Programme (US$)*
Thailand, rice	50%	-	5-10 million
Philippines, rice	62%	110%	5-10 million
Indonesia, rice	34-42%	105%	50-100 million
Nicaragua, maize	25%	93%	-
Bangladesh, rice	0-25%	113-124%	-
India, groundnuts	0%	100%	34,000
China, rice	46-80%	110%	400,000
Vietnam, rice	57%	107%	54,000
India, rice	33%	108%	790,000

Value Addition

Agricultural crops are processed for many different purposes. These range from the removal of anti-nutritional components and increasing the storage life of the final product to adding value to increase both employment and income generating opportunities. Value addition can be achieved through

1. Processing
2. Fermentation

Processing

Many agricultural crops can be processed mechanically into chips, flour, pellets, starch, jam, jelly, etc. A few examples are cited here to elucidate the value-addition of agricultural produce through processing.

Chips: Root and tuber crops like potato, tapioca, sweet potato, arrowroots, etc. can be sliced into chips. These chips can either be sun-dried or oven-dried to reduce moisture contents so as to prevent them from spoilage. The chips are mainly used for preparation of animal feeds.

Flour: Grains of cereals and dried chips from roots and tuber crops are pounded or grinded to obtain flour. It is usually regarded as a difficult product to preserve in storage.

Pellets: Most of the chips or flour for animal feed is now handled as pellets. Hard and glossy pellets can be stored without spoilage for 4 months.

Starch: Most of the commercial starch of global interest is obtained either from maize or from cassava. Other sources of commercial starch are from arrowroot, canna, sweet potato and yams.

There are three general areas in which starch is mainly used by the textile industries—(1) sizing operations, (2) finishing operations and (3) printing operations.

Paper Industries: Though the basic component of paper production is cellulose fibre, a number of other materials are used to process and modify the finished products to suit various end uses. Starch accounts for 97 per cent of these materials.

Adhesive Industry: Starch is commonly used in making gums and adhesives.

Dextrins are a large varied group of D-glucose polymers, which are obtained from starch. They are used as back-steam and front-steam gums for envelopes as bottle labelling adhesives, postage stamps, lined cardboard boxes and photographic mounting materials.

Food Industry: Starch may be incorporated into food in native form or a gelatinised form. Sago is an excellent example of a gelatinised food product from starch. Starch also finds use in various other foods and has diverse and far-ranging functions. Starch functions as an adhesive in breaded products. It is a binder in processed meats and extruded foods. The starch imparts cloudiness to cream filling and glazing to nuts. In baked foods, starch provides anti-staling character.

Sweetener Industry: Starch is the primary source for glucose and glucose syrups which are sweetner. Glucose is converted into fructose syrup, which is 20 times more sweetner than glucose.

Miscellaneous Uses: In addition to the above major industries which uses starch, there are many other applications of starch such as

Soap and detergent industry, Laundry starches, cosmetic uses, pharmaceutical uses and horticultural sprays, in explosives and plastics from starch.

Juice, Jam, Jelley and Ketchups: Fruits are processed into various value-added products like juice, Jam, jelly and ketchups. The process products offer handsome returns as compared to raw materials. Further, the processed products can be substantiated with vitamins, minerals, etc. to enhance either its nutrient content or its aroma and flavour.

Pigments and Natural Colourants: As alternate to synthetic colourants, natural colourants are being derived from plants and microbial sources. Beta-carotene (yellow and orange colour) and anthocyanins (purple colour) are two major natural colourants extracted from carrots, beet root and grape pomes, respectively.

Fermentation

Fermentation is one of the oldest forms of food preservation technologies in the world. Indigenous fermented foods such as bread, cheese and wine have been prepared and consumed for thousands of years. Fermenting fruits and vegetables can bring many benefits to people in developing countries. Fermented foods play an important role in providing food security, enhancing livelihoods and improving the nutrition and social well being of millions of people around the world. Fermentation is carried out by microorganisms, i.e. yeasts (yeast fermentation), bacteria (bacterial fermentation) and very often, jointly by yeasts/moulds and bacteria (mixed fermentation). Fruit based fermentations are grape wine and others like toddy from coconut palm.

Dosa, iddli, dholka, jilabi are traditional fermented foods from rice Similarly tapioca and sweet potato pulp are fermented and various fermented foods, i.e. gari, futu, dumby, manicuera (all from tapioca) and sauce, sochu (alcoholic beverages) from sweet potato are prepared. Basi is sugarcane wine made in the Philippines by fermenting boiled, freshly extracted sugarcane juice (Battcock and Ali, 2001). Muratina is an alcoholic drink made from sugar cane and Muratina fruits in Kenya (Dirar, 1993; Fellows, 1997).

Most traditional fermented food products are made by a complex interaction of different microorganism. One of the prominent examples is the production of vinegar.

- Vinegar is a product of a mixed fermentation of yeast followed by acetic acid bacteria. It can be made from any fermentable carbohydrate source, for example, fruits, vegetables, syrups and wine. The basic requirement for vinegar production is a raw material that will undergo an alcoholic fermentation. Apples, pears, grapes, honey, syrups, cereals, hydrolysed starches are all ideal substrates for the production of vinegars.

Fermentation technologies play an important role in ensuring the food security of millions of people around the world, particularly marginalised and vulnerable groups like women and children. This is achieved through improved food preservation, increasing the range of raw materials that can be used to produce edible food products and removing anti-nutritional factors to make food safe to eat.

Income and employment generation

The production of fermented fruit and vegetable products provides income and employment to millions of people around the world. Food processing is probably the most important source of income and employment in Africa, Asia and Latin America. The FAO has stated that value added through marketing and processing raw products can be much greater than the value of primary production. For instance in Sub-Saharan Africa, more than 60 per cent of the workforce is employed in the small scale food processing sector, and between one third and two thirds of value added manufacturing is based on agricultural raw materials (Odunfa, 1985). This is particularly important, as agriculture and the formal sector are unable to absorb the growing labour force in many countries.

Improving cultural and social well being

The strong flavours of fermented food products can enhance a dull diet. Fermented vegetables such as pickles, and sauerkraut are used as condiments to enhance the overall flavour of the meal. A small amount of pickle can make a bland starchy diet (like dahl and rice in Asia) much more appealing.

Strategies for Sustainable Agriculture

Technology Generation

- Change in research focus from commodity based to agro-ecosystem based research.
- Participatory technology development using bottom-up and interactive processes.
- Farming systems research embody a whole farm or farming system orientation with individual farmers.
- Efficient research management system managing man, material and processes in an efficient and sustainable way.
- Market oriented research to develop and popularise appropriate technologies.
- Developing and maintaining functional linkages with technology transfer, utilisation and support systems.

Technology Transfer

- Use collaborative problem solving as the development mode of influence on the farmers behaviour.
- Use extension resources to support the development of independent farmers organisations (Self-help groups, farmer interest groups, commodity associations, etc.) to improve feedback.
- Encourage and facilitate planning and action at group and community levels.
- Encourage learning, which will enable farmers to manage with minimal extension support in the future and to identify critical points which support is needed.
- Participatory communication strategies to provide relevant messages and technologies to the farmers.
- Harness the power of information technology to promote sustainable technologies.

Utilisation System and Value Addition

- Develop farmers understanding of the ecological system, eco-technologies and their impact on agriculture and human life.
- Develop farmers knowledge and skills in marketing intelligence, weather interpretation, production management and marketing skills.

Supporting System

- Timely supply of quality inputs in adequate quantities at a reasonable price.
- Timely supply of adequate credit.
- Easy access to input and credit facilities.
- Well-knit price control mechanism and innovative marketing strategies.
- Good infrastructure development—transport, irrigation, power supply etc.
- Farmer friendly policies which facilitate easy adoption of eco-technologies.
- Legislative measures to protect natural resources, farmers rights, market regulation and indigenous knowledge.

Conclusion

The world has the capacity to feed itself. It can be done, however only if environment degradative trends can be reversed and sustainable agriculture can be restored. We must develop a coordinated and multidisciplinary approach to assess soil and agricultural resources and evaluate their potential and restraints. New technological innovations must not only be high yielding but also compatible with sustaining acceptable standard of environmental quality. The world community therefore must develop a resource management policy. This is particularly true when dealing with marginal, fragile and ecologically sensitive ecosystems. Multidisciplinary teams should derive resource management policies for agriculture that should be implemented through sound ecological and economic incentives.

17

Community Participation in Management of Forest Resources and Sustainable Development

N. SUBBA RAO

Environment preservation and economic development are the two important issues that have been intensively deliberated globally and nationally ever since the United Nations sponsored historic meeting on environment held at Stockholm in 1972.[1] Basically, they are the two alternatives that can strike a balance between them from the societal point of view. Unbridled consumerism, which is the universal outcome of modern economic growth, does lead to the use of natural resources at a level, which is not sustainable. Over and above the direct demands on the natural resources, the life-style generally accompanying economic growth has led to serious pollution and resource degradation (Vyas, 1996). In more recent years, attention has been shifted from 'development' to 'sustainability'. The task of integrating environmental concerns in development is not as complex as is widely believed. The success of development invariably depends on people's cooperation and participation which would be forthcoming more easily if development projects are sensitive to the purity of soil, forests, air and water. The wise use of natural resources alone would guarantee sustainable development (Singh, 2001).

Forests constitute one of the important renewable natural resources of the biosphere and contribute substantially to economic development. They play a major role in enhancing the quality of environment. However, excessive exploitation of forest wealth has led to deforestation and land degradation, and consequent problems of environment. The global environmental problems are direct or indirect consequence, of local and individual actions. Unfortunately, there is complete lack of effort to educate and organise people around environmental issues regionally and locally. This paper is an attempt to examine the state of forest resources and the changes in forest cover and the role of various agencies in forest management. It also highlights the need for sustainable management of forest resources through community participation and the ways and means to create awareness among various sections of population.

Sustainable Development—Some Conceptual Issues

The sustainable development is not a new paradigm. It had origins in 1980s and came into prominence with the highlighting of the concept of Sustainable Development by the UN World Commission on Environment and Development (WCED) popularly known as Brundtland Commission (1987). It is the latest expression of a long-standing ethic involving people's relationship with the environment, and responsibilities of the present generation to the future. Sustainable development has been defined variously by different authors and institutions. The popular among these include that of WCED and Food and Agriculture Organisation (FAO).

The WCED defined sustainable development as 'meeting the needs of the present without compromising the ability of future generations to meet their needs'. This means that, the present resource base is the base for the survival of the future generations too. So, the nature has entrusted us with a hard task of preserving the environment while exploiting and pass on to the next generation as we have borrowed from our elders. The definition of Food and Agriculture Organisation (FAO) goes a step further. According to it "sustainable development is the management and conservation of the natural resource base, and the orientation of technological and institutional change in such a manner as to ensure the attainment and continued satisfaction of human needs for present and future generations. Such sustainable development (in agriculture, forestry and fisheries sectors) conserves land, water, plant and animal reservoirs, is environmentally non-degrading, technically appropriate, economically viable and socially acceptable".

All these definitions strike at a common point that is responsible utilisation of resources as "natural capital" with the due care for environment and biodiversity for an ecologically viable and equitable development as "sustainable income" fully from the balance of nature and development. This again calls for an overall horizon of sustainability in terms of temporal viability, biological ability, economical feasibility, environmental stability and social equity as a measure of real time development.

Randal O'Toole of the environmental think-tank, Thoreau Institute, divides the modern-day environmental movement into two groups—preservationists and conservationists. In the preservationists' view, nature knows best and nature should be preserved at any cost. In this context no system of food production or other has much growing room. The question for preservationists is simple: how can six billion people survive on this planet with "no impact" from development? Humanity's need to breathe, eat, create waste, and shelter itself has a profound impact on the earth's ecosystem. We can seek to attenuate the negative aspects of that impact as much as possible, but there will always be some impact. On the other hand, Conservationists are more realistic about sustainability. Their goal is to maintain ecosystems through collaborative management by public and private stakeholders at the local level. Regardless of the preservationist or conservationist leanings, environmental groups make an important contribution by alerting the public to hazards and risks. However, as environmental groups proliferate and compete with one another to capture public attention and funding, there is a tendency to reduce facts to quick ideas and clichés, known in the mass media trade as "sound bites." Reality does not lend itself well to sound bites, but exaggeration and emotion do. This challenge of sound bites has to be faced by insisting on a review of facts.

Thus, the paradigm of sustainable development incorporates environmental sustainability on the one hand and economic sustainability on the other. Then there are two other elements of sustainability, viz., social and institutional. But one needs to understand the meaning of sustainable development in the context of differences across countries pertaining to the levels of socio-political and economic developments. Unless these dimensions are taken into account the weaknesses and contradictions of sustainable development come into fore. The imperfect understanding of the link between poverty and environmental degradation often results in propagating linear policies, i.e., concentrating on either one or the other problem, rather than following an integrated approach which would address both the problems (Vyas, *et al.*, 1996; Ratna Reddy, 1996).

Many of the issues of environment and sustainable development are diffuse, multi-disciplinary, multi-agency, multi-stakeholder and multi-sector in nature that needs a more collaborative and holistic system approach for a better resolution. Hence, the environmental solution no longer comes as a simple "top down" plan or Governmental mandate. The goal of sustainable forest management through a set of realistic steps is a responsibility of all participants in the system and indeed, substantive, practical solutions will require the concerted efforts of a host of stakeholders across the society. More so in forest environments, given various user conflict, it is impossible for the Government to formulate and protect the eco-system solely by means of policing—control and enforcement. It is we, the whole society, who are responsible for the accomplishment. Here in this perspective, a co-operative responsibility falls upon all of us—scientists, politicians, managers, resource users and concerned citizens to develop and implement a comprehensive management strategy to ensure the sustained production into consideration, not just economically important ones (Muruganandam and Sastry, 1998).

Status of Forest Resources and Changes in Forest Cover

Forests form an integral component of the biosphere. They have been the green frontier of mankind since time immemorial—a seemingly limitless resource for human expansion. They are home for countless plants and animals that are vital elements of our life-supporting systems, as well as for millions of forest dwellers. They provide goods for direct consumption (including recreational activities) and land for food production. They also represent capital when converted to shelter and infrastructure. With their supply of timber, fuel wood, game, and a rich variety of other products they were, and are, a crucial source of raw materials for human society. But increasingly we are realising that they offer more than that. They offer more land when we need it; they balance and manage our water supplies and the flow of our rivers; they are a major force in determining our climate. They are essential to the stabilisation of global climate and the management of water and land (Sharma and Rowe, 1992 and ICIHI, 1989).

The area of the world's forests, including natural forests and forest plantations, was estimated to be 3,454 million hectares in 1995, or about one-fourth of the land area of the Earth. While 97 per cent of the world's forests are natural or semi-natural forests, only about 3 per cent are plantations. About 55 per cent of the world's forests are located in developing countries, with the remaining 45 per cent in developed countries (FAO, 1999).

The world's forests are almost equally divided between tropical/subtropical forests and temperate/boreal forests. While the former are rich in biodiversity and valuable tropical hardwood, the latter serve as the world's primary source of industrial wood. The tropical forests (both moist and dry, totaling about 1.5 billion hectares each) stretch across the developing countries. While two-thirds of the tropical moist forests are in Latin America, with the remainder split between Africa and Asia; three quarters of the tropical dry forests are in Africa. On the other hand, the temperate forests (1.5 million ha) can be found mainly in the developed world.

India's forest cover which includes dense forest, open forest and mangrove was estimated in 1991 at 63.9 million hectares or about 19.27 per cent of the country's total geographical area. Out of these, the dense forest land with a crown density of 40 per cent or more covers only 38.5 million hectares accounting for only 11.7 per cent of India's total area. The open forest represents 7.95 per cent while mangrove forest 0.15 per cent and scrub area 1.74 per cent. In spite of efforts during the last 45 years, only a modest annual increase under forest cover was achieved, which, however is ascribed to the technical changes in assessment techniques rather than to any actual increase (Rathore, 1996).

Change in Forest Cover

Over the period, there have been changes in the forest cover the world over. Data published in the State of the World's Forests, 1997 (FAO, 1997) provide a picture of the trends in the forest cover in a 15-year interval (1980-1995) and allow a comparison between the 1980-1990 and 1990-1995 periods. Between 1980 and 1995, the extent of the world's forests (including both natural forests and forest plantations) decreased by some 180 million hectares. There was a net increase of 20 million hectares in developed countries, but a net loss of 200 million hectares in developing nations (FAO, 1997).

Between 1990 and 1995, there was an estimated net loss of 56.3 million hectares of forests worldwide. This represented decreases of 65.1 million hectares in developing countries and an increase of 8.8 million hectares in developed countries. Although the global loss of forests was still very high, the figures suggest that the rate of deforestation might be slowing. The estimate of forest cover change in natural forests of developing countries (which is where most deforestation is taking place) was an annual loss of 13.7 million hectares between 1990 and 1995, compared with 15.5 million hectares per year over the decade 1980-1990 (FAO, 1997).

But in recent years, there has been an alarming increase in destructive deforestation and land degradation in developing countries, reflecting the earlier development experiences of industrial countries, when large areas of the world's temperate forests were cleared for agriculture, timber, and fuel wood. Recent studies show that deforestation, especially in the tropics, has risen to an estimated 17-20 million ha annually—almost equivalent in area to the United Kingdom or Uganda—from around 11.4 million ha in 1980. Those hardest hit include Costa Rica, Cote d'Ivoire, Ghana, Honduras, India, Nepal, Nigeria, Thailand, and the Philippines. In the temperate region, old-growth forests are also at risk. Furthermore, forest degradation, largely from acid precipitation, is harming large areas of temperate forests, especially in Eastern Europe.

In respect of India, the annual deforestation is estimated at about 47 thousand hectares in the early eighties. Though the forest area is currently not shrinking, forest degradation continues because of the increasing urban and rural demands for fuel, fodder, timber and other industrial use. The declining forest wealth and productivity would be the inevitable outcome of these trends.

The major causes of change in forest cover in the tropics appear to be expansion of subsistence agriculture in Africa and Asia and large economic development programmes involving resettlement, agriculture and infrastructure in Latin America and Asia (FAO, 1997). The net increase in forest area in developed countries is largely a result of afforestation and reforestation, including natural regrowth on land abandoned by agriculture. This increase has more than compensated for the clearing of some areas of forests in various developed countries, mainly for urban expansion and infrastructure development (FAO, 1999).

Already, the misuse of forests has brought with it significant social, economic and environmental costs (e.g., lost soil and watershed protection, local climate change, and destruction of habitat). Many developing countries, especially in Africa and South Asia, face acute shortages of fuel wood, fodder, timber, and other forest products, not to mention the displacement of their forest dwellers. There has been a loss of biological diversity, possible global climate change, degradation of watersheds, and desertification. The loss of tropical moist forests is especially worrying, as they provide habitats for more than 50 per cent of the world's plants and animal species, genetic materials for food and medicine, and influence the climate, both at the regional and global level (Sharma and Rowe, 1992; Subba Rao, 2001).

The heavy dependency on wood fuels has combined with rapid population growth to contribute to accelerating forest and woodland destruction, especially around major urban centres. Since fuel wood is generally considered a free good, taken largely from land to which everyone has access, efficient markets for fuel wood have not developed, despite its increasing scarcity. Commercial logging has been directly responsible for only 10 to 20 per-cent of forest destruction in Sub-Saharan Africa, but it usually leads to a second phase of destruction: logging roads provide access for settlers who continue the deforestation the loggers have begun. The degradation and destruction of forests and woodlands accelerates soil degradation and erosion and harms local and regional climates and hydrological regimes, which in turn negatively affect agriculture. The worsening fuel wood and water supply situation also forces women and children to spend more time collecting these necessities (Cleaver and Schreiber, 1992; Dixon, 1986).

What is to be done?

Clearly, new approaches are needed. But what form should they take? Deforestation needs to be slowed and the area of forests, woodlands, and wilderness gradually stabilised. This will require that further expansion of cropped land be limited necessitating rapid agricultural intensification. And the average total fertility rate needs to be lowered by 50 per cent over the next 30 years, so as to reduce population growth to 2.2 per cent annum. Further, effective agro forestry activities can have a major impact on the environment, farming, the rural energy economy, and women's time. Wood fuel markets will develop more rapidly if open access to fuel wood is eliminated, people can freely market wood from their own land, and communities and farmers have uncontested ownership of local forests and woodlands (Cleaver and Schreiber, 1992).

Role of International Agencies and Civil Servants in Forest Management

Over the period a number of international organisations have showed interest in the conservation of forests and trees in developing countries. Prominent among these include International Tropical Timber Organisation ITTO), Yokohama; Tropical Forestry Action Programme of FAO; United Nations Environment Programme (UNEP), World Bank, U.N. Commission for Sustainable Development and so on (Ravi Sharma, 1995). Conserving forests and trees in developing countries is now a fad in the bureaucracies based in the above organisations. The civil servants working in these organisations are confident that to conserve tropical forests, their power and budgets have to increase. But the billions of dollars allocated to forestry are in large part a façade as is evident from the continuing deforestation. The felling of trees remains a profitable venture and even industrialised countries make money out of it. The credit for this situation goes to the international civil servants who have failed to make a dent on the economics behind deforestation. They have not developed an economic model, which will make it profitable to keep forests intact rather than clear them. Moreover, it does not look for ways to correct market failures but instead increases the number of international civil servants to monitor and channel funds for forestry activities in the developing world. It continues the old game of either dangling the false hope of increased aid or threatening to cut the existing aid to help arrest tropical deforestation. At the same time it does not seriously consider the legitimate demand of developing countries to compensate them for the loss of revenue from stopping commercial activity. And despite the obvious failure of these international initiatives in correcting market failures related to forestry, backed by countries like Canada, USA, attempts are made time and again for fresh agreements on forest conservation (Ravi Sharma, 1995).

Commenting on the failure of TFAP of FAO, Mr. Ullsten remarked in his review that despite its wide-ranging aims, in practice, the plan had "too narrow an approach to the forestry sector, especially with regard to ecological and environmental issues, and too little attention to its linkages with other sectors." Mr. Ullsten also found that foreign experts often outnumbered local professional staff on field missions, which cost $700,000 per country and concluded, "the approach savours of arrogance with foreign experts telling the country what is good for it instead of creating a dialogue aimed at working out solutions". It was also pointed out that non-governmental organisations were consulted in only seven out of the 25 countries. (Ravi Sharma, 1995).

Further, these agencies and civil servants at the international level have undertaken a number of initiatives[2] in recent years. These include guidelines (ITTO, 1990) and Criteria and indicators for sustainable forestry management (FAO, 2001) that have been promoted by various international agencies. Criteria and indicators are tools used to define, assess and monitor progress towards sustainable forestry management. At the national level they may be used to guide countrywide policies, regulations and legislation. The ultimate aim is to promote improved forest management practices over time, and to further the development of a healthier and more productive forest estate, taking into consideration the social, economic, environmental, cultural and spiritual needs of the full range of stakeholder groups in the countries concerned. However, to date, there has been only limited application of both the guidelines and criteria and indicators and, hence, only limited impact on field practice (Cassells and Hall, 2000; Vandana Shiva, *et al.*, 1981). Another instrument used for achieving the goal of sustainable management is the auditing and certification system. But this applies to those countries where well-developed forestry planning and legislation exist. It was observed that current auditing systems are inadequate for the effective monitoring of forestry legislation enforcement in general and sustainable forest management in particular. Where forest legislation is inadequate, it was felt that strict adherence to bureaucratic requirements could easily lead more to corruption than to effective law enforcement (Nsenkyiere and Simula, 2000). Other initiatives contemplated in the Asia-Pacific Region are the imposition of logging bans (Sarry, 2000) and the Code of Practice for Forest Harvesting that has been initiated by FAO (APFC, 2000). However, successful implementation of all these initiatives and national forest plans and policies will be possible only when there is a well-formulated forest policy and strategic planning[3] supported by resource allocation and forethought.

State Control and Bureaucratic Approaches

Under British rule in India, the State established monopoly control over forests, reserved large tracts for timber extraction, severely restricted the customary rights of local populations to these resources and encouraged commercially profitable species at the cost of species used by the local population. There was also large-scale forest clearance and felling by railways, ships, bridges, tea and coffee plantations, crop cultivation to increase the Government's land base and so on (Guha, 1989). After independence, state monopoly over forests continued, as did the practice of forestry in the interests of commercial gain, while the local people's rights to non-timber forest produce were further curtailed (Agarwal, 1995). Today, the state apparatus (Civil Servants and Forest Department Officials) is in charge of the entire development process. It controls the natural resource base of the entire country just like any other Government/ landholders, controlling one-fifth of the landmass. The state has draconian powers to acquire private lands and displace poor and tribals, without providing them alternative livelihoods. So the process is one of state controlling all nature resources, organising their exploitation, more often than not in non-attainable wasteful ways, leaving the local communities high and dry. This apparatus then attempts to alleviate rural poverty by providing a variety of handouts. It also tries to deliver health care and education to the poor. This whole process of organising state patronage is riddled by corruption; so, much of what is expected to percolate down is lapped up on the way (Gadgil and Seshagiri Rao, 1995; Pashupati Nath and Siddha Nath, 1990).

The state apparatus is instead engaged in taking bamboo away from basket weavers, who have depended on it for generations for a livelihood, and handing it to paper mills at throwaway prices. It is engaged in throwing out tribals of Madhya Pradesh to construct dams that will benefit the sugar barons of Surat. Its performance has tended to worsen social inequities and regional disparities. In consequence, it has today lost all legitimacy to claims of promoting social equity and regional balance (Gadgil and Seshagiri Rao, 1995). This can also be attributed to the absence of a well-defined forest policy and its implementation.

Over the years the forest policy in India has changed. Until the early seventies, the objective was to increase state revenues and to obtain sustained yield of timber from government forests by planting non-browsable and market-oriented timber trees. Emphasis was laid on the conversion of low value mixed forest into high value plantation of commercial species mainly to meet industrial requirements. This policy led to reduction in the diversity of forest species and also deprived the poor people who depended traditionally on forests for their livelihood products, which they were able to obtain from mixed forests. This neglect of people's demands further exacerbated biotic pressure and made regenération of natural forests more difficult. Recognising these problems a policy change was made in the mid-seventies and Social Forestry (SF) on village and private lands was introduced. This was seen more as a programme, which would release industry forestry from social pressure. Unfortunately, the SF programme failed to take off not only because of various technical and operational reasons but more significantly because of lack of involvement of local people in the programme (Saxena, 1994).

The policies regarding government forests until 1990 have neither led to improved productivity nor to improved welfare of the people. Several alternatives were suggested, including leasing of forest lands to user industries. However, instead of solving the problem, the policy led to the emergence of a new set of issues, such as industrialists grabbing good and wastelands in the name of afforestation. Despite policy interventions the present position is that forestlands suffer from extreme biotic pressure. They require not capital investment, nor even higher technology but protection and recuperation, which can be done only by working with the people (Saxena, 1994).

Forest Policy and Strategic Planning

Successful implementation of various kinds of international initiatives and national forest policies mentioned above, therefore, will be possible only when there is a well-formulated forest policy and strategic planning and its meticulous implementation.[3] A good forest policy should have three essential characteristics. It must be global and take into account economic, ecological and social interests. It must look into the long term and be linked to the other public policies which have an impact on forest resources. Finally it has to be the result of a compromise between the various stakeholders, who should participate actively both in the formulation of the forest policy and in the subsequent stages of implementation, monitoring and evaluation.

There are two main approaches to forest policy formulation. These are the so called administrative approach, where the forest administration plays the major role, and the so called negotiation approach, which is a participatory process that allows the various stakeholders to negotiate between themselves in order to reach a compromise. However, there is a mixed approach which combines the advantages of the first two and calls upon facilitators/mediators/organisers to help in the expression of individual positions, the dialogue and the negotiation so as to reach a compromise. Although the formulation process can be perceived as a participatory process of research and negotiation towards a compromise between several stakeholders with divergent interests, the negotiated solution should however be considered by all as a consensual measure, the application of which also requires the active participation of all parties (Buttoud and Samyn, 1999).

Traditional Indigenous Systems of Forest Development and Management

Thus forestlands suffer from extreme biotic pressure, and require not capital investment, nor even higher technology, but protection and recuperation, which can be done only by working with people basing on their knowledge and information. The restoration of trees and forests on degraded lands will require knowledge about the best ways to efficiently and effectively plant various species of woody plants, and this knowledge will not come easily because the woody flora of South Asia and other regions is very diverse. For many tree species, we do not have sufficient information about even basic features of reproduction like the formation, maturation and germination of seeds, the growth of seedlings, and the conditions under which seedlings survive (Rai, 1999). Moreover, the rate at which the information is accumulated about our native forest trees is slow at a time when natural habits and their biota are disappearing at a rapid pace. The success of our efforts to green the earth, to restore degraded lands, to sustainably utilise our precious forest resources and to conserve our natural endowment would be greatly enhanced by such information.

Basically where community management existed, responsibility for resource management was linked to resource use. Government takeover of forests and the privatisation of the village commons lands have effectively broken this link, and eroded the social base of these protective systems. Forests and village commons are no longer the collective responsibility of villagers they have become a commodity to be individually exploited (Agarwal, 1995).

The process of satisation and privatisation indicated above have not only concentrated natural resources in the hands of a few, they have also contributed to their depletion by undermining traditional institutional arrangements of communal resource use and management which existed in many regions. Traditionally, all villages, irrespective of gender, had same rights of collection of fire wood collection and others in village common lands. People have traditionally enjoyed access to government forests including the reserve forests, but they were alienated from the management of forests. Traditional systems of forest management and gathering was typically not destructive of nature. Even today, 75 per cent of firewood for rural domestic use in northern India is gathered in the form of twigs and fallen branches, which does not destroy the forest. Some religious and folk beliefs also helped preserve nature, as in the sacred groves still found in North-east India (Agarwal, 1995, Nadkarni, 1996; Borah, 1999). Cultural practices of the indigenous people also seem to have stronger influence on the conservation of natural systems[4] (Ratna Reddy, 1996).

The gathering of food and medicinal items from forests and village common lands demands an elaborate knowledge of the properties of plant species, which the women, who are gatherers, gained through long experience. The disappearance of forests and village commons is destroying the material basis of this knowledge.

Also in many regions peasant women were responsible for indigenous seed collection and preservation. With the large-scale shift to hybrid seed varieties this control has passed into the hands of national and international laboratories. While traditional knowledge systems are being devalued, the women who possess and depend on this knowledge have little access to the institutions, which create what is seen as scientific knowledge and modern technology. In this sense, what we see today is not just a crisis of sustenance for the poor and for women; it is also the loss of knowledge critical for generating sustainable livelihoods (Agrarwal, 1995). People who are nearer to nature understand environment much better than those who are away. The first such view was expressed by people through 'Chipco Movement' started at the Alakananda catchment areas of Himalayas, later it was spread to different areas. Similarly, there is another movement in Western Ghats near Karnataka, viz., 'Appiko Movement'. These movements spread environmental awareness among people of the regions and also conduct Eco-camps (Iyengar, 1993).

Participatory Management

Forestry is one of the most critical factors of life supporting systems. Protecting forests and other conservation areas stabilises local and regional climate and hydrology, stimulates agricultural intensification, and ensures the provision of forest products and environmental services (Kevin Cleaver, *et al.* 1992). Keeping this in view the World Commission on Forests and Sustainable Development (WCFSD) demands a conscious effort by societies to take bold political decisions and develop new civil society institutions so as to improve governance and accountability regarding forest use. Innovation is desperately needed if the world is to prevent a deepening of the forest crisis.

Managing forests sustainably involves more than technical solutions. It must get to the human issues-betterment of the human condition., social equity, poverty reduction, power relations, gender roles, which lie at the heart of forest resource problems and conflicts. Embracing these human issues requires the participation of a broad cross-section of people in planning for and making decisions about forest management.

All the on-going forest development and management projects, therefore, rely on forest conservation technology built upon accumulated wisdom of the people. This will not only enhance the people's participation but also assist in adopting conservation measures, which are necessarily to be adopted on community basis/collectively by group action. Thus the success of forest management programmes mainly depends upon the level of participation of the people living in the area.

The WCFSD extends strong support for greater participation in decision-making and management by communities who closely depend on forest resources, and also by other elements of civil society. This approach reduces centralised bureaucratic determination and control. It is also consistent with the themes of community management and empowerment of local people. It believes that achieving sustainable rural livelihoods and alleviating poverty is more likely through the localised management of forest resources; it results in a more equitable sharing of benefits compared to centralised or corporate management. Localised management manifested through community forests, village woodlots and tree plantations on farms reduce poverty by: providing fuel wood, fodder and non-timber products; increasing food security; preventing land degradation; and providing rural employment (Krishnaswamy, 1999; Silver, 1991; Bakouma and Buttoud, 1999).

In other words, sustainable development and management of forests can be a reality only with the involvement of the people concerned and it should not be imposed. As rightly pointed out by United Nations Development Programme (UNDP, 1993) "peoples' participation is becoming central issue of our times". Of late, there is a change in the attitude and thinking of policy makers, administrators and donor agencies, which hovers around people's participation as a central component in any rural development programme.

Concept and Meaning of People's Participation

A participatory approach is an essential mechanism for the protection of the public interest. Key issues in the participatory approach are: defining the participants (or stakeholders) and their interests; willingness and ability to have a dialogue; presenting scientific information in a form which can be easily understood; reconciling local, national and global interests; and the political will to respect and enforce tough decisions. Neither governments nor aid agencies are equipped to make judgments about how local people value their environment.

Development projects that have not built upon the strengths of existing practices have often failed. Local participation also has high economic and environmental returns in implementing programmes in afforestation, soil management, park protection and so on (Andrew Steer, 1992; Bakouma andButtoud, 1999).

The participation in a development programme is not only the involvement of people in rendering financial assistance, giving one's own labour (shramdan), or resource mobilisation. In real sense participation of people can only be considered if they had also a role to play in the planning of a programme. The people involve themselves in thinking, in need-identification, fixing priorities of the needs, planning, decision-making, implementing and evaluating the socio-economic development programmes. So, this is both mental and physical process. People's participation, therefore, can be defined as an individual's mental and emotional involvement in group solutions that encourage him to contribute to group goals and to share responsibility for them. Similarly, the United Nation's Social Development Division (UNSDD) defined participation as a process of activities comprising people's involvement in decision-making, contributing to development efforts and sharing equitably the benefits therefrom. More deliberately participatory development can be explained as those development programmes which have in-built mechanism for complete involvement of people in decision-making process about what would be done and how; in implementing programmes and decision by contributing various resources; in sharing of benefits accruing out of development programmes; and in evaluating such programmes. Taken together, all these four kinds of involvement of people in a programme lead to an innovative kind of development approach called participatory development (Sah, 1995).

The Commission realises that simply opening up the decision-making process will not by itself reverse the decline of forests. Most of the causes of forest decline are due to policies and actions that originate outside the forestry sector. However, the Commission advocates the participatory approach as a necessary means of achieving greater social equity, which is essential for sustaining human societies. New forms of governance and institutions to permit wider and more equitable participation therefore have to be high on the political and social agendas of the 21st century.

Further, People's participation can also be seen as employing a method where the associated communities are motivated to function and contribute as a group to perform a pre-determined task All adults, living and making their livelihood from within the forest area, are referred to as the 'community'.

The important question that may arise is why should people participate? It is generally agreed in many quarters that unless the direct and visible benefits of the programmes are in congruence with the interest of the people, participation comes slowly. Experiences of many have also shown that it is not very difficult to organise people around a profitable activity for a while, but, sustaining of such interest over a long period has been difficult. Mobilising people's participation would require much more intensive interaction wherein the communities would be required to be involved in the process of planning, implementation and management of programmes to the extent possible (Venkattakumar, *et al.*, 2000).

Need for Extension Education and Creation of Awareness

The problem confronting many forest conservationists is how do we induce the people to participate. Generally there are two schools of thought on inducing people's participation. One school advocates that a well-designed and executed education and extension campaign would suffice to convince most people to join such a programme. They don't think incentives or subsidies are necessary, because most developing countries have severe financial constraints and people may develop a subsidy-dependent mentality for every government-generated programme. The other school considers that it is not fair for people to have to share the total cost of conservation when their meager income could be reduced in the first few years and benefits may accrue only to the next generation or to others downstream. Hence, incentives, either direct or indirect, should be given to those forestry dependent people who participate in the programme. This is deemed as a cost-sharing programme or a system to implement equitable income distribution.

These views are not necessarily mutually exclusive. To induce people to participate in a programme requires good extension. Unless people understand well that forest conservation will do them good in the long run, they may not maintain the practices even after they have done the work. On the other hand, to convince a majority of people to join a programme only by means of education may need many years. Many people simply have no resources and time to start the work unless some tangible incentives are given. Experience shows that in addition to extension and education, giving proper incentives, in cash or in kind (including food) has promoted people's participation and speeded up the Protection of land.

Environmental education and awareness are the prerequisites for effective tackling of environmental degradation. It is therefore, need of the hour to inculcate forestry based ecological consciousness among the masses, general public, students and others. A two-pronged approach needs to be adopted towards this end, (1) creation of awareness among the rural people and general public through extension education and (2) imparting curriculum based education.

1. People should be educated to make them aware of their rights and privileges and organising themselves into groups for undertaking productive activities. In the interests of informing and educating the rural masses to enable them to participate effectively in the conservation and management programs they should have access to all shades of opinion. Mass media such as the Radio, the Television, the Newspaper, the Journal, the Satellite and the Cinema may be used to educate literate as well as illiterate people of India and other Third World countries about the hazards and remedial measures of deforestation. Other avenues like distribution of pamphlets, leaflets, booklets, folktales, enactment of street plays, playlets, involvement of Non-governmental organisations (NGOs), charitable trusts, environmental agencies, conducting of Eco-camps, organising movements like that of Chipko, etc should be used and every effort must be undertaken in this gigantic task to preserve and conserve the forest environment.
2. Curriculum based environmental education in general and forestry education in particular should be initiated right from the school level. Forestry education is an educational program, which provides for a study of forestry, trees and vegetation, community, nation and world. It tries to inculcate ecological consciousness among the students. It creates in them basic awareness of the dynamics of forestry and trees, its importance, status and trends and its impact on people and the nation. The most important goal of forestry education should be to stabilise and maintain ecological balance of the biodiversity. However the burden of curriculum should not remain restricted at any level, but it should spread to higher classes also with advanced information. Special education and research-based education in forestry should also need to be undertaken. For the development of healthy society and for building superstructure of civilisation we need physically fit, mentally healthy, emotionally stable, socially adjusted, aesthetically sensitive and intellectually alert individuals, which can be possible only when the environmental and forestry based biodiversity is well maintained. Forestry based environmental education serves as a beacon light to enlighten people and make their attitudes and thinking scientific, rational and logical, so that they are free from biases and prejudices. It is the need of the hour, therefore, to eradicate this global crisis of deforestation through environmental education.

Conclusions

Forests must and will be used to feed, clothe, house and otherwise satisfy basic human needs. The concern is about the extent to which forests are used in relation to their capacity for renewal; the challenge is to manage forests so that they continue to satisfy human needs and at the same time are able to sustain the planet through their ecological functions. Based on the existing evidence, humans can no longer use forests in the way they have in the past. Some radical adjustments have to be made in order to sustain them in the 21st century and beyond. Therefore, sustainable forest management puts an obligation on forest managers (forest officials and other civil servants) and other forest conservationists to evaluate and mitigate the negative impacts of forest resource use on forest biodiversity. There is a need to integrate biodiversity into forestry planning and management. Further, the forest managers need exposure and deep involvement of strategies and programmes for sustainable management because technical forestry education is no longer enough to equip the foresters for challenges facing today. Given the economic, political and social institutions that will confront the world in the near future, there is a need for them to be socially active and appreciate the need for urgent conservation.

Summary

The world's forests are almost equally divided between tropical forests and temperate forests. While 97 per cent of the world's forests are natural or semi-natural forests, only about 3 per cent are plantations. About 55 per cent of the world's forests are located in developing countries, with the remaining 45 per cent in developed countries. India's forest cover which includes dense forest, open forest and mangrove was estimated in 1991 at 63.9 million hectares or about 19.27 per cent of the country's total geographical area. Between 1980 and 1995, the extent of the world's forests (including both natural forests and forest plantations) decreased by some 180 million hectares. But in recent years, there has been an alarming increase in destructive deforestation and land degradation in developing countries. Attempts to conserve the forest resources through national and international initiatives have not yielded any fruitful results. Successful implementation of various kinds of international initiatives and national forest policies will be possible only when there is a well-formulated forest policy and strategic planning and its meticulous implementation. People have traditionally enjoyed access to government forests including the reserve forests, but they were alienated from the management of forests. Traditional systems of forest management and gathering was typically not destructive of nature. All the on-going forest development and management projects, therefore, rely on forest conservation technology built upon accumulated wisdom of the people. Therefore people's participation plays a pivotal role in the sustainable management of forest resources. People involve themselves in thinking, in need-identification, fixing priorities of the needs, planning, decision-making, implementing and evaluating the socio-economic development programmes. But the problem confronting many forest conservationists is how to induce people to participate. This requires good extension education among the general public as well as people nearby areas and those who depend on forests for their livelihood by creation of awareness through multimedia. Similarly, curriculum based environmental education in general and forestry education in particular should be initiated right from the school level. There is a need to integrate biodiversity into forestry planning and management. Further, the forest managers need exposure and deep involvement of strategies and programmes for sustainable management because technical forestry education is no longer enough to equip the foresters for the challenges facing today.

NOTES

1. The UNO Conference on Human Environment held at Stockholm in June, 1972, has created an impact on ecologists, politicians and public alike at inter-governmental, governmental and non-governmental levels to formulate strategies of environmental conservation particularly of the ecosystems that are stress and strain of biotic and other forces (Ambasht and Singh, 1989).
2. The various international initiative processes for laying down criteria and indicators of sustainable forestry management include the Pan-European Forest Process, the Montreal Process, the Amazon Cooperative Treaty, the Dry-Zone Africa Process, the Near East Process, the Lepaterique Process of Central America, the Dry-Zone Asia Initiative, International Tropical Timber Organisation (ITTO), African Timber Organisation (ATO), the Centre for International Forestry Research (CIFOR) and International Union of Forestry Research (IUFRO) FAO, 2001, http://www.fao.org/forestry).
3. In the 1980s under the impetus of donors and the FAO, several countries embarked on exercises of national forest plan formulation. The same passion also followed the Earth Summit held in Rio de Janeiro in June, 1992, when countries had to adapt their forest policies to the guidelines that emerged during the Summit. However, several exercises in forest policy formulation stopped short, or did not succeed in establishing real credibility. Several forest policies, apparently well formulated, did not produce expected results (Buttoud and Samyn, 1999).
4. For instance, in parts of arid and desert regions of Rajasthan one sees plenty of trees in the areas predominantly of Bishnoi community which is

traditionally a nature friendly community. This community forbids cutting trees and eating non-vegetarian food. In fact, they worship the *khejdi* tree. Though firewood is a major problem in these areas one sees people picking dry stems in the open field (Ratna Reddy, 1996).

18

Women and Environment
The Gender Difference

DIPAK DE

Environmental issues have emerged as a major global concern for human survival in the present century. A large number of International and Global organisations with the collective wisdom of scientists, economists and planners have come up to settle the environmental issues confronting the nations and the physical world. The basic life support system—land, air, water, flora and fauna and the atmosphere are under severe stress both in the developed and developing countries. The environmental crisis has convinced the world to use technologies and the resources to repair the damage already done to environment and also to protect and preserve nature and natural resources. The consumption pattern of the rich, the gross economic inequalities, ecologically unsustainable exploitation of natural resources, lack of concerted efforts in the sustainable management of the national and global communities, poor technology, mounting pressure of population and the political and social indifference to the problems of poverty and pollution are all threatening a happy common future which modern science and technology have brought within the realms of possibility. In the present day world, environment has become a major international topic and has become an important benchmark, in the process of universal awareness of the importance of the environment.

In 1972, a United Nations conference on the Human Environment was held in Stockholm, Sweden. The Stockholm plan of action—a set of 109 recommendations designed to lay down a basis for concrete actions and measures—aimed at increasing universal knowledge of the environment improving the quality thereof and preserving it for future generations.

"Environment is a subject of deep concern in the international community. Many feel that if there is any issue on which the industrialised countries can discuss with the third world is non-other than environment.

It is so because; there is now a perceptible burning danger, an increasing growing threat to the global ecosystem as a result of global warming and other factors. Most of them have emanated from the industrial countries themselves. There is no doubt about that. But there is the growing fear that as the third world countries proceed along the same path of development, the burden on the ecosphere on the world ecological system will become intolerable and endanger the future of the planet itself (Coeria, 1990). So, there is a serious issue and an issue on which there is a readiness to talk among affected countries. The problems of India, indeed of developing countries are massive. The country has fast growing populations, 40 per cent of which depend on the nature's gift of land, water and forest for food, fuel, shelter and materials to provide them employment. The prosperous segments of the population to meet its demands turn to industrial units, which cause heavy pollution and degradation of natural resources.

Due to catastrophic population explosion and its subsequent effects, our environment is changing day by day, which leads to global warning, ozone depletion, acid rain and resource degradation in many countries. The people should be well educated and informed about the hazardous effects of environmental pollution and the methods to protect it. To achieve this, certain re-orientation is needed in the present education, research and extension system.

In developing countries gender plays an important role (Dash, 2005) to protect environment. Expert in environmental and related areas should play a key role in the society to make aware of environmental issues through education and training to gender. How does gender feel concerned about environmental issues? How do they differ in environmental issues? How do they feel committed in the environmental protection? Broadly to answer these questions an attempt has been made to study gender difference in environmental awareness and their commitment to environmental protection.

Empirical Study

(i) *Locale of Research*

The present study was conducted in Varanasi district of Uttar Pradesh, which is situated on the bank of river Ganga. Banaras Municipal area has three universities, namely; Banaras Hindu University, Kashi Vidyapith and Sanskrit University. Out of these three universities, Banaras Hindu University (B.H.U.) has been selected purposely for the study. The main campus of the University is situated on an area measuring 1300 acres which houses 112 departments of which 98 departments provide instruction leading to Postgraduate degree, forming part of 14 faculties. In addition, there is Mahila Mahavidyalaya, situated in the main campus and three school level institutions at the Kamachha campus.

B.H.U. has been chosen purposely due to following reasons:

- Convenience in data collection
- Easy accessibility of the students
- The limited resources and time available at the disposal of the researcher
- Acquaintance of the researcher with the scientists, who helped for proper and prompt response.

(ii) *Selection of Respondents*

Respondents of the study were male and female postgraduate students of science and arts faculties of the University. Fifty male and 50 female postgraduate students were selected from each of science and arts faculties of the university. Thus, the total number of respondents was 200. Postgraduate implies the stage of higher education after having completed graduation, e.g. Master Course of any subject. In this study M.A., M.Sc., M.Sc. (Ag.), M.Tech. and M.D. students had been sampled.

(iii) *Knowledge of Respondents about Environmental Pollution*

Knowledge in the present study has been referred to as a body of understood information possessed by an individual. It has been defined as "those behaviours and test situations which emphasise remembering either by recognition or recall of ideas, materials or phenomena" (Bloom *et al.*, 1956).

Knowledge of the respondents about environment was measured with the help of a knowledge index, specially developed for the study purpose. The items included in the knowledge index were 'definitions and terminologies related to environment'. Under it following items were included.

Different dimensions of pollution; air pollution; water pollution; soil pollution; sound pollution; ozone depletion and global warming; acid rain and radiation ecology.

(iv) *Self Commitment*

Self theories attempt to integrate the various parts of the personality structure into a meaningful whole. Roger (1959) is the most closely associated with this approach. He defined the self or self concept of an "organised, consistent conceptual gestalt composed of the characteristics of 'I' or 'me' to others. and to various aspects of life, together with the values attached to these perceptions. The 'I' is the personal self, the self that one believes in and strives to be. It consists of the individuals psychological process (perception, learning and motivation which in contribution, result in a unique whole).

The 'me' represents the social self. The 'me' is the way a person appears to others and the way this person thinks he or she appear to others. In the present study self-commitment means involving oneself for the betterment of social and personal surroundings, through environmental protection.

(v) *Data Collection*

Data were collected with the help of a structured schedule.

Findings and Discussion

Knowledge level of P.G. Students, i.e. Science Boys and Arts Boys About Environmental Issues:

The knowledge level of PG. Students—science boys and arts boys, was found out and categorised into four levels. The data have been presented in Table 18.1.

Table 18.1: Knowledge Level of Science Boys and Arts Boys about Environmental Issues

Knowledge Score	*Science Boys (N = 50)*			*Arts Boys (N = 50)*		
	No.	*%*	*Rank*	*NO.*	*%*	*Rank*
0-25	–	–	–	6	12	3rd
26-50	11	22	3rd	23	46	1st
51-75	25	50	1st	19	38	2nd
76-100	14	28	2nd	2	4	4th

Table 18.1 shows that maximum number of science boys (50 + 28) = 78%) were in high knowledge level category while only 2 in moderate knowledge level. But in Arts boys only (38 +4 = 42%) were in high knowledge level category, but maximum 46 per cent were in moderate and 12 per cent were in low knowledge category. So science boys had more knowledge than Arts boys.

It may be due to the fact that environment is itself as the subject of science.

Knowledge Level of P.G. Students, i.e. Science Girls and Arts Girls about Environmental Issues

The knowledge level of P.G. students, i.e. Science girls and Arts girls were worked out and categorised into four levels. The data have been presented in Table 18.2.

Table 18.2: Knowledge Level of Science Girls and Arts Girls about Environmental Issues

Knowledge Score	*Science Girls (N = 50)*			*Arts Girls (N = 50)*		
	No.	*%*	*Rank*	*NO.*	*%*	*Rank*
0-25	1	2	3rd	5	10	3rd
26-50	10	20	2nd	24	48	1st
51-75	38	76	1st	20	40	2nd
76-100	1	2	4th	1	2	4th

Table 18.2 shows that maximum number of Science Girls (76 + 2 = 78%) were in high knowledge level category while in Arts girls only 40+2 = 42 per cent were in high knowledge level category. In Arts maximum 48 per cent girls were in moderate knowledge level and 10 per cent were in low knowledge level but in Science girls only 20 per cent were in moderate knowledge level and 2 per cent were in low knowledge level category. It may be due to the fact that girls belonging to science faculty might have direct link with the subject matter related to environment.

Knowledge Level of P.G. Students, i.e. Total Boys (Science + Arts) and Total Girls (Science + Arts)

The knowledge level of P.G. students, i.e. total boys and total girls were worked out and categorised into four levels.

The data have been presented in Table 18.3.

Table 18.3: Knowledge Level of Total Boys and Total Girls about Environmental Issues

Knowledge Score	*Total Boys (N = 50)*			*Total Girls (N = 50)*		
	No.	*%*	*Rank*	*NO.*	*%*	*Rank*
0-25	6	6	4th	6	6	3rd
26-50	34	34	2nd	34	34	2nd
51-75	44	44	1st	58	58	1st
76-100	16	16	3rd	2	2	4th

Data in table shows that maximum boys (Science + Arts) were in high knowledge level (44+16 = 60 %) category while 34 per cent were in moderate and 6 per cent were in low knowledge level category. Similarly, among girls, maximum 58+2 = 60 per cent were in high knowledge level while only 34+6 = 40 per cent were in low knowledge level category.

But in high knowledge level category between 51-75 per cent there were maximum 58 per cent girls as compared to boys (44 %).

Difference of knowledge Level of different P.G. Respondents About Environmental Issues

Paired 't' test was used to test the difference in knowledge level between different respondents, i.e.,

(i) Science boys vs. Arts boys;
(ii) Science girls vs. Arts girls;
(iii) Science boys vs. Arts girls;
(iv) Science girls vs. Arts boys
(v) Total boys (Science + Arts) vs. Total girls (Science + Arts).

The results have been presented in Table 18.4.

Table 18.4: Difference in Knowledge Level between Different Respondents about Environmental Issues

Sl No.	*Respondents*	*Over all Knowledge Level Mean Score*	*Difference in Mean Score*	*'t' Values*
1.	Science boys	201.44		
	vs.		57.68	6.42**
	Arts boys	143.044		
2.	Science Girls	178.06		
	vs.		27.64	3.32**
	Arts Girls	150.42		
3.	Science Boys	201.44		
	vs.		51.02	5.50**
	Arts Girls	150.42		
4.	Science Girls	178.06		
	vs.		34.52	4.15**
	Arts Boys	143.44		
5.	Total Boys	164.34		
	vs.		8.36	1.26
	Total Girls	172.60		

* Significance at 0.01 level of probability.

(i) *Difference of Knowledge between Science Boys vs Arts Boys*

Table 19.4(i) shows that there was a significant difference in over all knowledge level between science boys and arts boys about environmental issues. The computed 't' value was 6.42, which was significant at 1 per cent level of probability.

It is clear from table that science boys possessed higher knowledge as compared to arts boys about environmental issues. It may be due to the fact that environment is considered as a subject of science stream.

(ii) *Difference of Knowledge Level Between Science Girls and Arts Girl*

Data in Table 18.4(ii) reveals that there was a significant difference in over all knowledge between science girls and arts girls. The computed 't' value was 3.22 which was significant at 1 per cent level of probability.

Table clearly shows that science girls had more knowledge than arts girls. This may be due to the fact that environment is itself a subject of science.

(iii) *Difference in Knowledge Level between Science Boys and Arts Girls*

Data in Table 18.4(iii) reveals that there was a significant difference in knowledge level between science boys and arts girls about environmental issues. The computed 't' value was 5.50, which is highly significant at I per cent level of probability. It is evident from Table that the science boys possessed more knowledge as compared to arts girls. It may be due to the fact that environment is itself a subject of science.

(iv) *Difference of Knowledge Level between Science Girls vs. Arts Boys*

Data in Table 18.4(iv) shows that there was a significant difference of knowledge level between science girls and arts boys. The computed 't' value was 4.15 which was significant at I per cent level of probability. Data in table clearly shows that science girls possess higher knowledge as compared to arts boys. It may be due to the fact the environment is itself a subject of science.

(v) *Difference in Knowledge Level between Total Boys (Science + Arts) vs, Total Girls (Science + Arts)*

Data in Table 18.4(v) show that there was insignificant difference in overall knowledge level between total boys and total girls. The computed 't' value was 1.20 which was non-significant. So over all there was no difference in knowledge level between total boys (science + arts) vs. total girls. It may be due to the fact that all students might be conscious about environment.

Self commitment of Respondents towards Environmental Protection

Self-commitment means how far one is involved for the betterment of social and personal surroundings. The results of boys, i.e. 100 (Science and Arts Faculties) and the girls, i.e. 100 (Science and Arts Faculties) have been presented in Table 18.5.

Table 18.5: Self Commitment of Different Respondents (Boys + Girls)

Sl. No.	*Particulars*	*Boys (N=100)*	*Girls (N=100)*
1.	Participation in environmental protection programme like N.S.S. Vriksharopan	62	76
2.	Participation in the Universities' environmental programmes like plantation etc.	43	58
3.	Member of environmental organisation likc N.S.S. young intach	65	39
4.	Participation in afforestation and plantation outside university	9	4
5.	Hour to be devoted for participation in environmental protection programme		
	(a) upto ½ hr./week	20	25
	(b) ½-1 hr./week	5	2
	(c) ½ hrs./week	2	5
	(d) more than 2 hrs./week	2	8
	(e) whole life	15	5
6.	Participation in different educational programmes to check pollution		
	(a) public awareness	32	52
	(b) cleanliness of surroundings like roads channels	5	2
	(c) Use of pollution free vehicle	2	–
	(d) deforestation should be checked	15	25
	(e) proper garbage disposal	5	2

Data in Table 18.5 shows that in Sl. No. I, girls participated more in environmental protection programmes than boys. In Sl. No. 2, also girls were more interested in environmental programmes of the universities than boys. In Sl. No. 3, it vividly shows that girls were having more membership of different organisations like N.S.S., Young Intachs and other environmental organisations. It might be due to the fact that Science girls possessed more knowledge than Arts boys and Arts girls possessed more knowledge than Arts boys. In Sl. No. 4 of the Table 19.5, it is observed that boys participated more in afforestation and plantation programmes. In Sl. Nos. 5 and 6, i.e. hours to be devoted for participation in environmental protection programmes and participation in different educational programmes to check pollution, the girls participated more than boys. It may be concluded that girls were more committed for protecting environment than boys. But the participation of boys and girls in protecting environment is must for sustaining development in the light of changes taking place in our global context. It is an oceanic process of sustaining peoples development. Oceanic process refers to circulating and participatory character of interaction in the social system. In this process of interaction there will be ever-widening, never-ascending circles. Interaction will not be an oceanic circle whose centre will be the individual sharing information. This is in line with the Gandhian concept of oceanic circle as referred by Pantham and Dentsch (1986).

Conclusion

The increasing population, massive industrialisation, agricultural transformation, etc. are the major crucial factors that have resulted in massive exploitation of natural resources, i.e. air, water, soil, etc. For fulfilling the objectives of the sustainable development, the commitment of the students, who are the future of the nation is a must. Therefore, special programme is to be launched for imparting training and involvement of students for sustainable development. Unless the human resources are well oriented and trained, their brains are shaped by education and the attitudes are modeled to environmental protection policy, not much gains would be reaped by slogans.

19

Community Awareness for Sustainable Development

A Case Study from Bhubaneswar

A.K. PATRA and PARAMITA PRAMANICK

India is a land of villages and in spite of increasing urbanisation over the past many years, villages continue to exist in large numbers and still form a significant component of socio-cultural life of our country. It is said (Mandelbaum, 1972) that the village is a principal unit for understanding the society.

However, the craze for urbanisation is on the rise. Ever since the rural areas started converting into urban, an in-between zone was always in sight. Whether the urban form is of the nature of a town, city, metropolis or megalopolis, the fringe phenomenon, is found everywhere, with almost identical characteristics (Mohan, 1999). Urbanisation in India remains as a fringe phenomenon. There is existence of a partially integrated, semi-urban slum squalors, and stagnant settlements at the periphery of large urban metropolitan centres.

Bhubaneswar, the capital city of Orissa, popularly known as the City of Temples, located on 20°15 North Latitude and 85°50 East Longitude in the Eastern Coastal Plain of India, is characterised by its lush green environment and a mixture of rural and urban life. This well planned capital city encompasses an area of 57,326,128 acres comprising of 93 revenue units, including the present municipal limits of the city. Breaking up this data there are 28 villages comprising of 42 units coming under the Bhubaneswar Municipality and 65 villages outside the Municipality. Villages like Nuagaon, Mancheswar, Patia, Samantarapur, Dhauli exist independently outside the Municipality but within the Master Plan Area. But there are certain villages like Nilakanthanagar, Paiknagar, Baramunda, Jagmara, Sunderpada, Pokhariput, and Damana, which exist within the Municipal units. They are a part of the posh urban units, which derive their names from these villages. These villages exist within the heart of the city, amidst urban premises and yet continue to have independent existence. Baramunda village is one of such type. It is situated on the borderline of the National Highway No. 5 and is flanked by the New Bus Stand and Orissa University of Agriculture, and Technology (OUAT) on either side. The Baramunda Housing Board Colony (a recent product of Bhubaneswar Development Authority) who derives its name from this village is located on its outskirt

Environment awareness is the term very much in use today. It is the need of the hour and is the main solution to the environmental problems encircling us. The area of environmental awareness requires large-scale participation of people, which often is a difficult, task. In developing countries where literacy is low and workget delayed, no government can do every thing unless it is worked out in partnership with its people and local institutions. Environment movement can be a people's movement only when they understand the problem and realise its cause. In this connection, the proper understanding of the environment issues by human being is highly essential in order to save it (Mishra, 1999). This article attempts to reveal the necessity of community awareness towards various environmental issues in Baramunda village of Bhubaneswar.

Objective

The present study aims at focusing on the living patterns of city village people and and their need for community awareness.

Methodology

A wide range of survey was conducted on the village environment with special emphasis on the life style and living patterns of the residents. Collected data on the education and addiction habits were analysed to derive the desired conclusions.

Observation

1. *Type of House*

Type	*Average (%) Before Cyclone*	*Average (%) After Cyclone*
RCC	69	83
Straw	28	14
Asbestos	3	3

2. *Fuel Used*

LPG (%)	Wood (%)	Kerosene (%)
42	50	8

3. *Source of drinking Water*

Well (%)	Pond (%)	Hand pump (%)	Tap (%)
95	–	4	6

4. *Garbage Disposal*

Open (%)	Closed Landfill (%)	Dustbin (%)
56	24	20

5. *Drainage System*

Open (%)	Closed (%)
60	40

6. *Addiction*

Category	Tobacco Smoking (%)	Alcohol Consumption (%)	Paan Chewing (%)	Gutkha Chewing (%)
General	20.8	13.4	54.04	18.04
Male	42.8	28.0	55.04	24.5
Female	0.62	–	56.24	12.8
Youth	17.04	12.2	32.5	48.7
Adult	26.5	16.4	73.15	10.3

7. *Education*

	Below Matric Matric (%)	Metric (%)	Graduate (%)	Post Graduate (%)	Uneducated (%)
Male	30	16	26	1	28
Female	21	18	16	–	45

8. *Role of Media*

	Newspaper (Oriya) %	Newspaper (English and Oriya) %	Radio (%)	Television (%)
Present	80	20	48	74
Absent	20	80	52	26

Before the super cyclone of 1999, Baramunda village comprised of 69 per cent RCC houses; 28 per cent trawl houses; and 3 per cent asbestos houses. The super cyclone did not cause any damage to the RCC houses; however, it partially damaged 22 per cent and completely destroyed 6 per cent of the straw houses. The asbestos houses remained unaffected. After the cyclone, 14 per cent of the straw house dwellers built themselves RCC houses, while the remaining 14 per cent repaired and continued living in the straw houses.

Ventilation is satisfactory in 70 per cent of the RCC houses, 25 per cent of the straw houses and 100 per cent of the asbestos houses. Forty two per cent of the villagers use LPG as the fuel for cooking purposes, 50 per cent still rely on wood, while 8 per cent use kerosene.

Wells within the household premises and nearby form the source of drinking water for 95 per cent of the inhabitants, 4 per cent of the folks fetch their water from the adjacent hand-pump while 6 per cent use the tap water. Pond water is not used for consumption.

Disposal of garbage in the open area is a regular habit of 56 per cent of the population, 24 per cent dump their wastes in closed landfills while, 20 per cent use dustbins. Open drains run through the premises of 60 per cent of the houses, 40 per cent have proper drains.

The population of Baramunda village comprises of 20.8 per cent smokers, 13.4 per cent alcohol consumers, 54.04 per cent paan chewing and 18.04 per cent gutkha-chewing addicts. Within the male community, 42.8 per cent are habitual smokers, 28 per cent are heavy drinkers, 55.04 per cent and 24.5 per cent are heavy addicts of paan and gutkha respectively. Among the females, 0.62 per cent smoke tobacco, while 56.24 per cent chew it as paan and 12.8 per cent chew it as paan masala (gutkha). The category of smokers also includes 17.04 per cent youth and 26.5 per cent adults. Alcohol consumption is a practice prevalent among 12.2 per cent of the youth and 16.4 per cent of the adult population. 32 per cent of the youth community has taken to regular chewing of paan and 48.7 per cent have taken to regular chewing of gutkha. Chewing of tobacco in paan is an old practice of 73.15 per cent adults while, chewing, of gutkha is a practice of 10.3 per cent adults.

Twenty eight per cent of the men and 45 per cent of the females are illiterate; 30 per cent of the former and 21 per cent of the latter are under matriculates, while, 16 per cent and 18 per cent are matriculates respectively. Graduate population is only 26 per cent and 16 per cent men and women respectively. 38 per cent of the total population is aware of the environment while, 62 per cent have no environmental awareness.

Oriya newspapers are subscribed by 80 per cent of the families while both English and Oriya news papers are taken by 20 per cent of the families. Forty eight per cent of the homes possess radio while, 74 per cent have television.

Discussion

Over recent years, the increasing challenge to identify missing factors to contribute towards sustaining resource management efforts has brought to light the significant role of community participation in sustainable development programmes. Community based sustainable development programmes work on the basic premise that people have the innate capacity to improve their quality of life and the problems confronting them can be overcome through their own efforts with some assistance from government and non-government agencies.

Our country is burdened with several problems like population explosion, illiteracy, unemployment, poverty, etc. Rapid industrialisation and increasing urbanisation have triggered a chain of reactions, turning fertile lands and forests into vast barren waste lands, pollution of the vital air and water resource, posing danger to health and economic welfare of man (Lambert, 1962). During this process of urbanisation, the rural urban interaction results in the occurrence of a 'fringe'. This fringe is a transitional or twilight zone situated between well-recognised land uses of the city and the agricultural tracts of the village (Mohan, 1999).

Baramunda village located in the heart of the capital city Bhubaneswar is a twilight zone between urbanisation and rural life. Encircling an area of 200 hectares, the village comprises of an approximate human population of 5682. There are 900 to 1000 houses, 83 per cent of which are concrete built (RCC). The super cyclone, therefore, could not cause much damage to this city village. It is only the straw houses, which suffered damage to some extent. The partially damaged straw houses got repaired soon and began their existence in no time. The completely damaged straw houses got converted into RCC houses. There are only 14 per cent straw houses in the village now, which are located within the RCC houses. The RCC houses have been beautifully constructed and handsomely decorated giving the impression of posh urban lifestyle. However, ventilation is not satisfactory in these houses because they are situated very close to each other.

The village area had once been a dense forest, including the urban surroundings. Due to increase in population, the forests had to be cleared away to produce adequate space for shelter. The establishment of housing colonies, roads, highway and so on has led to the decrease in floral population. The greenery of Baramunda village has therefore become quite scanty. The population of plants and trees is on decline, as the need for more shelters is on the rise due to increase in human population. However, trees surround the village, which protect it from the heavy pollution of National Highway. But with numerous electric poles and wires being set up, the tall trees are also on the verge of being felled down.

Since the area had once been a dense forest, numerous animals had existed in the habitat. However, now the faunal population has been restricted to the domestic animals like cows, buffaloes, bulls, oxen, goats, dogs, cats and the like. One thousand seven hundred and fifty animals exist in the village. Almost every house owns a cow or a bull; some have two or more. The cattle are usually required for ploughing and tilling on the farms, which are located on the village outskirts, i.e. around the houses. Most of the families own farms and land, which they sell off in their time of need.

With rise in environmental pollution, sanitation carries greater importance than other things in life as only a healthy atmosphere can banish the dreaded pollutants. In this context village sanitation is now the most sought after field of social activists. The main form of insanitation in the villages is the stinking atmosphere as the villagers ease them here and there unmindful of the unhygienic situation. It is a fact that the economic conditions of the people living in the villages are not so well up as urbanites to go in for better sanitary and health standards. But, given the assistance and guidance, they can keep up and contribute to the establishment of a non-polluting region.

The drainage system is however not satisfactory in Baramunda village. Most of the drains are open running in between the houses and even inside the houses, giving rise to foul smell, flies and mosquitoes. However, a majority of the residents are least concerned about these open drains and it makes no difference to their living patterns. They dump their wastes in these drains and even sit beside them for any work. Some have been even found to eat near these drains, the odour and the flies have no impact on them.

Garbage is also dumped in the open area and some of the open land area has got converted into vast garbage pits, again giving rise to flies and mosquitoes. Closed bins are rarely visible and the municipality seldom cleans those present.

There are five ponds, of which three are swamp ponds. The other two ponds are used by the natives of this city village for bathing, washing clothes or utensils, bathing animals and also for throwing wastes. All these activities are carried out on the basis of a simple and phenomenal logic: the pond water is not stagnant and hence is unlikely to remain polluted. It is this inadequate knowledge, which is the root cause of all health problems.

Most of the villagers are suffering from skin ailments. There are many victims with acute ringworm infestations and several with eczema from head to toes. Nail eczema is the most common skin infection prevalent. However, these people are least bothered and continue bathing in the common ponds, thus neglecting their health problems. They are not convinced that the dirty pond water is the root cause of all dermal infections. It is for this reason that all medical aid fails as the people continue using the pond, which they call as sacred. Moreover, they do not use the sophisticated bathrooms in their homes and go out to the fields for defecation. When they defecate in the open, barefoot, they invite all infections as hookworms easily penetrate into the body through the feet. After this when they directly enter the pond for washing and bathing, they not only contaminate the pond water, but also spread infections. This regular practice aggravates the infections and their body becomes a breeding ground of parasites. In spite of all suffering and widespread infections, the people remain adamant, mentally backward and highly superstitious. The surrounding urban life has no effect on their thoughts and sanitary habits. They are not ready to accept any changes in their lifestyle.

Their homes, however, have all luxurious amenities like refrigerator, television, radio, tape-recorder, grinder and costly furniture. They cannot be called poor or backward, and the presence of electricity and telephone shows that the government does not neglect them either. They feed upon all the food items, rice, dal, fish, eggs, meat, milk, etc. but their mode of preparation is unhealthy and unhygienic. They fetch their drinking water from wells and hand-pumps located in the village. Every one out of five homes encloses a well or a hand-pump. This well water is used for drinking and cooking. The most interesting fact here is that the water of these wells varies a lot in their tastes from place to place. There is a marked difference in the taste of water of two adjacent wells.

The villagers have a high rate of addiction for tobacco. They consume tobacco in the form of 'beedi', betel leaves called 'paan' and as gutkha or paan masalas. While the former along with alcohol consumption is prevalent among the male community only, the latter two are favourites of both men and women. Some of the elderly females consume about twenty-five paans' in a day. One acute case shows blisters and lesions in the mouth and gums, with oozes of pus, which may lead to oral cancer. In spite of all this, chewing tobacco continues to be a regular habit. During the heavy working hours, tobacco in the form of 'beedi' is supposed to be a relaxant and source of strength. Similarly, alcohol seems to provide relief after the hard day's exhaustion and labor. The inhabitants are least bothered to change their habits for a healthy living. Most of them are not aware of the consequences, and for those who are it is too late to drop the habit.

The villagers are regular sufferers of gastro-intestinal and respiratory ailments. Every family reports of at least one victim, there may be more also. This is mainly because of their lifestyle and addiction towards tobacco. They visit the local village dispensary or the government hospital for their treatment but do not go ahead for further tests and check-ups. Whenever they are advised any pathological tests or consultation of a specialist, they back out for fear of exposure to a big disease and to avoid expenditure. They feel that the declaration of a disease would embarrass them in front of the entire village community. Further they also feel that it would be a huge expense. They can spend money on lavish goods and on their addicted products but not on their health. Good health and hygiene have no importance in their life.

The root cause of all these problems is their narrow mentality based on their illiteracy. Most of the older generation (60 years and above) are either uneducated or educated up to the matric level. The middle age group (35-60) has studied till the secondary level. The younger generation (20-35) is mostly graduates. It is the middle and the older groups, which are orthodox. Education is restricted within the three elementary schools in the village. The status of these schools is not adequate for shaping their personalities. Higher education in town is a rare occurrence as the age-old belief of losing the child and disowning him from the village community prevails. The educated lot, however, does not utilise its knowledge in services of any kind. Most of them end up owning shops or working in the Bus Stand. Very few are serving in public and private sectors. The low education and occupational status of this city village is a matter of grave concern.

It is education, which only can help in the upliftment of the life of an individual by improving his knowledge, understanding, ethics and morale. The people of K. Rampura, small villages in the drought prone Pavagada Taluk of Tumkur district in Karnataka have proved this. The village is a combination of rocky terrain, parched lands, barren Fields, scanty rainfall and a relentless sun beating down throughout the year. The villagers had been poverty stricken and living hand to mouth. Things perhaps would have been the same had it not been for *Akshara Kalpavrelksha* a district wide Total Literacy Campaign that had been sweeping through K. Rampura in the past two years. The campaign is bringing along an avalanche of changes in their attitudes and thinking towards environment and development. Literacy has galvanised the 570 odd village residents into recognising environmentalists as a panacea for their ills.

Fired by the desires to green their village and its surroundings, many of the K. Rampura residents have donned the mantle of environmentalists. The conservation strategy was simple but effective: *Conserve whatever one can.* To begin with Rampart Gouda or the village hillock was recognised as a community asset and conservation priority. Next, villagers cordoned off the hillock for afforestation and natural rejuvenation. Animals were prevented from grazing there. Tree felling was totally prohibited. Two years of stringent conservation has paid off dividends. Today thick foliage covers the entire hillock making it look like an emerald in Pavagada's star and rocky landscape. The neo-literate villagers have christened their new green exhibit *Akshara Vana*, a forest created by literacy imparted knowledge (Anonymous, 1993).

Eco-volunteers, a joint programme of the United Nations Volunteers and ELCI is an initiative which has been designed to identify and support community leaders in their efforts to tackle local environmental problems. They motivate the community of villagers through action and education of community and environment development programmes (Anonymous, 1996).

Growing concerns over the activities of Australian mining companies in developing countries has led to collaboration between environment and development. NGOs in Australia and in Asian Pacific spearheading such collaboration is a partnership formed between Australia's largest environment NGO the Australian Conservation Foundation (ACF) and the Papua New Guinean Malenesian Environment Foundation (MEF), an indigenous environmental organisation dedicated to community education (Rosenbaum, 1996).

Canadian communities and NGOs are also engaged in a struggle to protect their vital natural resources. Local environmental activities along with larger environmental groups like the Western Canada Wilderness Community have been battling multinational logging companies over the fate of Clauyoquot's giant treed forests for more than two decades (Carr, 1996).

Designed to build public support for sustainable development in the Republic of Estonia, a proposed new pilot communications programme is focused on audio/visual media and the educational system. The programme has attempted to strengthen environmental awareness and harness the environmental education sector by running a sustained public environmental information and education campaign (MeGean, 1995).

The importance of public understanding through education, awareness and training for environment was recognised at Rio de Janeiro (1992) by United Nations Conference on Environment and Development known as Earth summit. The principle 10 of Rio declaration states.

Human beings are the centre of concern for sustainable development. Environmental issues are best handled with the participation of all concerned citizens at the relevant level, each individual shall have appropriate access to information concerning the environment that is held by public authorities including information on hazardous materials and activities in their communities and the opportunities to participate in the decision making process. States shall facilitate and encourage public awareness and participation by making information widely available. Thus orienting education towards improving the capacity of the people to address environment and development issues can help in solving environmental problems of the society.

In the state of Orissa, National Environmental Awareness Campaign has been carried out through the participation of voluntary organisations, Government agencies, educational institutions and the government of Orissa.

The Centre for Environmental and Multicultural Communication, Orissa (CEMC), working in the field of environment and human development has tried to create awareness on environment through the children environment activists. These children, through their paintings have made an appeal to all the intellectuals, social activists, environmentalists, politicians and common man to save the environment for future generations like them to lead a better life.

The environmental concerns as a whole show a clear picture of the crisis which man has created for himself through his own action. Growing population, increasing consumption, and poor management of existing resources are leading to a decline in natural resources and decreasing the sustaining capacity of the environment. To ensure the healthy growth and development of man and other forms of life, there is an urgent need to avoid any conflict between development and environment. Natural resources should be wisely conserved and fairly distributed, besides being used judiciously for the sake of the well being of both present as well as future generations.

The residents of Baramunda village with their combined efforts can save their environment. Education can generate awareness of the self and surroundings and enable them to save the ship from sinking. From a study on the women of Orissa, it has been found (Dash and Satapathy, 2004) that women have strong concern for environmental protection. As such women education and empowerment can help to expedite the situation as women are more concerned about environmental conservation (Dash, 2005; Jaggi *et al.*, 2005) than men who have more interest on commercial aspect. In promoting the active participation of the citizenry for sustainable development, non-government organisations can act as (Balagot, 1990) the central vehicle in mobilising people to participate, since they are the segments of population which work through the organising community, public information campaigns, research/situation assessment, environmental surveillance and monitoring.

References and Bibliography

ACTH, M. (1988), A case for developing an environmental curriculum adapted to the needs of the learners. International School Seminar, Nairobi.

Agarwal, Anil (1982), For an alternative development. *The UNESCO Courier*, August-September, pp. 23-26.

Agarwal, B. (1995) Women and natural resources. *The Hindu Survey of the Environment,* 7-14, Madras.

Agarwal, S.K. (1997), *Environmental Issues and Schemes*. APH Publications, New Delhi.

——(1998), *Population and Environment: Environmental Issues and Researches in India.* Himansu Publication, Udaipur, p. 397.

Agrawal, A. and Narain, S. (1989), *'Towards Green Village: A strategy for Environmentally sound, Participatory Rural Development.* Centre for Science and Environment, New Delhi.

Ahmad, Karuna (1979), Studies of educational working women in India: Trends and Issues. *Economic and Political Weekly,* VXIV (33) 34-43.

Ahmadi A.M. (1997), The strength of character. *University News*, 35(7): 23-24.

Alam, M.U. (1998), Education Innovation for Sustainable Development: An Indian Experience. *Indian Journal of Adult Education*, 59(4): 29-36.

Alexander, M. (1977) *Introduction to Soil Microbiology*, 2nd edn., Wiley, N.Y.

Altekar, A.S. (1973), The position of women in Hindu civilisation, Delhi, Motilal Banarasidas.

Ambannavar, J.P. (1975), Changes in economic activity of males and females in India, 1911-61. *Demography India*, 4(2): 344-364.

Ambasht, R.S. and M.P. Singh (1989) Conservation and management of a degrading riparian wasteland. (in) Pramod Singh (ed.) *Problem of Wasteland and Forest Ecology in India,* Ashish Publishing House, New Delhi: 29-44.

Andrew Steer (1992) The environment for development, *Finance and Development,* 20(2): 18-21.

Andrew, D.M. (1987), The interrelationship among the cognitive, affective and behavioural domains in an outdoor environmental programme, Dissertation Abstracts International, December, p. 4196.

Annual Report (1994-95). Central Soil and Water Conservation Research and Training Institute (CSWCRTI), Dehradun, pp. 86-87.

Anon (1992) Environmental problems and developing countries. *Finance and Development,* 20(2): 22-23.

Anonymous (1968), Conference of African Educators, EDC and CREDO Report, Nairobi: African Social Studies Programme.

—— (1969), National Antipollution Law, Japan.

—— (1976), International environmental education workshop, "The Belgrade Charter—A Global Framework for Environmental Education". *Connect,* 1(1): 1-2.

—— (1985), WWF, *'Sustainable Development: an approach to development assistance which integrates conservation and development'*, World Wildlife Fund, Washington D.C.

—— (1987), World Commission on Environment and Development', *'Our Common Future,* Oxford University Press, London.

—— (1988), 'Technical Advisory Committee (TAG) of CGIAR', *Soil Management for sustainable Agriculture in Dry land Areas'* (Bulletin No. 16), Published in 1994 by Indian Society of Soil Sciences, New Delhi, p. 2.

—— (1990), *'The Manila Declaration on People's Participation and Sustainable Development',* lfda Dossier, 75/76, Jan./Apr.

—— (1991), IUCN, UNEP and WWF, *'Caring for the earth: a strategy for sustainable living.* Gland, Switzerland: The world conservation Union, United Nations Environment Programme and World Wildlife Fund.

—— (1992), Rio declaration on environment and development. *Tiger paper,* 19(2): 4-5.

—— (1993), Connect, UNESCO-UNEP Environmental Education *Newsletter,* Vol. VIII, No. 2, June, 1993.

—— (1993), Hyderabad Bachao: Association for preservation of society and Quality of Life, August-November, 1993, Vol. 3, No. 8.

—— (1993), The Chamber's Dictionary.

—— (1993), *The New Shorter Oxford English Dictionary*: Thumb Index Edition, Clarenndon Press. Oxford, London.

—— (1996), Annual International Conference in Sustainable Development and Environment, 15-17 March, 1996 at Calcutta, Organised by National Environmental Science Academy.

—— (1996), Ecoforum: Working for the Earth, Profile of an Ecovolunteer in India, March, 1996.

—— (1997), "Defining Sustainability": Special issue. *Land Economics,* 73(4): 448-60.

—— (1999), Children's Participation in Environment Awareness Campaign, CEMC Newsletter, Vol. 1, No. 2.

—— (2002), One planet, one community. *Earth focus,* 13: 1-35.

—— (2002), Some critical environmental issues of the 21st century. Third world Resurgence, No. 139/140: 44-48.

—— (2004), Environment Matters: At the World Bank Annual Review 2004, Washington DC, USA, p. 64.

—— (2005), Tsunami. *Environmental Awareness* 28(1): 7-11.

APFC (2000) Report of the Committee on Code of Practice for Forest Harvesting in Asia and Pacific, *Asia-Pacific Forest Commission,* Bangkok.

Ariyaratne, A.T. Gandhian thoughts in the educational perspectives, *University News*, 35(12): 17-20.

Armson, K.A. (1977). *Forest Soils, Properties and Processes*. Univ. Toronto Press, Toronto.

Arora, G.C. and Panda, P. (2000), Teacher Education in the crossroads: Issues and Emerging Trends. *Teacher Education in India*, University Grants Commission, New Delhi, p. 179.

Asthana, Pratima, (1974), *Women's movement in India*. Vikas Publishing House Private Ltd., New Delhi.

Atchia, M. (1988), A case for developing an environmental curriculum adapted to the needs of the learners. International School Seminar, Nairobi.

—— (1990), Biology and the quality of life. In *selected issues in Biological education* (ed. by Mayer, Rex), IUBS-CBE.

Atlas, R.M. (1981), Microbial degradation of petroleum hydrocarbons: An environmental perspective. *Microbiological Reviews*, 45: 180-209.

Awasthy, Indira (1982), *Rural women of India* B.R Publishing Corporation, New Delhi.

Ayres Robert, U. (1999), Eco-restructuring: Implications for Sustainable Development. United Nation University Press. *Current Science*, 76(7): 1045-48.

Bakouma, J. and G. Buttoud (1999) Sustainable forest management in Africa: Constraints, costs and conditions, *Tropical Forest Update,* 9(3): 4-5.

Bala Ravi, S. (2006), Biodiversity and food security. *Yojana* 50: 69-70.

Balagot, B.P. (1990), Environmental Management in the context of Sustainable Development. In "*Source Book in Environmental Education for Secondary School.*

—— (1990), Environmental Management in the context of Sustainable Development. pp. 141-48 In *Source Book in Environmental Education for Secondary School Teachers.* (Ed. by R.C. Sharma and M.C. Tan), UNESCO, Bangkok.

Baliga, B.B. (1996), Environmental concerns in the late nineties of the present century. *Science and Culture,* 62(5-6): 107-09.

Bandhu, D., Singh, H. and Maitra, A.K. (1990), *Environmental Education and Sustainable Development* [ed.]. Proceedings of the Third International Conference on environmental Education, Indian Environment Society, New Delhi, pp. 5-9, 23-29, 61-67.

Bardhan, Kalpana (1977), Rural employment, wages and labour market in India: A survey of research. *Economic and Political Weekly*, VXII (26): 34-48.

Bardhan, Pranab (1978), Some employment and unemployment characteristics of rural women: an analysis of NSS data for West Bengal 1972-73. *Economic and Political Weekly*, XIII (12): 21-26.

Barnabus, J. (1966), Women as Agents of Social Change, *Social Welfare,* 13(9) December, pp. 22-28.

Barrell, G.W. and Odum, E.P. (2000), The twenty first century: The world at carrying capacity. *Bioscience*, 50(4): 363-68.

Barrett, G.W. (1985), A problem-solving approach to resource management. Bioscience, *American Institute of Biological Sciences*, 35(7): 423-27.

Basu, A.K. (1995), *Technology for Sustainable Development.* Paper presented at National Training on Sustainable Development, organised by NCDC, Varanasi from 1-13 April, 1995.

Basu, Shreelekha (1979), Role of women in rural economic development. *Yojana*, XXIII (21): 23-25.

Batanouny, K.H. (1990), 'Problems of Environmental Education for sustainable Development in the Developing Countries', In *'Environmental Education and Sustainable Development'* (ed. by Desh Bandhu, Hrjit Singh and A.K. Maitra), Indian Environmental Society, New Delhi, pp. 23-29.

Battcock, M. and Ali, S.A. (2001) *Fermented Fruits and Vegetables—a Global Perspective.* FAO Publications, Rome.

Beeby, C.E. (ed.) (1969), *Qualitative Aspects of educational planning.* Paris, UNESCO/IIEP, Harvard University Press, Massachusetts.

Bhagwati, P.N. (1990), The crucial Condition "Environment-90", 165-167.

Bhardwaj, S.P. and Dhyani, B.L. (1994) Achievements and prospects of operational research projects on integrated watershed management in India. *Indian J. Soil Cons.*, 22, 255-62.

Bhel, R.K. (1993), Environmental Education and Sustainable Development *J. of Indian Education*, XIX (2): 18-21.

Birdsall, N.D. Ross and R. Sabot (1995), Inequality and growth reconsidered: Lesson from East Asia. *The World Bank Economic Review*, 9(3): 7-11.

Bisoyi, R.N. (2002), Factors affecting microbial transformation in soil microhabitat. In: *Microbial Transformations in Soil.* (Eds) K. Chandrayan, KIlumuraju, Z. John Kennedy and K. Govindarajan, Tamil Nadu Agril. Univ. Coimbatore, India, pp. 13-19.

Bloom, B.S., M., Ecoctbarelt; S. Frust; W. Hill and D. Kranthwhol (1956), *Taxonomy of educational objectives.* The Cognitive Doman, Longman's Green and Co., New York.

Borah, J. (1999) Women, domestic fuels and environment: A study of rural North-East, *Kurukshetra,* 47(12): 9-13.

Bosch, R. Van den, (1978), The Pesticide Conspiracy. Doubleday & Company, Inc. U.S.A., p. 226.

Botkin D. and E. Keller (1995), *Biological diversity and Biogeography.* John Wiley and Sons, Inc. New York.

Botkin, J.W., M. Elmandjra, and M. Malitza, (1980), *No Limits to Learning. Bridging the Human Gap.* A Report to the Club of Rome, Pergamon Press, New York, p. 159.

Broeker, W.S. (1970), Enough Air. *Environment*, 2: 27-31.

Brown, L.R. (2000), Saving the planet: No time to lose (pp. 7-14) in The Hindu. *Survey of the Environment*, p. 224.

Buringh, P. (1989) Availability of agricultural land for crop and livestock population. In: *Food and Natural Resources*, Pimental, D. and Hall, C.W. (eds.), Academic Press, San Diego, pp. 69-83.

Burns, R.C. and R.F. Hardy (1975), *Nitrogen Fixation in bacteria and Higher plants*. Springer Verlog, New York.

Buttoud, G. and J.M. Samyn (1999) Politique et planification forestieres: Guide pour la formulation et l'elaboration, Intercooperation, Berne, Switzerland (Review by E. Ze Meka (2000), *Tropical Forest Update,* 9(4): 28-29.

Caldwell, L.K. (1991), *'Population, Resources, Energy and Development', International Environmental Policy: Emergence and Dimensions*; East-West Press Edition, 1991, New Delhi, pp. 168-210.

Cammack, R. (1995), Splitting molecular hydrogen, *Nature*, 373: 556-558.

Carr Adriane (1996), Western Canada Wilderness Committee, Ecoforum, March, 1996.

Carson, R. (1962), *Silent Spring*. Houghton Miffin, Co., Boston, p. 368.

Cart Write. D. (1949), Some principles of mass persuasion. *Human Relations*, 2: 253-67.

Cassells, D.S. and C.A. Hall (2000) A structure for sustainability, *Tropical Forest Update*, 10(3): 2-4.

Cassidy, K.J. (1987), Securing lasting world peace through education. *Education*, 45: 17-21.

CEE (1994), Essential learning in Environmental Education. Centre for Environmental Education, Ahmedabad, India, p. 150.

Census of India, (Paper I of 1981), Prov. Population total, page/43 census of India, Paper 2 of 1992, Final population total excluding J.&K. 53nl round NSSO, December, 1997.

Ceria, G. (1990), "An International Development Strategy for the govs: global Stakes Requires a New Consensus*", life dossier*, 78 July-September, 82-85.

Charjan. Y.D. and Hajre. T.N. (2002) Ecological agriculture solves the problems of Indian agriculture. *Kisan World*, 29(7), 43-44.

Chatterjee, A.S. (1992), Social Dimensions of Sustainable Development, Awareness Workshop for a Sustainable Future. Centre for Scientific Research, pp. 75-76.

Chhokar, K.B. (2000), Sharing concerns in environment education. *University News*, 38(26): 26-29.

Chiappo, Lepado (1978), Environmental Education and the Third World, Prospects. *Quarterly Review of Education*, 3(4): 456-65.

Chidambaram, R.M. (2005), Environmental Accounting. *Social Welfare,* June, 2005, 13-15.

Chopra, K. and Kadekodi, G. (2001), Environment and Development, Operationalising Sustainable Development, *Yojana*, 45: 45.

Chowdhry, K. (1987), Waste lands and rural poor, essentials of a policy framework, *Tiger paper,* 14(2): 1-6.

Ciferro, O. (1983), Spirulina, the edible microorganism, *Microbiological Reviews*, 47: 551-78.

Clark, C. (1996), *Mathematical Bio-economics*, John Wiley, New York.

Clausen, A.W. (1982), Sustainable development: The global imperative. *Environmentalist*, 2(1): 23-28.

Conway, G.R. (1990), 'The challenge of Sustainable Agriculture, In

'Environmental Education and Sustainable Development' (ed. by D. Bandhu, H. Singh and A.K. Mitra). Indian Environmental Society, New Delhi, pp. 181-90.

Costanza, R. (1996), Ecosystem, Biodiversity and Ecological Services, *International Society for Ecological Economics,* 92-98.

Costanza, R.. Cumberland, J, Day, H.; Goodland, R. and Nigard, R. (1997), An Introduction to ecological economics. St. Lucie Press, Boca Raton, Florida (USA), p. 275.

Crawford, J.W. (1983) Composting of agricultural wastes—a review. *Process Biochem.*, Jan/Feb., 14-18.

Dalby, S. (2003), Environmental Insecurities: Geopolitics, Resources and Conflict. *Economic and Political Weekly*, 38(48): 5073-79.

Dandapani, S. (2002), Value attainment and self image. *Edutracks*, 2(4): 6-11.

Dandin, S.B. (2000) Food security through agro-biodiversity. In: *Krishi Prativa,* Hiremath, K.C., Raghavendra Rao. K. and Gunjetti. B.V. (eds.), University of Agricultural Sciences, Dharwad, India.

Das, B.C. (1980), Population, food, energy, environment, science and technology—A hopeful strategy for reduction of poverty. In *Man and his Environment* (Ed. By I.P. Singh and S.C. Tiwari). Concept Publishing Company, New Delhi, p. 276.

Das, P. (2003), *Study of teacher's perceptions of curricular and pedagogical issues underlying education for sustainable development.* Academic Report, Regional Institute of Education, Bhubaneswar, p. 35.

Dash, D. (2005), *Women, Environment and Health.* Mangal Deep Publications, Jaipur, p. 243, 268.

Dash, D. and M.K. Satapathy (2004), Public participation in environmental protection: An analysis of the attitude and concerns of the women of Orissa. *Man and Development* XXV(2): 39-56.

Dash, D. and M.K. Satapathy (2006), Education for Sustainable Development: Teaching of values for conservation of Environment through 3Rs. *Edutrack* May, 2006, 9-13.

Datta, N.C. (1990), Expanding horizon of Ecology—An introspection (Presidential address in the Section of Zoology, Entomology and Fisheries at the 77th Session Indian Science Congress, Cochin. *Indian Science Congress Association,* Calcutta, p. 21.

—— (1993), Ecology and quality of life—Platinum Jubilee Lecture in the Section of Zoology at the 80th Session of *Indian Science Congress,* Goa.

—— (1996), Ecodegradation, Sustainable Development and World Conservation Strategy—An appraisal from philosophical perspective (Keynote address at the 11th Annual International Conference of National Environmental Science Academy held at Calcutta). *Science and Culture,* 62(5-6): 110-112.

—— (2000a), Endangered Environment—A Global Enigma. *Science and Culture*, 66(5-6): 169-70.

—— (2000b), Environment as a common concern for mankind and his civilisation. In: Environmental Pollution and individual man. *Mother Publishing House*, Calcutta, Ed. A.K. De: 1-6.

—— (2001), Ecology and a Dialogue on Linkage between Biodiversity and Biomonitoring. In: Emerging Disciplines in Contemporary Zoology—*Proc. VIth Refresher Course in Zoology*, Department of Zoology, University of Calcutta (in Press).

Dave, N.R. (1998), What makes Universities great. *University News*, 36(16): 1-4.

Davis, J.R., Huisman, O.C., Westermann, D.T., Hafez, S.L., Everson, D.O., Sorensen, L.H. and Schneider, A.T. (1996) Effects of green manures on *Verticillium* wilt of potato. *Phytopathol.*, 86, 444-53.

Deacon, J.W. (1983), Microbial Control of Plant Pests and Diseases. *Aspects of Microbiology*, No 7, American Society of Microbiology, Washington.

Deevey, E.S. Jr. (1970), Mineral Cycles. *Scientific American*, 223(5): 148-58.

Desh Bandhu; Bongartz, H.; Ghaznawi, A.G. and Gopal, B. (eds) (1994), *Environmental education for sustainable development*. Indian Environmental Society, New Delhi.

Desinger, J. (1983), Environmental Education's Definitional Problem, *ERIC Information Bulletin*, No. 2. ERIC, Ohio.

Dhaka, A.K. (1999). *Organic Farming*, 2nd Edition. Agrobotanica, Bikaner, p. 294.

Dhar, U.; R.S. Rawal; S. Airi; I.D. Bhatt and S. Samant (2002), Promoting outreach through conservation education programmes—case study from Indian Himalayan region. *Curr Sci*. 82(7): 808-15.

Dhurva Narayan, V.V. and Ram Babu (1983) Estimation of soil erosion in India. *J. Irrig. Drain. Engg.*, 109(4), 419-434.

Diaz, L.F., G.M. Savage, L.L. Eggerth and C.G. Goleuke (1993), Composting *and recycling: Municipal Solid Waste* CRC Press, Boca Raton, FL.

Disinger, John F. (1990), Environmental Education for sustainable development. *The Journal of Environmental Education*, 21(4): 3-6.

Dixon, J.A. (1986) Selected policy options for fuelwood production and use in the Philippines. (in) J.A. Dixon and M.M. Hufschmist (eds.) Economic Valuation Techniques for the Environment, *The Johns Hopkins University Press*, Baltimore: 163-176.

Dobson, Andrew (1998), *Justice and the Environment*, New York, Oxford University Press.

Drechsel, P., Steiner, K.G. and Hagedorn, F (1996) A review on the potential of improved fallows and green manure in Rwanda. *Agrofor. Syst.*, 33, 109-36.

Dubai, V.K. and Dead. (1993), Development Communication: Challenges in the Nineties for Developing Nations: *The Journal of Development Communication*, 1(4): 39-49.

Ediger, M. (2005), The Innovative Science Curriculum. *Edutracks*, 4(6): 17-20.

Edwards, C.A. and Thompson, A.R. (1973) Pesticides and the soil fauna. *Residue Res.*, 1, 45.

Ehriich, H.L. (1995), *Geomicrobiology*, Marcel Dekkar, New York.

Ehrlich, Anne H. and Paul R. Ehrlich (2005), Helping to make a global society sustainable: millennium assessment of human behaviour. *Environmental Awareness* 28(3): 83-92.

Ehrlich, Paul R. (1978), Preface, In: *The Pesticide Conspiracy*, Doubleday and Company. Inc. U.S.A., p. 226.

Elliott, A. Jennifer (1994), An introduction to sustainable development, Routledge, New York, 65-66.

Elwin, V. (1960) *Elwin Verrier's reports on Indian Tribes*. Govt. of India, Publ. New Delhi, p. 86.

Engfeldt, Lers-Goran (2002), The road from Stockholm to Johannesburg. *UN Chronicle*, 3: 14-18.

Evans, H., G. Stacey and R.H. Bums (1991), *Biological Nitrogen Fixation*, Chapman Hall, New York.

Ezadiaro, S.D. (1971), Review of the legal aspect of International water pollution control, *Howard Law Journal*, 7(1): 69-90.

FAO (1990) FAO activities related to environment and sustainable development. *FAO Council Document,* CL 98/6, September, 1990.

—— (1992), *Sustainable Development and the Environment: FAO Policies and Actions, FAO* publication, *Rome* pp. 7-8.

—— (1992), *Sustainable development and the Environment: FAO Policies and Actions*. FAO Publication, Rome.

—— (1993). *Strategies for Sustainable Agriculture and Rural Development* (SARD): *The Role of Agriculture, Forestry and Fisheries*. FAO, Rome.

—— (1997) State of the world forests, 1997, *Food and Agriculture Organisation*, Rome.

—— (1999) State of the world forests, 1999, *Food and Agriculture Organisation,* Rome.

—— (2001) Criteria and indicators for sustainable forest management, Forestry Information Notes, *Food and Agriculture Organisation,* Rome, http://www.fao.org/forestry.

Fellows, P. (1997) *Traditional Foods*. Intermediate Technology Publications, U.K.

Fowler. C. and Mooney. P. (1990) *The Threatened gene: Food policies and the loss of Genetic Diversity.* The Lutterworth Press, Cambridge.

Freedman, Bill. (1995), Environmental Ecology, *Academic Press.* San Diego, New York, London, p. 606.

Futuresco (1993), A UNESCO Bibliographical Bulletin of Future-Oriented Literature, *Environment*, Nos. 2-3, July, 1992, June, 1993.

Gadgil, M. and P.R. Seshagiri Rao (1995) Nature, health and learning, *The Hindu Survey of Environment,* 1995: 37-41. Madras .

Garforth. C. and Lawrence. A. (1997). Supporting sustainable agriculture through extension in Asia. *Natural Resources Perspectives, Paper No. 21*. Overseas Development of Natural Resources Institute, London.

Gautham Hari (2000), The objectives of higher education. *University News*, 38(26): 56-59.

Ghanta, R. and Bhaskar Rao, D. (1998), *Environmental Education: Problems and Prospects*. Discovery Publishing House, New Delhi, p. 308.

Ghosh, A.K. (1997), Redefining the ideals of education. *University News*, 35(3): 9-10.

Ghosh, P. (2004), Harmonising Environmental Concerns and Economic Growth—The Indian Perspective. *Environment Matters (Annual Review), World Bank,* pp. 10-11.

Gill, J.S. and Lahiry, D. (1999), *Environmental education Trends and Developments in India*. In Desh Bandhu and R. Dyal (Eds) *Environmental Education for a sustainable future*, Indian Environmental Society, New Delhi.

Gill, Manmohan S. (2005), Problems of Sustainability in Third World Countries. *Guru Nanak Journal of Sociology*, 26(1): 73-82.

Gnanam, A. (2000), From Knowledge to competency. *University News*, 38(46): 51-55.

Goodland, R.; Daly, H.; Serafy, S.E. and Von Droste, B. (1991), *Environmentally Sustainable Economic Development*: Building on Brundtland. Paris: United Nations Educational, Scientific and Cultural Organisation. Paris.

Gore, A. (1992), *Earth in the Balance: Ecology and the Human Spirit*. Boston, Houghton Mifflin.

Gore, A.L. (1992), *Earth in the balance*: *Ecology and the Human Spirit*. Haughton Mifflin, Boston.

Government of India (1959), Report of the National Committee on Women's Education, 1958-59, New Delhi.

—— (1975), *Women in India: A Compendium of Programmers*, New Delhi.

—— (1986), *National Policy on education*, Ministry of Human Resource Development, Govt. of India, New Delhi.

—— (1988), National perspective plan for women 1988-2000 A.D. Department of Women and Child Development, Govemment of India, New Delhi.

—— (1998), National Perspective Plan for Women 1988-2000 A.D. *op. cit.*, pp. 97-98.

Govil, S. (2003), Application of Biotechnology for clean environment: Indian Success Stories. *Value Education*, 3(2): 14-26.

Guenzi, W.D. (1974) *Pesticides in Soil and Water*. Soil Sci. Soc. Amer. Madison, W.I.

Guha, R. (1989) The unquiet woods: Ecological change and peasant resistance in the Himalaya, *Oxford University Press,* New Delhi.

Gupta, Arvind (1998), Science and sustainable development. *Science Reporter*, 35(12): 60-63.

Hamilton and Lawrence, C. (1985), Who cares about water pollution? Opinions in a small town crisis. Socio-logical Inquiry, 55, 2. Spring 170-181.

Haque, M.Z. (1999), Sustainable Development in the 21st Century: A Review Book Mission Control. *Down to Earth*, 7(8): 61.

Hawkes, H.A. (1997), The ecology of activated sludge. In: *The Oil Industry and Microbial Ecosystems* (Eds.) K.W.A. Chafer and H.J. Somerville, Institute of Petroleum, London, pp. 217-33.

Hawking, S.W. (1988), A brief history of time from the Big Bang to Black Holes. *Bantam Book*, London, p. 211.

Hazell, P. and Ramasamy, C. (1991) *The Green Revolution Reconsidered: The impact of High Yielding Varieties in South India.* The Johns Hopkins University Press, Baltimore.

Hermann, Rohrs (1992), Securing lasting world peace through education, *Education*, pp. 1-17.

Hesselink, F., P. van Kempen and A. Wals (2000), ES Debate: International Debate on Education for Sustainable Development, Gland, IUCN.

Heyn, M., Lythgue and C. Myers, C. (1997), Education and economic development: Sustainability, thresholds and equity. In *report of the third UNESCO-ACEID International Conference. Educational Innovation for Sustainable Development*, 1-4 December, 1997, Bangkok, Thailand.

Heyzer, N. (2005), Making the links: Women's rights and empowerment are key to chieving the Millennium Development Goals. *Gender and Development*, 13(1): 9-12.

Hillari, J. Abramovitz, C. Bright, G. Gardner, A. Mc Ginn, M. Renner, D.M. Roodman and L. Starke (1997) State of the World. A World Watch Institute Report on progress toward a sustainable society. *W.W. Norton & Company*, New York, p. 229.

Himesh, S. (2001), Dilemma of development and environment: A-perspective. *Current Science*, 80(9): 1101-02.

Homan, R. (1992), The ethics of open research. *British Journal of Sociology*, 43(3): 321-31.

Hopkins, Charles (1998), Educational innovation for environmentally sustainable development. In *report of the third UNESCO-ACEID. International Conference. Educational Innovation for sustainable development*, 1-4 December, 1998, Bangkok, Thailand.

Hopper, D.R. (1989), Cleaning up contaminated waste sites. *Chemical Engineering*, 96: 94-110.

Houghton, R.A., J.E. Hobbie, J.M. Melillo, B. Moore, B.J. Peterson, G.R. Shaver and G.M. Woodwell (1983), *Changes in the carbon content of terrestrial biota and soils between 1860 and 1980: A net release of CO_2 to the atmosphere*. Ecological Monographs, 53: 235-62.

Howkins, Donald, E. and Dennis, A. Vinton (1973), *The Environmental Classroom*, U.S.A., Prentice Hall.

Hudson, S.J. (2001), Challenges for environmental education: issue and ideas for the 21st century. *Bioscience* 51(4): 283-88.

Independent Commission on International Humanitarian Issues (ICIHI, 1989) *The vanishing forest: The human consequences of deforestation*, Popular Prakashan, Bombay, p. 89.

ITTO (1990) Guidelines for sustainable management of tropical forests, *International Tropical Timber Organisation*, Yokohama, Japan.

IUCN (1980), International Union for Nature and Nature Conservation. World Conservation Strategy, IUCN.

IUCN. UNEP and WWF (1991), Caring for the Earth: A strategy for sustainable living. IUCN, Gland, Switzerland.

IUCN/UNEP/WWF (1991), *Caring for the earth. A strategy for sustainable living*. Gland, Switzerland.

Iyengar, R.N. (1993) Role of forests in environmental conservation. in B.P. Chaurasia (ed.) *Environmental Degradation and Global Awakening*, pp. 339-47, Chugh Publications, Allhabad.

Jackson, E.A. (1976), Brazil's national alcohol programme. Process Biochemistry II: 29-30.

Jackson, M.G. (2001), Environmental education in India, What has been achieved? *Indian Educational Review,* 37(1): 20-30.

Jacobs, P. and D.A. Munro (1978), *Conservation with Equity Strategies for Sustainable Development* IVCN Publication, U.K.

Jaggi, P., N. Chako and E. Grover (2005), Mothers and the Earth. *Social Welfare,* 52(3): 9-12.

Jain, Revaki (1975), *Indian women.* India Publication Division, I&B: New Delhi.

Jain, V.P. (2002), Sustainable Development: Issues and Perspectives, *Mainstream,* 40(37): 5-6

Jalal, K.F. (1990), 'Environmental Education of Sustainable Development: Role of ESCAP'. In *'Environmental Education and Sustainable Development'* (ed. by D. Bandhu, H. Singh and A.K. Maitra), Indian Environmental Society, New Delhi, pp. 23-29.

Jha, U.C. (1974), *Communication Behaviour of Small Farmers and its Influence on Knowledge.* Ph.D. thesis. Division of Extension Education, IARI, New Delhi.

Jodha, N.S., Banakota, M. and Pratap, T. (1990), Strategies for Sustainable Development of Mountain Agriculture: An Overview'. *Sustainable Mountain Agriculture: Perspectives and Issues* [ed.] International Centre for Integrated Mountain Development, Katmandu; Oxford and IBH Publishing Co. Pvt. Ltd.; New Delhi, p. 30.

John, P.S., George, M. and Senthil, S. (2001) Integrated nutrition management. *Kisan World,* 28, 27-28

Johnson, L.M., C.S. McDowell and M. Krupha (1985), Microbiology in pollution Control: From bugs to biotechnology, 26: 365-76.

Jorgensen, B.B. (1989), Biogeochemistry of chemoautotrophic l) Bacteria. In: H.G. Sclilegel and B. Bowien (Eds.) *Autotrophic Bacteria.* Springer-Verlag, Berlin, pp. 117-46.

Joshi, A.P. (2003), Resource education. *Kurukshetra,* 21: 12-13.

Joshi, S.M. and Pushpanadham, K. (2000), The vision for learning at higher education. *University News,* 38(12): 1-3.

Kale, R.K. (2006), Higher education and Development of the Nation. *Univ. News,* 44(3): 1-11.

Kanniyan. S. (2000) Biofertilisers: Key factor in organic farming. *The Hindu Survey of Indian Agriculture,* pp. 65-173.

Kantowsky, D. (1934), Gandhi—coming back from West to East. *Ifda dossier,* 39, January/February.

Kanwar, J.S. (1994), 'Relevance of Soil Management in Sustainable Agriculture' Soil Management for Sustainable Agriculture in Dryland Areas, (ed. by T.D. Biswas *et al.,*) Indian Society of Soil Science, IARI, New Delhi.

—— (1994), Management of Soil and Water Resources for Sustainable Agriculture and Environment: Keynote address at Diamond Jubilee Symposium of Indian Society of Soil Science, IARI, New Delhi.

Kapoor, K.N., Rathore, V.S. and Rai, A.K. (194). Basic concept of integrated pest management. pp. 52-61 in V.N. Shroff, (eds.) *Organic Farming*, College of Agriculture, Indore.

Kasturiranga, K. (2000), Towards a sustainable society. *University News*, 38(25): 14-15.

Katyal. J.C. (1997) Sustainability: Relevance of integrated concept. *The Hindu Survey of Indian Agriculture,* pp. 25-31.

Kaur, N., J.N. Kaur and R. Kaur (2003), To save life, save earth. *Agrobios*, 1(9): 36-37.

Kendeigh, S.C. (1974), Ecology. Englewood Cliffs, J.J., *Prentice Hall,* p. 468.

Kerr, R.A. (1994), Iron fertilization: A tonic but no cure for the green house. *Science*, 263: 1089-90.

Kevin Cleaver and Gotz Schreiber (1992) Population, agriculture and the environment in Africa, *Finance and Development*, 20(2), June: 34-35.

Khan, W. (1996), Family and sustainable development. *Science and Culture*, 62(5-6): 151-53.

Khandal, H.K. (2003), Value oriented approach from Primary to University Education. *University News*, 41(13): 9-11.

Khoshoo, T.N. (1990), "Towards a Sustainable Society". *The Times of India*, New Delhi, 2 March.

—— (1994), India's biodiversity: Tasks ahead. *Current Science*, 67(8): 557-82.

—— (1996), India needs a National Biodiversity Conservation Board. *Current Science*, 71(7): 506-13.

—— (1998), Sustaining development in the developing countries. *Current Science* 75(7): 652-60.

Khosla, A. (1999), Science and technology for sustainable development. *Current Science*, 76(8): 1080-86.

Kimmins, J.P. (1987) *Forest Ecology*, Mac Millan, N.Y.

Kirk, John (1992), Environmental education in the United States. *Environmental Education,* 41: 10-11.

Kiss, A. (2004), Sustainable development and policy reform-Implementing MDG7, Target 9. Environment Matters: At the World Bank. *Annual Review*, p. 64.

Knimiller, G.W. (1983), Environmental education for relevance in developing countries. *The Environmentalist,* 3: 173-79.

Knowles F.G. (1949), Man and other living things (An introduction to Human Biology). George G. Harrap & Co. Ltd., London, p. 355.

Kormondy, E.J. (2000), Concepts of ecology, *Prentice-Hall of India, Pvt. Ltd.*, 4th edition (tenth printing), p. 559.

Kothari, A. (1999) Agro-biodiversity: The future of India's agriculture. In: *Challenges of Agriculture in the 21st Century*, Pillai, G.M. (ed.), Maharashtra Council of Agricultural Education and Research, Pune, India.

Krebs, C.J. (1985), Ecology: The Experimental Analysis of Distribution and Abundance, 3rd ed. *Harper & Row*, New York. p. 800.

Krishna Nand (2002) Biomethanation from agro-industrial and food processing wastes. In: Biochemistry: Food Fermentation (Vol. II), Joshi, V.K. and Pandey, A. (eds), pp. 1349-1372, Indus Publishing Company, New Delhi.

Krishnamoorthy, B. and Veerabhadraiah, V. (2001). Constraints in adoption of IPM practices by rice farmers. *J. Exten. Edn.*, 12(3), 12.

Krishnaswamy, A. (1999) A global vision for forests in the 21st century, *Tropical Forest Update,* 9(4): 7-9.

Kumar U. and A.K. Sharma (2001), Plant Biotechnology and Biodiversity Conservation. Agro bios (India).

Kwapata, M.B. (1991) Response of contrasting tomato cultivars to depth of applied mulch and irrigation frequency under hot, dry tropical conditions. *Trop. Agr. (Trinidad)*, 68, 301-03.

Laflin, M. (1980), Environmental Communication: New Roles. Hard Choices, Development Communication Report, No. 65, Arlington, USA.

Lakshmipathy, V. (2003), Poverty Reduction Strategies-Micro level Participatory Planning for Sustainable Development: Rural Hinterland-ICT Applications-*Kuppam. Asian Economic Review*, 45(3): 440-47.

Lakshmisree, E. (2000), Promoting environmental ethics. *The environmental Review*, 106:(1): 9-10.

Lal, R. and Lal, S. (1988) *Pesticides and Nitrogen Cycle*, Vols. 1-3, CRC Press, Boca Raton, Fl.

Lambert (1962), India's Urban Future: The impact of urban society on village life, University of California Press.

Lamberth, E. (1996) ,A Bibliographic review of Civic Journalism, *National Civic Review*, 85(1): 36-48.

Leibenstein, H. (1957), Economic Backwardness and Economic Growth, Berkely.

Litchfield, J.H. (1977), Comparative technical and economic aspects of single cell. Protein processes. *Advances in Applied Microbiology*, 22: 267-305.

Loveley, D.R. (1993), Dissimilatory metal reduction. *Annual Review of Microbiology*, 47: 263-90.

Lucas, R.E., Holtman, J.B. and Conner, L.J. (1977) Soil organic carbon dynamics and cropping practices. In: *Agriculture and Energy*, Lockertz, W. (ed.), Academic Press, N.Y.

Lundgren, R. and A. McMakin, (1998), *Risk Communication*, Battele Press, Ohio.

Lynan and Herdt (1988), *Soil Management for Sustainable Agriculture in Dry land Areas,* Bulletin No. 16, Published in 1994 by Indian Society of Soil Science, New Delhi, p. 2.

Mac Neill, J. (1996), Sustainable Development: Meeting the Growth Imperative for the 21st century. *Sustaining Earth,* pp. 191-201.

Mahalinggam, P.K. (1973). Ameliorative properties of lignite fly ash in reclaiming saline and alkali soils. *Madras Agric. J.*, 60, 1055-57.

Malaisamy, A. (2002) Sustainability of agriculture in the 21st century. *Kisan World*, 29, 32-34.

Manahori, (2002) Organic farming for sustainable agriculture. MANAGE. *http://manage.gov.in/managelib/faculty/manohari.htm*

Mandelbaum (1972), Society in India, Vol. I & II, Popular Prakashan Pvt. Ltd. Bombay.

Mangal, S.K. (2002), Educating the teacher educators. *Edutracks*, 1(2): 6-12.

Mayor, Federico (1997), The Raja Roy Singh keynote address In *Third UNESCO-ACEID International Conference in Educational Innovations for sustainable development*, 1-4 December, 1997. UNESCO Principal Regional Office for the Asia and the Pacific, Thailand.

Mc Neely, J.; A., K.R., Miller; W.V., Reid; R.A. Mittermier and T.B., Werner, (1990), *Conserving the World's Biological Diversity*, Gland, Switzerland.

Menon, M.G.K. (1997), Our Heritage. *University News*, 35(26): 12-16.

Miller, G.R. and M. Steinberg (1975), *Between People*. CA: Science Research Associates, Palo Alto.

Mishra, A.K. (2000), Development and Education. *School Science*, 38(1): 1-7.

Mishra, B.P. (2002), Analysis of the knowledge, attitude and perception regarding sustainable development among pre-service and in-service teachers at secondary level. Ph. D Thesis, Utkal University, Bhubaneswar, Orissa, p. 231.

Mishra, N. (2005), Ecofeminism: A global concern. *Social Welfare*, 52(3): 3-8.

Mishra, P.N. and Airen, G. (1994), A model for environmental education. *University News*, 32(16): 1-3.

Mishra, R. (1999), Mass awareness for environmental problem, CEMC Newsletter, Vol. I, No. 1.

Mishra, S. and Dhaka, R.S. (2001), Final Declaration "Education 21—Learning for fair and sustainable future development". *Adult Education and Development*, 57: 45-51.

Mittal, S.P. (2001), Towards sustainable development. *Kurukhetra*, 48(5): 42-43.

MoEF (1998), *India: Sustaining development*. Ministry of Environment and Forest, Government of India, p. 107.

Moore, Sylvia (1986), Participatory Communication in the Development Process. The *Third Channel*, 2(2) 4: 586-623.

Morris, R.A., Furoc, R.E. and Dizon, M.A. (1986) Rice responses to a short duration green manure. I. Grain yield. *Agron. J.*, 78, 409-12..

Moses, V. and D.G. Springham (1982), *Bacteria and the enhancement of Oil Recovery*. Applied Science Publishers, London.

Muraleedharam, S. (1997), Gandhian Way Of Development: The Indian Experience *ISDA Journal*, 7(2-3): 139-46.

Muruganandam, M. and G. Sastry (1998) The concept of environment and sustainable aquaculture development, Proc. of Workshop on Environmental Impact Assessment of Aquaculture Enterprises, organised by *Rajiv Gandhi Centre for Aquaculture*, Kochi, at Chennai, during 10-12 December, 1997: 44-61.

Nadkarni, M.V. (1996) Forests, people and economics, *Indian Journal of Agricultural Economics*, 51(1&2): 1-24.

Nag, V.K. and Saingal, V.R. (1986), A Case Study of Air Pollution Status in Bombay Metropolitan Region. *Indian Env. Agric.*, 1(1): 72-83.

Nagchaudhuri, B.D. (1983), Introduction to Environmental Management. Interprint, New Delhi, p. 156.

Nair, N. Balakrishnan (1994), Strategies in environmental planning. *Biology Education*, 11(4): 248-51.

Naoss, A. (1990), *Sustainable Development and Deep Ecology, Ethics of Environment and Development—Global Challenge and International Response* (Ed. by Engel, J.R. and Engel, J.B.) Belhaven Press (a division of printer publisher), 25 floral Street, London.

Narain, P. (1998), A Dialectical Perspective of Agricultural Research for Sustainable Development. *Current Science*, 74(8): 663-65.

Narayan, K.K. (1999), Gap between plan and action. *University News*, 37(3): 18-19.

Natarajan, S. (2001), Commitment for the less fortunate ones. *University News*, 39(11): 15-17.

National Academy of Sciences (1977), *Methane generation from Human, Animal and Agricultural Wastes.* National Academy of Sciences, Washington, D.C. National Research Council (1979), *Microbial Processes: Promising Technologies for Developing Countries.* National Academy of Sciences, Washington, D.C.

Nayak, A.K. and Kanungo, A.P. (1993), Sustainable Agriculture: Some Observations. *Yojana*, 37(22): 7-8.

NCERT (1981), Environmental Education and NCERT. *National Council of Educational Research and Training*, New Delhi, p. 30.

—— (1984), National Council of Educational Research and Training, 1984, Educational backwardness of girls in eight selected states (Unpublished Report), New Delhi.

—— (1988), *National Curriculum for Elementary and Secondary Education*, NCERT, New Delhi, p. 16.

—— (2000), *National Curriculum Framework for School Education.* National Council of Educational Research and Training, New Delhi, p. 128.

—— (2001), *Environmental orientation to school education: a training module for eastern region.* National Council of Educational Research and Training, New Delhi, p. 316.

—— (2004), *Environmental education in schools.* National Council of Educational Research and Training, New Delhi, p. 112.

—— (2005), *National Curriculum Framework,* 2005. NCERT, New Delhi, p. 140.

NCTE (1998), *Curriculum Framework for Quality Teacher Education.* National Council for Teacher Education, New Delhi, p. 137.

Nealson, K.H. and D. Safiarini (1994), Iron and manganese in anaerobic respiration. Environmental significance, physiology and regulation. *Annual Review of Microbiology*, 48: 311-43.

Neelima, B.N. and K.R. Nair (2001), Environmental education through media. *Journal of Indian Education*, XXVII (2): 59-65.

Nelson D.C. (1990), *Physiology and Biochemistry of filamentous sulphur bacteria. In Autotrophic Bacter,* (Eds.) H-G. Schlegel and B. Bowein., Springer-Verlag, Berlin, pp. 219-38.

Nelson, W.A., Kahn, B.A. and Roberts, B.W. (1991) Screening cover crops for use in conservation tillage systems for vegetables following spring plowing. *Hort. Sci.*, 26, 860-62.

Nicholson, A.G. and Wien, H.C. (1983) Screening of turf grasses and clovers for use as living mulches in sweet corn and cabbage. *J. Am.Soc. Hort. Sci.*, 108, 1071-1076.

NIEPA (1990), National Institute of Educational Planning and Administration, 1990, Education for All by 2000: India perspective, NIEPA.

Nsenkyiere, E.O. and M. Simula (2000) Developing auditing systems for SFM, *Tropical Forest Update*, 10(3): 5-7.

Obiefuna, J.C. (1991) The effect of crop residue mulches on the yield and production pattern of plantain (*Musa* sp.). *Biol. Agr. Hort.*, 8, 71-80.

Odum, E.P. (1971), Fundamentals of Ecology. 3rd ed. W.B. Saunders Co., p. 574.

—— (1993), Ecology and our endangered life support systems. (2nd Ed.) Sunderland Mars, Sinauter.

Odum, H.T. (1971). Environment, Power and Society. *John Willey and Sons, Inc.,* New York. p. 331.

Odunfa, S.A. (1985) African fermented Foods, In: *Microbiology of Fermented Foods,* Elsevier Applied Science Publishers, USA

Okada, T. (1991). Environment-friendly insect pest control. Special Volume on Agriculture and Environment. Farming Japan, 25: 39-44.

Padmanaban. S. (2001) Energy efficiency in Indian agriculture. Available at: http://www.usaid.gov/in/whatsnew/articles.htm.

Palmer, Joy (1993), A model for teaching and learning in the environmental education. *Environmental Education*, 12: 8-10.

Panayotou, T. (1992), The integration of economy and ecology in sustainable development and its implications for policy. In Keynote address for the conference on the role of environmental economics in national development, Colombo, Sri Lanka.

Pandey, S. (1998), Teacher for the 21st century. *University News*, 36(6): February 9.

——(2000), Status of Environment Education. *University News*, 38(39): 26-31.

Panigrahi, S.K. (2004), Environmental Education: Need of the hour. Jojana, 48(6): 13-22.

Pantham, T. and K.L. Dentsch (1986), *Political Thought in Modern India.* Sage Publication, New Delhi.

Parashar, M. (1996), Environmentally sustainable development and education. *School Science*, 39(4): 7-12.

Paroda, R.S. (1998), Excellence in science and education. *University News*, 36(10): 9-10.

Parton, W.J., Persson, J. and Anderson, D.W. (1982) Simulation of organic matter changes in Swedish soils. In: *Proc. Third Int. Conf. State of the Art in Ecological Modelling*, Fort Collins, CO.

Pashupati Nath and Siddha Nath (1990) *Environmental pollution: Conservation and planning*, Vol. II, p. 212. Chugh Publications, Allahabad.

Pati, Jagannath (2000), Women, Environment and Sustainable Development. *Kurukshetra*, 48(12): 22-27.

Patil, V.S. and Kolekar. H.D. (2002). Genetic uniformity and agriculture. *Kisan World*, 29(9), 35-36.

Pawar, J.D.S., Saikia, S.P. and Naidu, V.S.G. (2001). Biofertilizers for enhancing crop productivity and environmental security. *Indian Farming*, January, 2001, pp. 56-60.

Pearce, D.W. (1996), The Limits of Cost Benefit Analysis as a Guide To Environmental Police, Kyklos, 29, Fass 1.

Powell, C.L. (1980) Mycorrhizal infectivity of eroded soils. *Sol Biol Biochem.*, 12, 247-50.

Prasad, M. (1990), Inaugural Address, Third International Conference on Environmental Education, Goa, in *Environmental Education and sustainable Development* (Ed. by D. Bandhu, H. Singh and A.K. Maitra), Indian Environmental Society, New Delhi, pp. 5-9.

Pretty, J.N. (1996). *Regenerating agriculture: Policies and strategies for sustainability and self-reliance*. Vikas Publishing House Pvt. Ltd., Bangalore.

Proulx, G. (2004), Integrating scientific method and critical thinking in classroom debates on environmental issues, *The American Biology Teacher*, 66(1) 26-33.

Pushpangadan, P. and K.N. Nair (2001), Future of systematics and biodiversity research in India: Need for a National Consortium and National Agenda for systematic biology research. *Current Science*, 80(5): 631-37.

Rai, S.N. (1999) *Nursery and Planting Techniques of Forest Tress in Tropical South Asia*, Punarvasu Publications, Dharwad. India.

Rajagopalan, R. (2005), *Environmental Studies: From Crises to Cure*. Oxford University Press, New Delhi.

Rajendraprasad, M; P.N. Krishnan and P. Pushpangadan (1997), Role of sacred groves in conservation of biodiversity and protection of the environment. *Kurukshetra*, (XLVI): 19-22.

Rajput J.S. (1997), Role of teacher in 21st century. *The Progresas of Education*, 22(1): 22-23.

—— (2003), The values context in environmental education. *Journal of Value Education*, 3(2): 5-13.

Ram Babu, Dhyani, B.L., Agarwal, M.C. and Samra, J.S. (1997) *Economic evaluation of watershed management projects*. CSWCRTI, Dehradun, India, Bulletin No. T.33/D-23.

Ramamurthy, V.V. (2004), Biodiversity and Sustainability in food production—Tasks ahead. *Indian Farming* 48: 37-40.

Raman, A., S. Raghu and S. Sreenath (2000), Integrating environment, education and employment for sustainable society: An HRD agenda for developing countries. *Current Science*, 78(3): 241-47.

Ramasamy, A.S. (1996), Population, Environment and Development. *Kurukshtra*, 44: 28-31.

Ramesh, G. (1998), Environmental education: The need and the challenges. pp. 1-4. In *Environmental education: Problems and prospects*. (Eds. Ghanta, R. and Baskar Rao, D.), Discovery Publishing House, New Delhi.

Rana, R.S. (1992), Conservation of plant genetic resources: Holding the seeds of the future gene revolution. *Indian Farming*, 3-13.

Rao, D.N. and Mikkelsen, D.S. (1977) Effect of rice straw additions on production of organic acids in a flooded soil. *Pl. Soil.*, 47, 303-311.

Rao, P.N. (1999), Protection of environment and basic needs of mankind. *Environment and people* 6(4): 5-12.

Rao, T.V.S, Ramamohan and S. Kar, (2003), An Approach to Sustainable Development, *Indian Journal of Economics*, 84(333): 333-42.

Rathore, M.S. (1996) Environment and development: Areas of conflict and convergence. In M.S. Rathore (ed.) *Environment and Development*, pp. 15-44. Rawat Publications, New Delhi.

Ratna Reddy, V. (1996) Environment and sustainable agricultural development: conflicts and contradictions. In M.S. Rathore (ed.) *Environment and Development,* 58-87. Rawat Publications, New Delhi.

Ravi Sharma (1995) International forest management: Sincerity in question, *The Hindu Survey of the Environment*, 1995: 55-59. Madras

Ray, J.G. (1999), Significance of environment education and ecological studies in the news century. *University News*, 37(37): 14-15.

—— (2001), Environmental Science Vs. Ecology. *University News*, 39(4): 30.

Ray, P.K. (1997), Our Environment—present status and future perspectives. *Science and Culture*, 63(5-6): 96-97.

Reddy, D.N. (2002), Sustainable development: Environment education is the key. *Edutracks*, 1(4): 35-37.

Reddy, K. Kranthi Kumar (2002), Economic Growth and Environment Sustainability. *Third Concept*, 16(185): 38-41.

Reddy, M.R. and Rajanikanth, G. (1998), Peoples' Participation for Sustainable Development. *Yojana*, 42(4): 30-32.

Reddy, P.M., H. Spiller, S.L. Albrecht, and K.T. Shanmugam (1996), Photo dissimilation of fructose to Hz and CO_2 by a dinitrogen fixing Cyanobacterium, Anabaena variabilis. *Applied and Environmental Microbiology*, 62: 1220-27.

Reigntzes, C., Haverkert, B. and Waters Bayer, A. (1992), *Farming for the Future: An Introduction to Low-External Input and Sustainable Agriculture*. The MacMillan Press Ltd., London, pp. 2-3.

Remadevi, V.S. (2001), Education, the enduring means of empowerment. *University News*, 39(9): 6-12.

Rodgers, P.B. (1993). Potential of bio-pesticides in agriculture. *Pestic. Sci.*, 39,117-29.

Rogers, C. (1959), A theory of Therapy, Personality, Inter-personal Relationships as Developed in the Client-centered framework, in *Psychology: A Study of Social Control.* By S. Koch, pp. 184-256, Mc-Graw Hill, New York.

Rolland Romain (1924), *Mahatma Gandhi—who became one with the universal being*. Publ. Division, Ministry of I & B, Govt. of India, New Delhi.

Rose, A.H., (1979), Microbial biomass. Economic Microbiology, Vol 4, Academic Press, London.

Roux, C. and J.G. Ferriera (2005), Enhancing environmental education teaching skilis through in-service education and teaching. *Journal of Education for Teaching*, 31(1): 3-14.

Sah, A.K. 1995. Participatory Development—Concept, Need and Psychology, *Kurukhetra,* 48(3) December, 1999, pp. 31-35.

Sahai, R. (1993) Animal Genetic Resources Scenario of India. *Paper presented at the National Seminar on Animal Genetic Resources and their Conservation, 22-23* April, 1993, National Bureau of Animal Genetic Resources, and Nature Conservators, Karnal, India.

Samir, A. (2006), The Millenium Development Goals—A critique from the south. *Review of the month* 57(10): 1-15.

Samra, J.S. (1997) *Status of Research on Watershed Management.* CSWCRTI, Dehradun, India.

Sanginga, N., Mulungoy, K. and Swift, M.J. (1992) Contribution of soil organisms to the sustainability and productivity (sic) cropping systems in the tropics. *Agr. Ecosyst. Environ.*, 41, 135-52.

Santra, S.C. (2001), *Environmental Science.* New Central Book Agency (P) Ltd., Calcutta, p. 944.

Saradamoni, (ed.) (1985), *Women, Work and Society,* Indian statistical Institute, New Delhi, pp. 275-308.

Saradamoni, K. (1988), Statistics on employment of women, presented in the Seminar of Social Statistics, C.S.O., Government of India.

Sarre, A. (2000) The role of log bans, *Tropical Forest Update,* 10(3): 24-25.

Sathe, M. (1997), Development sans literacy; Unsustainable. *Indian Journal of Adult Education,* 58(1): 16-28.

Saxena, A.B. (1993), *Environment centred education, Journal of Indian Education,* 9(4): 10-18.

—— (1996), Students' Concept of Energy and its Implication for Curriculum. *School Science*, XXXIV(4): 33-38.

—— (2000), Science and Technology: Education for sustainable development. *Journal of Indian Education*, 26(1): 24-30.

Saxena, N.C. (1996) Policy issues in forestry. In M.S. Rathore (ed.) pp. 88-116, *Environment and Development*, Rawat Publications, New Delhi: 88-116.

Schaefer, G. (1989), Biology an Integrating Science, IUBS-CBE Meeting, Moscow.

Schmidt, E.L. (1982) Nitrification in soil. In: *Nitrogen in Agricultural Soils,* Agronomy Monograph 22, Madison, W.I.

Schneider, S. (1989), The changing climate. *Scientific American*, 257: 70-79.

Schramm, Wilbur (1972), The Nature of Communication Between Humans. In W. Schramm and D.F. Roberts (eds.) *The Process and Effects of Mass Communications*. University of Illinois Press, Urbana.

Schuyler, Arint H. (1983), Population, resources and environment: All one problem *The Journal of Environmental Education*, 15(1): 1-2.

Sehgal, J.L. and Abrol, I.P. (1994) *Soil Degradation in India: Status and Impact.* Oxford and IBH Publishing Co. Pvt. Ltd., New Delhi, India.

Sen, Amartya (1989), *Standards of living*. Oxford University Press, London.

Sequcira, J. (1997), Innovation in educational management in selected countries experiencing rapid transition to market economics. In *Educational Innovation for sustainable development. Report of the third UNESCO-ACEID International Conference* 1-4 December, 1997, Thailand.

Shah, K.T. (ed.) (1947), Women's role in planned economy, national planning committee, Indian National Congress, pp. 1-18.

Sharma, E.A.S. (1998), The challenge of 21st century. *University News*, 36(12): 41-44.

Sharma, H.S. and Chattopadhyay, S. (2000), *Sustainable development: Issues and case studies*. Concept Publishing Company, New Delhi, p. 307.

Sharma, N. (1997), Nehru's vision of Sustainable Development. *Kurukshetra*, XLV(8): 53-54.

Sharma, N. and R. Rowe (1992) Managing the world's forests, *Finance and Development*, 20(2): 31-33.

Sharma, S. (2005), Rethinking Teachers Education *Yojana*, 49: 41-44.

—— (2005), Role of teacher in curriculum construction and Implementation. *Edutracks*, 4(6): 6-11.

Sharma, S.L. (ed.) (1986), Changing Conceptions of Development: An Analytical Search for Missing Dimensions, Rawat Publications, Jaipur.

Shiva, V. (1991) *Ecology and the politics of Survival: Conflicts over natural resources in India*. Sage Publication India Ltd., New Delhi.

—— (2005), Voice from the south: Tsunami lessons. *Resurgence*, 230: 6-8.

Shiva, Vandana (1991), Ecology and the politics of survival: Conflicts over natural resources in India. Sage Publication India Ltd., New Delhi.

Shiva, Vandana, H.C. Sharatchandra and J. Bandyopadhyay (1981) Social, economic and ecological impact of social forestry in Kolar, *Indian Institute of Management*, Bangalore, p. 83.

Shoenfeld, Clay (1971), The Third American Revolution. *Everybody's Ecology*, Barn.

Shribbs, J.M. and Skroch, W.A. (1986) Influence of twelve ground cover systems on young Smoothee Golden Delicious apple trees: II. Nutrition. *J. Am. Soc. Hort. Sci.*, 111, 529-33.

Shroff, V.N. and Menon, T.G.K. (1994). Basic concept of organic farming. Page 2-4 in V.N. Shroff, (eds.) *Organic Farming*. College of Agriculture, Indore.

Silva Victor (1996), Bulldozer Diplomacy, Ecoforum, March, 1996.

Silver, C.S. (1991) *One earth, one future: Our changing global environment*, p. 196. Affiliated East-West Press Pvt. Ltd., New Delhi.

Singh, A. (1988), *Scientific temperament among postgraduate students of different regions of India.* Ph.D. Thesis, Faculty of Education, B.H.U., Varanasi.

—— (1995), Concept and Philosophy of Sustainable Development. Paper presented in National Training on Sustainable Development, Organised by National Council of Development Communication (NCDC), Varanasi, 13 April, 95.

Singh, A.K., Jain, S.C., Dabhalkar, A.R., Raghuvanshi, R.K.S. and Mishra, O.R. (1994). Basic concept of integrated nutrients supply management. pp. 7-16 in V.N. Shroff, eds., *Organic Farming*. College of Agriculture, Indore.

Singh, B.K. (1982), Environment Man and Society. *Yojana* 26:19-20.

Singh, B.M. and P.L. Gautam (1997), Bioresources of medicinal and aromatic plants in India: their conservation and related issues. *Kurukshetra*, (XLVI): 9-13.

Singh, B.P. (2001) Democracy and culture, *Span*, 52(3): 38-39.

Singh, G.B. (1999) Natural resource management for sustainable agriculture. In: *Fifty Years of Natural Resource Management Research*, Singh, G.B. and Sharma, B.R., (eds.), pp. 4-11. Indian Council of Agricultural Research, New Delhi.

Singh, H.P. (1996) Watershed as a unit for sustainable development. In: *Land Resources and their Management for Sustainability in Arid regions*, Kolarkar, A.S. (ed.), Scientific Publishers, Jodhpur, pp. 105-16.

Singh, J.S. (2002), The biodiversity crisis: A multifaceted review, Curr. Sci., 82(6): 638-47.

Singh, M. (1998), Towards sustainable development. *Man and Development*, 20(1): 28-32.

Singh, N. and Titi, V. (1993), Empowerment for Sustainable Development, working paper of JISD, Winnipeg.

Singh, P. (2001). Sustainable crop production—limitations and strategies. *Indian Farming*, January, 2001, p. 7-10.

Singh, P.K. and R.N. Bisoyi (1992), Restoration of soil fertility through biofertilizers. *In: Land Restoration: Concepts and Strategies* (Ed) J.S. Singh, Rastogi Publ. Meerut, India, pp. 25-47.

Singh, R.B. (1995). Research and developmental strategies for intensification of rice production in the Asia-pacific regions. Page 25-44 in K. Muralidharan and E.A. Siddiq, eds., New Frontier in Rice Research. Directorate of Rice Research, Hyderabad.

Singh, R.K. and Lal, R.B. (1985) Contribution of legumes to the fertiliser nitrogen economy in a maize-based cropping system. *J. Agr. Sci., Camb.*, 105, 491-93.

Singh. S.P. (2000) Integrated pest management: Bio-intensive approach helpful. *The Hindu Survey of Indian Agriculture*, pp. 159-63.

Sisodia (2001), Size of Higher Education System in India by 2011 A.D.

Smith, Robert L. (1992), *Elements of Ecology* (3rd Ed.) Hozper and Low, New York.

Solow, R. (1992), *An Almost Practical Step Toward Sustainability, Address to Resources for the Future*, Washington.

Southwick, C.H. (1976), Ecology and the quality of our environment. 2nd ed. D. Van Nostrand Co., New York. Lond, p. 426.

Srivastava, A. (2001), Feminist re-definition of Sustainable Development. *Social Welfare*, 48(9): 8-14.

Srivastava, G. (1995), Environmental Awareness: A historical prospective. *Journal of Indian Education*, XIX (2): 29-32.

Srivastava, O.N., Das. P.K. and Bidari, D. (1998) Impact of IPM training in India. http://www.panasia.org.sg/nird/clic/reshigh17-1998.htm

Stapp, W.B. (1970), The concept of environmental education. *American Biology Teacher*, 32: 14.

Steinkraus, K.H. (1996) *Handbook of fermented Foods*, Marcel Decker Inc, N.Y.

—— (1992) Lactic acid fermentation. In: *Application of Biotechnology to traditional fermented foods. II. Report of an ad hoc panel of the Board on*

Science and Technology for International Development, National Academy Press, Washington D.C.

Sterling, S. (2001), Sustainable Education: *Revisioning learning and changes.* Totnes, Green Books.

—— (2005), An analysis of the Development of Sustainability Education: Evolution, Interpretation and Transformation potential In "*The Sustainability Curriculum: The challenges for Higher Education.* (Ed. by: John Blewitt and CedRic Cllingford) Earthscan, London, Sterling.

Stewart, W.D.P. (1975) *Nitrogen Fixation by Free Living Microorganisms*. Camb. Univ. Press, Camb., U.K.

Subba Rao, N. (2001) Sustainable forest management, *Kurukhetra,* 49(6): 28-32.

Subramaji, S. (1986), Pollution control at Bharat Petroleum Refinary Chemi. *Eng. World*, 21(1): 101-03.

Susanne Charles; Luc Hens and Dimitri Oevuyst (1989), Integrated Environmental Education into General University Teaching in Europe, UNESCO-UNEP, p. 394.

Swaminathan, M.S. (1984), Genetic conservation—Microbes to Man. *Science Age* January 1984, pp. 17-20.

—— (1996). *Sustainable Agriculture, Towards an Ever Green Revolution.* Konark Publishers Pvt. Ltd. p. 220.

—— (1997), State of Sustainable Agriculture Five Years after Rio. *Kurukhetra,* XLV (11): 8-11.

—— (2000), Science and Sustainable Food Security. *Indian Farming*, 50(10): 4-6.

—— (2001), Sustainable Livelihood and freedom from hunger. *Indian Farming*, 51(8): 6-9.

—— (2005), Tsunami: Rehabilitation efforts for sustainable human security. *Environmental Awareness*, 28(2): 45-52.

Sweetman, C. (2005), Editorial, *Gender and development* 13(1):3-8.

Syriac, V. (2002), The Earth is an organism? The daily *Deccan Hearald, Science & Technology Supplement*, 12 February, pp. III.

Talba, M.K. (1991), Population, Resources, Energy and Development, In *International Environment policy: Emergence and Dimensions* (Ed. By L.K. Caldwell) East-West Press Edition, New Delhi.

Tansley, A.G. (1935), The use and abuse of vegetational concepts and terms, *Ecology*, 16: 284-307.

Teachers (Edited by R.C. Sharma and M.C. Tan). UNESCO Principal Regional Office for Asia and the Pacific, Bangkok, p. 311.

Teasdale, J.R. and Abdul-Baki, A.A. (1997) Growth analysis of tomatos in black polyethylene and hairy vetch production systems. *Hort. Sci.*, 32, 659-663.

Tewari, D.N. (2000), Population and sustainable development, *Yojana*, 44(8): 5-6.

Tiessen, H. and J.W.B. Stewart (1985), The biogeochemistry of soil phosphorus. In: *Planetary Ecology* (Eds.) D.C. Caldwell, J.A. Brierley and C.L. Brierley, Van Nostrand Reinhold, New York, pp. 463-72.

Tilak, J.B.G. (1986), *Education in an unequal world. National Institute of*

Educational Planning and Administration, Concept Publishing Company, New Delhi.

Tindall, J.A., Beverly, R.B. and Radcliffe, D.E. (1991) Mulch effect on soil properties and tomato growth using micro-irrigation. *Agron. J.*, 83, 1028-34.

Tiwari, K.K. (1998), Education and Training for Rural Women. *Employment News*, 5-11 September 1998, New Delhi.

Tompkins, L.J. (2005), A case for community based education: Students turn partnership to tackle local environmental issues. *The Science Teacher*, 72(4): 34-36.

Treguer, P., D.M. Nelson, A.J. VanBennekom, D.J. DeMaster, A. Leyaert and B. Queguiner (1995), The silica balance in the world ocean: A re-estimate. *Science*, 268: 375-79.

Tu, C.M. and Miles, J.R.W. (1976) Interactions between insecticides and soil microbes. *Residue Rev.*, 4, 17-65.

Tuovinen, O.H. (1990), Biological fundamentals of mineral leaching processes, In: *Microbial Mineral Recovery* (Eds.) R.L. Ehrlich and C.L. Brierley, M.C. Graw-Hill, New York, pp. 55-78.

Udagawa, T. (1991). Agriculture and environmental problems in Japan. *Special Volume on Agriculture and Environment*. Farming Japan, 25: 10-19.

Udai Pareek (1982), *Education and Rural Development in Asia*, Oxford and IBH Publications, New Delhi.

UHL, Christopher and Anderson, Amy (2001), Green Destiny: Universities leading the way to a sustainable future. *Bio-science*, 51(1): 36-42.

Ulluwishewa, R. (1993), Indigenous Knowledge, National I.K., Resource Centers and Sustainable Development, Indigenous Knowledge and Development Monitor, CIRAN, Hague, Netherlands, 1(3): 11-13.

UNDP (1993) *Human development report*, 1993, United Nations Development Programme, New York.

UNESCO (1974), Seminar on Environmental Education, Jammi: Finnish National Commission for UNESCO, 1974.

—— (1978), *Intergovernmental conference on environmental education.* Tbilisi (USSR), 14-26 October, 1977, Final Report, Paris.

—— (1985), *Environmental Education: Principles of teaching and learning. Environmental Education series,* 20, UNESCO-UNEP. International Environmental Education Programme. Division of Science-Technical and Environmental Education Absts.

—— (1986), *Procedures for developing an Environment Education Curriculum Env. Edn. Series No. 25,* UNESCO-UNEP. International Environmental Education Programme. Division of Science-Technical and Environmental Education Absts.

—— (1987), Strategies for Training of teacher in Environmental education. Env. Edn. Series No. 25, UNESCO-UNEP. International Environmental Education Programme. Division of Science—Technical and Environmental Education Absts.

—— (1988), *Environmental Education: A process of pre-service teacher training curriculum development. Environmental Education* series 26,

UNESCO-UNEP International Environmental Education Programme. Division of Science-Technical and Environmental Education Absts, p. 175.

—— (1990), Source book in environmental education for secondary school teachers. (In R.C. Sharma Merle C. Tan) UNESCO Principal Regional office for Asia and the Pacific. Bangkok, Thailand.

—— (1998), *Educational innovation for sustainable development*. Report of the third UNESCO-ACEID International Conference, 1-4 December, 1997, Bangkok, Thailand.

—— (1998), *Higher education in the 21st century, Vision and action—Report,* UNESCO, Bangkok.

—— (1998a), Higher education in the 21st century, Vision and action—Report, UNESCO, Bangkok.

—— (1998b), *Educational innovation for sustainable development*. Report of the third UNESCO-ACEID International Conference. 1-4 December, 1997, Bangkok, Thailand.

—— (2002), *Education for sustainability—From Rio to Johannesburg: Lessons learnt from a decade of commitment*, UNESCO, Paris.

UNESCO-UNEP (1978), Teacher training in environmental education. *Connect*, 6(4): 1-8.

UNICEF (1989), *Children and Environment: A UNICEF strategy for sustainable development.* UNICEF, USA 121P.

Usha Rao, N.J. (1983), *Women in Developing Society*, Ashish Publishing House, New Delhi.

Veer, K. (1989), "*A study on factors affecting teleological gaps in the adoption of chemical fertilizer (NPK) with special reference to cultivation of wheat and bajra crops.* M.Sc. Thesis (Unpub.), S.K.N. College of Agril. Jobner, Rajasthan.

Venkatachalam, M., Selvaraj, G. and Philip, H. (2001) Maladies and remedies in the use of bio-control agents. *J. Exten. Edn.*, 12(3), 3184-90.

Venkataiah, N. (1998), Value education. *University News*, 36(25): 1-4.

Venkattakumar, R., P.N. Ananth, N. Sriram and K.B. Sripal (2000) People's participation in Watershed Management, *Kurukhetra*, 48(11): 22-30.

Verma, D.K and A. Schrot (2003), The concept of social Justice in post-modern society: Some reflections on sustainable development. *Prasthasnika*, 30(2): 39-59

Vijayalakshmi, G. (2002), Teachers perception of school children's values. *Edutracks*, 2(4): 22-24.

Viro, P.J. (1974) Effects of forest fire on soil. In: *Fire and Ecosystems,* Kozlowski, T.T. and Ahlgree, C.E. (eds.), Academic Press, N.Y.

Voroney, R.P., Van Veen, J.A. and Paul, E.A. (1981). Organic carbon dynamics in grassland soils. II. Model validation and simulation of the long term effects of cultivation and rainfall erosion. *Can. J. Soil Sci.*, 61, 211-24.

Vyas, S.C. and A.C. Vyas (1994). Potential of biofertilizers in crop production in Indian agriculture. pp. 19-27 in V.N. Shroff,(eds) *Organic Farming,* College of Agriculture, Indore.

Vyas, V.S. (1996) Foreword. In M.S. Rathore (ed.) *Environment and Development*, pp 5-7. Rawat Publications, New Delhi: 5-7.

Vyas, V.S. and V. Ratna Reddy (1996) Environmental policies and policy implementation in India: An assessment. (in) M.S. Rathore (ed.) Environment and Development, pp. 167-92. Rawat Publications, New Delhi.

Wang, C.W., Lien, T.H. and Mibkelsen, D.S. (2001) Development of sulphur deficiency as limiting factor for rice production. *IRI Bull.* 47, N.Y.

WCED (1987) World Commission on Environment and Development. Our *Common Future,* Oxford University, Press, New Delhi.

WCMC, (1993), *Global Biodiversity*. Chapman and Hall, London.

Westing, A.H. (1996), Core values for sustainable development *Environmental conservation* 23(3): 219-25.

——(1999), Towards a universal recognition of environmental responsibilities. *Environmental Conservation*, 26(3): 157-80.

Wheatley. C, Scott. G.J., Best. R. and Wiersema. S. (1995) *Adding value to root and tuber crops: A manual for product development (CIAT Publication No. 247),* CIAT, Cali, Columbia, p. 166.

World Bank (1997), *Social Indicators of Development*. John Hopkins Univ. Press, London.

World Commission on Environment and Development (1987) *Our Common Future*, Oxford University Press, New York.

—— (1989), World Commission on Environment and Development "Our Common Future", Oxford University Press.

——(1990), "The Manila Declaration on People's participation and sustainable development", *lfda dossier*, 75/76 January/April.

Wright, N.G. (1995), Indicators for sustainability, paper presented in National Training on Sustainable Development, organised by NCDC, Varanasi, 1-13 April, 1995.

Yodamani, S. (1997), Environmental issues of considerations affecting sustainable development in the Asia-Pacific region. In *Educational Innovation for sustainable development*. Report of the third UNESCO-ACEID. International Conference, 1-4 December, 1997.

Index

Acharya Rama Murthi Committee 114
Acid rain 8, 45, 273-74
Adult education 142, 144, 158
  centres 143
  courses 199
  Programme 143-44, 159
Adventure Education 44
Air pollution 2, 8, 37, 45, 105, 118, 205, 209, 274
Animal
  diversification 212-13
  food production 215, 218
  genetic resources 54, 212, 227
Arts teacher 83-85
Atmospheric nitrogen 182-83, 242
Azolla 221-22, 241-42
Azospirillum 182, 186, 222, 232, 241, 243
Azotobactor 221-22

Bacillus 183-84, 187, 236, 242
Basic Concepts of Environment-friendly Agriculture 215
Belgrade Chárter 12, 81
Bio-banks 135-36
Biodegradation 86, 180, 188
Biodiversity 65, 109, 122-31, 133-39, 161-63, 165, 167, 169-71, 173, 175, 177-78, 192, 212, 229-30, 268-70
  conservation 131, 133-34, 136, 138, 229, 234
  erosion 37, 134
  forest 269
  global 125, 127
  loss of 86, 129-32, 136, 169, 171, 212
  massive loss of 205, 212
  utilisation of 136-37
Biological diversity 90, 96, 124, 129, 133-34, 139, 170, 234, 258
  Components of 133-34, 234
Biomass 96, 190, 237
  microbial 190, 237
Biopesticides 204, 216-17, 223
Bioremediation 188, 191
Biosphere 33, 53, 64, 78-79, 90, 108, 162, 165, 167-68, 173, 175, 179-85, 189-91, 206, 253
Biotechnology 135, 137-39, 190, 215, 229
Biotic-Environment Contamination 211
Burning, disqualify forest 101

Carbon dioxide 101, 181, 210, 230
Centre for Environmental Education 90, 200
Centre for International Forestry Research 270
Centre for Science and Environment 15
Children environment activists 290
Climate change 8, 112, 124, 166, 169-70
Closed Landfill 283-84
Colleges of Teacher Education 26
Commission on Sustainable Development 96, 259
Communication Support for Environmnetal Education 196

Community Awareness for Sustainable Development 281, 283, 285, 287, 289, 290
Community Participation Management of Forest Resources 253, 255, 257, 259, 261, 263, 265, 267, 269, 271
Conservation and Sustainable Development 161
Conservation education 12, 44, 108
Conservation of natural resources 54, 56, 59, 90, 105, 109, 225, 227, 234, 238
Council for Environmental Education 11
Crop
  cultivated 131, 135
  damage 211, 224
  dry land 238
  hybrids of 207, 213
  legumes 221
  management 205
  non-leguminous 220, 222
  Range of Nitrogen Fixation 222
  species 203, 214, 220, 229
Cyanobacteria 182, 186, 189-90, 222, 241-42
Cyclone 213, 282, 284

Day education system 30
Deforestation 17, 25, 77, 86, 104, 166, 169, 204-45, 230, 253, 257-59, 268, 279
Degradation 6, 27, 58, 96, 132, 137, 152, 167, 185, 194, 204, 206, 209, 237, 258
  biological 236
  chemical 231
  forces 231
  of Land Resources 230
Depletion
  massive 212
  ozone 17, 41, 101, 169, 273-74
  of ozone layer 118, 166, 186
  unabated 192
  of water resources 231
Deterioration of soil health 208, 231
Development education 12, 44
Dimensions
  of Environmental Education 20
  of Sustainable Development 84-85
Disaster
  environmental 1
  natural 3, 37

Eco-friendly Environment 228-9, 231, 233, 235, 237, 239, 241, 243, 245, 247, 249, 251
Ecological Programmes in Higher Education 28-29, 31, 33, 35, 37, 39
Ecological Themes in Education 32
Education
  campaign 289
  commission 13, 86
  formal system of 142
  global environmental issues 12
  professional 86, 143
Education Developmental Focus Appropriate 75
Education Programme 26, 77, 89, 90
  environmental 12, 22, 46, 176, 196-97, 199
  higher 28
  in-service teacher 88
  international Environmental 11
  secondary 200
Education system
  formal 198
  non-formal 11
Educational authorities 24
Educational Backwardness of Women 147
Educational facilities 142, 158
  expansion of 142, 159
  female literacy 144
Educational Status of Women in India 142
Effective environmental education 22
Elementary education 142-43, 158
Environment
  awareness 282
  classroom 14
  development programmes 289

education orientation 89
Education Programmes 25
preservation 10, 253
Environmental
Agenda 12
awareness 7, 8, 11, 24, 33, 81, 105, 167, 178, 196, 202, 264, 273, 282, 284, 289
Awareness Programme 49
case studies 27
Consciousness 4, 8, 11, 13, 27, 29, 36, 39, 72
Consequences, 78
Conservation and Sustainable Development 92, 100, 192
Cost of Modern Intensive Agriculture 206
Curriculum 46
Education
in England 42
in Schools 14, 17
Ethical Element 46-47
European Resolution on Environmental Education 42
Extension Education and Creation of Awareness 267

Female literacy, education facilities 159
Forest
conservationists 267, 269-70
managers 269-70
policies, national 262, 269
resources, sustainable management of 254, 270
Forestry
education 268, 270
planning 269-70

Gandhi, Mahatma 13, 36, 37, 38, 117
Garbage disposal 279, 283-84
Gene banks 134, 138, 234
Genesis and History of Environmental Education 10
Genetic
diversity 115, 125, 129, 171-73, 230
variation 122
Goals of Environmental Education 42
Green
house gases 102, 166, 210
manures 208, 214, 217, 221, 240-41
revolution 204-08, 216, 218, 224, 233-34
Ground water 179, 188, 193, 205-11, 232
contamination 186, 209
depletion 205, 210, 231
pollution 118, 209

habitats 3, 96, 123-25, 128, 132, 136, 138, 179, 184, 191, 227, 258
heritage education 12
Higher Education System 145

Indispensability of environmental education 178
industrial effluents 166, 208-09
Inequality and Sustainable Development 98
Institutes of Advanced Studies in Education 26
Inter-governmental conference on Environmental Education 12, 42, 81
International Congress on Environmental Education 12
International Education Commission 38
International Environmental Education 44, 81
International Union for Conservation of Nature (IUCN) 11, 42, 53, 58, 64, 88, 112, 132, 136, 167, 168, 172
International Workshop on Environmental Education 42
Inter-related Components of Environmental Education 48
IUPN 11, 167

knowledge index 274
Knowledge Level of Science
Boys and Arts Boys 275
Girls and Arts Girls 276
Knowledge of ecological concepts 36

life-support systems 77
local environmental issues 26, 106, 289

macro learning 175-76
man-environment interaction 73
Mass Media and Environmental Education 197
Microbes for
  Maintenance of Sustainable Agriculture 185
  Protection of Crops 186
  Treatment of Liquid Wastes 187
  Treatment of Solid Wastes 186
Millennium Development Goals 5, 13, 83
Ministry of
  Education 102, 108
  Environment 90
  Environment and Forestry 15
  Human Resource Development 14
Model for
  Environmental Education 9
  Sustainable Development 56-57
model syllabus 109

Narmada Bachao Andolan 201
National Biodiversity Conservation Board 136
National Commission on Self-Employed Women 150
National Council of Educational Research and Training (NCERT) 14, 17, 19-23, 25, 72-73, 81, 89-90, 109, 143, 147
National Council of Teacher Education (NCTE) 26, 79-80, 90
National Curriculum Council 101
National Curriculum Framework 14, 19, 72-73
National Environmental Awareness Campaign 15, 290
National Environmental Policy Act 167
National Policy on Education 13-14, 19, 71, 113-14, 143, 147, 159
Natural tropical forests 124
NGOs 5, 15, 27, 44, 49, 74, 99, 109, 137, 139, 201, 268, 289
NIEPA (NUEPA) 143
Non-biological agents 182
non-formal education streams 12
Nuclear Polyhedrosis Viruses 186
nutrients 128, 133, 180, 186-87, 190, 204, 208, 214-15, 221-22, 236, 238-39, 241, 243
Nutrition and Health Care 147, 157

Odum 60, 63, 112, 117, 165, 172
organic
  farming 118, 120, 206, 215-19, 225
  manures 204, 208-09, 214, 216-17, 220-21
  wastes 128, 204
Oslo Conference on Sustainable Development 168
Ozone
  Conference in London 168
  hole 8
  layer 3, 77, 118, 166, 168, 186

Papua New Guinean Malenesian Environment Foundation 289
Pedagogical Issues 22
Perspectives of Environmental Education in College and University 41
pesticides 20-21, 95, 128, 131, 169, 186, 188, 205-09, 211-13, 216-17, 223, 225, 231-32, 238, 244, 247
  attack 204, 211
  control 86, 223, 229
plant species 58, 102, 115, 126, 132-33, 229-30, 244, 264
pollution control 41, 90, 185, 191
pond water 286-87
Population
  Bomb 11
  control 54, 217
pre-service education 90
primary education 5, 71
Principles of Sustainable Development 57, 69

Professional development of teachers 90
Proposal for Planet Protection Fund 169
public information campaigns 290
Publication of National Curriculum Documentation for Environmental Education 42

quality of environment 11, 17, 24, 51, 55-56, 63, 80, 82, 111, 169, 234, 253

Radhakrishnan Commission 38
rain forest 101
RCC houses 284-85
Recent Trends in Higher Education System 31
Recombinant DNA technology 188
recycling of wastes 6, 89, 102
Red Data Book 11, 167
renewable resources 10, 65, 87, 95, 133, 172, 200, 233
Reorienting education 82
Rhizobium 182, 186, 221, 232, 241-42
rice 181, 204-05, 207, 210, 212, 221, 230, 233-34, 239-43, 249-50, 287
-pulse system 243
Rio
Conference 169
declaration 73, 113, 170, 289
Earth Summit 83
Rishis and Vedic masters 35
Role of
Education 100
International Agencies and Civil Servants 259
Mass Media in Promoting Environmental Conservation 192
Microbes in Maintaining Ecological Sustainability 180
Rural-Urban Literacy Rates 145

salinisation 104, 161, 208
Sanginga 240-41
Sardar Sarovar Dam 201
school curriculum 19, 73, 75, 109, 159
science education 90
Scientific Committee on Problems of Environment 168
sewage treatment processes 187
Silent Spring 4, 11, 167, 169, 178
Size of Higher Education System in India 146
smokers 284
socio-ecological problems 44
socio-economic
category 83-85
problems of Women 153, 155
socio-environmental problems 44
Soil and Water Conservation 236-37
soil conservation 120, 210-11
soil degradation 2, 208, 236, 258
soil erosion 104, 166, 205, 208, 231, 238, 240
soil fauna 232
soil fertility 102, 208, 214-15, 217-18, 220-21, 236-38, 240
level 221
soil pollution 118, 177, 274
solar oven 225
solar treatments 223
solid wastes 186, 239
solubilising 186, 208, 236, 241, 243
Special education 268
State Control and Bureaucratic Approaches 261
State Councils of Educational Research and Training 26
sustainable development 5-6, 12-13, 15, 17, 47, 51-59, 61, 63-70, 72-76, 78-79, 82-83, 85-86, 89-91, 95-96, 100, 110, 112-14, 120, 133, 138, 152, 170, 173-74, 180, 185, 192-93, 200-01, 228, 253-55, 265, 280, 285, 289-90
Concept Map of 57, 67
Conservation Strategies for 122
education plans 74
framework 78
Issues Organised 69

Major Dimensions of 68
sustainable human settlements 70
Sustainable utilisation of species 172-73
Swami Vivekananda 35-36
Sweetener Industry 248

tea wastes 240
teacher education 25, 78, 86, 88-90
Teacher Training and Instructional Material 25
Third International Conference on Environmental Education 52
time education programmes 158
Total Literacy Campaign 288
Toxic compounds 189
Training of Women 156
Transformative Role of Environmental Education 25
Trends in
Environmental Education 44
Higher Education 29
tropical forest species 130
Tropical Forestry Action Programme of FAO 259
tropical forests 2, 126, 130, 132, 230, 256, 259, 269
TRYSEM 157
tsunami 3

UNESCO 11-13, 16-18, 21, 38, 42, 44, 63, 66, 74, 79, 80-82, 105, 114, 152, 167, 172, 175
Biosphere Conference 42, 167
United Nations
Commission on Sustainable Development 82
Conference on Environment and Development 82, 96, 169, 289
Conference on Human Environment 4, 270
Environment Programme 11, 44, 132, 168, 171-72, 259
World Commission on Environment and Development 254
United States Senate report on Environmental Education Act 198
Universal Declaration of Human Responsibilities 71, 138
Universal Declaration of Human Rights 62, 113
Upanishads 35
Utilisation System and Value Addition 251

Value Education and Development 114
Value of Biodiversity 171
Vedic and Upanishadic concepts of human dependence 111

waste disposal 111, 128, 187
Water and Air Pollution 209
water conservation measures 236-38
water erosion 231, 237-38
water management 14, 96, 237
water pollution 118, 120, 209, 274
wetlands 3, 125
Whooping Cough 104
Wild Fauna 168
wind erosion 231, 238
Women
Education and Sustainable Development 151
empowerment 152
job seekers 150
teachers 143, 159
World Charter for Nature 168
World Commission on
Environment and Development 5, 52, 64, 78, 81, 133, 168, 171, 173
Forests and Sustainable Development 264
World Conservation
Centre 168
Strategy 11, 42, 168, 172, 178
Union 132
World Meteorological Organisation 168
World Summit for
Children 70
Sustainable Development 13, 71

Worldwide Fund for Nature 42, 53, 58, 64, 112, 117, 167, 172

xenobiotics 166, 169, 18

yeasts 249

zoological gardens 134
Zoraster 38

List of Contributors

Prof. A.K. Patra, Environmental Biology Research Laboratory, School of Biological Sciences, Utkal University, Bhubaneswar-751004 (Orissa).

Dr. A.S. Dixit, Department of Environmental Science, North-East Hill University, Shillong, (Meghalaya).

Dr. (Mrs.) B.N. Neelima, Department of Communication and Journalism, Sri. Padmavati Mahila Visvavidyalayam, Tirupati, (Andhra Pradesh).

Dr. B.P. Sahu, Department of Adult and Continuing Education, North-East Hill University, Shillong-793002 (Meghalaya).

Dr. (Mrs.) D. Dash, Department of Education in Science and Mathematics, Regional Institute of Education (NCERT), Bhubaneswar-751022 (Orissa).

Dr. Dipak De, Associate Professor, Department of Extension Education, Institute of Agricultural Science, Banaras Hindu University, Varanasi-221005 (Uttar Pradesh).

Dr. J.G. Ray, Environmental Education Research Lab, Department of Botany, S.B. College, Canganacherry-686101 (Kerala).

Dr. K.K. Tiwari, Head, Post-graduate Department of Education, Government P.G. College, Ghazipur, (Uttar Pradesh).

Prof. M.K. Satapathy, Head, Dept. of Education in Science and Mathematics, North East Regional Institute of Education, Shillong-793003 (Meghalaya).

Dr. M. Nedunchezhiyan, Senior Scientist, Central Tuber Crop Research Institute, Bhubaneswar-751019 (Orissa).

Prof. N.C. Datta, Ecology Research Unit, Department of Zoology, University of Calcutta, Calcutta-700019 (West Bengal).

Dr. N. Subba Rao, School of Distance Education, Andhra University, Visakhapatnam-530003 (Andhra Pradesh).

Dr. P.S. Sivakumar, Scientist, Central Tuber Crop Research Institute, Bhubaneswar-751019 (Orissa).

Dr. (Ms.) P. Ghildyal, North East Regional Institute of Education, Shillong-793003 (Meghalaya).

Dr. Paramita Pramanick, Environmental Biology Research Laboratory, School of Biological Sciences, Utkal University, Bhubaneswar-751004 (Orissa).

Dr. R.N. Bisoyi, Director, Regional Biofertilizer Development Centre, (Govt. of India), 34-V Main, Hebbal, Bangalore-560024 (Karnataka).

Dr. R.C. Ray, Principal Scientist, Central Tuber Crop Research Institute, Bhubaneswar-7751019 (Orissa).

Dr. S. Singh, Principal Scientist, Division of Environmental Sciences, Indian Agricultural Research Institute, New Delhi-110012.

Prof. S.C. Santra, Head, Department of Environmental Sciences, Kalyani University, Kalyani-741235 (West Bengal).